The Madman and the Churchrobber

The Madman and the Churchrobber

Law and Conflict in Early Modern England

JASON PEACEY

OXFORD
UNIVERSITY PRESS

OXFORD
UNIVERSITY PRESS

Great Clarendon Street, Oxford, OX2 6DP,
United Kingdom

Oxford University Press is a department of the University of Oxford.
It furthers the University's objective of excellence in research, scholarship,
and education by publishing worldwide. Oxford is a registered trade mark of
Oxford University Press in the UK and in certain other countries

First Edition published in 2022

Impression: 1

Published in the United States of America by Oxford University Press
198 Madison Avenue, New York, NY 10016, United States of America

British Library Cataloguing in Publication Data
Data available

Library of Congress Control Number: 2021951369

ISBN 978–0–19–289713–8

DOI: 10.1093/oso/9780192897138.001.0001

Printed and bound by
CPI Group (UK) Ltd, Croydon, CR0 4YY

For Annette

Contents

List of Illustrations

Acknowledgements

This project took longer than expected to complete. Archival discoveries forced me to confront complex issues, and I came to identify with comments by one of the book's protagonists—John Smyth of Nibley. Official duties (my time as Head of Department) were like 'thieves in stealing much time from this', and the research was sometimes painful, as weeks were spent 'without the gleaning of a note to enlarge a line herein'. Like Smyth, I have reflected on how an immersion in legal complexities made me 'privy to mine own ignorance', and like him I am grateful for considerable support along the way.[1] Many people have mitigated my ignorance and taken time to engage with an unusual and perhaps risky project. These include: Ian Archer, Richard Bell, Alex Barber, Mike Braddick, Simon Brown, Bill Bulman, Tom Cogswell, David Como, Richard Cust, David d'Avray, Kenneth Fincham, Steve Hindle, Clive Holmes, Ann Hughes, Robert Ingram, Mark Jenner, Sean Kelsey, Chris Kyle, Peter Lake, Patrick Lantschner, Ed Legon, Noah Millstone, Nicholas Popper, Stephen Roberts, John Walter, Tim Reinke-Williams, John Sabapathy, David Harris Sacks, Christopher St John Smith, Jack Sargeant, Laura Stewart, Elliot Vernon, John Walter, and Andy Wood. This book would not have been possible without enthusiastic support from librarians and archivists, including Karen Davidson and David Smith at Berkeley Castle, Judith Curthoys at Christ Church, Oxford, and Julian Reid at Corpus Christi College, Oxford, and the wonderful staff at Gloucestershire Archives. I am also grateful to the Huntington Library for a fellowship that enabled me to put my findings into a wider context, and to Cathryn Steele at OUP for her wonderful help and support. Most of all I am grateful to Annette, who has heard more than anyone ought to about John Smyth and Benjamin Crokey, and who even came on pilgrimage with me to Nibley . . . twice.

[1] Smyth, *Lives*, ii. 440–1, 442–3.

List of Abbreviations

A&O	C. H. Firth and R. S. Rait, *Acts and Ordinances of the Interregnum, 1642–1660* (3 vols, London, 1911)
Add.	Additional
Admissions MT	H. A. C. Sturgess, ed., *Register of Admissions to the Honourable Society of the Middle Temple* (3 vols, London, 1949),
AHR	*American Historical Review*
AJLH	*American Journal of Legal History*
AJS	*American Journal of Sociology*
Al. Cant.	John Venn and J. A. Venn, *Alumni Cantabrigienses* (4 vols, Cambridge, 1922)
Al. Oxon.	Joseph Foster, *Alumni Oxonienses* (4 vols, Oxford, 1891–2)
APC	*Acts of the Privy Council*
BA	Bristol Archives
Beaven, *Bristol*	Alfred Beaven, *Bristol Lists* (Bristol, 1899)
Berkeley	Berkeley Castle, Gloucestershire
Bigland, *Gloucester*	Ralph Bigland, *Historical, Monumental and Genealogical Collections Relative to the County of Gloucester* (4 vols, London, 1791–2)
BIHR	*Bulletin of the Institute of Historical Research*
BL	British Library
Bodl.	Bodleian Library
Bossy, *Disputes*	John Bossy, ed., *Disputes and Settlements. Law and Human Relations in the West* (Cambridge, 1983)
Broadway, 'John Smyth'	Jan Broadway, 'John Smyth of Nibley: a Jacobean man of business and his service to the Berkeley family', *Midland History*, 24.1 (1999)
Broadway, 'Political appropriation'	Jan Broadway, 'Political appropriation: reading Sir Walter Raleigh's "Dialogue between a counsellor of state and a justice of peace"' (http://www.livesandletters.ac.uk/papers/SOTC_2006_01_001.pdf accessed 1 September 2021)
BRS	Bristol Records Society
Brooks, *Law*	C. W. Brooks, *Law, Politics and Society in Early Modern England* (Cambridge, 2008)
Brooks, *Lawyers*	C. W. Brooks, *Lawyers, Litigation, and English Society since 1450* (London, 1998)
Brooks, *Pettyfoggers*	C. W. Brooks, *Pettyfoggers and Vipers of the Commonwealth: the 'Lower Branch' of the Legal Profession in Early Modern England* (Cambridge, 1986)

Calamy Revised	A. G. Matthews, *Calamy Revised* (Oxford, 1934)
CCAM	M. A. E. Green, ed., *Calendar of the Proceedings of the Committee for Advance of Money, 1642–1656* (3 vols, London, 1888)
CCC	M. A. E. Green, ed., *Calendar of the Proceedings of the Committee for Compounding* (5 vols, London, 1889–92)
CD 1621	Wallace Notestein, Frances Relf and Hartley Simpson, eds, *Commons Debates 1621* (7 vols, New Haven, 1935)
Churches, 'Equity'	Christine Churches, '"Equity against a purchaser shall not be": a seventeenth-century case study in landholding and indebtedness', *Parergon*, 11.2 (1993), 69–87
Churches, 'Business at law'	Christine Churches, 'Business at law: retrieving commercial disputes from eighteenth-century Chancery', *HJ*, 43.4 (2000), 937–54
Churches, 'Putting women'	Christine Churches, 'Putting women in their place: female litigants at Whitehaven, 1660–1760', in Nancy E. Wright et al., eds, *Women, Property and the Letters of the Law in Early Modern England* (Toronto, 2004), pp. 40–65
Churches, 'False friends	Christine Churches, 'False friends, spiteful enemies: a community at law in early modern England', *HR*, 71.174 (1998), 52–74
CJ	*Commons Journals*
Commons 1604–1629	Andrew Thrush and John P. Ferris, eds, *The House of Commons, 1604–1629* (6 vols, London, 2010)
Commons 1660–1690	Basil Duke Henning, ed., *The House of Commons, 1660–1690* (3 vols, London, 1983)
Complete Peerage	G. E. C[okayne], *The Complete Peerage* (14 vols, London, 1910–59)
Crokey, *Briefe*	Benjamin Crokey, *A Briefe of a Bill* (1621)
Crokey, *Contents*	Benjamin Crokey, *The Contents and Short Briefe of this Book* (1646)
Crokey, *Complaint*	Benjamin Crokey, *To the Right Honourable the Higher and Lower Houses of Parliament, now Assembled: The Humble Complaint of Benjamine Crokey* (1640)
Crokey, *Petition*	Benjamin Crokey, *To the Right Honourable the House of Parliament. The Humble Petition of Benjamin Crookey and Sarah his Daughter* (1647)
Crokey, *Sacred Maiestie*	Benjamin Crokey, *To his Sacred Maiestie, the Lords Spiritual and Temporal, and the House of Commons* (1625)
CSPD	*Calendar of State Papers Domestic*
CTB	*Calendar of Treasury Books*
EcHR	*Economic History Review*
EHR	*English Historical Review*
Elrington, 'Survey'	C. R. Elrington, 'The survey of church livings in Gloucestershire, 1650', *TBGAS*, 83 (1964)

Fincham and Tyacke, *Altars*	Kenneth Fincham and Nicholas Tyacke, *Altars Restored: The Changing Face of English Religious Worship, 1547–c.1700* (Oxford, 2008)
Fincham, *Prelate*	Kenneth Fincham, *Prelate as Pastor: The Episcopate of James I* (Oxford, 1990)
FSL	Folger Shakespeare Library, Washington DC
GA	Gloucestershire Archives
Gardiner, *Reports*	S. R. Gardiner, ed, *Reports of Cases in the Courts of Star Chamber and High Commission* (Camden Society, new series 39, 1886)
GL	Guildhall Library, London
H&T	*History and Theory*
Harlow, *Religious Ministry*	Jonathan Harlow, *Religious Ministry in Bristol, 1603–1689* (Bristol, 2017)
Hart, Justice	James S. Hart, *Justice upon Petition. The House of Lords and the Reformation of Justice, 1621–1675* (London, 1991)
HEH	Henry E. Huntington Library, San Marino, California
HJ	*Historical Journal*
HMC	*Historical Manuscripts Commission*
Hopwood, *MT Recs*	Charles Henry Hopwood, ed., *Middle Temple Records* (4 vols, London, 1904–5)
Horn, *New World*	James Horn, *Adapting to a New World. English Society in the Seventeenth Century Chesapeake* (London, 1994)
Howes, 'John Smyth'	Russell Howes, 'John Smyth the younger of North Nibley and his papers', *TBGAS*, 121 (2003), 213–31
HR	*Historical Research*
Jansson, *Proceedings*	Maija Jansson, ed., *Proceedings in the Opening Session of the Long Parliament* (7 vols, Woodbridge, 2000–7)
JBS	*Journal of British Studies*
JMH	*Journal of Modern History*
Jones, *Chancery*	W. J. Jones, *The Elizabethan Court of Chancery* (Oxford, 1967)
JP	Justice of the Peace
Kingsbury, *Virginia*	S. M. Kingsbury, ed., *The Records of the Virginia Company of London* (4 vols, Washington, 1906–35)
LB	Library of Birmingham
Lindley, *Wotton*	E. S. Lindley, *Wotton under Edge: Men and Affairs of a Cotswold Town* (London, 1962)
LJ	*Lords Journals*
LMA	London Metropolitan Archives
LPL	Lambeth Palace Library
McGrath, *Merchants*	Patrick McGrath, ed., *Merchants and Merchandise in Seventeenth Century Bristol* (BRS, 19, 1955)
McGrath, *Records*	Patrick McGrath, ed., *Records Relating to the Society of Merchant Venturers of the City of Bristol* (BRS, 17, 1952)

Men and Armour	*Men and Armour for Gloucestershire in 1608* (Stroud, 1980)
MS	Manuscript
MSS	Manuscripts
NYPL	New York Public Library
ODNB	*Oxford Dictionary of National Biography*
P&P	*Past and Present*
PA	Parliamentary Archives
PH	*Parliamentary History*
Prest, *Barristers*	Wilfrid R. Prest, *The Rise of the Barristers: A Social History of the English Bar, 1590–1640* (Oxford, 1986)
Reynolds, *Godly Reformers*	Matthew Reynolds, *Godly Reformers and their Opponents in Early Modern England* (Woodbridge, 2005)
Rollison, *Local Origins*	David Rollison, *The Local Origins of Modern Society. Gloucestershire, 1500–1800* (London, 1992)
RS	Record Society
Rudder, *Gloucestershire*	Samuel Rudder, *A New History of Gloucestershire* (Cirencester, 1779)
Sacks, *Widening Gate*	David Harris Sacks, *The Widening Gate. Bristol and the Atlantic Economy, 1450–1700* (Oxford, 1991)
Smyth, *Lives*	John Smyth, *The Lives of the Berkeleys*, ed. Sir John Maclean (3 vols, Gloucester, 1883)
Stretton, *Women*	Tim Stretton, *Women Waging Law in Elizabethan England* (Cambridge, 1998)
TBGAS	*Transactions of the Bristol and Gloucestershire Archaeological Society*
TRHS	*Transactions of the Royal Historical Society*
UL	University Library
VCH Gloucester	*The Victoria History of the County of Gloucester* (13 vols, London, Oxford and Woodbridge, 1907–2016)
Vis. Gloucester 1623	John Maclean and W. C. Heane, eds, *The Visitation of the County of Gloucester 1623* (London, 1885)
Vis. Gloucester 1682-3	T. Fitz-Roy Fenwick and Walter C. Metcalfe, eds, *The Visitation of the County of Gloucester, 1682–3* (Exeter, 1884)
Walker Revised	A. G. Matthews, *Walker Revised* (Oxford, 1988)
Warmington, *Gloucestershire*	A. R. Warmington, *Civil War, Interregnum and Restoration in Gloucestershire, 1640–1672* (Woodbridge, 1997)
WCA	Westminster City Archives
Yorks Star Chamber	H. B. McCall and W. Brown, eds, *Yorkshire Star Chamber Proceedings* (3 vols, Leeds, 1909–14)

Note on Dates

All dates are Old Style unless otherwise indicated, but the new year is taken to begin on 1 January rather than 25 March.

Unless otherwise stated, London is the place of publication for works printed before 1800.

Legal terms: Michaelmas (October–December), Hilary (January–March), Easter (AprilMay), and Trinity (June–July).

For war's not equal to this battle:
That eats but men, this men and cattle.
Therefore no more this combat choose,
Where he that wins doth always lose,
And those that gain all, with this curse they receive it,
From fools they get it, to their sons they leave it.

Thomas Middleton, *The Phoenix* (1604)

'these quarrelsome folk by the Severn were the stuff of English history'

William B. Willcox

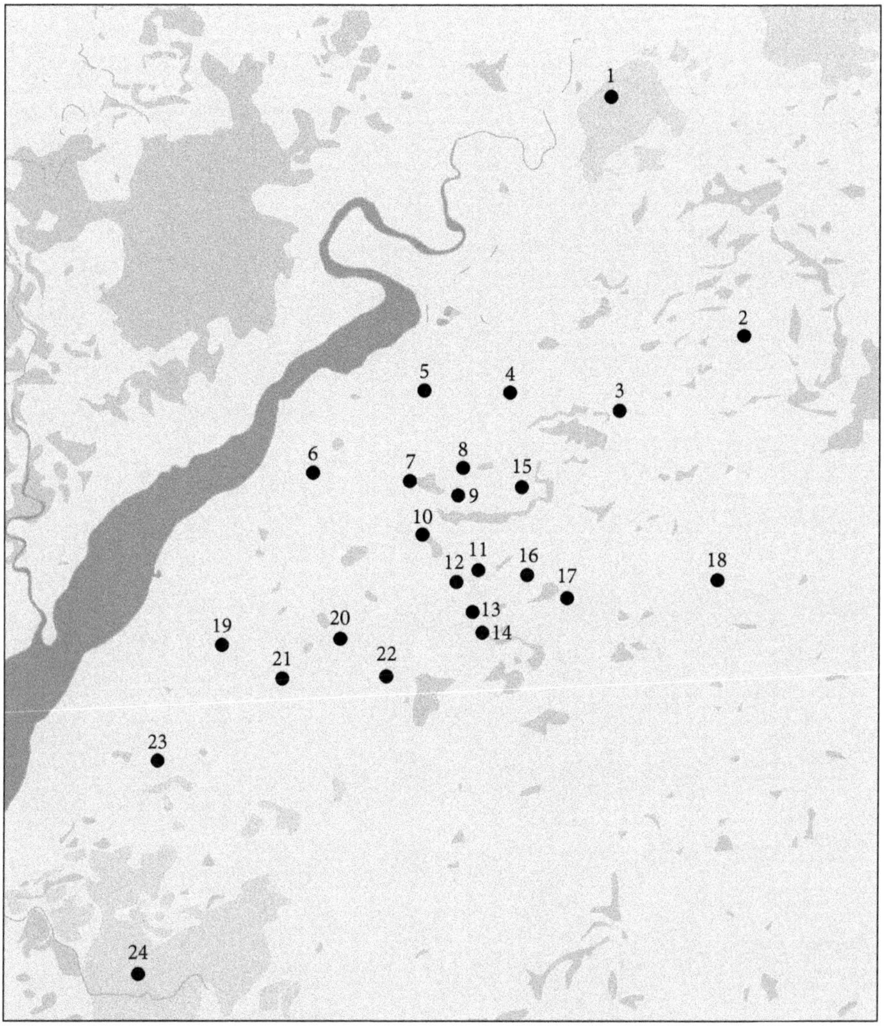

Key:

1. Gloucester
2. Bisley
3. Woodchester
4. Frocester
5. Slimbridge
6. Berkeley
7. Stinchcombe
8. Cam
9. Dursley
10. Nibley
11. Coombe
12. Wotton-under-Edge
13. Wortley
14. Alderley
15. Uley
16. Ozleworth
17. Boxwell
18. Tetbury
19. Thornbury
20. Cromhall
21. Tytherington
22. Boxwell
23. Almondsbury
24. Bristol

Introduction

On 25 June 1626, a cousin of John Smyth of Nibley called Samuel Trotman visited the house of a brewer's clerk, William Burford, near the Black Griffin tavern in St Giles in the Fields, on the fringes of London. Struck by what he saw, Trotman reported to Smyth that 'there was fixed . . . like a ballad on the wall' a printed sheet in folio. This might not seem extraordinary. Historians recognise that cheap print was ubiquitous in the seventeenth century, and that it was accessible to, and popular with, people from all walks of life. They also recognise that, in homes and alehouses alike, printed sheets with ballads and merry tales were displayed in precisely this fashion.[1] On this occasion, however, all is not what it seems. This is intimated by Trotman's comment that, upon entering the house, Burford's wife Susan 'pulled down' this broadside 'in a rage', suggesting that it was no ordinary text, and that possessing it was risky.[2] The item in question, a single sheet by Benjamin Crokey, does not fit with scholarly appreciation of the kinds of text favoured by humble readers. Its title was *A Briefe of a Bill in the most high and honourable House of Parliament* (Fig. 1), and it was the kind of thing used to lobby MPs and peers about petitions and reforming notions. Such works have begun to receive attention within analyses of Parliament's role as a participatory forum, and this particular work had actually been around since 1621, when print first became a common method for drawing attention to grievances, demands, and ideas, and when Crokey himself launched an unsuccessful bid to influence the legislative agenda.[3] Here, in short, is curious evidence of humble readers treating a parliamentary 'breviate' with the veneration usually afforded to popular verse.

It also became clear that another of Crokey's texts, a substantial sixty-four page pamphlet from 1625, addressed *To his sacred maiestie, the lords spiritual, and temporal, and the House of Commons*, had become the talk of the town.[4] Christopher Stokes saw a copy lying on a table at the chamber of Mr Chester, near St Clement Danes, read it 'in part', and discussed it with his host. Gyles Bird was offered a copy by a soldier called John Leigh, who asked 'whether he would

[1] Adam Fox, 'Ballads, libels and popular ridicule in Jacobean England', *P&P*, 145 (1994), 47–83; Tessa Watt, *Cheap Print and Popular Piety, 1550–1640* (Cambridge, 1991).

[2] GA, D9125/1/12014.

[3] Chris R. Kyle, *Theater of State. Parliament and Political Culture in Early Stuart England* (Stanford, 2012), ch. 6; Jason Peacey, *Print and Public Politics in the English Revolution* (Cambridge, 2013), chs. 8–9; Crokey, *Briefe*; *CD 1621*, i. 84–6.

[4] Crokey, *Sacred Maiestie*. For Smyth's copy of this tract, see: GA, D9125/1/12007.

The Madman and the Churchrobber: Law and Conflict in Early Modern England. Jason Peacey, Oxford University Press.
 DOI: 10.1093/oso/9780192897138.003.0001

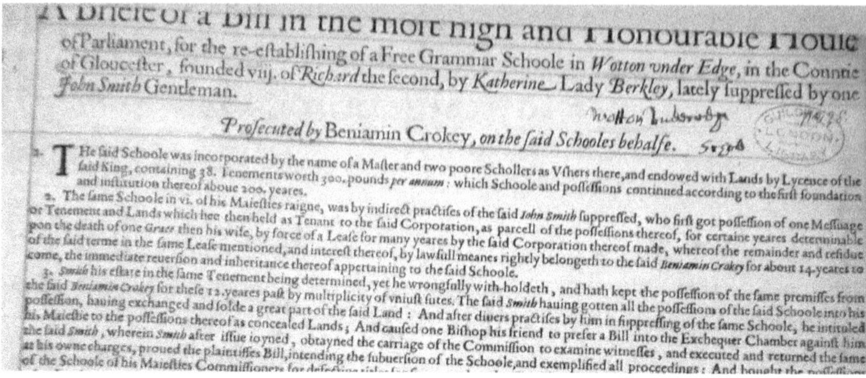
A Briefe of a Bill in the most high and Honourable House of Parliament, for the re-eſtabliſhing of a Free Grammar Schoole in *Wotton vnder Edge*, in the Countie of Glouceſter, founded viij. of *Richard* the ſecond, by *Katherine* Lady *Berkley*, lately ſuppreſſed by one *John Smith* Gentleman.

Proſecuted by Beniamin Crokey, *on the ſaid Schooles behalfe.*

1. THe ſaid Schoole was incorporated by the name of a Maſter and two poore Schollers as Vſhers there, and endowed with Lands by Lycence of the ſaid King, containing 38. Tenements worth 300. pounds *per annum*: which Schoole and poſſeſſions continued according to the firſt foundation and inſtitution thereof aboue 200. yeares.
2. The ſame Schoole in vi. of his Maieſties raigne, was by indirect practiſes of the ſaid *John Smith* ſuppreſſed, who firſt got poſſeſſion of one Meſſuage or Tenement and Lands which hee then held as Tenant to the ſaid Corporation, as parcell of the poſſeſſions thereof, for certaine yeares determinable vpon the death of one *Grace* then his wife, by force of a Leaſe for many yeares by the ſaid Corporation thereof made, whereof the remainder and reſidue of the ſaid terme in the ſame Leaſe mentioned, and intereſt thereof, by lawfull meanes rightly belongeth to the ſaid *Beniamin Crokey* for about 14. yeares to come, the immediate reuerſion and inheritance thereof appertaining to the ſaid Schoole.
3. *Smith* his eſtate in the ſame Tenement being determined, yet he wrongfully with-holdeth, and hath kept the poſſeſſion of the ſame premiſſes from the ſaid *Beniamin Crokey* for theſe 12. yeares paſt by multiplicity of vniuſt ſutes. The ſaid *Smith* hauing gotten all the poſſeſſions of the ſaid Schoole into his poſſeſſion, hauing exchanged and ſolde a great part of the ſaid Land: And after diuers practiſes by him in ſuppreſſing of the ſame Schoole, he intituled his Maieſtie to the poſſeſſions thereof as concealed Lands; And cauſed one Biſhop his friend to prefer a Bill into the Exchequer Chamber againſt him the ſaid *Smith*, wherein *Smith* after iſſue ioyned, obtayned the carriage of the Commiſſion to examine witneſſes, and executed and returned the ſame at his owne charges, proued the plaintiffes Bill, intending the ſubuerſion of the Schoole, and exemplified all proceedings: And bought the poſſeſſions of the Schoole of his Maieſties Commiſſioners for defective titles [illegible]

Fig. 1. Benjamin Crokey, *A Briefe of a Bill in the most high and Honourable House of Parliament* ([London,] 1621). Guildhall Library, London, Bside 24.43. Reproduced by permission of the Guildhall Library, City of London.

read a piece of *news*'. Copies were doing the rounds at the Three Cups inn in Bread Street, as well as at Blackwell Hall, the centre of the wool and cloth trade, where Richard Poole heard it read aloud by a 'factor', Edward Tanner, before borrowing it and reading it himself. More alarming still was news that the tract had reached Gloucestershire, Smyth's own county, where it was talked about at the Bell tavern in Gloucester, and seen in more rural areas, by men like Thomas Brinkworth, a tailor from Coombe, near Wotton-under-Edge. Philip Langley of Mangotsfield received a copy from his maid, and another man, Albane Saunders, obtained one from his son, a pupil at Wotton's grammar school. Another Wotton tailor, Edward Brinkworth, saw Edward Olyver's maid 'reading one of them', and promptly borrowed a copy, and in that part of the world there was 'a notable bruit and wonderment . . . at the first coming of the books'.[5]

Such evidence is odd, not just in terms of why Smyth was so interested in Crokey's use of print, but also because Crokey's texts were being treated like the trashiest kinds of literature.[6] There has always been a temptation to suggest that 'ordinary' people—the 'lower orders', especially outside London—did not read such things, because of illiteracy or lack of engagement with parliamentary and political affairs, or because printed pamphlets were simply not available in the provinces. Such assumptions have been challenged in recent years, in terms of the geographical and social 'reach' of print, but there remains something intriguing about the attention that Crokey's texts received from a diverse group of people,

[5] GA, D9125/1/12014.

[6] Some trashy literature contained serious messages: Peter Lake, 'Deeds against nature: cheap print, Protestantism and murder in early seventeenth-century England', in Peter Lake and Kevin Sharpe, eds, *Culture and Politics in Early Stuart England* (Basingstoke, 1993), pp. 257–74.

many of whom were far removed from Parliament.[7] These texts were primarily aimed at legislators, were legalistic, and, in the case of the 1625 pamphlet, rather long. We appear to be confronted by a mystery, and it is precisely this mystery that this book seeks to solve.

At the same time, this study also has a much broader remit. It analyses civil litigation, based upon the idea that existing studies, which have rightly alerted us to an explosion in disputation during the early modern period, have not done enough to understand the phenomenon. This reflects the difficulties involved in getting to grips with the *stories* behind legal action, which means that we only have a limited understanding of what went on during litigation, what it meant for those involved, and what effects it had. This study argues that it is only by means of a deeply contextualised case study that the nature and importance of early modern litigation can be recovered. As such, the approach taken here—as with other episodes that disorient historians—is microhistorical, at least in certain ways. 'Microhistory' might now be regarded as a debased methodology, for reasons that will become clear, but it has ongoing relevance for grappling with apparently inexplicable things, by reducing the scale of observation and undertaking microscopic analysis of very particular phenomena, and by using a circumscribed archive. Very often this involves unusual incidents and strange characters; attending to neglected sections of society, recognising the 'agency' of ordinary people, and recovering alien mentalities. The aim is often to reveal things—ways of doing, being, and thinking—that are incapable of being observed using other approaches, and to shed new light upon the wider world of a particular age.[8] Central to understanding the characters in any number of microhistories have been legal proceedings, and understanding Benjamin Crokey certainly involves analysing legal records. Crokey's printed texts referred to, and reflected the fortunes of, a legal dispute that had been ongoing for a very long time. The litigation to which they related—the contested fate of a hundred-acre estate called Warrens Court in Nibley, Gloucestershire—began in the 1560s, and did not grind to a halt until the early 1660s. Its central issues were then revisited in renewed contestation fifty years later, in the early eighteenth century.

It is this litigation that explains John Smyth's interest in Crokey's printed texts. Smyth was the man with whom Crokey was in dispute, and the man against whom both the bill and the book were targeted. Such legal manoeuvring, however,

[7] Peacey, *Print and Public Politics*, chs. 1–3.

[8] The literature here is vast, but see: Sigurdur Gylfi Magnusson and Istvan M. Szijarto, *What is Microhistory?* (London, 2013); Edward Muir and Guido Ruggiero, eds, *Microhistory and the Lost Peoples of Europe* (London, 1991); Giovanni Levi, 'On microhistory', in Peter Burke, ed., *New Perspectives on Historical Writing* (Cambridge, 1991), 97–119; Jill Lepore, 'Historians who love too much: reflections on microhistory and biography', *Journal of American History*, 88.1 (2001), 129–44; Thomas Robisheaux, 'Microhistory today: a roundtable discussion', *Journal of Medieval and Early Modern Studies*, 47.1 (2017), 7–52; John-Paul Ghobrial, ed., *Global History and Microhistory* (*P&P* supplement 14, 2019).

merely throws up another mystery, in terms of a legal contest that might be thought to have defied good sense. It is—and was—hard to establish the extent and value of the land in question, and while Crokey generally claimed that it was worth £300–500 per annum, others valued it at as little as £30–70.[9] As such, and given that litigation revolved around a *lease*, rather than freehold land, the amount of money that litigants spent on the dispute seems fundamentally disproportionate: Smyth regularly spent far more than this *per year* in pursuing the matter through the courts, and by the mid-1640s Crokey claimed to have spent over £3,000 on the affair.[10] This book examines why this particular affair was contested for so long, and why it was a dispute that Smyth and Crokey both inherited, pursued with great vigour, and then passed on to their children. Doing so involves understanding the logic of litigation, and paying attention to the everyday aspects of disputation, as much as to apparently extraordinary episodes and characters. The aim is to demonstrate that the battle over Warrens Court reveals how waging law could spin out of control, and that by establishing how both men thought about disputation, conducted litigation, and reflected on the legal system, it is possible to discern the affair's deeper meaning, for the disputants as well as for contemporary onlookers. Doing so will shed light upon the wider world of legal wrangling in early modern England.

Put another way, this book demonstrates how and why to interrogate a neglected legal dispute that seems to be both insignificant *and* extraordinary. Contestation over Warrens Court has been noted only briefly by historians, in terms of the 'trouble and expense' involved, although attention has occasionally been paid to the fact that Crokey was one of the first people to capitalise upon the decision to reconstitute the House of Lords as a court of judicature in the 1620s, and an early adopter of print as petitioner and lobbyist.[11] More obviously, the dispute has played a minor part in debates over early modern censorship, because Crokey was ultimately prosecuted for libel in Star Chamber (1631). For S. R. Gardiner, Crokey's treatment was indicative of the repressive policies that marked the 'personal rule' of Charles I, and that helped to bring about constitutional crisis, civil wars, and revolution.[12] More recently, it has been used to bolster 'revisionist' claims that early modern governments were preoccupied with authors who breached 'civility rules', rather than with silencing all forms of criticism.[13]

[9] *VCH Gloucester*, ii. 400; Crokey, *Briefe*; Crokey, *Sacred Maiestie*, sig. H3v; *LJ*, iii. 171; PA, HL/PO/JO/10/1/37; HL/PO/JO/10/1/24; TNA, C 3/338/8; STAC 8/107/7, STAC 8/274/8; SP 23/196, p. 513; C 21/625/4; GA, D9125/1/11989/1, 11996; Crokey, *Contents*, sig. A; GA, D8887/6/87.

[10] TNA, C 3/338/8; PA, HL/PO/JO/10/1/24, 37, 274, 296; Crokey, *Briefe*. See below, Chapter 3.

[11] William B. Willcox, 'Lawyers and litigants in Stuart England', *Cornell Law Quarterly*, 24 (1938–9), 545–6; James Herbert Cooke, 'The Berkeley Manuscripts, and their author, John Smith', *TBGAS*, 5 (1880–1), 214; Broadway, 'John Smyth', p. 89; *Commons 1604–1629*, vi. 350–2; Lindley, *Wotton*, pp. 224–30; William Bradford Willcox, *Gloucestershire: A Study in Local Government, 1590–1640* (New Haven, 1940), p. 64; *CD 1621*, i. 82; Hart, *Justice*, p. 39; Kyle, *Theater*, pp. 160–1.

[12] Gardiner, *Reports*, pp. 37–40.

[13] Debora K. Shuger, *Censorship and Cultural Sensibility* (Philadelphia, 2006), p. 174.

Whether or not Crokey's case provides a useful means of analysing early modern censorship, it certainly provides vivid evidence about the manner in which legal disputes could be contested. Such disputes were defined not just by the matters that came before the courts, but also by dramatic tales that emerged about forgery, bribery, and corruption, as well as about riots, assaults, and kidnapping. Surviving evidence includes eye-witness accounts of hot words in London inns, of houses being besieged, and of witnesses being intimidated, not to mention an extraordinary scene in which a messenger was taken captive and put on 'trial' by the inmates of King's Bench prison. Wild claims were made by litigants on both sides. One was called a 'churchrobber' and a 'jesuitical fellow', and was likened to a 'toothdrawer', while another was called a 'madman' and 'that idiot'. Both men were accused of bad behaviour and sharp practice. Such language explains the book's title, which provides a flavour of the contemporary rhetoric, indicates the animosity involved, and highlights the serious issues at stake. Central to the book's argument is the idea that this most perplexing of disputes can be comprehended not just by placing litigation at the heart of contestation over Warrens Court, but also by exploring a broader pattern of disputatious behaviour, within which legal proceedings were enveloped.

A key aim is to suggest that close analysis of a rich, complex, and vibrant dispute—a 'micro-legal history' of a 'hard case'—makes it possible to tease out aspects of early modern litigation that are otherwise hidden from view. Contests like this one offer rare examples of how to delve beneath the surface of litigation that might easily be regarded as trivial, formulaic, and mundane. They open up new ways of scrutinising other cases, and the wider phenomenon of litigation, and also provide more general insights about the 'lawmindedness' of contemporary society, as well as about its fractures and fissures. Ultimately, the book suggests that litigation provides valuable evidence about the prevalence, severity, and *visibility* of social and ideological conflict in post-Reformation England, and one particular value of the Warrens Court dispute is that its longevity permits engagement with long-term trends, with contemporary awareness of those changes, and with people's memories and sense of connection with the past. The Warrens Court dispute thus provides a fresh perspective upon debates about whether the early seventeenth century was blessed by 'consensus' or riven by 'conflict', and about problems that provided the backdrop to the English revolution and survived its passing. Key here are reflections upon the methods needed for recovering evidence of conflict and division, and the book argues that solving the mysteries surrounding Crokey—why the dispute lasted so long and why it fascinated contemporaries—has implications for how historians think about the period's political, religious, and socio-economic tensions. My argument is that ideological conflict can sometimes only be brought into focus with a microhistorical approach, by subjecting legal cases and the legal system to particularly close scrutiny, by being sensitive to the thinking of those involved, and by identifying the local issues with which they were embroiled, and how these developed over time. As such, this book involves what might be called a *longue durée* microhistory.[14]

Such a study is only made possible by the survival of a neglected and extraordinarily rich cache of papers, the exploration of which should be considered not as an indulgent fetishisation of archival novelty, but rather as an opportunity to subject early modern litigation to deep contextualisation, and to undertake the kind of granular analysis that sheds light upon the wider world of law and politics. As is so often the case, it is the density of surviving archival material that makes it possible to fulfil the central aim of all true microhistories: connecting specific and apparently peculiar phenomena to a much bigger picture. What appears below is an introduction to the archive regarding Warrens Court, to the dispute's main protagonists, and to the methodological and conceptual issues with which subsequent chapters grapple.

I

As with so many microhistories, this book is reliant upon a rich but scrappy body of archival material, which came to light serendipitously, and which highlights the value of reading, rather than merely searching, catalogues. It was generated by calling up manuscripts more or less speculatively, from collections that are voluminous but fragmentary, and by tapping into the knowledge and enthusiasm of professional archivists, and it demonstrates the value of letting new research projects emerge more or less organically out of earlier work.

The fortuitous discovery that prompted this book occurred while working on the 'print revolution'. That project analysed how print culture transformed political life for ordinary citizens, by providing access to new kinds of information, as well as new opportunities to express opinions and exert influence over political processes, and it involved—in part—examining how even humble people began to use print to express grievances and set out demands, so that these could be presented to MPs in the hope of getting cases heard. This was a story of how familiar practices—petitioning and lobbying—underwent change as a result of technical innovations, and it was tracing such tactics that first revealed an obscure Bristol merchant called Benjamin Crokey, who was one of the first people to do this—in the early 1620s—and who did so repeatedly.[15] By their very nature, such texts pose significant challenges for historians. For a long time they eluded scholarly attention, not least because they tend to survive within archival

[14] Cynthia B. Herrup, *A House in Gross Disorder* (Oxford, 1999), p. 152; Guillaume Calafat, 'Jurisdictional pluralism in a litigious sea (1590–1630)', in Ghobrial, ed., *Global History*, 142–78. For questions of scale, see: Jan De Vries, 'Playing with scales: the global and the micro, the macro and the nano', in ibid., 23–36.

[15] Peacey, *Print Culture*.

collections, rather than in libraries, and although this rapidly became a popular genre, individual items are not necessarily easy to find. It was the chance of tracking down one particular item that prompted a visit to the Gloucestershire Archives, the catalogue of which indicated that it possessed a copy of Crokey's *Humble Petition* from 1640, the only other known copy of which was somewhat further away in Trinity College Dublin.[16] Unfortunately, this document turned out to be missing, although it was possible to locate copies of other texts that he printed, in 1621, 1625, and 1629, as well as in the 1640s. It was at this point that, in the hope that the tract might simply have been mis-shelved, it seemed worthwhile to scour the catalogues for boxes where it might be lurking, and to draw upon the cheerful assistance of archivists, who offered expert guidance regarding collections that have had more than one home over the centuries, and that have been re-catalogued and re-arranged over time. The upshot was that, although this particular pamphlet might genuinely be lost, the dispute to which it related can be documented in phenomenal detail, not least within the papers of Crokey's nemesis, John Smyth of Nibley.

This book contains the story that such papers reveal, and what can be wrought from them—imperfectly but dramatically—through a tortuous process of reconstruction. Before commencing such analysis, however, it is worth reflecting upon the nature of the surviving evidence, which likewise involves a story of good fortune. This is partly a matter of Crokey's texts, which are rich and tendentious, and partly a matter of the official records, including legal proceedings, parliamentary papers, and state archives, which are voluminous and valuable, albeit frustrating. What really underpins this project, however, is John Smyth's incredible archive, which can now be pieced together even though it is dispersed throughout numerous repositories. When Smyth reflected upon the dispute with Crokey in his well-known history of the Berkeley family, he claimed that he chose to 'write the less, referring him that desireth more to the records themselves', and the possibility of using these papers to resolve the affair's mysteries reflects not just the extraordinary story that they reveal, but also the fortunate way in which they have come down to us.[17] The latter is a tale worth telling—briefly—because it reinforces the sense that the papers provide an extremely rare opportunity to subject such a dispute to intense scrutiny.

The story of Smyth's papers involves the tendency for private papers to migrate around the country, in response to the fluctuating fortunes of gentry families. We know that Smyth bequeathed 'evidences and writings in my study at Nibley' to his son (1641), and that the papers remained with Smyth's descendants in Gloucestershire until the late eighteenth century. The death of Nicholas Smyth in 1790 saw the archive pass to his widow, Anna Maria, with whom they moved to the

[16] Crokey, *Petition*.   [17] Smyth, *Lives*, iii. 402.

estate that she inherited at Condover Hall in Shropshire, where they became integrated with the papers of the Cholmondeley family, following the death of Nicholas Smythe-Owen without heir in 1804.[18] It was at Condover that the papers were examined by the Historical Manuscripts Commission, which published an invaluable calendar in 1876, doubtless as part of the process by which the archive—and then the house—was put up for sale.[19] That sale—by Puttick and Simpson in 1887—could easily have been fatal for any historian of the Warrens Court dispute, because the bulk of the papers—some 3,000 documents that formed lot 976—were purchased by a specialist dealer, Bernard Quaritch, for £43, and immediately broken into smaller lots, which were then dispersed in another sale (1888).[20]

In such circumstances it is remarkable that almost all of Smyth's papers are now housed in public libraries. Papers relating to Virginia were acquired by Alexander Maitland, and given to the New York Public Library, before being published by S. M. Kingsbury.[21] The volumes that comprised 'Men and Armour'—Smyth's record of Gloucestershire men who could bear arms in 1608—were acquired by Lord Sherborne, whose family enabled them to be published in 1902.[22] Papers relating to Kingswood Abbey made their way to Bristol University Library, while another portion was bequeathed to Birmingham Central Library as the Fletcher Collection. Other choice items—including historical and literary works by Smyth, as well as his parliamentary diary—were acquired by the British Library, the Bodleian Library, the Folger Shakespeare Library, Yale University Library, and Chicago University Library.[23] Most aptly, but most impressively, the bulk of the collection made its way into what is now Gloucestershire Archives, via Gloucester City Library. Many of these were acquired from the Quaritch sale by F. A. Crisp FSA (*d.*1922), a prolific genealogist, from whose Grove Park Press they were acquired in 1921 by the Gloucester city librarian, Roland Austin, with the help of Alderman Edwin Lea (1848–1931).[24] Crisp's assistant thereupon expressed satisfaction that the papers were 'together . . . where the public can consult them', even if Austin himself was a little disappointed by what they contained.[25] The transfer of these materials to what was then Gloucestershire Record Office took place between 1952 and 2005, since when they have continued to receive the curatorial care they deserve. Yet another portion of the Condover papers turned up at Sotheby's in 1956, including a letter from Robert Burton, the author of *Anatomy of Melancholy*, which was acquired by the British Library after being

[18] Irvine Gray, 'Smith of Nibley's will', *TBGAS*, 78 (1959), 130; Smyth, *Lives*, i. pedigree; Herefordshire Archive and Records Centre, BB2/223.

[19] *HMC 5th Report* (London, 1876), pp. 339–60.

[20] Chicago UL, MS 1465, folder 1.

[21] NYPL, *ZL-214; Kingsbury, *Virginia*, i. 55.

[22] *Men and Armour*.

[23] Bristol UL, DM104; LB, MS 3549; BL, Add. MSS 33588–9, Add. MS 34121; Bodl. MS Eng.Misc. e.6; FSL, Z.e.1; V.b.298; Z.c.13, Z.c.30; Beinecke Library, Yale, Osborn a22; Chicago UL, MS 1465.

[24] R. Austin, *Catalogue of the Gloucestershire Collection* (Gloucester, 1928). See: GA, D9125/2/7644. Another document was donated in 1922: D9125/1/12024.

[25] GA, D9125/2/7644/15.

refused an export licence, as well as a volume about the civil wars that was acquired for Berkeley Castle, and the so-called 'Crewe albums' of correspondence and official papers, which were added to the 'Gloucestershire Collection'. The extraordinary upshot of such sales and acquisitions is that, while some of the papers identified by the HMC were thought to be missing as recently as 1961, they all now seem to be accessible.[26]

The moral of this story involves the fragility of the historical record, as well as the services of unheralded donors and archivists, and while it would be naïve to think that this constitutes a full record of the dispute between Crokey and Smyth, even when supplemented by material from other sources, what survives nevertheless constitutes a phenomenal archival seam. The importance of Smyth's papers has been widely recognised. They have been subjected to bibliographical enquiry, used to reconstruct Smyth's biography, and mined for documents that could be edited in specialist journals, and they have also been crucial to four book-length studies of early modern Gloucestershire.[27] Hitherto, however, they have not been used to analyse the Warrens Court dispute, even though they make it possible to resolve the mysteries with which we began, to shed light on a large cast of obscure characters, and to subject Smyth and Crokey to detailed reappraisal.[28]

II

The most famous of these protagonists is John Smyth of Nibley (1567–1641), who has been familiar to antiquarians since the late eighteenth century, including Thomas Fosbroke, who described his 'well known' papers as being 'of the first archaeological quality'.[29] Smyth's fame, however, rests mainly upon his literary significance, partly for his friendship with Robert Burton, but more obviously for his scholarly 'recreations', including the *Lives* of the Berkeley family.[30] This monumental work was lauded in its own time, and has been well used ever since, given that Smyth's analysis was historically and sociologically sophisticated, and given that his papers also reveal working practices and working notes. Smyth's *Lives* was described in commendatory verses as the work of 'a dextrous mind', and

[26] BL, Add. MS 49381; Berkeley, Select Books 87; GA, D7115/1–2; E. S. Lindley, 'A John Smyth bibliography', *TBGAS*, 80 (1961), 121–31.

[27] Willcox, *Gloucestershire*; Warmington, *Gloucestershire*; Rollison, *Local Origins*; Horn, *New World*.

[28] Howes, 'John Smyth', pp. 213–31; E. S. Lindley, 'William Archard: an unrecognized Gloucestershire worthy', *TBGAS*, 68 (1949), 190–8.

[29] Robert Atkyns, *The Ancient and Present State of Gloucestershire* (London, 1678), pp. 302–4; Rudder, *Gloucestershire*, pp. 574–5; Thomas Fosbroke, *Berkeley Manuscripts* (London, 1821), p. v; Thomas Fosbroke, *Abstracts of Records and Manuscripts Respecting the County of Gloucester* (2 vols, Gloucester, 1807), p. i. sig. a2.

[30] T. C. Skeat, 'A letter of Robert Burton', *British Museum Quarterly*, 22.1–2 (1960), 12–16; Smyth, *Lives*, iii. 410.

of 'unwearied industry'.[31] His pioneering census of Gloucestershire's adult males proved invaluable to social historians, and prompted R. H. Tawney to opine about 'the learned, lovable, pedantic John Smyth of Nibley'.[32] Somewhat less well understood are Smyth's career, his religious and political views, and his mental outlook.

Crucial here is Smyth's loyal service—as steward and 'man of business' for over fifty years—to the Berkeleys of Berkeley Castle, one of England's oldest noble families.[33] Having begun his life as the scion of an obscure Leicestershire family—albeit one whose home at Hoby fell within the Berkeleys' orbit—Smyth became a household servant to Henry, 7th Lord Berkeley (*d.*1613) in the early 1580s, accompanied his heir, Thomas (*d.*1611) to Oxford, and became steward to the family's estates in the 1590s.[34] Such service—during much of which Berkeley was lord lieutenant of Gloucestershire—is amply documented in Smyth's papers and the records at Berkeley Castle, in myriad accounts, receipts, acquittances, and bonds, as well as occasional letters, all of which were maintained in meticulous fashion. Smyth evidently became a trusted ally at a difficult time in the family's history, amid claims of recusancy, as well as indebtedness, intestacy, and exile, not to mention contested wardships and sexual scandal, and his loyalty was evident not just in the gifts he presented to his employers, but also in his service as the family's 'fixer', not least during the widowhood of Lady Elizabeth Berkeley (1613—22). Smyth railed against other servants who proved to be unreliable—one was described as 'a drunken rogue... a thief, a liar and a perjured fellow', while another was 'fitter for fairs and markets of cattle... than to grapple with a watchful adversary'—and the debts that the family incurred to him were financial as well as figurative.[35]

More importantly, after being called to the bar at the Middle Temple, Smyth also undertook a phenomenal amount of the work—as what Lord Berkeley called 'solicitor of my law causes'—that had 'beaten smooth the pavements between Temple Bar and Westminster Hall'.[36] In 1609, he negotiated an end to the family's 'great cause', a ferocious and violent dispute with the Lisle family that lasted for

[31] John Maclean, 'The manor of Bosham in the county of Sussex', *TBGAS*, 10 (1885–6), 250–77; LPL, MS 3512, fos 21–38; BL, Add. 33588, fos 1–43, 58, 63–8, 69 (quoted), 71; Beinecke Library, Osborn fb151; GA, D9125/1/6942, 12268; D8887/1/53–77; Chicago UL, MS 1465, folder 2/3–4.

[32] *HMC 5th report*, p. 339; R. H. Tawney, 'An occupational census of the seventeenth century', *Economic History Review*, 5.1 (1934), 27.

[33] Smyth, *Lives*, iii. 410–12.

[34] *Vis. Gloucester 1623*, p. 149; *Vis. Gloucester 1682–3*, pp. 171–3; *Al. Oxon*, iv. 1374; *Admissions MT*, i. 66; Smyth, *Lives*, i. pedigree, pp. iii–iv, ii. 378, 386, 394–5; Berkeley, BB107, fos 13v, 54, 94, 98v, 99v; BL, Add. MS 33588, fos 44–9v, 50v–1.

[35] GA, D9125/1/6945, 6948–50, 6954, 6958, 13609–10, 13615, 13617; D8887/1/29–32, 78–119; D8887/2/1–88; D8887/3/1–15, 51–5, 79–80; D8887/4/44, 56, 108–16; D8887/5/30, 44–5; D8887/9/31, 40; D8887/10/46, 51–2, 63; D9125/1/13608, fos 30, 41, 46, 52v; D9125/1/13612/8–10; D9125/1/13611/3–4; Berkeley, BB109, fo. 94v; BB10, fo. 82; Bodl. MS Eng.Misc.e.6, fos 41v, 83v; Smyth, *Lives*, ii. 310–11; Chicago UL, MS 1465, folders 3–4; BL, Add. MS 33588, fo. 60.

[36] GA, D8887/1/83; Smyth, *Lives*, ii. 37. See also: GA, D8887/2/42.

almost two hundred years, the settlement of which enabled the family to regain huge swathes of Gloucestershire land, including the manors of Nibley and Wotton-under-Edge, which became central to Smyth's life and the dispute with Crokey.[37] Smyth described such work as 'the most toilsome of all my labours', and it clearly had huge personal significance. This is not just because his services—what Lady Berkeley called his 'love and zeal', and his 'continual and effectual endeavours'—were handsomely rewarded, as his salary of between £10 and £17 was supplemented with traditional feudal gifts—a doe from the Berkeley estates once a year—as well as financial bonuses, and timber for 're-edifying' his Nibley residence.[38] It is also because, as his papers document in breath-taking detail, Smyth became a hugely experienced and well-connected litigant, whose knowledge of the legal system, its possibilities and its pitfalls, was probably unrivalled outside the profession.

What also seems clear is that Smyth gradually emerged from a position of dependency within an aristocratic household to become an established member of the Gloucestershire gentry, worth perhaps £500 *per annum*.[39] This complex relationship with the Berkeleys was certainly recognised by the family's fool, who responded to news that Smyth was building a grand new house—Smalcombe Court—with a quip that it would be advisable to anchor Berkeley Castle very firmly to the local church, lest Smyth should try and take it away to Nibley.[40] It is also evident from the zeal with which Smyth developed his estate, in highly controversial ways, as well as from his assumption of official duties beyond Berkeley Castle. Smyth served as Gloucestershire's escheator (1601–3), as steward of the local vice-admiralty court (1603–13), as commissioner of sewers (by 1615), and as subsidy commissioner (1629). He also became a 'projector', as a member of the Virginia Company, an investor in the Somers Island Company (1615), and a member of the Fisheries Society (1632).[41] In 1616, Smyth even contemplated purchasing the office of Keeper of the Records in the Tower of London (for £1,000), and by 1621 he was sufficiently well established to secure a seat in Parliament, where he kept the diary of proceedings that has helped to cement his fame.[42]

[37] Smyth, *Lives*, ii. 288–356, 372; GA, D8887/2/12, 77; D9125/1/13617; Berkeley, BB10, fo. 206. See: James Herbert Cooke, 'The Great Berkeley law-suit of the 15th and 16th centuries', *TBGAS*, 3 (1878–9), 305–24.

[38] GA, D8887/1/108; D8887/2/17, 20, 35, 39, 55, 64, 75; D9125/1/13615, 13617; Smyth, *Lives*, ii. 321–2, 333, iii. 42; Berkeley, BB107, fos 15v, 50, 64v, 65, 92; BB10, fos 118, 145v, 154, 260; LB, MS 3549/153. For Lady Berkeley's comments, see: BL, Add. MS 33588, fos 52, 54.

[39] TNA, STAC 8/107/7; Bodl. MS Eng.Misc.e.6, fos 15, 19v.

[40] Fosbroke, *Abstracts*, i. 468–9.

[41] LB, MS 3549/122; Smyth, *Lives*, ii. 372, iii. 9; TNA, C 181/2, fo. 240v; C 181/3, fo. 172v; GA, D8887/1/34; D8887/2/76; D8887/3/68; D8887/4/55, 79, 80, 105–6; D8887/5/20–1, 29, 31, 49; D8887/7/52; D9125/1/1103, 13608/72; Kingsbury, *Virginia*, i. 469, 472–3, 490, 496, 556; J. E. Gethyn-Jones, 'Berkeley plantation Virginia', *TBGAS*, 94 (1977), 5–17; TNA, SP 16/221, fos 1–8; Bodl. MS Eng.Misc. e.6, fo. 97v.

[42] GA, D8887/5/22; BL, Add. MS 34121; *CD 1621*, v. 249–420.

Smyth's election demonstrated that he had come a long way since 1608, when he described himself as 'an utter barrister' who could furnish 'three swords and one halberd' for the king's service, as well as 'one corslet furnished, one birding piece, one crossbow and [a] gauntlet'. Indeed, there are many ways of highlighting Smyth's hard-won status, and the pride he took in being a local powerbroker, albeit one who never rose high enough to merit appointment to the county bench.[43] These include sources as diverse as tailors' bills and the documents he prepared when fitting out a new house in 1640.[44] They involve meticulous records relating to gifts—from silver bowls to fish and fowl, worth perhaps £50 per year—that were presented to friends, clients, servants, and tenants, as well as to the seating plan that he devised for Nibley Church, both of which projected his dominant position within the local community.[45] They also involve the fine monument that Smyth erected to his first wife, Grace Drew (costing £6 13*s*.4*d*.), the portraits he commissioned of his second wife, and the coat of arms he engraved onto the rings that passed down through the family.[46] Ultimately, Smyth's position also ensured that he was able to send at least three of his five sons to Oxford (the expenses were naturally recorded in great detail), to educate John Smyth junior at the Middle Temple, and to secure for his heir an impressive marriage to the daughter of Sir Edward Bromfield, lord mayor of London. More obviously than his father, Smyth junior not only served as steward to the Berkeley family for life—referring to his 'duty' and their 'many favours'—but also did so as a leading member of the county elite.[47]

However, while Smyth's rise to prominence is easily documented, it is much harder to illuminate his mental outlook and his political and religious beliefs. Writing in 1821, Fosbroke described him as a 'violent Puritan', and this interpretation has proved remarkably resilient.[48] Smyth's parliamentary diary and reading habits have been used to align him with 'the political opposition to Stuart autocracy', and he has been described as someone who stood uneasily between 'the two worlds of feudalism and capitalism', but who betrayed evidence of a 'bourgeois soul', and who was 'sternly practical, intensely personal and individualistic'. Although this did not involve labelling him as a Puritan, it certainly involving characterising him as someone who held moderate and proto-secular views of the church, and whose outlook and financial interests—in colonial adventures, coal mining, and cloth working—reflected those of an

[43] *Men and Armour*, pp. 173–5.
[44] GA, D8887/5/47, 50; D8887/10/107; D9125/1/13619.
[45] GA, D9125/1/13618; D9125/2/5821.
[46] GA, GDR/1692/240; Bodl. MS Eng.Misc.e.6, fo. 48v.
[47] Smyth, *Lives*, i. pedigree; GA, D8887/5/32, 34, 80; D8887/9/122, 134; D8887/10/79–80; D8887/2/91, 93, 94, 96, 98, 103, 110; D8887/3/64; D8887/4/56–8, 62–3; D8887/11/3–4, 36, 42, 53, 116, 118; D2957/216/5–7.
[48] Fosbroke, *Abstracts*, i. 468; Fosbroke, *Berkeley Manuscripts*, p. vi.

emerging 'middle class'.[49] What unites these different accounts of Smyth's outlook is recognition that, in the absence of overt statements about his ideas and beliefs, it is necessary to analyse his outlook by focusing upon his behaviour. However, doing this more systematically, and focusing much more closely on Smyth's responses to the political and religious developments of the age, generates a rather different picture of his mental world, and reveal that he was anything but a Puritan.

III

The challenge with Smyth's adversary, Benjamin Crokey, is similar and different at the same time. He too requires careful scrutiny, given that evidence about him is not just allusive but also elusive, and it is hard to deny that surviving documentation about the Warrens Court dispute is asymmetrical, and very heavily weighted towards Smyth. Nevertheless, if data about Crokey is uneven then it is hardly negligible, and this book challenges how he has been characterised hitherto, and the 'enormous condescension' with which characters from outside the elite are still apt to be treated. From the brief accounts we have of his battle with Smyth, Crokey emerges as a failed merchant, who became 'obsessed' with the dispute, and who 'let himself go'. In one account, Crokey was little more than 'wayward', and even 'unbalanced'.[50] The aim here is to rescue Crokey from obscurity, reveal his attitudes and motivations, and revise such claims about his character.

The place to start is the idea that Crokey was a failed merchant, since this is not straightforwardly true. At his most successful, Crokey was a far from humble tradesman. He claimed armigerous status, and was apparently descended from William Crokey of Yorkshire, who was granted arms in 1496.[51] This man, or more likely his son, served as a customs officer in Hull in the 1540s, and although the family's genealogy remains obscure, they subsequently moved to London, where Robert Crokey (*d.*1597) lived in the parish of St Katherine's by the Tower, and held property in St Katherine's Dock from at least the 1550s.[52] Unfortunately, as a royal 'peculiar' St Katherine's is less well documented than other London parishes, but this was clearly Crokey's father, who was made freeman of the Ironmongers' Company in 1560 or 1561, became a liveryman in 1562–3, and died in 1597. In the

[49] *CD 1621*, i. 76, 82–3; Broadway, 'Political appropriation', pp. 3–5; D. Rollison, 'The bourgeois soul of John Smyth of Nibley', *Social History*, 12.3 (1987), 309–10, 318, 321–2, 325–6, 327, 330; Broadway, 'John Smyth', p. 89. For Smyth and the clothiers: GA, D9125/1/13612/3, 13881; D8887/9/2, 4, 11, 15–17, 27, 29, 33, 44, 46–9, 51, 58–9, 62. For coal mines: Smyth, *Lives*, iii. 42.

[50] Lindley, *Wotton*, p. 229; F. Hornsby and P. Griffin, *Katherine Lady Berkeley's School* (Wotton, 1984), p. 44.

[51] W. Harry Rylands, ed., *Grantees of Arms* (London, 1915), p. 66.

[52] *Letters and Papers Henry VIII* (23 vols, London, 1862–1932), 19 part 2 (1544), p. 69; TNA, C 3/34/29; C 3/38/24; C 3/46/122; E 133/7/955.

years between 1560 and 1597, Robert Crokey left only occasional marks on the papers of the Ironmongers' Company. He took on an apprentice in 1561–2, occasionally attended the company's court from 1565, and served as steward of one lord mayor's dinner (1569), but he was only sometimes listed as providing funds for charitable collections and assessments. Nevertheless, he was an established figure, who stood for election as company warden on five occasions between 1584 and 1596, even if he was never chosen.[53]

Benjamin Crokey (born *c.*1574) was thus the scion of a successful mercantile family, and although this status was newly won its impact was significant. As will become clear, Robert Crokey's marriage to Katherine Powell—at some point before 1574—explains the family's involvement in the Warrens Court dispute, but it also enabled Benjamin Crokey to launch his own mercantile career in 1593, by becoming apprentice to a Bristol draper called Thomas Watkins.[54] This was not an uncomplicated development, because Watkins soon found himself imprisoned in relation to a violent dispute with John Dowle of Bristol's custom house, which meant that Crokey only completed part of his training.[55] Nevertheless, he acquired his freedom by redemption in 1599, settled in the parish of St Mary Le Port, and became involved in overseas trade.[56] Crucially, in October 1600 Crokey married Elizabeth, the sister of Robert Aldworth (*d.*1634), thereby forging an alliance with one of Bristol's most powerful mercantile families. The effective heir of Thomas Aldworth, the city's MP in 1586 and 1589, Robert Aldworth became immensely wealthy, partly on the back of the emerging slave trade, and also became a dominant figure within the civic community, as sheriff, alderman, and mayor.[57]

Aldworth's network would be hugely important to Crokey's fortunes, even if not always in positive ways, and it was almost certainly with his help that Crokey joined a fast track to mercantile success.[58] Crokey's later claim, that he traded in cloth and 'other merchanidizes . . . to divers foreign countries', can be substantiated by Bristol's port books, which reveal frequent shipments of bays, Irish rugs, friezes, kerseys, and 'Polonia cloth', as well as iron and sugar, from 1600 to around 1612, sometimes in partnership with Aldworth and Humphrey Fitzherbert.[59] Like

[53] GL, MS 16988/2, fos 117v, 122, 126, 136v, 145, 160v, 206v, 231v; MS 16967/1, fos 44, 47, 52v, 55, 61v, 63, 75, 75v, 78, 83v, 86, 92v, 95v, 98-v, 102, 107v, 118v, 157, 172, 200, 201v, 203; A. W. Hughes Clarke, ed., *The Registers of St Katherine by the Tower* (7 vols, London, 1945–51), i. 125.

[54] TNA, STAC 8/274/8; GA, D8887/6/2–3; D9125/1/11989/1; BA, FC/AB/1(b)15. Benjamin Crokey was 44 in 1618: GA, D8887/6/66.

[55] TNA, SP 12/267, fos 53–65v; SP 12/274, fos 85–99; BA, M/BCC/CCP/1/1, pp. 30–1.

[56] BA, F/Au/1/15, p. 17.

[57] T. Colyer-Fergusson, ed., *The Marriage Registers of St Dunstan's Stepney* (3 vols, Canterbury, 1898–1901), i. 45; Beaven, *Bristol*, pp. 184, 196, 275; GA, D3439/1/442, unfol.

[58] Crokey's daughter, Elizabeth, married one of Aldworth's kinsmen, George Payne: TNA, PROB 11/167, fo. 21.

[59] TNA, C 3/338/8; E 190/1133/1, fos 11, 13, 19v; E 190/1133/3, fos 23, 29; E 190/1133/5, fo. 13; E 190/1133/9, unfol.; E 190/1133/11, fos 14, 17v, 19v, 36v, 38v; E 190/1133/12, fos 17v, 22, 24, 24v, 43v, 45; E 190/1134/2, unfol.; E 190/1134/3, fos 1v, 9v; Susan Flavin and Evan Jones, eds, *Bristol's Trade with Ireland and the Continent, 1503–1601* (BRS, 61, 2009), p. 939.

Fitzherbert, Crokey became a member of Bristol's Society of Merchant Venturers, where Aldworth served as master on three occasions, thereby joining a small and highly elite group of citizens, which comprised only seventy-two men by 1618.[60]

Crokey thus became a successful and well-established merchant, who might easily have gone on to join Bristol's civic elite, had it not been for the difficulties that drove him out of trade sometime between 1612 and 1615. Although there are gaps in the city's port books, it appears that Crokey was much less active after 1612, something that is confirmed by Bristol's Staple Court and Tolzey Court papers. These two bodies were empowered to resolve disputes between local merchants without recourse to common law, and thus provide an indication of an individual's economic activity, rather than their litigiousness. Like most local merchants, Crokey's name appears in these records with some regularity—usually in relation to debts of between 20*s.* and £200—but only until 1615, which fits with his later claim that, having 'lived in good credit and reputation', he became a victim of pirates 'upon the seas', and that £2,000 worth of goods were 'violently taken... to his utter undoing'.[61] This is certainly credible: the Merchant Venturers recorded that forty-five ships were 'taken by the Turks' in 1610, and by 1613 the city's prisons housed many captured pirates, who operated as close to home as the Severn estuary. In 1619 and 1620, local merchants contributed significant sums towards expeditions 'against the pirates of Algiers', although Crokey's name is not listed among the subscribers. By that stage he had almost certainly ceased trading, lacked funds, and was preoccupied with other matters.[62]

Such evidence suggests that with Crokey, as with Smyth, there is scope to reflect upon his background, status, and circumstances, upon the circles in which he moved, and upon the motivations and attitudes that underpinned his involvement in litigation. From his upbringing on the fringes of London, in a parish notorious for heterodoxy, to his encounters with merchants whose business interests have been linked with a certain kind of 'Laudianism', hints will emerge that litigation and disputation reflected Crokey's ideological outlook, and one that involved both puritanism and parliamentarianism.[63]

IV

Introducing the key protagonists in a dispute that seems so mysterious indicates that Smyth's papers are invaluable, but also that they require careful handling if they are to shed light upon motivations, attitudes, ideas, and beliefs. The same can

[60] McGrath, *Records*, p. 27; BA, SMV/3/1/1.
[61] BA, JStap/1/3, fos 15v, 49v, 90; JTol/J/1/10, fos 63v, 85, 89v, 114v, 116, 226; TNA, C 3/338/8.
[62] BA, SMV/2/1/1/34, pp. 74, 78; M/BCC/CCP/1/2, fos 32, 79v, 80v, 87; SMV/3/1/1, fos 10v, 131v, 132; McGrath, *Records*, pp. 185–6.
[63] Sacks, *Widening Gate*, pp. 221–46.

also be said about the most important challenge of all: analysing the litigation at the heart of the Warrens Court dispute. The final task in setting up this book involves addressing the methodological issues and conceptual tools relevant for a study of this kind. This is because the aim is not simply to reconstruct the dispute—its events and episodes, and the people and places involved—in great detail, let alone to assess which side had the best claim.[64] A proper appreciation of why Crokey's printed works proved to be so fascinating, and why the dispute went on for so long, requires understanding what was at stake, in terms of the different social, mental, and ideological worlds that Smyth, Crokey, and their respective networks inhabited. This can be achieved—and used to understand early modern litigation more generally—by embracing the insights of certain kinds of micro-historian, and of the political and legal anthropologists with whom they have much in common. This involves addressing 'micro-events', 'micro-sociology', and 'micro-politics', and the everyday practices, processes, and behaviour associated with disputes, as well as larger issues relating to social conflict. It means exploring the relationship between 'structure' and 'agency', not least by distinguishing between the ostensible issues involved in litigation and what was 'really going on'.[65] Ultimately, it is argued that exploring a precise and localised affair, albeit one that was protracted, makes it possible to solve the mysteries surrounding the dispute, and to reveal insights into contemporary legal and political culture that would otherwise not be possible.

That this book involves only a certain kind of microhistory reflects the fact that the genre encapsulates different kinds of scholarship. First, microhistories are sometimes associated with the 'revival of narrative', involving a determination to make history accessible by telling 'captivating' stories, bringing neglected episodes 'alive', focusing on their 'colour', 'immediacy, intimacy and concreteness', and offering 'entertainment'. Some are even accused of imposing narrative coherence upon historical evidence, and of succumbing to the temptation to use speculation to 'fill the gaps'.[66] Alan Macfarlane recognised that, while legal records provide a wealth of dramatic stories, they might also result in a 'literary mode of pure description', 'almost like the plays of Webster', as Penry Williams noted. Robert Darnton bemoaned the emergence of 'incident analysis', in which discrete moments are explored in terms of how observers at the time construed them,

[64] Tim Stretton, 'Social historians and the records of litigation', in Solvi Sogner, ed., *Fact, Fiction and Forensic Evidence* (Oslo, 1997), pp. 26–7. Cf. Carlo Ginzburg, 'The inquisitor as anthropologist', in *Clues, Myths and the Historical Method* (Baltimore, 1986), pp. 156–64.

[65] Victor Turner, *Schism and Continuity in an African Society* (Manchester, 1957), p. xxiv; Victor Turner, *Dramas, Fields and Metaphors* (London, 1974), p. 63.

[66] Holly Tucker, *Blood Work. A Tale of Medicine and Murder in the Scientific Revolution* (London, 2011), pp. xix–xxii; Thomas V. Cohen and Elizabeth S. Cohen, *Words and Deeds in Renaissance Rome* (Toronto, 2000), pp. ix–x; Gene Brucker, *Giovanni and Lusanna* (Berkeley, 1986), p. ix; Thomas Cohen, *Love and Death in Renaissance Italy* (Chicago, 2004), p. 5; Thomas Kuehn, 'Reading microhistory', *JMH*, 61.3 (1989), 512–34.

and how they were remembered over time.[67] This is not the same as exploring how protagonists constructed narratives to comprehend the more or less unscripted events with which they were involved, or as subjecting events to thorough historical contextualisation and analysis.

Secondly, microhistories are sometimes methodologically unreflective, and have been criticised for 'theoretical poverty'. This means doing too little to address the 'research process' or 'craft', in terms of how to deal with 'clues, signs and symptoms', and while exemplary microhistories like *The Voices of Morebath* demonstrate that dealing with such issues overtly is not essential, explicit methodological reflection is more or less important with certain kinds of material, not least legal sources. Particular challenges exist in terms of how sources were generated, which perspectives they record, and how to avoid taking documents at face value. If legal sources are to be used for more than merely analysing legal issues, in terms of exploring the assumptions and motivations of those involved, and the conflicts with which they were involved, then it is important to confront such methodological challenges head-on.[68]

Thirdly, not all microhistories demonstrate a determination to 'scale up', by connecting micro- and macro-level analysis. This requires ensuring that 'gripping' stories are properly contextualised, that narrative is complemented by attention to the complexities of contemporary lives and worlds, and that unique individuals and episodes are used to tease out 'deeper historical resonances'.[69] How to achieve this 'change of scale' has been a matter of debate, given the problem of demonstrating that specific incidents or individuals are 'representative' of wider phenomena, but it commonly involves ideas about what constitutes a 'normal exception'. This is the idea that obscure episodes and mysterious characters are worthy of study because what appears to be 'exceptional' might actually have been 'normal', especially for those on the periphery of society. As such, they help to illuminate the 'boundaries of the ordinary', and thus the wider historical landscape.[70] The claim advanced here is that the Warrens Court dispute represents the 'normal exception' in the world of early modern litigation; an extreme case that, by virtue of being susceptible to close scrutiny, illuminates the wider landscape of litigation, revealing things that were more or less common to other disputes, and tendencies that might

[67] Alan Macfarlane, 'History, anthropology and the study of communities', *Social History*, 2 (1977), 636–7; P. Williams, 'The Star Chamber and the Council of the Marches of Wales, 1558–1603', *Bulletin of the Board of Welsh Studies*, 16.4 (1956), 288; Robert Darnton, 'It happened one night', *New York Review of Books* (24 June 2004).

[68] Anthony Molho, 'review of Brucker, *Giovanni and Lusanna*', *Renaissance Quarterly*, 40.1 (1987), 99; Levi, 'On microhistory', p. 106; Kuehn, 'Reading microhistory'; Eamon Duffy, *The Voices of Morebath* (New Haven, 2001).

[69] Paul Boyer and Stephen Nissenbaum, *Salem Possessed. The Social Origins of Witchcraft* (Cambridge, Mass., 1974), pp. xii, 179.

[70] Cohen, *Love and Death*, pp. 74–5.

easily have led other disputes to spin out of control. That is why attempts are made throughout to draw parallels with other disputes, and with the rhetoric involved.

Precisely how to overcome such problems—how to blend narrative and analysis, grapple with legal sources, and use unusual cases to address bigger issues—remains a matter of debate, not least between 'cultural' and 'social' microhistorians, and it is the latter whose work seems most relevant. The key point is that social microhistorians have followed a path identified by Giovanni Levi, rather than the one chosen by Carlo Ginzburg, which means moving beyond insights from symbolic anthropology, recognising that contemporary contexts reveal multiple experiences of, and perspectives on, specific phenomena, and emphasising human 'agency', and also producing accounts that are diachronic rather than merely synchronic.[71] 'Social' microhistorians obviously recognise that 'agency' is a problematic term, but they understand the need to focus upon lived experience, to examine the decision-making that individuals undertook in daily life, and to consider the constraints under which they operated.[72] They also recognise the need to explore not just curious individuals and incidents, but also specific communities and phenomena over fairly protracted periods, using a variety of 'regular' records relating to society, the economy, and the law. Unlike many famous microhistories, in other words, this book only superficially grapples with extraordinary episodes and peculiar people, and a key aim is to stress that this particular dispute involves an exaggerated instance of commonplace activities. It highlights how a normal activity—civil litigation—could become protracted and problematic, and it involves legal suits that might easily be regarded as routine and unimportant, were it not for the extraordinary archival evidence which reveals their real significance. The goal is to demonstrate how the meaning and significance of particular disputes can be recovered, and it makes sense to reflect upon the methods and approaches employed in this book, each of which is mentioned briefly in setting out the book's structure, before being set out more thoroughly at the start of each of its three main sections.

Part One establishes the narrative arc of the dispute, in terms of the apparently interminable and self-destructive legal suits contested between 1545 and 1661. The first two chapters use Smyth's papers, court records, and the petitions and pamphlets that emerged from litigation, to reconstruct a complex series of events and initiatives, and to trace the dispute's twists and turns. The approach here is different from most other studies of early modern litigation, which tend to focus

[71] Levi, 'On microhistory', pp. 98, 103; Simona Cerutti, 'Microhistory: social relations versus cultural models', in Anna-Maija Castrem et al., eds, *Between Sociology and History* (Helsinki, 2004), pp. 17–40; Jacques Revel, 'Microanalysis and the construction of the social', in Lynn Hunt and Jacques Revel, eds, *Histories: French Constructions of the Past* (New York, 1995); Francesca Trivellato, 'Microstoria/microhistoire/microhistory', *French Politics, Culture and Society*, 33.1 (2015), 122–34.

[72] Thomas V. Cohen, 'The macrohistory of microhistory', *Journal of Medieval and Early Modern Studies*, 47.1 (2017), 59–60; Guido Ruggiero, *Binding Passions: Tales of Magic, Marriage and Power at the End of the Renaissance* (Oxford, 1993), p. 13.

on particular courts or localities, and on official records and synoptic analysis. This section, by contrast, explores one protracted dispute across time and across multiple jurisdictions, and focuses on the legal basis upon which successive cases were brought and fought, and the legal decisions reached by the courts, not to mention how litigants responded to success and failure in procedural terms. It argues that an apparently incomprehensible battle like the Warrens Court dispute can begin to be understood by recognising that both sides had reasons to believe they were making progress, and that the nature of the dispute changed dramatically over time, in ways which involved issues larger than merely the financial interests of contending parties. As a legal dispute, the battle for Warrens Court demonstrates how litigation could involve mutation, frustration, and escalation.

Part Two turns from lawsuits to the strategies and tactics of disputants, and the ideas and practices associated with dispute resolution. It approaches some of the episodes outlined in Part One from different angles, to develop a multi-perspectival and thematic account of the contest. It is this possibility of recovering different perspectives on specific disputes, and the thinking of all sides, that is so often lacking from studies of litigation, and the claim advanced here is that grappling with how litigants planned, perceived, and portrayed disputation is crucial to our appreciation of what was involved—and invested—in early modern litigation. This means observing how protagonists thought about how best to proceed, and how they understood—and perhaps bent—the 'rules of the game'. It also means analysing how each litigant's approaches were viewed and discussed by contemporaries, in terms of a discourse of 'practices' and 'power', naivety and ineptitude, not least to demonstrate that claims about vexatious litigation, sharp practice, and even violence sometimes involved more than exaggerated rhetoric. It is argued that contemporary practices, thoughts about 'practice', and reflections on success and failure reveal litigants' motivations and help to explain their determination to press on with the dispute. Litigants' reflections on the case also indicate what they made of, and expected from, the legal system.

Finally, Part Three picks up this idea—that disputation was rooted in, revealed, and generated different ideas—by addressing the 'structural' issues at stake, and the values, beliefs, and ideologies of those involved. It argues that the Warrens Court dispute went on for so long because it was underpinned by religious and political tensions, and that the ideas of Smyth and Crokey are recoverable even though they were not expressed overtly, not least by scrutinising their respective networks. Key here is the need to situate the affair within at least three distinct communities, in London, in Bristol, and in the Vale of Berkeley. The latter is particularly important, since the dispute revolved around people and property in Nibley and Wotton-under-Edge; small divided communities nestling under the Cotswold hills, only a few miles from Berkeley Castle. Smyth's beloved Nibley was a village of a few hundred people, which he cherished for its 'sweet salutary air', its 'pretty river', and its mixture of 'arable, meadow, pasture, wood'. It was also intimately linked to its larger neighbour, Wotton, which Leland described as 'an attractive market town' that 'clings to the hillside' under the Cotswold escarpment. Nibley's chapel belonged to the church of St Mary in Wotton, and with its clutch of tuck mills and grist mills the village also shared with Wotton a significant involvement in cloth working.[73] What makes these places interesting is their convoluted manorial history, as well as the social, economic, and religious changes they witnessed, from the development of the cloth trade to the Reformation and the civil wars, and like the nearby city of Bristol they were at the heart of the dispute between Crokey and Smyth, in terms of both personnel and contested property. Moreover, while the dispute resembled a feud or vendetta, something that was well known to lots of contemporaries, it also involved broader groupings that linked and divided particular families and communities. While the worlds of John Smyth and Benjamin Crokey were different, they also overlapped and intersected in fascinating ways, through work, marriage, and kinship, and as their dispute developed and escalated, the localities and networks to which they were connected were mobilised and weaponised, as the tussle over Warrens Court became an expression and manifestation of wider and deeper divisions.

V

Teasing out the religious and political ideas that underpinned the Warrens Court dispute eventually makes it possible to resolve one of the mysteries that inspired this book—contemporary fascination with Crokey's texts—by highlighting how the dispute involved ideological tensions, which affected everyday life and coloured people's reflections on current affairs. Contemporary fascination with the dispute is indicative of deeper ideological issues, and for participants and onlookers alike it mattered not so much because of its ostensible issues, in terms of matters that came before the courts, and how they were described in legal bills, petitions, and pamphlets, but rather because it was emblematic of profound fault lines within contemporary society. These were familiar, important, and long-lasting, and the dispute was informed by people's memories of ideological division, within the region and their own families. Ultimately, the case attracted attention and interest because an apparently innocuous, if protracted and acrimonious dispute, was fraught with political and religious issues.

Of course, this is not the first study to employ microhistorical methods, or even litigation, to explore political and religious conflict.[74] Bernard Capp has shown

[73] GA, D3439/1/299; Smyth, *Lives*, iii. 85, 260, 269; Elrington, 'Survey', p. 95; John Chandler, ed., *John Leland's Itinerary* (Stroud, 1993), p. 184; *Men and Armour*, pp. 163–5, 173–5.

[74] Peter Lake, *The Boxmaker's Revenge: 'Orthodoxy, 'Heterodoxy' and the Politics of the Parish in Early Stuart London* (Manchester, 2009); John Walter, *Understanding Popular Violence in the English Revolution* (Oxford, 2008).

how local legal disputes could dominate the affairs of specific communities, and how they shed light upon bigger issues.[75] John Walter has demonstrated the value of 'thick description' for exploring tensions within local communities, and for demonstrating that they were connected to 'deeper structures and longer term processes', and informed by political and religious divisions at 'national' level. In studying the response to Laudian innovations within the parish of Radwinter, he argued that local disputes represented the 'visible tip of a denser pattern of... everyday conflict' and revealed the 'depth of politicisation that made the English revolution possible'. He also argued that the introduction of Laudianism revealed and exacerbated existing tensions.[76] This book also shares the instincts and approaches of David Underdown's *Fire from Heaven*, a diachronic microhistory of a particular place—Dorchester—which explores political culture, religious tensions, and the relationship between local and national issues, by examining local disputation and litigation, looking for 'deeper' issues beneath 'surface' problems, and reading 'between the lines' to recover contemporary mentalities.[77] In other words, this book is consciously positioned alongside a body of scholarship that takes seriously the possibility of detecting tension and conflict in the decades before the civil wars, not least within local communities.[78]

With this dispute, however, something rather different is involved. Rather than simply demonstrating that ideological tensions affected all levels of society and all parts of the country, it highlights the need to rethink activity that is not ostensibly ideological. In part this is a matter of litigation, a thoroughly commonplace activity, and one that is sometimes used to demonstrate the opportunities that ordinary people had for problem-solving. It is argued that, while the dispute was unusually long and well documented, it was not fundamentally out of the ordinary, and that it highlights how litigation could reveal, reflect, and generate disharmony, even along ideological lines. However, reflecting on the ideological dimensions of the Warrens Court dispute is also a matter of how historians interpret the relationship between local and national affairs, not least as reflected in parliamentary business. Central here is the idea that a local dispute involving deep political and religious divisions was not expressed in ideological terms. Ideological division is shown to have been something that contemporaries could see even though it was not made clear from texts that reached Parliament, the Privy Council, and the Court, a finding at odds with much recent scholarship on political and ideological conflict in early modern Britain, and on the role of the

[75] Bernard Capp, 'Life, love and litigation: Sileby in the 1630s', *P&P*, 182 (2004), 55–84.

[76] John Walter, 'Affronts and insolencies: the voices of Radwinter and popular opposition to Laudianism', *EHR*, 122.495 (2007), 36, 55, 60.

[77] David Underdown, *Fire from Heaven* (New Haven, 1992), pp. 30, 32–3, 46, 153.

[78] Thomas Cogswell, *Home Divisions* (Manchester, 1998); Ann Hughes, *Politics, Society and Civil War in Warwickshire, 1620–1660* (Cambridge, 1987).

Westminster system.[79] It is this conclusion—that ideological conflict may have been more prevalent in the localities than it appears to have been at the centre—that justifies the use of 'thick description' and a microhistorical approach, in terms of the possibility for seeing something new about something big through the lens of something small and mysterious.

[79] Conrad Russell, *Unrevolutionary England, 1603–1642* (Woodbridge, 1990); Conrad Russell, *Parliaments and English Politics, 1621–9* (Oxford, 1979).

PART ONE
SUITS

> Men are grown to be far more contentious than they have been in times past, and readier to revenge their quarrels of small importance, whereof the lawyers complain not.
>
> William Harrison, *The Description of England* (1577)

> Innumerable children have been born into the cause; innumerable young people have married into it; innumerable old people have died out of it.
>
> Charles Dickens, *Bleak House* (1853)

Introduction

Luckily, John Smyth of Nibley had a reliable London base in the 1610s and 1620s. He generally lodged, at the sign of the Blue Anchor in St Clement Danes, with Michael Moseley, a King's Bench clerk with whom he had worked since the 1590s. Smyth was fortunate because he needed to stay in London a lot; for most or all of almost every legal term for twenty years, either on his own or with one or more servants. This reflected the volume of legal cases in which he was embroiled, and while some of these certainly involved his employer, Lord Berkeley, most involved his own affairs, particularly the protracted dispute with Benjamin Crokey. This contest dated back to 1610 but was something that both men inherited. It had been dragging on since at least the 1560s, relating to land transactions from the 1540s, and it was a fight that both men would pass on to the next generation; Smyth to his son and namesake, Crokey to his daughter Sarah, who finally gave up the ghost in the early 1660s. This section begins the process of making sense of this 'scarecrow' dispute, and of early modern litigation, in terms of why it went on so long and became so acrimonious. This can only be done through analysis of litigation. Writing in 1625, Crokey referred to no fewer than thirty-three suits emerging from the will of William Thomas, 'whereupon there were verdicts, decrees, nonsuits, and dismissions'.[1] It would later be noted that Crokey was imprisoned no fewer than four times before 1641, involving twenty years in detention, and Smyth too found himself in prison more than once.[2] Both men referred to the vast sums of money spent in contesting the matter.

Understanding such a dispute means building upon historical understanding of legal contestation and the early modern legal system, in terms of patterns of litigation, the ways in which the system did and did not work, and how contemporaries reflected upon the perils and pitfalls of legal processes. Historians have recognised the dramatic increase in litigation that occurred during the early modern period, and traced it to population growth and socio-economic change, and they also understand that legal mentalities became prevalent across both the nation and the social spectrum. Such change was not universally welcomed, and while some contemporaries saw opportunities for the exercise of 'agency' by ordinary people, and effective methods for maintaining the rule of law, others feared that litigation betrayed social stress, conflict, and disharmony. Contemporaries quickly became anxious about a series of interconnected problems with the legal system, which meant that the growing popularity of litigation went alongside mounting complaints and grievances.[3]

Firstly, while going to law was fairly cheap, such that poor and humble citizens were not systematically excluded, and litigation could be a 'pastime', financial issues were complicated. Common law was cheaper than equity, while certain procedures could be extremely expensive, and concerns emerged that fees were rising, and that costs could mount very quickly if cases dragged on, and 'racket the subject lamentably'.[4] Secondly, litigants were confronted by procedural complexities, and the uncertainties that arose from 'overlapping and ill-defined jurisdictions'.[5] Thirdly, contemporaries worried about 'procedural deceleration' caused by courts being overburdened, and in 1617 it was reckoned that there were 8,000 Chancery cases awaiting resolution. The danger was that individual cases might drag on for years or even decades, 'as long as a buff coat will endure wearing',

[1] Crokey, *Sacred Maiestie*, sig. B4. See: Berkeley, BB109, fo. 29v; BB110, fo. 1; GA, D2404/13; GA, D8887/7/21; D8887/6/44; D8887/5/2; D9125/1/13612/8.

[2] GA, D9125/1/12028, p. 8.

[3] Brooks, *Pettyfoggers*, pp. 57, 78–9, 132, 203; Hart, *Justice*, p. 23; Brooks, *Lawyers*, pp. 36, 66, 86, 91; John Walter, '"Law-mindedness": crowds, courts and popular knowledge of the law in early modern England', in Michael Lobban, Joanne Begiato and Adrian Green, eds, *Law, Lawyers and Litigants in Early Modern England* (Cambridge, 2019), 164–84; Richard J. Ross, 'Commoning of the Common Law', *University of Pennsylvania Law Review*, 146.2 (1998), 323–461.

[4] HEH, EL2749.

[5] Hart, *Justice*, pp. 3–4; Jones, *Chancery*, p. 19; James McComish, 'Defining boundaries: law, justice and community in sixteenth-century England', in Fernanda Pirie and Judith Scheele, eds, *Legalism: Community and Justice* (Oxford, 2014), pp. 125, 131.

something that was intimately connected to a fourth concern: lawyers.[6] The rise of litigation dramatically transformed the legal profession, and litigants encountered not just barristers but also scriveners, solicitors, and attorneys, and the 'lower branches' of the profession included people who lacked formal training, and perhaps anything more than familiarity with William West's *Symbolaeographia*, one of a number of printed texts that brought legal understanding within the reach of ordinary citizens. Concerns mounted about a 'pestiferous generation' of lawyers; about the unscrupulous 'pettyfogging' lawyer, the 'mercenary fellow' that 'crams up crowns/from hobnailed boors and sheepskin country clowns', who was incentivised to provoke and prolong bad cases rather than to serve his client's interests.[7] This was the world of Tangle in Middleton's *The Phoenix*, a 'villainous law-worm that eats holes into poor men's causes', who offered 'knavish counsel', and who 'found such sweet pleasure in the vexation of others'.[8] It was a concern that John Smyth appreciated from reading *A Summons for Sleepers*. This decried how 'the law' had become a 'spider's web, where great flies pass easily through but little flies are strangled', and it likened lawyers to 'a bramble bush standing in the midst of a plain field, whereunto the poor sheep in time of cold storms furrow and harbour so long, till at the last by little and little, being robbed of their fleeces, are sent away naked'.[9] The danger was a proliferation of frivolous and hopeless suits, with clients—particularly 'poor suitors' and 'common rustics'—being led astray by misleading advice. Taken together, such problems made litigation a risky and expensive business, involving 'rubs and wrenches' and 'the great toil and impoverishing of many subjects'.[10]

The upshot of such concerns was adaptation and reform, although the latter was more often demanded than achieved. Attempts were made to make legal processes more efficient, and in the 1620s the House of Lords responded to perceived failures of justice by establishing committees to consider reform, and by reviving private party judicature. This meant dealing with petitions for justice, and with apparently insoluble legal problems that required extraordinary remedy, thereby creating a sense that Parliament provided an affordable remedy for personal grievances. More generally, demands for concerted reform mounted

6 Thomas Barnes, 'Due process and slow process in the late Elizabethan-early Stuart Star Chamber', *AJLH*, 6 (1962), p. 226; Hart, *Justice*, pp. 3–4, 22; Jones, *Chancery*, pp. 147, 162; Brooks, *Pettyfoggers*, p. 134; William Cole, *A Rod for the Lawyers* (1659), p. 9.

7 Brooks, *Pettyfoggers*, p. 57; W. Prest, 'Lay legal knowledge in early modern England', in Jonathan A. Bush and Alain Wijffels, eds, *Learning the Law* (London, 1999), 303–14; Prest, *Barristers*, pp. 17–19, 21, 23, 160–3, 182, 283, 286–7, 290–3, 301–2; Jones, *Chancery*, pp. 314–15; Hart, *Justice*, pp. 3–4; Cole, *Rod*, p. 3; Thomas Powell, *Tom of all Trades* (1631), sig. Bv.

8 Thomas Middleton, 'The Phoenix', in *The Collected Works*, ed. Gary Taylor and John Lavagnino (Oxford, 2007), 4.43–5, 63, 115–24, 126, 171–5; Thomas Middleton, 'Michaelmas Term', ibid., pp. 337–8.

9 Leonard Wright, *A Summons for Sleepers* (1589), sigs B2–3: Bodl. MS Eng.e.3400, fo. 8.

10 George Norburie, 'The abuses and remedies of Chancery', in Francis Hargrave, ed., *A Collection of Tracts* (London, 1787), i. 436, 444.

steadily until the 1650s, and such demands, like the revival of the Lords' judicial function, are certainly relevant to our story.[11]

However, while historians like Christopher Brooks and Wilfrid Prest have explored the nature and limitations of the legal system, and recognised the need to integrate the history of litigation, legal institutions, and the legal profession into wider social, cultural, and political histories, significant areas remain under-explored.[12] Attention has generally focused on criminal rather than civil law, albeit in ways which have revealed the participatory nature of the legal system, and how high-profile cases raised fundamental social, religious, and political questions.[13] Scholarship on litigation has tended to involve top-down administrative studies, analysis of individual courts, and the views of establishment figures, playwrights, and pamphleteers, much more obviously than 'the routine process of litigation'. Investigations of litigation and litigants' experiences are limited to synoptic studies, which are extremely valuable, but which tend to involve myriad fragmentary cases and formal legal records, even in studies that drill down into the relationship between litigation and social relations in particular communities.[14] As such, even if it is possible to grapple with official records to establish the nature, length, and outcome of individual *suits*, scholars have rarely explored—or been able to explore—the history of the *disputes* to which they related, and the experiences and perspectives of litigants, particularly if disputes occurred over a protracted period, involved different kinds of legal action, and ranged across jurisdictions.[15] Ironically, historians have sometimes alighted on contemporary comments about the legal system without exploring the experiences of litigation from which they emerged, including those involved in the Warrens Court dispute. These include James Duport's comment that 'we are now fallen into the declining, or rather doting days of the world, which . . . setteth shifting, idle fellows on work to whet their wits, to dive into every man's estate to see if they can catch never so little colour to work upon, that they may draw some money

[11] Hart, *Justice*, pp. 3–4, 5, 12, 24.

[12] See also: Craig Muldrew, 'Rural credit and legal institutions in the countryside in England', in C. W. Brooks and Michael Lobban, eds, *Communities and Courts* (London, 1997), 155–77; Craig Muldrew, 'Credit and the courts': debt litigation in a seventeenth-century urban community', *EcHR*, 46.1 (1993), 23–38.

[13] Cynthia B. Herrup, *The Common Peace* (Cambridge, 1987); Cynthia B. Herrup, *A House in Gross Disorder* (Oxford, 1999).

[14] Richard L. Kagan, *Lawsuits and Litigants in Castile, 1500–1700* (Chapel Hill, 1982), p. xx. See: Marjorie Blatcher, *The Court of King's Bench, 1450–1550* (London, 1978); Stretton, *Women*, p. 4; W. H. Bryson, *The Equity Side of the Exchequer* (Cambridge, 1975); Jones, *Chancery*; Thomas G. Barnes, 'Star Chamber litigants and their counsel, 1596–1641', in J. H. Baker, *Legal Records and the Historian* (London, 1978), 7–20; Martin Ingram, 'Law, litigants and the construction of 'honour': slander suits in early modern England', in Peter Coss, ed., *The Moral World of the Law* (Cambridge, 2000), 134–60; L. A. Knafla, *Kent at Law, 1602* (London, 1992).

[15] *Yorks Star Chamber*, ii. vii; Alison Wall, 'For love, money, or politics? A clandestine marriage and the Elizabethan Court of Arches', *HJ*, 38.3 (1995), 511–33.

from other men'.[16] They also include comments by John Smyth, who grumbled about 'troops of lawyers, attorneys and solicitors', and whose reference to the 'country malice and envy that rageth in this age with the inferior sort'—and to Westminster Hall as 'our cockpit of revenge'—clearly reflected his own experiences.[17]

Historians thus recognise that the legal system could become difficult for litigants, and that cases could drag on for decades, or even generations, at huge cost in terms of money and energy. They appreciate that protracted cases generated local interest—with legal papers being 'thrown about the town as thick as playbills'—and also understand that such cases could reflect 'long-standing disputes of considerable personal or social significance'. Nevertheless, intense and intractable disputes have proved difficult to analyse, not least in terms of the rationality of those involved and what was really going on.[18] This is partly a matter of the skills needed to interpret the 'mysteries' of early modern law, with its 'quagmire' of technicalities and legal fictions, and the historian who tackles legal issues risks being regarded as 'a fumbling amateur' or 'unwelcome interloper'. Such problems are exacerbated by the likelihood that litigants operated in and across multiple courts, and the process of reconstructing particular disputes is recognised as being 'tedious' and fraught with difficulties. Legally and procedurally it might be difficult to establish the outcome of individual suits, let alone protracted disputes, without even thinking about their meaning.[19]

A particular challenge is posed by the nature of surviving documentation. Extant official records are vast in scope, but case papers are generally fragmentary, asymmetrical, and 'jumbled'.[20] Court records tend to reveal what was being contested, and claims made by one or other side, and historians are confronted by the fact that 'disagreement was ubiquitous', as 'opposing parties exchanged volleys of assertions, denials and counter-assertions'. It is difficult to assess whether such claims were formulaic or literal, and it has proved tempting to suggest that the rhetoric of litigation—particularly regarding violence—was 'exuberant', 'picturesque', and 'exaggerated', and to despair about getting a 'correct

[16] GA, D9125/1/11990; William B. Willcox, 'Lawyers and litigants in Stuart England', *Cornell Law Quarterly*, 24 (1938–9), p. 538.

[17] Smyth, *Lives*, i. 242; Prest, *Barristers*, p. 21.

[18] Prest, *Barristers*, p. 300; Brooks, *Pettyfoggers*, p. 66. See: Thomas Kuehn, 'Nemo mortalis cognitus vivit in evo: moral and legal conflicts in a Florentine inheritance case of 1442', in Coss, ed., *Moral World*, 113–33.

[19] Stretton, *Women*, pp. 4, 11; J. H. Baker, 'Introduction', in Baker, *Legal Records*, pp. 1, 3–4, 5. See: Thomas G. Barnes, 'A Cheshire seductress, precedent and a 'sore blow' in Chancery', in M. S. Arnold, et al., eds, *On the Laws and Customs of England* (Chapel Hill, 1981), 359–82.

[20] Stretton, *Women*, pp. 11–12, 16. See: Thomas. G. Barnes, 'The archives and archival problems of the Elizabethan and early Stuart Star Chamber', *Journal of the Society of Archivists*, 2.8 (1963), 345–60; J. A. Guy, *The Court of Star Chamber and its Records to the reign of Elizabeth I* (London, 1985), pp. vii, 19, 21, 23–4, 29, 49–50.

opinion', particularly where verdicts are unknown.[21] Such problems are significant even if the aim is not to 'play at being magistrate', or arbitrate between rival claims, and even if the goal is to understand how and why people went to court, the experiences they encountered, and the implications of litigation.[22] Evidentially, lawsuits are difficult to interpret, and official records provide a poor way of reconstructing and comprehending complex and protracted disputes over time and across different courts.

This exploration of the Warrens Court dispute seeks to overcome such problems, and to build upon the work of historians—notably Christine Churches—who have sought to 'untangle' complex disputes, and to explore what Steve Hindle calls the 'micro-spatial dynamics of litigation'. This means moving beyond formal legal records, exploring evidence from local archives, and analysing litigation and legal processes from the perspectives of litigants, less in the hope of assessing the truth about rival claims, than of recovering the purposes, aims and experiences of disputants, and of getting beneath the surface of cases as presented in court.[23] This is precisely what can be achieved with documentation that extends far beyond the evidence surviving within the National Archives, and the range of documentary sources that Smyth preserved is dizzying. In addition to original 'bills' from a range of different courts, as well as occasional decrees, there survive copies of legal bills, rejoinders, and decisions that are no longer extant in official repositories.[24] Smyth also preserved other forms of legal paperwork, including notes made in the preparation of cases, the opinions of counsellors,[25] and certified copies of orders, writs, affidavits, and summonses,[26] as well as copies of jury verdicts and jury lists.[27] On the numerous occasions when courts established commissions of enquiry to be executed in Gloucestershire, Smyth's papers supplement official records with copies of the interrogatories upon which witnesses were examined, and of the depositions they generated,[28] as well as various surveys of the disputed land.[29] Smyth even compiled lists of legal suits, and the progress that had or had not been made, which provide an invaluable skeletal history of the dispute.[30] Like any good man of property, moreover, Smyth preserved indentures, together with wills, inventories, and letters of administration.[31] Very occasionally, there survive

[21] Stretton, *Women*, pp. 14, 17; *Yorks Star Chamber*, i. viii; ii. vii; iii. v.

[22] Stretton, *Women*, pp. 18, 20; Jones, *Chancery*, p. 194.

[23] Churches, 'Equity', pp. 69–70; Churches, 'Business at law', 937–54; Churches, 'Putting women', p. 51; Churches, 'False friends', pp. 52–3, 58; Steve Hindle, 'The micro-spatial dynamics of litigation: the Chilvers-Coton tithe dispute, Barrows vs Archer (1657)', in Lobban, Begiato and Green, eds, *Law, Lawyers and Litigants*, 140–63. For these issues, see: Frances Dolan, *True Relations: Reading, Literature and Evidence in Seventeenth-Century England* (Philadelphia, 2013).

[24] GA, D9125/1/11989/4, 9; D9125/1/11994, 11996–7, 12002.

[25] GA, D8887/6/27–8, 32, 56; D8887/7/21, 53; D9125/1/11989/10, 13.

[26] GA, D8887/6/2, 3, 5, 26.

[27] GA, D8887/6/34.

[28] GA, D9125/1/11989/11–12; D9125/1/11992.

[29] GA, D9125/1/11998–12000.

[30] GA, D8887/6/17, 26, 44–5; D9125/1/11989/2.

[31] GA, D9125/1/9790, 9791; D8887/6/43, 46.

letters to or from Smyth, which relate to the dispute and describe specific incidents in detail.[32] Finally, it is possible to consult the accounts of the dispute that both men prepared, not just in petitions and breviates, but also in pamphlets, some of which were printed, and some of which—like Smyth's 1626 reply to Crokey's allegations—were not.[33] Such evidence makes it possible to reconstruct the narrative of the dispute, and to demonstrate that, having begun in the Council of the Marches, the affair eventually made it to every major national court, as well as to Parliament and the Privy Council.

Reconstructing the narrative of the Warrens Court dispute makes it possible to begin the process of understanding why it lasted so long, and why people remained involved, beyond the obvious possibility that it involved 'path dependency', whereby the affair's very longevity provided perverse incentives to fight on. This means employing the insights of legal anthropologists, in at least two respects. First, the dispute can be treated as an 'extended case study' of dispute resolution, in terms of mapping the 'social drama' involved. This involves placing particular legal battles within the context of relations between litigants over time and in the round, in order to trace the path from a 'breach' to a 'crisis' that witnessed dramatic and public phases of disputation, with 'ritually heightened' elements and escalation through different judicial processes. It also means examining whether 'redressive mechanisms' repaired relations or resulted in an 'irreparable breach', and a more or less permanent change in social relations.[34] Thus, rather than simply examine the narrow legal issues involved in particular suits, it is important to consider the 'total history of relations' between litigants. This means examining how things found their way to court, rather than just what happened in court, and it means recognising that litigation could both reflect and precipitate ill-feeling, and that litigants might move matters from court to court, perhaps aware that they might not win.

Secondly, legal anthropologists have emphasised that the law involves a 'process' by which cases are tried and rulings given, rather than simply the application of 'rules', such that judges are recognised as having discretion in how laws are applied, to the point where they introduce uncertainty and even change the law.[35] The 'processual turn' in legal anthropology is helpful for thinking about how litigants dealt with situations in which the law might prove unpredictable, and how they used the legal system to advance their interests and ambitions, and also for recognising that litigation was not pathological, but actually integral to 'the ongoing flow of community life'. Such an approach makes it possible to recover

[32] GA, D9125/1/11990. [33] For Smyth's reply to Crokey, see: GA, D9125/1/12008.

[34] Victor Turner, *Schism and Continuity in an African Society* (Manchester, 1957), pp. 89–94; J. Van Velsen, 'The extended-case method and situational analysis', in A. L. Epstein, ed., *The Craft of Social Anthropology* (London, 1967), 129–49.

[35] Max Gluckman, *The Judicial Process among the Barotse of Northern Rhodesia* (Manchester, 1967), pp. 20–1, 196, 234, 326–8, 345, 353.

the 'cultural logic' of particular disputes, and how litigants engaged in litigation as part of the process of waging and resolving disputes, and of managing social relations.[36]

Such ideas provide ways of thinking about the nature and shape of disputes, and about attempts to resolve them, and they have been useful for historians who seek to understand the contests recorded in legal records.[37] They are certainly valuable for comprehending a dispute as long as the one with which Smyth and Crokey became involved, and in the first instance this means fathoming why litigants persisted in contesting the dispute over such an extended period, in legal terms. Part One interrogates the legal rationale for ongoing litigation, and the degree of success that litigants achieved, which means recognising two crucial things. First, the nature of legal processes was such that—at least at times—everyone involved felt that they were winning or had grounds for thinking that they might win. This reflected the legal advice they received, opinions expressed by officials, and judgments in court, as well as the possibilities that existed for making progress in one legal forum or another, and by one means or another. As anthropologists show, some disputes are incapable of resolution, because they are diffuse and embedded within larger battles, and historians recognise that the early modern legal system did not revolve around the discovery of truth, but more obviously around courts deciding which version of the truth was most 'compelling', and that legal decrees tended not to end disputes definitively.[38] Lord Chancellor Bacon and Lord Chancellor Ellesmere both worried that 'it was no longer possible for litigants to be certain when, if ever, their causes had reached a final conclusion', and some felt that decisions which validated the power of equity courts 'diminished the value and finality of judgments at law', and made it more likely that 'suits would be infinite', so that 'no one could be in peace for anything that the law had given him by judgment'.[39] The law could be unpredictable and uncertain, in ways that made it plausible, or even sensible, for litigants to fight on, even in the face of apparent setbacks.

Secondly, in protracted legal wrangling it was possible for different suits to invoke different issues, for the nature of a dispute to change over time, and for disparities to exist between the form in which matters were brought to court and the substance of the original quarrel.[40] What becomes clear is that Crokey and

[36] John L. Comaroff and Simon Roberts, *Rules and Processes* (London, 1981), pp. 14, 131; Peter Just, 'History, power, ideology and culture: current directions in the anthropology of law', *Law and Society Review*, 26.2 (1992), 373–4, 375.

[37] For example: John Putnam Demos, *Entertaining Satan* (Oxford, 1982); Chris Wickham, *Courts and Conflict in Twelfth-Century Tuscany* (Oxford, 2003).

[38] Just, 'History, power', pp. 383–4; Stretton, *Women*, p. 14; J. Oldham, 'Truth-telling in the eighteenth-century English courtroom', *Law and History Review*, 12.1 (1994), 95–121.

[39] Brooks, *Pettyfoggers*, p. 109; Hart, *Justice*, p. 28.

[40] Jones, *Chancery*, p. 306; Comaroff and Roberts, *Rules and Processes*, p. 117; Simon Roberts, 'The study of dispute', in Bossy, *Disputes*, p. 22.

Smyth were participants in a protracted dispute, but not really one single issue or case. Their contest involved an evolving series of cases, which saw new claims emerge over time, as protagonists died, and as new ones became involved. This was partly a matter of different allegations being deployed at different stages, but it was also a matter of a fundamental change in the basis on which the dispute rested. Crucially, what began as an inheritance dispute between fractious siblings (one of whom married Crokey's father, while the daughter of another married Smyth), was transformed into a case about a tiny school, Lady Katherine Berkeley's Grammar School in Wotton-under-Edge, founded in 1384 and flourishing to this day. The school had always been funded by profits from the Warrens Court estate, and over time the dispute came to centre upon the status of the land, upon claims that Smyth was misappropriating resources, and upon the idea that the school needed to be re-founded. Demonstrating how this happened goes a long way towards explaining why Crokey and Smyth were incentivised to pursue their dispute for such a long time, why it became so contentious and so enthralling for contemporaries, and why such disputes were prone to become bogged town in the courts.

1

'Strange passages in divers suits'

Waging Law over Warrens Court, 1560–1615

By the time Crokey produced his printed breviate in 1621—the one seen hanging like a ballad on William Burford's wall—he had been involved in the Warrens Court dispute for seven years, but litigation had been ongoing since the 1560s, regarding land transactions undertaken in 1545. Any attempt to understand what the case meant by the closing years of James I's reign involves comprehending where it began, how it generated a bewildering variety of lawsuits, and what kind of dynamic and complexity was involved. This means tracing the dispute as it unfolded and developed, across courts and across time. This challenging task is essential for understanding any legal dispute, and a well-documented affair like this one highlights a series of ways in which contestation could become protracted, and key factors that affected whether lawsuits resolved differences or generated further wrangling.

The contestation with which Smyth and Crokey became involved originated with an eighty-eight-year lease made by Robert Coldwell—the master of Wotton-under-Edge grammar school—to William Thomas of Wickwar (May 1545). This involved an estate called Warrens Court, which consisted of a house and around 100 acres of land.[1] That there was scope for litigation reflected Thomas's determination to assist with the upbringing of his step-children, the offspring of his wife, Alice, by her first husband, John Moore. This involved promising that Moore's legacies to his children—amounting to 120 marks—would be paid, and Thomas's 1556 will not only made provision for his and Alice's own daughter, Grace, but also for his step-children, including a Bristol Grocer called Richard Moore, by stipulating that the lease of the Nibley lands should pass first to Grace, and then to her half-siblings.[2]

This apparently straightforward bequest set in train the entire Warrens Court affair, which seemed at first to involve a straightforward inheritance dispute between the children and descendants of William Thomas, involving branches of the family to which Smyth and Crokey became connected through marriage. What follows represents an attempt to map litigation down to the 1610s. This is

[1] GA, D2957/216/24. For Coldwell and his successors, see: GA, D9125/1/11996; S379/2/2/1/2; D4431/2/128/4; D8887/6/56; LB, MS 3549/49–50, 60–1, 63.

[2] GA, D8887/6/13, 26, 45; GA, GDR/1556/143; D9125/1/11994, 12008, pp. 10–11; TNA, PROB 11/68, fo. 391v.

The Madman and the Churchrobber: Law and Conflict in Early Modern England. Jason Peacey, Oxford University Press.
 DOI: 10.1093/oso/9780192897138.003.0002

not straightforward, and it is not always possible to be confident about the moves being made, or about the decisions reached in court, and for the period before the early seventeenth century there are significant evidential gaps. The reader might also despair about the possibility of keeping track of a convoluted story and wonder why it needs to be related in such detail. Every effort has thus been made to summarise as much as to narrate, and to bring out the explosive, scandalous, and farcical accusations that emerged, the animosities that arose, and the wider relevance of such manoeuvres for our understanding of early modern litigation. The twists and turns of disputation are essential in permitting conclusions to be reached about the manner in which contestation took place, and the reasons that were found for pursuing specific issues. While it might seem odd that such straightforward commitments provided the basis for litigation lasting over a century, this chapter argues that such disputation is explicable not just because inheritance cases were prone to generate protracted contestation, but also because circumstances changed, new people became involved, and new claims materialised. What emerges is that even if the original reasons behind a dispute—and the goals people sought to achieve—remained stable, legal claims could vary dramatically over time.

I

The disputes that bedevilled the Warrens Court estate began not long after the death of William Thomas, with the marriage of his widow, Alice, to her third husband, Reginald Ap Powell (May 1560). Although the issues and protagonists at this stage are unclear, and the paperwork patchy, the matter came to the attention of Sir Edward Saunders, Chief Baron of the Exchequer, by 1566, and within a few years the issue of Alice's title was taken up by her son, Richard Moore, in what proved to be a decisive move. Moore's involvement came in the wake of Powell's death (June 1571), and involved a lawsuit in the Court of the Marches, and a challenge to a deathbed manoeuvre by which the 'original lease' of Warrens Court was conveyed to a Bristol apothecary, John Sprint, the husband of another of John Moore's children, Joyce. This was controversial because Sprint promptly re-conveyed the property to Alice following Powell's death, thereby ensuring—as Smyth later recognised—that Richard Moore's reversionary interest was 'extinguished'.[3]

Although details about these early machinations are hazy—the records of the Council of the Marches have been lost—Alice's relatives were clearly protecting their reversionary interest. This comes into sharper focus through a more richly

[3] TNA, C 78/84/20; GA, D9125/1/11989/4, 9–10, 13–14; D9125/1/11996, 12002, 12008, pp. 11–12; D8887/6/44–5; D8887/7/1. For Sprint: TNA, PROB 11/73, fo. 216.

documented Chancery case, brought against Alice and her daughter (Grace) by Richard Moore and his three sisters (Katherine, Mary, and Joyce), together with their respective husbands (1584).[4] In the long run, the significance of this manoeuvre was that it signalled the first involvement of the Crokey family, since Robert Crokey was married to Moore's sister, Katherine, and was one of the plaintiffs. At this stage, however, the key figure was Moore, and the case coincided with the expiration of a twenty-one-year lease that he acquired from Powell in 1563, and reflected a concern that moves were being made to deny him his inheritance.[5] This was something Moore expected to receive as a 'token and remembrance' of William Thomas's 'good will', and he protested that his half-sister, Grace, sought the estate for herself, and wanted to avoid liability for Thomas's legacies. Moore insisted that, while Alice still held the property, she was 'aged and sickly', and 'altogether ruled and directed' by Grace, 'who hath the keeping and disposition of the . . . original lease and only seeketh her own gain and commodity'. Moore's litigation was predicated upon his 'interest', which involved the remaining term of the original lease (around fifty years, and land worth £30 *per annum*), as well as an 'unkindness' done to him, and his failure to protect his inheritance by other means.

Litigation represented the failure of informal mediation. Moore referred to having visited Alice and Grace 'divers times', asking them—'gently and earnestly'—not to 'frustrate him of his legacies', to 'deliver' the lease to an 'indifferent friend' for safe keeping, and to preserve his 'interest'. He claimed that Alice—'by the counsel and persuasion' of Grace—used 'secret and sinister means' to 'defraud and defeat him'. This allegedly involved 'forfeiting', 'aliening', and 'encumbering' the lease, and Moore made particular reference to grants of the lease made to Grace in 1584, for forty-one years. Moore insisted that these transactions were 'void and of no effect', and that they fell foul of the 'statute of fraudulent gifts'—a statute he apparently read aloud to Alice and Grace. His reasoning was that Alice could only claim the estate as a legacy from, rather than as executor to, William Thomas, and that this made her incapable of granting leases to Grace. At this stage, therefore, the quarrel over Warrens court involved questions over who would inherit the land, and technical issues relating to how Alice acquired it and what she could legitimately do with it. Such issues quickly generated real tension. Alice responded to Moore's complaint by denying that any 'secret or sinister' means had been used to 'defraud or defeat' him, and by expressing willingness that the 'original lease' should be held in safe custody by an 'indifferent or substantial' person. She insisted, however, upon having proved Thomas's will as

[4] Mary married William Cox of Monmouth; Joyce married John Sprint; and Katherine married Robert Crokey.

[5] GA, D9125/1/11989/1, 4, 9–10; D9125/1/11996, 12002, 12008, p. 11; D8887/6/32; LB, MS 3549/66.

executor, and that the new lease—like an earlier gift to Grace of goods and chattels—was perfectly valid.[6]

Moore's suit ended in defeat, and it was decided that Alice and Grace should enjoy possession 'without let or interruption' (October 1584). As such, the matter might well have ended there and then, but instead Moore instigated a protracted run of cases 'touching the . . . original lease', in an unsuccessful campaign to secure the estate. At one point, he referred to the contestation of seven suits in Chancery, three cases in Star Chamber, and two more in the Court of the Marches, as well as ten more 'at common law'. That this was possible reflected the legal complexities involved, and matters that remained unresolved, as well as how new problems arose when familial circumstances changed. The effect was to give Moore grounds for optimism that his fortunes might change.

First, questions remained regarding William Thomas's unpaid debts, and John Moore's unpaid legacies, which led to the unearthing of acquittances which were said to show that sums of money had indeed been received by Moore, Robert Crokey, John Sprint and others, alongside evidence that Alice and William Thomas had provided for John Moore's children.[7] More importantly, renewed impetus for legal manoeuvres was provided by Grace's marriage to John Drew (February 1585), and by Alice's death, intestate (April 1585). The significance of a change in circumstances was that it led to a change in Richard Moore's legal argument.[8] His response involved taking administration of his mother's estate (April 1585), and then securing administration of the estate of William Thomas (November 1585), some three decades after his death. Moore thus took possession of Warrens Court, which meant—as John Smyth later recognised—that the case now turned on whether Moore, as administrator, had a better title than Alice and Grace, who claimed the estate by gift. One detailed document weighed up the arguments—'on both sides'—about whether Alice claimed the estate as executrix or legatrix and recorded the legal opinion of Serjeant John Savile of the Middle Temple. What Moore had done was to transform the grounds of his complaint: he no longer claimed the estate 'by any remainder or legacy', but rather as administrator of Alice's estate, recognising that, if Alice could claim the estate as executor to William Thomas, then the 'remainders'—i.e. his reversionary interest—would be 'destroyed'.[9]

Such evidence reveals the impact of contingencies—deaths and marriages—upon legal disputes, and the apparent ease with which litigants shifted the basis of

[6] GA, D9125/1/11989/1, 4, 9–10; D8887/6/9, 13, 17, 26, 32, 34, 44–5; D9125/1/12008, pp. 11, 13; TNA, C 78/84/20; STAC 5/M50/37.

[7] GA, D9125/1/11989/1–2, 4, 9; D9125/1/11996, 12008, pp. 13–14; D8887/6/17, 26, 32, 45.

[8] GA, D9125/1/11989/2, 9; D9125/1/11994, 12008, p. 12; D8887/6/2–3, 12, 16–17, 45.

[9] GA, D8887/6/2–3, 13, 16, 23, 26, 32, 44; D9125/1/11989/2, 4, 9–10; D9125/1/11996; D8887/7/3–4; D2957/216/4; TNA, PROB 6/3, fo. 139; PROB 11/68, fo. 391v; C 2/Eliz/M3/53; STAC 5/M15/20; STAC 5/M50/37; Chicago UL, MS 1465, folder 2/1. See also: GA, D8887/6/32; D9125/1/12008, pp. 11–14; TNA, STAC 5/M13/19.

their claims. The most obvious ramification was that Moore submitted a new Chancery suit (November 1585), exploiting recent developments by pointing out that Alice's claim to the estate rested on her being executor to William Thomas, rather than merely being his legatee. On this occasion, his gambit paid off, and a judgment gave him control of the estate (December 1585).[10] His victory was short-lived, however, because Grace and her husband leased the property to Edward Perrin in April 1586, in a deliberate attempt to 'try the title'. The upshot was a new Chancery ruling, that Moore's recent proceedings were 'fraudulent and covenous' (May 1586). This followed a decision by the Court of the Arches that administration of Thomas's estate had been secured 'fraudulently', and by 'untrue significations'. As a result, John and Grace Drew secured control of Warrens Court once again.[11]

This flurry of activity provided clear evidence that the judicial process could involve uncertain judgments, which gave litigants cause for optimism even in the face of legal setbacks, particularly if they found new pathways through the system. This was precisely how Moore reacted, and he quickly identified a different means of resuming his campaign, in terms of his chosen forum and preferred argument. This involved a perjury suit in the Court of the Marches (begun in September 1586 and still taking evidence in January 1588), which alleged that the March 1584 lease from Alice to Grace was 'blotted and defaced', with key names 'razed and put out', in ways that made it void, and that a new version was made after Alice's death. Moore's contention was that John and Grace Drew 'wrongfully entered' the estate on the basis of a lease 'lewdly and falsely amended', and that they had no 'just or lawful title'. Although this particular claim was quickly dismissed—with costs being awarded against him—further cases followed in 1587 and 1588, including Moore's third suit in Chancery, as well as bills in Star Chamber and Common Pleas, not to mention proceedings at the Gloucestershire assizes, for at least some of which documentation survives. These cases involved Moore reiterating his earlier claims, but ongoing litigation involved more than merely 'forum shopping', the deliberate attempt to pursue a particular matter through different channels to find the most amenable court. It also revealed new allegations. This meant claims about due process, and Moore protested that the May 1586 Chancery hearing was improperly conducted, that witnesses were not examined, and that he incurred significant expense raising his siblings, not least because William Thomas 'refused' to provide them with adequate education, training, and preferment, 'as he was bound to do'. Moore also protested that he was unable to regain control of the estate despite a successful case at the Gloucestershire assizes. On that occasion he

[10] GA, D9125/1/11989/4, 9; D8887/6/17, 32.

[11] GA, D9125/1/11989/2, 4: D8887/6/2–3, 12, 17, 27–8, 55; TNA, STAC 5/M5/23; C 2/Eliz/M3/53; STAC 5/M13/19. See: TNA, PROB 11/69, fo. 55.

accused Grace of making a forcible entry onto the estate, and the result was an order that the sheriff should assist him in repossessing the lands.

Once again, Moore's legal claims—and the hopes raised by the ability to secure official support—were quickly dashed, not least because his opponents adapted to new circumstances. This is not to say that John and Grace refrained from rehearsing earlier claims. Their lawyer, George Snigge, sometime Bristol MP and lawyer for the Berkeleys, reiterated Alice's rightful title as executor to William Thomas, insisted that she 'made probate' of his will, and demonstrated that Thomas's debts were paid. Claims that the lease from Alice to Grace was 'falsified or corrupted' were dismissed as slanderous, and Moore's attempt to secure administration of the two estates was decried as 'fraudulent and subtle', as 'maliciously intended and executed', and as a 'practice' to 'defraud and divest' them of their 'lawful title'. John and Grace also justified their entry into the estate in September 1586 by adding new claims, protesting that Moore refused to submit to the order granting them possession, and that the assize judgment was overruled in King's Bench. The result was another setback for Moore, whose claims were once again dismissed in Chancery (February 1589), which ruled that he had unfairly 'interrupted' Grace's possession of Warrens Court with claims that were 'utterly confuted'. This ruling also hinted at the bitterness that already surrounded the dispute, noting that Moore was upbraided by the judges 'for his busy speaking in his evil matter'.[12]

Even at this stage Moore refused to concede defeat, almost certainly because of the manner in which his Chancery case was 'dismissed'. This involved a ruling—and a fairly standard judgment—that Moore should be 'left at his liberty to take what remedy he can by the ordinary course of the common law', which made it possible to find other avenues along which to resume his campaign, and perhaps encouraged him to do so. Whether or not he pursued the common law is unclear, but he certainly instigated two new Star Chamber cases (1590 and 1591), reiterating his allegations that Grace sought to defraud him by means of the 1584 lease, and that she, John Drew and George Snigge 'practiced and conspired' to defeat him. This was a fairly standard claim in Star Chamber, but it was substantiated with the allegation that they engaged in a 'false and wicked' move to 'frame, devise, contrive, forge and counterfeit' a new lease, which was 'published' in various law courts, and which resulted in them claiming the estate on the back of erroneous legal judgments. Moore continued to insist, in short, that they 'compassed' possession by 'indirect false practices', and that they held the Nibley lands by 'false deed only'. At the same time, Moore also pursued two new claims. The first was that 'corrupt and wilful perjury' was committed in the Court of the Marches

[12] GA, D9125/1/5826, 11989/2, 4, 9; D9125/1/12030/23; D8887/6/4–5, 7, 9, 11–13, 17, 29, 31–2; D2404/2; TNA, STAC 5/M5/23; STAC 5/M50/37; STAC 5/M15/20; C 2/Eliz/M3/53. For Snigge: *Commons 1604–1629*, vi. 371–2; Prest, *Barristers*, p. 392; Berkeley, BB109, fo. 58.

in September 1586, and in claiming that the 1584 deed was 'purposely razed and defaced' Moore alleged that Grace made an untrue deposition. At this point, things began to sound prosaic, Grace having apparently claimed that the 'blotting' of this document happened 'by chance', when George Snigge 'let a drop of ink fall out of his pen'. However, Moore also alleged that Snigge lied about whether the document was 'blotted and defaced', and that Drew supplied false testimony, 'purposely to defraud'. Moore's second claim was that John and Grace Drew made entry onto his estate in September 1586 in a 'riotous' fashion.[13]

By this stage the dispute was producing more heat than light, given that claims about 'riot' were *de rigueur* in Star Chamber. Drew's response—delivered by Snigge in late 1590—involved a familiar mixture of assertions and denials. He reiterated earlier claims—that Alice's title to the estate was sound, that William Thomas's debts were paid, and that the lease to Grace was made 'for her better advancement and preferment in marriage'—while also denying the accusation of riot. The only novel element of his response involved the admission that, while Grace's lease was not 'forged', and while there was no conspiracy aimed at 'impeaching' Moore's right, the lease had indeed been 'blotted', although it was still 'legible', and had merely been amended to make it more 'plain'.[14] The outcome of these cases is unknown, although they may well have dragged on for some time; Drew was called before Star Chamber in October 1591, and spent considerable amounts of time in London until early 1593.[15] What does seem clear is that Moore felt justified in devising yet another line of attack, renewing his suits with a fourth Chancery case (1592), even if he merely reiterated long-standing claims regarding Alice's intestacy, and about Grace's 'sinister and cunning shifts' to obtain the estate, and even if John and Grace Drew predictably responded with a demurrer regarding the settlement of William Thomas's debts and the legitimacy of Grace's lease. Thus, although this case took time to resolve—a November 1593 order referred to hearings being delayed 'through other great business'—it was understandable that Moore's case was dismissed once again in 1595.[16]

By 1595, John and Grace Drew might reasonably have sensed that their battle with Richard Moore was finally coming to an end, as Moore ran out of new arguments and new legal channels. However, at precisely the moment when their opponent seemed badly weakened, two new developments kept the dispute alive, even if one of them was to herald Moore's final defeat.

The first development was the death of John Drew, sometime between September 1596 (when his will was written) and April 1597 (when it was proved). Grace duly inherited his Gloucestershire lands, but Moore evidently sensed an

[13] TNA, STAC 5/M15/20; STAC 5/M13/19; GA, D9125/1/11989/4; D8887/6/12, 17–18. See also: LB, MS 3549/97; GA, D8887/7/9.

[14] TNA, STAC 5/M13/19.

[15] GA, D9125/1/13608/2.

[16] GA, D9125/1/11989/2, 9; D8887/6/6, 16, 18, 21–2, 32, 39; D2404/6; TNA, C 78/84/20. In May 1592 the 'original lease' was ordered to be held by the court: GA, D9125/1/12008, pp. 37–8.

opportunity to submit a new suit in the Exchequer Court, which led to the empanelling of a jury. That this did not proceed any further probably reflected a much more decisive development: Grace's re-marriage, within months, to John Smyth of Nibley, on the very day of which a new lease of Warrens Court was hastily prepared (5 October 1597).[17] This exemplifies the link between familial events, property ownership, and litigation, and the significance of these developments lay in ensuring that disputation would continue. Smyth later noted that Drew's death, and his 'intermarriage' with Grace, immediately provoked new suits over the 'original lease', and the years that followed witnessed intense litigation. Moreover, while the surviving documentation—formal legal papers, Smyth's legal notes, and notarised court orders—does not enable a thorough reconstruction of suits that were numerous, complex, and interwoven, Moore now faced a much more formidable adversary. Smyth subsequently boasted that he had not merely been to content to 'ward his blows', but that 'sometimes, as I saw cause, I struck back'.[18]

This final phase of Moore's campaign began confidently. A Chancery motion sought to reverse earlier decrees, and resulted in a decision that, since wrangling had been ongoing for three decades, both sides should 'set down' their cases in writing. As Moore explained to his brother-in-law, John Cotterell, new proceedings were also instigated in Star Chamber, where he laid claim to 'the whole interest' as 'administrator to my mother', and insisted that the legacies granted by William Thomas were void, 'because all his goods were not sufficient to discharge his debts' (October 1597). Moore recognised that Smyth had 'appeared for my sister', but remained confident that the case would soon 'draw... to some perfection', not least because a 'commission is agreed upon between us... here in the country'.[19] Moore challenged the legitimacy of the 1587 King's Bench order, which prevented the sheriff of Gloucestershire from ejecting John and Grace from Warrens Court, insisting that it was secured by 'confederacy, combination, forgery [and] counterfeiting'. Indeed, while the clerk who prepared this particular order—Edward Willan—protested that it was lawful, Grace Smyth eventually conceded that it was indeed procured by John Drew (June 1598).[20]

This new case was heard in late 1597 and early 1598, and was eventually dismissed because Moore failed to sustain his suit.[21] This signalled the waning of his fortunes, if not his energy, and the following two years witnessed a blizzard of cases in Chancery, King's Bench, and Common Pleas, as well as at the Gloucestershire assizes. Writs flew in all directions, and a range of bills, petitions, and demurrers were submitted by both men, amid claims about 'trespass' and 'rebellion'. The affair generated at least one 'outlawry', which declared someone to be outside the protection of the law, and a

[17] LB, MS 3549/100–1, 103; GA, D8887/6/20; D8887/3/94; D9125/1/12008, p. 12; D8887/5/43; Smyth, *Lives*, ii. 319–20.

[18] GA, D9125/1/11996, 12008, pp. 13–14.

[19] GA, D8887/6/23.

[20] TNA, STAC 5/M50/37; STAC 5/M52/22; STAC 5/M13/19.

[21] GA, D8887/6/36.

multitude of hearings, delays, and dismissals, some of which resulted in Moore being declared 'non suit' (i.e. that he failed to make a legal case), while others involved both sides being ordered to submit better answers. There were occasional respites—at one point Moore and Smyth agreed to 'stay' their business in Star Chamber—but Smyth was clearly gaining the ascendency, and by the end of 1599 Moore was a prisoner in the Fleet for non-payment of costs. His incarceration and sickness, and unsuccessful bids to secure writs of *habeas corpus*, made it difficult to appear at hearings, even though he was repeatedly summoned to court. Even when Moore secured his freedom in early 1600, Smyth confronted him with new legal actions. By the end of October 1600, Moore had been returned to the Fleet for defaulting on debts, and although Smyth responded to pleas regarding his adversary's health by agreeing to 'remit him of his close imprisonment', the failure to prosecute a writ of error (or appeal) resulted in further financial penalties. Subsequent attempts to broker a settlement probably reflected Moore's physical and financial weakness, and when arbitration failed Moore soon found himself close prisoner again. To make matters worse, the financial penalties awarded against him continued to mount, and in March 1601 a jury at Dursley imposed yet further damages (£50) and costs (53*s*.4*d*.) to Smyth and his allies.

Moore was now suffering a legal drubbing. Although he did not stop bringing new suits, Smyth secured a decree granting him possession of the lands (May 1601), after which Lord Keeper Ellesmere ruled that Moore's ongoing proceedings—he still had seven bills in Chancery, three in Star Chamber and two in the Court of the Marches, not to mention eight cases at common law—should be dismissed as 'vexations'. Moore was ordered to pay an additional £10 in costs and following further proceedings in King's Bench a full hearing in the last months of Elizabeth I's reign led to a final dismissal of the case against Smyth, with costs (November 1603). In May 1604, the 'original lease' was delivered to Smyth, 'to be enjoyed during the years to come'.[22]

Moore was now a broken man, and in November 1604 he wrote to Smyth from the Fleet with an admission of defeat, promising to 'desist' from further suits 'all my life henceforth'.[23] He did not have long to live, however, and Smyth, who pursued him to the very end, noted that Moore died on 27 February 1606. Having left no will, letters of administration were granted to Moore's daughter, Elizabeth, and her husband George Proctor (13 March 1606), and Moore's personal estate was subsequently valued at a mere £14 11*s*.8*d*. As Smyth later reflected, his approach to Moore had been relentless: 'I stroke back... never desisting' until he was 'dead in the Fleet' for 'non-payment of costs'.[24]

[22] GA, D8887/6/30, 32, 34–7, 44, 55, 109; D8887/7/21, 53; D9125/1/11989/3–4, 8–10; D9125/1/11991, 11994, 12008, pp. 37–9, 12030/23; D2404/7–10, 13; D2957/216/15.

[23] GA, D8887/6/109.

[24] GA, D8887/6/41, 43, 46; D9125/1/11996, 12008, pp. 13–14; LMA, P69/BRI/A/004/MS06538, unfol.

II

This story about Richard Moore's long and largely fruitless dispute with his family over Warrens Court is tortuous and repetitive, but its twists and turns are important for revealing how and why legal cases could drag on. It might be tempting to conclude that Moore persisted with litigation in the face of overwhelming odds, but he secured favourable verdicts, which gave him hope for the future and reasons to persevere. Legal verdicts did not always settle matters definitively, or to everyone's satisfaction, and sometimes recommended the pursuit of alternative legal channels. Litigants also found new grounds upon which to base their claims, and new reasons to fight on, not least when opponents died or found new partners, something that was particularly pertinent in a case which revolved around the law of property and inheritance. That the Warrens Court dispute dragged on for almost all of Elizabeth I's reign, and then into the reign of James I, entailed more than merely 'forum shopping'; it involved logical steps regarding, and possibilities offered by, different legal channels, modified arguments, and new circumstances.

This affair also suggests that disputes could endure because of the personalities involved. Moore was clearly a driven man, and the nature and course of his litigation presumably impacted upon subsequent generations. It would be simplistic to suggest that the subsequent battle was overdetermined, and yet Benjamin Crokey was clearly aware that he was picking up the reins from someone—his uncle—who had pursued a vigorous campaign to the ruin of both his estate and his health. It is also apparent that, by the time Crokey became embroiled, Smyth had been involved in the dispute for almost two decades, and had proved a dogged adversary, who was acutely conscious that his wife and her mother had been fighting off claims for nearly four decades.

What also seems clear is that Smyth's comprehensive victory over Richard Moore was vital for the history of Warrens Court, not because it brought an end to litigation, but because it affected the affair's subsequent trajectory. This was because Smyth seized the opportunity to re-develop the estate, thereby sowing the seeds of further controversy. His aim was to acquire additional property, including leases of other lands owned by Wotton school as part of a charitable bequest by Lady Katherine Berkeley in 1384.[25] In October 1604, he secured a ninety-year lease on land from Henry Duport of the Inner Temple, who was described as a 'farmer' of the school lands.[26] Subsequently, he purchased the

[25] GA, D9125/1/11985–6; S379/2/1/1–5; *VCH Gloucester*, ii. 396–400; FSL, Z.c.13(18); Bodl. MS Eng.Misc.e.6, fos 94-5v, 98v.

[26] GA, D9125/1/9790–1, 11996, 11999, 12002, 12008, pp. 17–18; LB, MS 3549/75; Bodl. MS Eng. Misc.e.6, fos 4–45.

remainder of a ninety-nine year lease of other school lands that been made by the master (John Duport) in the 1590s, for £300 (October 1608).[27]

Such deals were to have important repercussions, making it hard to know how to value Warrens Court, as distinct from other school lands. Of more immediate importance, however, was the death of Smyth's wife Grace (9 November 1609). As at other times, Grace's death provided new incentives for her family to revive old grievances, and on this occasion the cudgels were taken up by her aunt, Joyce Cotterell, the last of John Moore's children, to whom William Thomas had wanted the estate to pass after Grace's death.[28] However, while this did not generate the level of controversy witnessed subsequently, even at this point the affair continued to mutate. Unlike her brother, Joyce claimed the 'remainder' of the original lease, and the manner in which the affair was conducted added new levels of complexity, thereby prolonging the dispute and creating a sense of embitterment.

In other words, Grace Smyth's death ensured that a dispute that appeared to have been settled could be revived, in the form of a Chancery suit brought by Joyce and her husband, John Cotterell of Winford, Somerset (1610). This episode is poorly documented, but the outcome seems clear, and Smyth later claimed to have made 'answer and a plea in bar', with which 'Mr Cotterell seemed satisfied', and although nothing then happened for two years—what Smyth called 'a sufficient time for consideration'—the case was eventually dismissed 'for want of prosecution' and 'replication', with costs being awarded against the Cotterells (November 1613).[29] Such a setback did not deter Joyce, however, and it was her pursuit of the matter after her husband's death that prompted the fateful step of enlisting help from her nephew, Benjamin Crokey.[30] This resulted in Crokey becoming her adoptive heir—and taking administration of her estate—and in the preparation of 'divers deeds and writings', which conferred upon him her claim to the years left on the 'original lease'. The upshot was an episode wherein her solicitor, John Price, made a 'secret entry' onto the estate, where papers were signed conveying the lands to Crokey (1 January 1614).[31]

By 1614, in other words, there were rival claimants to Warrens Court, and claimants who were prepared to *transact* the property. Joyce Cotterell's decision to convey her 'title' made it possible for Benjamin Crokey to begin his epic legal battle, by instigating Chancery proceedings in Hilary term 1614 (hereafter, Case 1). Although formal documentation does not survive, his aim was to retrieve Coldwell's 'original lease' from 1545, and to pick up where Joyce had left off,

[27] GA, D2957/354/5, 6; D9125/1/7633, 9790, 11989/13–14, 11990, 11995, 11996, 12002, 12008, pp. 9, 18, 12030/23; S379/2/2/1/2; S379/2/4/1; S379/2/3/2/2; D4431/2/128/2; D8887/6/47–8; D8887/7/76.

[28] For Grace's death: Bodl. MS Eng.Misc.e.6, fo. 48.

[29] GA, D9125/1/11989/8–10, 11992, fo. 4, 11994, 11996, 12008, p. 14; D8887/6/50.

[30] GA, D9125/1/11989/8, 11991, 11994, 12008, p. 14. The absence of John Cotterell's will makes it hard to know what Crokey inherited.

[31] GA, D9125/1/11989/8, 11994, 11996, 12008, p. 14; Crokey, *Sacred Maiestie*, sig. B3v.

by claiming the remaining years as heir presumptive of the last beneficiary of William Thomas's will. This can be deduced from later references to the case, as well as from Smyth's surviving 'answers'. These pointed out that legal decisions had already been made in his favour (in 1601, 1604, and 1613), and reiterated that Alice had inherited the estate as executrix of Thomas's will (long before Richard Moore's attempt to take control in the 1580s), and that she was able to lease Warren's Court to Richard Moore. He also insisted upon the validity of the transactions involving Alice, her husband Reginald Ap Powell, and John Sprint in the 1570s, which undermined the reversionary interests of John Moore's descendants. He even pointed out that these deals had been *witnessed* by Richard Moore and Joyce Cotterell. Smyth also highlighted the significance of Grace's marriages, which seemed to prove that it was no longer possible to uphold the terms of William Thomas's will.[32]

Whether or not Smyth had the chance to deploy these arguments remains unclear, but Crokey had cause for hope in 1614, even if his suit ultimately came to nothing. On 15 July, the court signified that the case would at least need to be considered, insisting that Smyth should demonstrate why the 'original lease' should not be handed over to the court. It also appointed commissioners, who met at Gloucester in September 1614, to undertake an investigation, ahead of a hearing on 21 October. While Smyth produced old evidence about decisions that allowed him to keep the lease in his possession, the court insisted that Crokey should at least be given sight of it. Nevertheless, while another hearing was held at Thornbury to consider the case 'between the said parties', it failed to produce a definitive judgment (January 1615).[33]

More importantly, Smyth countered with three claims of his own, which took the case in entirely new directions. First, he made a pragmatic argument, about improvements he had made to the Warrens Court estate, at a cost of £4,000. (Smyth's accounts reveal that he was an avid purchaser of books on husbandry, and on 'the manner of planting, preserving and husbanding young trees.[34]) He also claimed that the lands formed part of the jointure for his second wife, Mary, the daughter of John Browning of Coaley, whom he had married in January 1610, only weeks after Grace's death, and before her funeral expenses had even been paid. Crucially, Smyth also explained that these lands had been 'intermingled' with the school lands, or else conveyed to tenants on long leases, such that 'infinite suits must needs arise' if Crokey proved victorious. Smyth insisted that further litigation would be messy, even if this was because he had deliberately made the school lands difficult to identify. Smyth's second argument

[32] Crokey, *Sacred Maiestie*, sig. B4; GA, D9125/1/11989/8–10, 12–14; D9125/1/11994, 11996, 12008, p. 41; D8887/6/23, 55, 62.

[33] GA, D8887/6/23, 51–3, 55; D9125/1/12008, p. 41; Bodl. MS Eng.Misc.e.6, fo. 89v.

[34] Bodl. MS Eng.Misc.e.6, fos 75v, 92; GA, D9125/1/13612/1, 12, 14; FSL, Z.c.13/18.

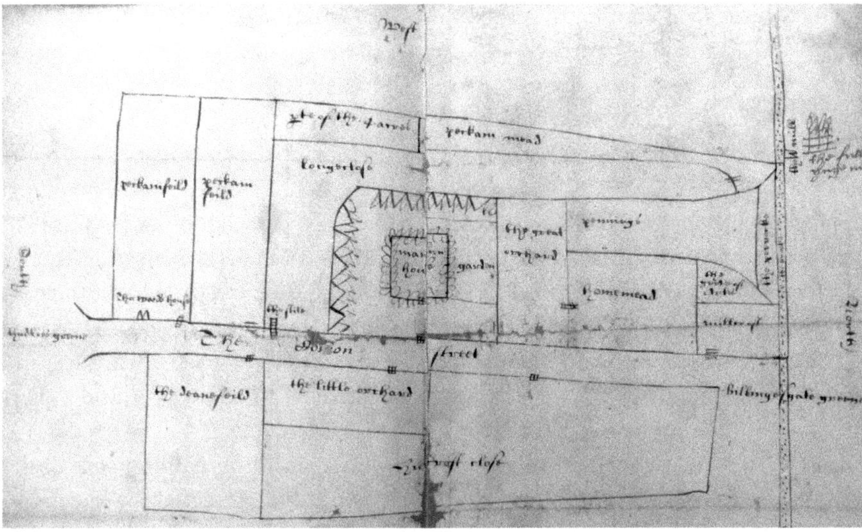

Fig. 2. Hand-drawn map of the Warrens Court estate, Nibley, Gloucestershire (*c.*1614). Gloucestershire Archives, D8887/5/98. Reproduced by permission of Gloucestershire Archives.

was technical. He claimed that Crokey's 'entry' onto his estate—and the conveyance of Joyce's title—did not take place on any part of the disputed lands. This move was evidently made in an attempt to demonstrate Joyce's possession, but Smyth prepared maps to show where different fields were located (Fig. 2). As such, Smyth had already secured a 'verdict of trespass' against Crokey—and £7 costs—at the Gloucestershire assizes (Summer 1614). Thirdly, Smyth made an explosive claim, by insisting that Joyce's assignment to Crokey 'appeared to be forged', because it failed to mention the £10 *per annum* that Crokey had allegedly agreed to pay in return for the title. Smyth asserted that Crokey's 'pretended title' rested on 'unlawful maintenance' and 'champerty', an illegal form of agreement by which someone with no prior interest in a lawsuit financed it for personal gain.[35]

Smyth's response sheds light on the Warrens Court dispute and on early modern litigation more generally. It demonstrates a new way in which litigation could be undertaken and disputes prolonged, involving aggressive claims regarding the manner rather than the substance of contestation. This enabled Smyth to move onto the offensive, and while Crokey's Chancery case was still pending

[35] GA, D2404/17; D9125/1/11989/8–10, 12–14; D9125/1/11994, 11996, 12008, pp. 14, 44–5; D8887/6/55, 62; Crokey, *Sacred Maiestie*, sig. B4; Bodl. MS Eng.Misc.e.6, fos 48v-9. For the map: Chicago UL, MS 1465, folder 5; GA, D8887/5/98. For Smyth leases: GA, D2957/216/2–3, 10, 28–9, 42–3; D2957/354/55; S379/2/2/1/4; D2404/14; D8887/3/100; D8887/4/9.

Smyth commenced champerty proceedings in Common Pleas, on 20 July 1614 (Case 2).[36] This actually proved to be unwise, because while Smyth submitted evidence in January or February 1615, a Gloucestershire jury ruled that Joyce Cotterell's conveyance represented 'a true and sufficient deed'. As a result Smyth was 'non-suited', and declared to have provided insufficient evidence to support his case (26 April 1615).[37] Fortunately for him, a mere three days later Lord Chancellor Ellesmere dismissed Crokey's Chancery case 'absolutely' (Case 1), having concluded that his associates had 'committed unlawful maintenance and champerty' (29 April 1615). According to Smyth, Ellesmere decided that the case had been 'perplexed by many suits', that Smyth had already secured 'divers verdicts, one decree and two dismissions' against Crokey's 'pretended title', and that Joyce Cotterell's own deposition indicated that 'if to come by a title in that sort were not maintenance, he knew not what maintenance was'.[38]

Here was dramatic evidence about the propensity for different branches of the legal system to produce conflicting verdicts, in ways that increased the likelihood of proceedings becoming protracted. Buoyed by this ruling, Smyth immediately commenced two new suits against Crokey (May 1615). One of these, in Chancery (Case 3), may have been more or less formulaic, and apparently involved an attempt to secure a deed—perhaps Joyce's 'forged' deed—from Crokey or his brother, Nathaniel. Smyth later reflected that he 'proceeded no further' as soon as he was satisfied by their answer, even if the case was not formally dismissed until July 1617.[39] The second and more serious suit was brought before Star Chamber almost simultaneously—writs were sent to witnesses on 22 and 25 May—to pursue in a different forum Smyth's claims about maintenance and champerty, and to target not just Crokey but also Joyce Cotterell, another relative (Anne Tempest), and two lawyers, William Porter and John Price (Case 4). Crucially, this also involved a suggestion that Crokey, having recognised that his original agreement to pay £10 per year to Cotterell was a 'badge or sign of champerty' (the 'buying of a pretended title'), had colluded with his co-defendants to 'forge a new deed'. According to Smyth it was this deed—omitting the offending clause—that had been produced during Crokey's Chancery hearing.[40]

Not content with these dramatic allegations, Smyth also petitioned James I about Crokey's forgery (13 May 1615). He alleged that the new deed contained the names—Deinton, Hathway and Lemon—of people who had not actually witnessed 'the signing, sealing and delivery of this false and forged deed'. Their

[36] Crokey, *Sacred Maiestie*, sig. B4v.

[37] TNA, STAC 8/274/8; GA, D8887/6/54, 67; D9125/1/11994; Crokey, *Sacred Maiestie*, sig. C.

[38] TNA, STAC 8/274/8; Crokey, *Sacred Maiestie*, sig. C; GA, D9125/1/11989/12–14; D9125/1/11994, 11996, 12008, pp. 15–16; D2957/216/14.

[39] Crokey, *Sacred Maiestie*, sigs C–Cv; GA, D9125/1/12008, p. 47.

[40] TNA, PRO 30/38/16, fo. 241v; GA, D8887/6/67; Crokey, *Sacred Maiestie*, sig. Cv; GA, D9125/1/11994.

signatures, he said, had been 'counterfeited and forged . . . to give countenance and credit' to the document, which Crokey then presented as a 'true and good deed'. Such 'wicked and wilful forgery' was undertaken to 'stir up and maintain suits and controversies', and to 'trouble, oppress and disinherit' him, and it deserved 'exemplary punishment'. Otherwise, 'other like ill-minded persons' would be encouraged to commit similar crimes.[41]

In their defence—May-June 1615—Crokey and his associates ignored the issue of forgery, but made allegations about earlier litigation and earlier rulings which demonstrate how contestation could become prolonged. They rehearsed earlier claims about the history of the lease, not least that Alice 'entered' and 'possessed' the estate as a legatee of, rather than as executor to, William Thomas; that Joyce Cotterell was entitled to the estate 'by survivorship'; and that the original lease should be brought back into court, from which it had been removed through 'false information'. They also denied the suggestion about maintenance and champerty, insisting that Joyce granted the lands out of 'natural love and affection' to Crokey, 'her sister's son', as well as for 'his preferment, and in satisfaction of his pains taken in her affairs and suits'. They also insisted that matters were settled by the earlier Common Pleas suit, 'wherein after full evidence the now plaintiff became nonsuit'. They protested that the dismissal of Cotterell's 1610 Chancery case was caused by 'the death of her husband', and that Joyce's claim to the estate—as 'remainderer'—was different from that of Richard Moore, with whose cases she had been uninvolved. They also pointed out that the only successful challenge to her claim—at the Gloucestershire assizes—had been secured 'by default, upon no evidence on the part of her title'. Joyce hoped to prove that 'divers verdicts' had been given 'in affirmance of her title', while Crokey insisted that his Chancery case was only dismissed because the Lord Chancellor 'thought it fitter to be tried at [common] law'.[42]

In other words, Cotterell and Crokey exploited the fact that earlier verdicts were technical rather than substantive, and it was at this point that the case (i.e. Case 4) became subject to considerable delays. It did not come to a hearing until early 1617—when a writ was sent to Crokey and his associates to appear in Star Chamber—but the process of gathering evidence was still ongoing, and it was not until May 1618 that it could be referred to a judge, Richard Hutton, after which witnesses were summoned and evidence was submitted.[43] Crokey sensed that this delay was deliberate, and in January 1619 his counsel moved the court—unsuccessfully—that the case should be dismissed if Smyth did not procure a speedy hearing. He implied that proceedings were being dragged out because

[41] GA, D9125/1/11989/8.
[42] GA, D9125/1/11994; TNA, STAC 8/274/8; Crokey, *Sacred Maiestie*, sig. B3v.
[43] LB, MS 3549/165; GA, D9125/1/11989/13–14; D8887/6/62, 66; D9125/1/12008, p. 49; TNA, STAC 8/274/8; PRO 30/38/17, fo. 221v.

Smyth had secured an injunction to prevent Crokey from pursuing his claims at common law.[44]

III

Whether Crokey or Smyth—or both—became frustrated by how the Star Chamber case was developing, neither party waited for its outcome. Both pursued other channels, thereby highlighting how a multi-jurisdictional legal system made it possible—perhaps necessary—to fight on more than one front simultaneously. Observing what this meant involves entering legal territory where absolute clarity is elusive, although it is certainly possible to observe developments that transformed the dispute profoundly and prolonged it yet further. Before exploring what these were, it makes sense to reflect on what has been learned thus far, in terms of the kind of dispute that Coldwell's 'original lease' provoked, how it changed over time, and why it continued for so long.

The death of Grace Smyth reinforced the sense that circumstantial change could have a significant impact on a prolonged legal dispute, and was the pivotal moment in a period that witnessed a decisive shift towards a new generation of protagonists, headed by John Smyth and Benjamin Crokey. New participants—like John Cotterell—were sometimes less litigious, creating an opportunity for watershed moments to lead to a reduction in legal activity, but the persistence of disputation was both logical and comprehensible. New people necessarily shifted the legal issues in subtle but important ways: Joyce Cotterell and Benjamin Crokey could not make the same claims as Richard Moore. The vagaries of the legal system ensured that inconsistent and inconclusive verdicts provided reasons to press on, offering validation and encouragement, and presenting opportunities to find alternative legal channels. Such circumstances made it likely that frustrations would grow, and that costs would spiral out of control, thereby ensuring that three overlapping and mutually reinforcing phenomena became more evident. First, there was a tendency for disputants to find new things to fight about, in terms not just of substance but also of process, and how the matter was being contested, including allegations about champerty, maintenance, and forgery. Secondly, there was a tendency to engage in 'forum shopping' within the legal system, and to appeal beyond the courts, to higher authorities, in ways that reflected frustration and an appreciation of which channels were likely to be most profitable. Thirdly, there were signs of frustration with a legal system in which carefully prepared cases could fall foul of legal technicalities and procedural hiccups. There is no reason to believe that such phenomena were unique to the Warrens Court dispute;

[44] GA, D8887/6/73.

dozens of petitioners in the early seventeenth century grumbled about long disputes that passed through many courts and 'could never yet be determined', about the frightening and damaging costs involved, and about the need to appeal beyond the courts, and to 'flee' and 'fly' to Parliament as a 'refuge'.[45] Rather, the Warrens Court dispute makes it possible to discern such phenomena, and to gauge their impact. Indeed, each one came into much sharper focus in the years that followed, in ways that revealed an intensification of the dispute, its capacity to be escalated in dramatic ways, and mounting bitterness and animosity.

[45] For example: PA, HL/PO/JO/10/1/10 (Richard Vaughan); HL/PO/JO/10/1/25 (John Freeman); HL/PO/JO/10/1/26 (Timothy Pinckney); HL/PO/JO/10/1/32 (Richard Wright); HL/PO/JO/10/1/33 (William Trollopp); HL/PO/JO/10/1/35 (Ralph Starkey); HL/PO/JO/10/1/37 (Richard Palmer, Anne Stone). See: Hart, *Justice*, p. 30.

2

'Given to superstitious uses'

Contesting Lady Katherine Berkeley's Grammar School, 1615–1662

In tracing the Warrens Court dispute, passing reference was made to people and places beyond Nibley, and beyond the descendants of Alice Moore. It was noted that the 'original lease'—the transaction that caused so much contestation—was made by Robert Coldwell, the master of Wotton's grammar school. It was also noted that one transformative moment involved the appearance of John Smyth and his aggressive policy of estate development. This involved the acquisition of further land from the Duport family, two of whose members had also served as schoolmasters. These transactions likewise related to land given by Lady Katherine Berkeley in 1384, when she established the grammar school that bore—and still bears—her name. The patent granted by Richard II for the erection of a free school—with a master and two scholars—decreed that the operation would be funded by profits from Lady Katherine's land, an estate consisting of 160 acres in Wotton, Nibley, and the surrounding villages. The school statutes stipulated that masters were to be presented by the bishop of Worcester and were to be priests operating out of Wotton church. What Smyth achieved in 1608 was control of the entire school estate, by acquiring from the master, James Duport of Medbourne, Leicestershire, and his brother (and predecessor), Dr John Duport (master of Jesus College, Cambridge), leases on lands not included in the 'original' Coldwell lease.[1] More importantly, Smyth also acquired the patronage of the school, at a cost of £60. He thus had power over the school's lands and budget, and the ability to appoint men who would teach and exert influence as local ministers.[2] Smyth's deal with the Duports—as revealed in correspondence and legal documents—was actually predicated upon the resignation of James Duport as master, whereupon Smyth nominated one Edward Cowper—'sometimes my

[1] GA, D9125/1/11985–6; S379/2/1/1–5; *VCH Gloucester*, ii. 396–400; Smyth, *Lives*, iii. 401–2; TNA, C 21/C25/4. See: LB, MS 3549/49–50, 60–1, 63; GA, D2957/216/24; D733/2/14; BL, Add. MS 33588, fo. 52.

[2] GA, D9125/2/7633. For the school's history: GA, D2957/354/1–4, 56–7, 317; D9125/1/11989/5–6, 13–14; D9125/1/11990/1, 11996–8, 12002, 12008, pp. 9, 16 17, 12030/23; D8887/6/1, 24–5; D2957/216/16, 25; S379/2/2/1/1–2; TNA, STAC 8/107/7; LB, MS 3549/57, 64, 75, 91, 94–5, 109, 117.

The Madman and the Churchrobber: Law and Conflict in Early Modern England. Jason Peacey, Oxford University Press.
 DOI: 10.1093/oso/9780192897138.003.0003

schoolmaster and tutor both in the country and in Oxford'—whose appointment was confirmed by Henry Parry, bishop of Gloucester (April 1609).[3]

Smyth's acquisition of the lease to the school lands, and of the patronage, provides the most significant example of a change in litigants' circumstances transforming the Warrens Court dispute. This chapter demonstrates how this became manifest in litigation, prolonging the affair, introducing new areas for contestation, and exacerbating tensions. It certainly scotched any hopes that Smyth might have harboured that victory over Richard Moore would bring contestation to an end.[4] Once again, this story has broader significance for our understanding of early modern litigation. It reinforces the idea that disputation was liable to be prolonged by new circumstances, new claims, and new protagonists, not to mention indeterminate verdicts, but it also reveals additional issues. These include different kinds of legal manoeuvre—injunctions, cross-bills, and proxy litigation—as well as extra-legal moves, which took matters out of the courts and into public arenas. Such things were not unique to the Warrens Court dispute, but they once again highlight the advantages of a case study that ranges across time and jurisdictions, and can only be made visible by contextualising litigation, plotting connections between apparently disparate suits and protagonists, and utilising evidence about the wider landscape of disputation. What makes them significant is that they reflected and exacerbated tensions, fostered aggressive behaviour, and forged connections with other contemporary controversies, some of which were explosive. They also drew in many more people, particularly in the local community.

In relating this phase, the aim is not to suggest that such developments were typical or inevitable, even if other disputes also revolved around allegations about charitable institutions and the misappropriation of funds.[5] Rather, they are indicative of how disputes might easily develop. The worsening of relations did not necessarily reflect conscious or deliberate decisions to antagonise opponents, even if prolonged litigation made escalatory gambits more likely, and this chapter argues that divisions could widen as a result of perfectly understandable moves, and that prolonged and embittered litigation could result from protagonists following sound legal logic.

I

Tracing this transformation of the Warrens Court dispute involves recognising that litigation was an iterative process, characterised by successive moves that

[3] GA, D2957/354/5, 6; D9125/1/9790, 11989/13–14, 11990, 11995–6, 12002, 12008, pp. 9, 18; S379/2/2/1/2; S379/2/4/1; D4431/2/128/2; D8887/6/47–8; D8887/7/76.

[4] See: *VCH Gloucester*, ii. 401–5.

[5] PA, HL/PO/JO/10/1/35 (Walgrave hospital).

represented logical responses to obstacles, setbacks, frustrations, and delays, but which could act like a ratchet, 'tightening' the dispute and making an amicable settlement less feasible. In this case, the ratchet effect was epitomised by the dispute becoming more public, and the issues becoming more general and controversial.

Crucially, in responding to Star Chamber delays and the injunction against common law suits, Crokey's legal gambit involved litigation by proxy, a novelty in this dispute, and a dimension of early modern litigation that is difficult to detect using formal legal records.[6] Following the dismissal of his Chancery case, Crokey made a lease of the disputed lands to a cooper's apprentice from Bristol, Thomas Baddam (September 1615), who made an 'entry' onto Smyth's lands. This was presumably a deliberate provocation, and Smyth predictably tried to 'eject' the new occupant with 'force and arms', to which Baddam reacted with a suit in Common Pleas—at Crokey's bidding—'for trial of the title', in the hope of securing a writ of 'ejectment' (Case 5).[7] Smyth responded with legal obstruction, and at the moment when his own Star Chamber case finally looked set to get a hearing, in early 1617, his counsel secured an injunction to halt Baddam's case. This insisted that there had already been 'divers verdicts' in Smyth's favour; that Crokey nevertheless 'exhibited three bills in Chancery', all of which were dismissed; and that Crokey and Baddam sought to 'prejudicate' the court, and 'premeditate the sentence'. For good measure, Smyth also suggested that Crokey sought to 'hinder' the Star Chamber case with 'many delays', before he could be 'brought to an answer and be examined'.[8] Crokey then responded to the prospect of further delay by trying to overturn the injunction, and following a ruling by the new Lord Keeper (Sir Francis Bacon)—that Smyth needed to demonstrate why it should remain in force (3 June 1617)—the case not only resumed in early 1618, but actually looked set to produce a ruling that Smyth should deliver up the estate. In the end, Crokey's hopes were dashed by two hearings at Serjeants' Inn, apparently granted at Smyth's request. This caused further delay, and while it was declared that a final verdict would not be possible before Michaelmas, the case was not finally resolved until 1620.[9]

Whether or not Smyth felt able to fend off Crokey's latest move, his response to suits and delays ratcheted up the dispute yet further, by placing the school at the heart of proceedings. This was a bold move, and one that could not be reversed, and like Crokey he sought to put distance between himself and the legal case submitted. In Easter 1616, it appeared that a new challenge was launched against his title, in the form of an Exchequer Court case by Edward Bishopp of the Middle

[6] Churches, 'Business at law', p. 947. For proxy litigation: PA, HL/PO/JO/10/1/32 (Peter Watson).

[7] GA, D9125/1/11989/9, 13–14; D9125/1/11996; Crokey, *Sacred Maiestie*, sig. C; GA, D8887/6/63–4.

[8] GA, D9125/1/11989/13–14; D9125/1/11994, 12008, pp. 48–9; D8887/6/63–4, 68; Crokey, *Sacred Maiestie*, sig. C2; LB, MS 3549/165.

[9] GA, D9125/1/11989/13–14; D9125/1/11996; D8887/6/63–5.

Temple (Case 6). The claim was explosive: that Warrens Court consisted of 'concealed' lands, which should have passed to the crown following the dissolution of the chantries in 1547. Bishopp insisted that the estate had formed part of a chantry establishment, and that the schoolmaster had traditionally been a priest who said prayers for the dead. The backstory here involved uncertainty over whether the Edwardian Chantry Act—an attempt to sweep away remnants of Catholicism—applied to places like Wotton school.[10] However, Bishopp argued that the Elizabethan regime actually made a grant of the lands (1589), that he recently inherited this claim, and that Smyth's possession of the estate served to 'defraud' him and 'deceive' the crown.[11] Smyth's response remains unclear, because the 'replication' in his papers is badly damaged, but Crokey insisted that this case was a charade—or 'mere practice'—involving 'combination and confederacy'. He alleged that Smyth 'procured' Bishopp to 'exhibit a bill' to prove that his estate consisted of former chantry lands.[12]

Whatever the origins of Bishopp's case, and whenever Smyth recognised the weakness of his title, the question of 'concealed lands' had much wider resonances, involving crown finance and the history of the Reformation. It made the Warrens Court dispute controversial, took it in new directions, and involved many more people. This was because it provoked an official inquiry—at the school and in the nearby village of Stone—in the summer and autumn of 1616, which investigated the existence of a chantry priest before the 1550s, and claims about the 'superstitious uses' that the lands had financed. This involved the memories of Wotton's oldest inhabitants: one of Robert Coldwell's former assistants (John Moore, parish clerk of Wotton, aged 86); past pupils (Jeffrey Mitchell, Thomas Plomer, and Thomas Hewes, aged 83, 85, and 87); and a former steward of the lands (William Phelps, aged 74). Agnes Adams deposed that Coldwell died at the house where she and her son Thomas now lived, and it transpired that the school was once known as the Chantry House, a name that only 'decayed' with the 'going down of the mass'. Witnesses apparently remembered—or had 'credibly heard'—that prayers were said for the dead, and that Coldwell was a 'morrow mass priest' (with loose morals), who lived 'half a bow shot from Wotton church' and 'kept a free school'. (According to Edwardian officials, Coldwell was 'unwieldy' and 'neither meet in discipline nor behaviour'.) Witnesses also confirmed that Smyth's lands belonged to the school, and earlier claims that the estate 'should belong to the crown' were evidently 'quieted' by successive schoolmasters, and by the Berkeley family.[13]

[10] *VCH Gloucester*, ii. 400. See: C. J. Kitching, 'The quest for concealed lands in the reign of Elizabeth I', *TRHS*, fifth series, 24 (1974), 63–78; A. F. Leach, *English Schools at the Reformation* (2 vols, Westminster, 1896), i. 67–70, 76, ii. 79–80.

[11] GA, D9125/1/11993, 11996; Crokey, *Sacred Maiestie*, sig. Cv; LB, MS 3549/77, 99, 163–4. For Bishopp (*d.*1633): TNA, PROB 11/164, fo. 258. See: LB, MS 3549/67, 73, 76.

[12] GA, D9125/1/11995–6, 12008, p. 19; TNA, STAC 8/107/7; C 93/8/21; Smyth, *Lives*, iii. 402.

[13] TNA, E 134/14Jas1/Mich28; STAC 8/107/7. See: Leach, *English Schools*, ii. 79–80; GA, D8887/2/52.

Bishopp's case took the dispute into murky territory, and provoked a series of Exchequer inquiries, which Crokey insisted were procured by Smyth to 'find the possessions of the said school to be concealed as chantry lands given to superstitious uses'. The first—according to an affidavit that Crokey later submitted—was held at Thornbury (20 April 1618), quickly followed by an inconclusive hearing at Tetbury (August), and then a third, overseen by Sir John Poyntz and Sir John Stafford at Wickwar (13 October).[14] The latter provoked serious contestation, because *Crokey* allegedly submitted evidence that enabled a jury to conclude that the lands should have passed to the crown, and that Smyth's title was 'defective'.[15] *Both* men subsequently claimed credit for reversing this decision, citing 'undue proceedings' and 'manifest imperfections' at the hearing (28 November 1618).[16]

Making sense of this episode will require delving further into the strategies of Smyth and Crokey in subsequent chapters, but the upshot—beyond heightened animosity—was that Smyth took advantage of legislation which provided relief for landowners whose 'defective titles' led to aggressive 'concealment-hunting', vexatious litigation, and 'intolerable charges'. Even before the outcome of the three commissions, Smyth secured new letters patent to the lands, at a cost of £50 (15 December 1617).[17] Raising the stakes, in other words, appeared to have paid off, albeit by raising tensions considerably.

II

There is scope to explore further Smyth's role in orchestrating Bishopp's suit and the subsequent investigations, but this episode is vital for understanding the Warrens Court dispute and contemporary litigation. This is because logical and successful legal moves could have unintended consequences, leading disputes in new and controversial directions. Invoking the history of Wotton school raised questions about whether Smyth had exploited his control over the charity's affairs, something strangely absent from previous litigation, even though he boasted about maintaining a schoolmaster with profits from the estate. Hereafter, Crokey made the school's fate a prime concern.[18] This meant insisting—as he allegedly failed to do at Wickwar—that the lands were *not* 'concealed', because the Edwardian chantry statute did not apply to leases made before 27 November 1545, as Coldwell's had (just) been. More importantly, it involved suggesting that Smyth sought to 'suppress' the school for his own financial benefit, and that it was Crokey

[14] Crokey, *Sacred Maiestie*, sigs. C3v–4v; GA, D8887/6/66; D9125/1/11996, 12002, 12008, p. 60.
[15] GA, D8887/6/70, 72; TNA, STAC 8/107/7.
[16] GA, D9125/1/11996, 12008, pp. 60–1; Crokey, *Sacred Maiestie*, sig. C4v; TNA, STAC 8/107/7.
[17] GA, D8887/6/96; D9125/1/11996, 12008, p. 20; TNA, C 93/8/21. See below, pp. C3.P51–C1.P53, C5.P22–C5.P24.
[18] GA, D9125/1/11992, 11989/10.

who had the school's best interests at heart. This made the contest more complex and more intense, in ways that were to prove decisive.[19]

Placing the school centre stage also created an opportunity to raise more general concerns about the 'public interest'. Crokey now sought to 're-establish' the school according to the 'true foundation' and secured a commission of enquiry based on the Elizabethan statute of charitable uses (43 Eliz.cap.4), albeit with considerable difficulty. Indeed, when two scheduled hearings were postponed, Crokey petitioned James I—in person, at Warwick—to expedite matters (August 1617). The king duly instructed the bishop of Gloucester and his fellow commissioners to 'finally determine' whether the lands had been 'misemployed', although the subsequent hearing proved abortive. Smyth was summoned to Gloucester Guildhall (or 'Boothall') on 2 September, where Crokey tried to give evidence, but commissioners concluded that they 'had not any power' to make a ruling, precisely because the lands had been concealed, and 'excepted' from the statute of charitable uses (11 September).[20]

Crokey's gambit was unsuccessful, but the school remained firmly at the heart of the dispute. This was partly because Smyth tried to enhance his credentials as a patron who sought 'the final settling and preservation of the school', by appointing twenty local men as trustees, and by providing twenty marks *per annum* for the schoolmaster (March 1618).[21] It was also because Crokey managed—again with difficulty—to secure a second commission of inquiry, with the aim of restoring the school's possessions and establishing that Smyth had 'drawn away' the lands 'under colour' of their 'concealment'. Once again, Crokey was stymied. Although he appeared at Thornbury with witnesses, only three of the seven commissioners attended, thereby making the hearing inquorate (April 1619).[22] Crokey's counsel asked Lord Chancellor Bacon for another commission, but Smyth's lawyer cited the outcome of the Gloucester hearing to ensure that this was denied, and Crokey was prohibited from obtaining further inquiries, and indeed 'disgraced' (June 1619).[23]

The Warrens Court dispute was becoming more intense, more acrimonious, and more likely to escalate. Crokey responded by appealing once again to the king, who immediately referred his petition—'in the school's behalf'—to the archbishop of Canterbury, the bishops of London and Winchester, and Sir Henry Hobart. As in 1617, this approach paid dividends, and a hearing at Lambeth resulted in a third inquiry, and a certificate setting out objections to Smyth's claims and behaviour, which survives as part of the 'answers' he prepared in

[19] Crokey, *Sacred Maiestie*, sig. Bv.
[20] GA, D9125/1/11996, 12008, pp. 58–9, 66–7; Crokey, *Sacred Maiestie*, sigs C3, D–Dv; GA, D8887/6/58a, 74–5; TNA, STAC 8/107/7.
[21] GA, D9125/1/12008, pp. 20–1; D2957/354/7; S379/2/2/1/3.
[22] Crokey, *Sacred Maiestie*, sigs C3–v; GA, D8887/6/74–5; D9125/1/12008, p. 67.
[23] GA, D8887/6/74–5; Crokey, *Sacred Maiestie*, sigs D–Dv; GA, D9125/1/12008, pp. 58–9, 68.

response.[24] This is a document to which it will be necessary to return, but it is worth noting here that Smyth was forced to defend his legal manoeuvres, his version of the school's history, and his oversight of its affairs. He denied that the school lands were worth £300 per annum, valuing them at no more than £131, and protested that many portions were held by others on long leases. He asserted that these had previously been put to 'superstitious' rather than 'good and pious... purposes', pointing out that schoolmasters had always been priests, and that an inquiry in the 1580s described the lands as 'concealed'. Smyth also denied acquiring the patronage in order 'to suppress the school' and 'convert the possessions to his own use', protesting that the master was 'a learned and religious divine', rather than someone appointed 'to serve his turn'. He insisted that the lands were not merely entrusted to 'friends', and that the schoolmaster's income had grown from 40*s*. to £12 *per annum*.[25]

III

Once the Warrens Court dispute became intertwined with the fate of Wotton school, new and controversial issues came into play, and novel options became available for securing favourable decisions. No amount of setbacks could conceal the fact that Crokey achieved some kind of validation, mostly from outside the courts, and that he had grounds for persevering, and perhaps for optimism, even if subsequent developments made it difficult to gain the ascendancy over Smyth.

First, in October 1619 Smyth's Star Chamber case regarding 'forgery, maintenance and champerty' (Case 4) was 'absolutely dismissed', with 'good costs', although this may merely have involved a judgment that it should be referred to common law, rather than an assessment about its substantive 'merits'.[26] Secondly, Crokey pursued the favourable outcome of the Lambeth hearing by petitioning Lord Chancellor Bacon for a third 'charitable uses' commission, even if the order in his favour—on 21 February 1620—did not lead to decisive action before the start of the 1621 Parliament.[27] Thirdly, Crokey revived Baddam's case (Case 5), leading to Common Pleas hearings in February and May 1620, when a Gloucestershire jury ruled in his favour.[28]

Unfortunately for Crokey, the lessons to emerge about the legal system were that each new sign of encouragement might generate new obstacles, that it was easy to make legal missteps, and that it was difficult to interpret legal decisions. Crokey struggled to get a favourable verdict translated into an official *judgment*,

[24] Crokey, *Sacred Maiestie*, sig. Dv; GA, D9125/1/11996.

[25] GA, D9125/1/11989/13–14.

[26] GA, D8887/6/76; D9125/1/11996, 12008, pp. 48, 50; Crokey, *Sacred Maiestie*, sig. C2.

[27] Crokey, *Sacred Maiestie*, sig. Dv.

[28] LB, MS 3549/175; GA, D9125/1/11996, 11989/9; Crokey, *Sacred Maiestie*, sig. C2v.

and after several sessions where Smyth and Crokey were 'heard at large' alongside their counsel, the judges—Sir Henry Hobart and Sir Peter Warburton—refused to proceed any further, citing a technical 'defect' (14 July).[29] This perhaps reflected the fact that, although the judges sought to 'finish the whole matter', Crokey chose precisely this moment to complain about his failure to obtain a judgment in Baddam's favour. This obviously reflected frustration, not just at another delay, but also at what he regarded as Smyth's refusal to abide by Common Pleas 'rules', agreed earlier in the year. Crokey interpreted these as binding both men to consent to whatever verdict emerged, and not to challenge it with writs of error. Crokey's allegation was that Smyth conspired to delay a judgment, not least by petitioning the king with 'misinformation', whereupon the judges had been ordered to 'compose the differences' between the two disputants. The problem, as Crokey saw it, was that neither man had agreed to accept the outcome of these new deliberations, and that, when the judges inevitably failed to broker a settlement, they merely 'left the same as they found it' and failed to set a day for another hearing.[30]

What emerges very clearly is that the reactions of both men were coloured by their ability to interpret developments. Smyth took a rather different line regarding the Common Pleas 'rules', insisting that Crokey—who was present when they were drawn up—had misinterpreted these provisions, 'understandeth not . . . the judges certificate', and pursued a fruitless legal manoeuvre.[31] At this stage, even Crokey's petition to the king was insufficient, and although judges were ordered to expedite the matter, the final judgment—ironically in Crokey's favour—was only reached after Baddam's lease had expired ('worn out'), thereby making it impossible to secure 'any writ for possession' (September 1620).[32] Whether because of his own missteps or Smyth's successful legal moves, Crokey was defeated, not by a legal judgment but by the legal *clock*, which had been ticking ever since his claim was conveyed to Baddam. This was doubtless a bitter lesson, and one that perhaps left him unsure how to respond, and it indicates that legal rules and legal processes did not always work in harmony.

To make matters worse, and to remind him that legal processes were complex, it then proved impossible for Crokey to secure the costs that were awarded when Smyth's Star Chamber case was dismissed in 1619 (Case 4). Crokey certainly submitted an account of money 'to be taxed' (Trinity term 1620), but this was blocked pending the outcome of Baddam's case. When the claim was re-submitted, following a royal order that the judges had made 'no end', and that 'the ordinary course of law should be observed' (30 November), this too was

[29] GA, D9125/1/11996, 12002, 12008, p. 54.
[30] Crokey, *Sacred Maiestie*, sigs D2–3; GA, D9125/1/11996; D8887/6/76.
[31] GA, D8887/6/82.
[32] Crokey, *Sacred Maiestie*, sigs D2–3.

rejected, the judges having insisted that they were actually still deliberating (December).[33]

Crokey was confronted not just by legal complexities, but also by Smyth's willingness to take further steps against him, and to point out his errors. First, Crokey was hampered by further legal proceedings, as Smyth pushed for a new trial in late 1620, to remove any suspicion that he was in contempt. Smyth noted that earlier cases failed, while verdicts were given in his favour, and rehearsed old claims about champerty and his development of the estate, before insisting that no judgment was possible once Baddam's lease had expired. He also protested, polemically, that the Common Pleas rules were drafted by Crokey's attorney, John Price (the 'drawer' of his breviates, 'instructor of his counsel', and 'bearer of part of the charges of this suit'), and that there was a risk of his being denied the 'liberty of a subject' if appeals were forbidden. Finally, Smyth explained that Crokey's earlier moves failed due a minute technical error—the 'defect' to which judges referred—whereby one juror was recorded as 'Richard Tippets' when the man sworn was 'Richard *Trippets*'. Smyth demanded a new trial on the basis of a spelling mistake, 'for that there was but eleven sworn of those which were returned'.[34]

Smyth's determination to instigate new legal proceedings indicates that the dispute now consisted of many interwoven strands—procedural, personal, principled, and public spirited—which meant that litigation was likely to become attritional and difficult to resolve.

IV

Quite what Smyth had in mind at this point is unclear, but the upshot of procedural complexity, heightened animosity, and controversial issues, and a willingness to appeal to the king, was official intervention. The dispute thus highlights the speed with which such factors could raise the stakes, and the likelihood that litigation would generate official anxiety, because of the tone of disputation and the invocation of contentious topics.

The result on this occasion was action against *both* men by Attorney General Coventry (9 October 1620).[35] This was undertaken in the interest of a well-established establishment, with a 'strong schoolhouse' for teaching local boys without 'stipend or salary', and Coventry noted that contest over the Coldwell lease—'whereof there are thirteen years yet to come'—had generated many 'suits and trials'. Crokey was said to have 'scandalised' Smyth, by accusing him of

[33] GA, D9125/1/12008, pp. 50–1; GA, D8887/6/60. [34] GA, D8887/6/65.

[35] Coventry did not formally become Attorney General until 1621 but assumed the responsibilities following the imprisonment of Sir Henry Yelverton in June 1620: *ODNB*.

'destroying the said school and converting the profits to his own use', such that Smyth sought 'the clearing of his reputation' and settlement of the case, 'to avoid multiplicity of suits'. Coventry recognised that this had proved impossible, because Crokey and Smyth accused each other of using 'indirect means' to secure possession of the estate, and he charged Smyth with acquiring an 'unreasonable' lease of former chantry lands, of securing the patronage or 'nomination', and of ensuring that lands were 'intermingled', as well as of making 'poor allowance to the schoolmaster'.[36]

In response, both men confirmed that many issues were now involved, while focusing attention upon the school's fate. Smyth denied Crokey's claims ('false pretences') that he 'went about' to 'subvert' the school, and he demanded the 'acquittal of his reputation so falsely scandalised'. He recounted the history of the lease, the litigation, and the 'intermingling' of school lands, and insisted that increasing the schoolmaster's stipend to £12 revealed 'his affection to the setting up of the said school'. He protested that, having long been 'ignorant of the crown's title', he belatedly discovered that teaching was traditionally conducted by a 'chantry priest', concluded that the estate ought to have passed to the crown, and decided to 'buy in' the lands. This was done, he insisted, to protect his 'undertenants', to ensure the 'quieting of his own possession', and to effect 'the better establishing of the said school'. Smyth also insisted that trustees were appointed to secure 'relief', or financial support, that timber from his own estate was used to 're-edify' its buildings, and that he was willing to do 'any further act for the preservation and continuance of the school'.[37]

Crokey, meanwhile, alleged that Smyth was intent on 'suppressing' the school and converting the lands 'to his own use', while also admitting a personal interest in the Coldwell lease, and rehearsing complaints about the handling of Baddam's case. He protested that the lands extended to 500 acres, worth £400 *per annum*, and that Smyth, 'fearing his title to be weak', used claims about 'chantry and concealed lands' as a prelude to securing a new grant from the crown. It was his discovery of 'manifest wrongs' that drove his attempts to expose Smyth's 'indirect practises', to prevent 'the subversion of good literature', and to address 'the grievance of all well-disposed persons', and he professed a 'charitable disposition' towards re-establishing the school on its 'true foundation'. Crokey described himself as the school's 'agent and careful solicitor', protested about being 'wronged by Smyth', and grumbled about being prosecuted 'as though he were a wrongdoer against the school'.[38]

At this stage, Crokey had no particular reason to fear the outcome of these proceedings. Following the submission of their responses, the court ordered both men to 'stay all suits' (November 1620), but if Crokey sensed that this was

[36] GA, D9125/1/11996, 12002, 12008, p. 54. See: Churches, 'Business at law', pp. 939, 949.
[37] GA, D9125/1/11996. [38] Crokey, *Sacred Maiestie*, sig. E; GA, D9125/1/11996–7.

intended to prevent him from pursuing the costs that remained due to him, he was probably heartened to learn that a new charitable uses commission was to survey the lands (with his input), that the case would be 'heard the next term', and that he would be able to examine witness statements, so long as these were not used 'against the... school' (December 1620). However, if Crokey dared to believe that his fortunes were changing, he quickly confronted yet another problem: official involvement caused procedural deceleration. In this case, the summoning of a new Parliament meant that both the commission and the hearing were seriously delayed.[39]

V

Whether or not Crokey feared the outcome of official hearings, he certainly appreciated that things were being kicked into the long grass. His response is revealing, because of the legal avenues he pursued, and because he—like others whose cases ground on without hope of resolution—concluded that the new Parliament provided an opportunity to go on the offensive, at the very moment when peers resumed their historic role as a court of judicature.

Notwithstanding the order to 'stay all suits', Crokey submitted a new Star Chamber case against Smyth and various associates (1 February 1621, Case 7). This lauded the school's achievements—its 'good literature and learning'—and bemoaned Smyth's 'plots and practices' to 'overturn' the original lease and deny the charity land worth £500 *per annum*. This allegedly involved acquiring the Duport lands and the patronage, conspiring 'corruptly and unlawfully' with Edward Bishopp to claim that the lands were concealed, and securing commissions of inquiry, as well as obtaining a patent under the statute of defective titles. Crokey's move was odd, given that Smyth's election to Parliament—as MP for Midhurst—brought immunity from prosecution, and Smyth invoked his privilege by declining to respond.[40] Indeed, when Crokey sought permission to recover his legal costs, Smyth appealed to Viscount Mandeville about yet another contravention of the order against further litigation (Easter 1621).[41]

More importantly, Smyth complained that Crokey 'betook himself' to 'other courses'. This meant taking matters out of the courts by submitting 'petitions to Parliament', and using 'scandalous' claims—that the school was 'suppressed'—to 'disgrace' his opponent, and turning to the House of Lords when the Commons proved unresponsive. Crokey asked for the recently appointed commission of

[39] GA, D9125/1/11996, 12002, 12008, pp. 23–4, 50–1; Crokey, *Sacred Maiestie*, sigs E–v.

[40] TNA, STAC 8/107/7; GA, D8887/6/84; Crokey, *Sacred Maiestie*, sig. F2; GA, D9125/1/12008, p. 63. The defendants were Peter Bird, William Archard, Sir John Poyntz, Sir William Guise, Robert Smyth (mayor of Wotton), John Browning, and Henry Minors.

[41] GA, D8887/6/97.

charitable uses to be annulled, but also submitted a draft bill for 'the establishment of the school' and 'private recompenses to himself', at a cost of £23. Here were echoes of other cases—including one regarding Thetford school—where claims about the misappropriation of charitable funds led to legal proceedings and private legislation, and it was this bill that Crokey promoted with a printed breviate—the text seen 'stuck on a wall like a ballad'—rehearsing recent events, his troubles with charitable uses commissions, and the 'multitude of unjust suits'. The breviate also suggested that Smyth, upon learning about the proposed bill, 'got himself to be a burgess of Midhurst in Sussex, 130 miles from his residence'. Crokey's demand, having apparently spent £1,600 in his dispute with Smyth, was that he should be 'restored' to the lands, that a new inquiry should be launched, and that the school should be reformed.[42]

Such interventions in the parliamentary process demonstrated that people like Crokey could pursue non-legal channels and feel vindicated by the responses they received. Thus, in addition to the possibility that different courts might produce different rulings, it also became clear that the political system might react differently to judges. Although Crokey later complained that his bill lay unread for six months, thereby echoing the complaints of others who grumbled about long and fruitless attendance at Westminster, the Lords granted him another commission—on 4 June—to be completed before Michaelmas term.[43] This was apparently the fifth commission Crokey was granted, and it was 'directed to several bishops'—of Worcester, Bristol and Gloucester—as well as gentlemen 'of good rank', and was 'executed' at Gloucester's Boothall, with the commissioners' report—and a 'true schedule' of the school's thirty-nine tenements—being returned on 19 September. Crokey himself was not present—having been arrested on 24 June—but the commissioners decided in his favour.[44]

Crokey probably felt that his efforts were being rewarded and his arguments validated. Having seen a range of evidence, the jury heard Crokey's counsel make allegations about a 'confederacy' between Smyth and Bishopp and were shown the archbishop of Canterbury's certificate regarding Smyth's 'practices'. When Smyth's counsel 'earnestly urged' that the Berkeley bequest involved 'superstition within the statute of chantries', Crokey's lawyers cited the opinions of Attorney General Yelverton and Solicitor General Coventry that the foundation was 'free from suspicion'. In the end, the jury agreed that Smyth sought 'the suppression of

[42] GA, D9125/1/6699, 6700, 11996, 12008, p. 68; Crokey, *Sacred Maiestie*, sig. Ev; GA, D8887/6/84; BL, Harl. MS 6803, fos 56v–7; Crokey, *Complaint*, sigs A3–v; Crokey, *Briefe*. For Thetford school: *The Eighth Part of the Reports of Sir Edward Coke* (London, 1738), fos 130v–31v.

[43] GA, D8887/6/85; Crokey, *Sacred Maiestie*, sig. Ev; HEH, EL7912; TNA, C 93/8/21. For delays at Westminster: PA, HL/PO/JO/10/1/17 (Francis Brode); HL/PO/JO/10/1/25 (Great Tewe); HL/PO/JO/10/1/33 (William Trollopp, Meredith Madey).

[44] GA, D8887/6/87; TNA, C 93/8/21. See: *LJ*, iii. 170–1.

the school', to which the lands should be restored, according to the 'charitable and pious foundation'.

As if to confirm that official rulings were rarely uncomplicated, however, the commissioners also noted issues which they could not 'determine'. They feared that the school 'corporation' was 'of late discontinued', and wondered whether any students were even being taught, and they were unsure about Crokey's demand for compensation, and about the significance of his parliamentary bill. These matters—'whereof we cannot judge'—were referred back to Chancery or Parliament, prompting Crokey to submit yet another petition, decrying Smyth's 'indirect practices' and the 'impoverishing of his estate', and asking for his bill to be considered (26 November). Once again, peers responded favourably and, after issuing a writ of *habeas corpus* to the keeper of the Marshalsea prison, Crokey appeared in person at Westminster (28 November 1621), and was released from prison.[45]

Even then, Crokey faced further setbacks. With matters unresolved by the time Parliament adjourned for the last time (19 December 1621), Smyth allegedly had Crokey arrested again 'for the same business' and submitted 'exceptions' to the commission's findings (3 December). Although Crokey was content to attend the subsequent hearing and was probably delighted when these 'exceptions' were deemed 'frivolous' (17 July 1622), he still could not secure 'determination of this cause'. Rather than upholding the commissioners' findings, the hearing merely paved the way for yet another commission, as mooted by the Attorney General (in 1620) but delayed by the calling of Parliament. This was charged with setting out 'the metes and bounds' of the disputed land, 'with speed'.[46] The commissioners undertook their work 'with great care and exactness', according to Smyth, employing five surveyors 'well known for their integrity and wisdom', and 'approved by both Smyth and Crokey'.[47] The fruits of their labour were revealed on 10 September 1622, attended by witnesses whose presence was required by Crokey, and they declared the findings—that the land lay 'in many small pieces and parcels'—'very just'. This paved the way for the Lord Keeper's order—at Smyth's behest—for the cause to be heard the following term (12 December 1622).[48]

[45] TNA, C 93/8/21; Crokey, *Complaint*, sigs A3–v; Crokey, *Sacred Maiestie*, sigs E2v–4v, Fv; GA, D8887/6/87; D9125/1/12002, 12008, p. 68; PA, HO/PO/JO/10/14/4, item 3363; HL/PO/JO/10/1/19; TNA, C 3/338/8; *LJ*, iii. 170–1, 173–4.

[46] Crokey, *Sacred Maiestie*, sigs E4v, Fv; GA, D9125/1/11996, 12002, 12008, p. 68; D8887/6/87; PA, HO/PO/JO/10/1/37. See: GA, D2957/354/8.

[47] GA, D9125/1/12000–1, 12021.

[48] GA, D9125/1/11996, 11999, 12002; Crokey, *Sacred Maiestie*, sig. G3v; TNA, C 21/C25/4.

VI

With issues of genuine complexity, clear verdicts were hard to reach, and there was always a chance that protagonists who appeared to be on the back foot might create new obstacles, or that officials would seek further evidence. This perhaps explains why Crokey sought to revive his recent Star Chamber case (Case 7), by issuing subpoenas to five defendants, perhaps more in hope than expectation, given that their despatch coincided with a hearing where evidence was 'at large debated' before Lord Keeper Williams (30 January 1623).[49] This involved counsel for the school (Williams and Solicitor General Sir Robert Heath), Smyth's nine counsellors, and Crokey's lawyers, and the outcome was controversial.[50] What became clear was that, once matters bounced between the courts and the higher authorities, even a decisive verdict might not settle matters, and recourse was always possible to Parliament, particularly given its willingness to intervene in legal proceedings.

The Lord Keeper's verdict suited Smyth more than it did Crokey. Williams declared that Crokey 'prosecuted' commissions 'upon the statute of charitable uses' for 'the advancement of his own ends', citing the claim that he gave evidence at Wickwar about the lands being 'concealed'. He also declared that the lands 'did *not* come to the crown by the . . . statute of chantries', because 'celebrating for souls departed'—while 'superstitious'—was not mandated by the original foundation, only being 'mentioned' in subsequent ordinances. Lady Katherine's principal aim had been 'teaching grammar'. However, 'long leases' made by Smyth were declared 'void in law and equity', being 'contrary to the pious and charitable intention of the founder', and tending to 'the destruction of the said school', and the lands needed to be 're-established in the said school'. Crucially, however, Williams acknowledged that Smyth had increased the schoolmaster's stipend, that his 'intention' was not to 'diminish' the school's income, and that existing leaseholders—including men of 'mean ability'—would face 'impoverishment' if agreements were revoked. They were to be granted new leases 'without fine', while Smyth—who had spent £700 on improving an estate that was 'intermingled' with other lands—was to have 'quiet possession' for 'three lives'. The *quid pro quo* was that rents were to be increased by one third, so that an additional £47 *per annum* could support the schoolmaster and scholars, although Smyth's rent was not to increase. Finally, the Lord Keeper refused to 'determine the said title between the said defendants', while insisting that 'all suits and prosecutions . . . shall be stayed and cease.'[51]

[49] Crokey, *Sacred Maiestie*, sigs F2–v.

[50] GA, D9125/1/12002; Crokey, *Sacred Maiestie*, sig. G3v.

[51] GA, D9125/1/12002, 12008, pp. 24–32, 55, 83, 12029/15; S379/2/3/2/1. See: Bodl. MS Eng.Misc. e.6, fo. 75.

Smyth was clearly satisfied with this judgment, commenting that uncertainty over the school was 'quieted' by the 1623 decree, after 'much trouble and expense'. He resolved to 'reverence and obey' the decision, although it apparently cost him 1,000 marks, and then played a prominent part in facilitating the school's re-foundation.[52] This involved petitioning the Lord Keeper almost immediately, to get a speedy resolution of outstanding matters, including the tenants' new leases, the number of scholars, and the new schoolmaster. By late February 1624, a plan was in place to raise rents, provide the master's income and support scholars financially, and in May Smyth successfully requested that fees for engrossing the new patent should be waived, thereby saving £10 7*s*.[53] The new charter named Edward Cowper as master, and George Lord Berkeley as patron, and the school was said to have 'such apt and exquisite ordinances' for its 'reglement' as would 'witness to after ages the wisdoms and cares' of those whose 'pains and pens' were involved in their preparation, notably Lord Keeper Williams, Sir Robert Heath, and the bishop of Bristol (Robert Wright).[54] Smyth rapidly secured a ninety-nine-year lease of Warrens Court from Cowper (September 1623), and once the dust had settled Lord Berkeley re-conveyed to him the advowson and patronage (December 1624).[55]

Crokey, meanwhile, was appalled by the outcome, complaining that the findings of the 1621 commission were ignored, that he was not allowed to 'produce any matter in behalf of himself', and that the hearing was perfunctory. He rejected the findings of the survey, and protested that the decree destroyed his title and altered the school's 'ancient foundation'.[56] He thus resumed the campaign to secure legal costs—due to him since 1619—resulting in rival petitions to Lord Keeper Williams. Smyth asked to have the matter 'discharged', on the grounds that it had already 'depended three years and a half' (February 1623); Crokey appealed to have them 'taxed' (May 1623), and then moved Star Chamber to the same effect (July 1623). Officials, however, disliked Crokey's 'troublesome and contentious disposition . . . in troubling this court for matters settled and determined', and Smyth was 'absolutely freed and discharged' from paying costs and being 'questioned for the same hereafter'.[57] More importantly, Crokey refused to accept that lawsuits should be 'stayed', resuming the Star Chamber case that had been ongoing since February 1621 (Case 7). Here too he faced problems, and in June 1624 Smyth's lawyers referred to a 'drooping prosecution', saying that Crokey had been slow in summoning witnesses. One defendant, Peter Bird, accused Crokey of having a 'troublesome conscience' for putting people to 'great and unnecessary charges and expenses . . . without any just cause exhibited', and it

[52] Smyth, *Lives*, iii. 402. GA, D9125/1/12008, p. 32.
[53] GA, D9125/1/12008, pp. 33–4; D8887/6/91–2.
[54] GA, D9125/1/12003, 12008, p. 36; TNA, C 66/2332/21.
[55] GA, D2957/216/23; D2957/354/9, 54. [56] Crokey, *Sacred Maiestie*, sigs F2v–H2.
[57] FSL, Z.e.1(27); Crokey, *Sacred Maiestie*, sig. C2; GA, D9125/1/12003, 12008, pp. 51–3, 58.

was also pointed out that Crokey had already been warned to 'proceed termly with effect'. Eventually, matters were referred to Sir Humphrey May, the deputy clerk of Star Chamber, who dismissed the case, awarding Smyth costs of £52 (February 1625).[58]

Legally, Crokey's options now seemed to be exhausted, but he knew that other avenues were available, and faced with such setbacks he became increasingly reliant upon Parliament as a forum for airing grievances, not least because the courts had offered at least some kind of validation. A petition to the 1624 Parliament—logged by clerks on 23 April—asked for his draft bill to be considered (without paying additional fees), claiming that it was 'not read at all' in 1621, that he had prosecuted five charitable uses commissions, and that he had spent £1,600 to his 'utter undoing'. It also complained about contradictory decisions: the failure to respond to the Gloucester inquiry which 'found for the school', and the Attorney General's decision to appoint a new commission even though the Lord Keeper had 'resolved to re-establish the school' once Smyth's objections were declared 'idle and frivolous'. As on previous occasions, this approach to Parliament was successful, and the Committee for Petitions referred matters to Serjeant Crew, to consider whether they could be considered in relation to 'the bill ... for the continuance of hospitals and free schools' (14 May). Progress was halted with the dissolution of Parliament on 29 May, but Crokey returned to Westminster at the opening of the 1625 Parliament, in the hope of promoting his bill and overturning the award of £52 to Smyth, as something obtained unduly.[59]

VII

The Warrens Court dispute reveals that escalatory gambits were possible and logical, even if they had a ratchet effect, worsening divisions and introducing issues which related to the public interest and could not then be removed from the table. Appeals to Parliament raised questions, not just about substantive legal issues, but also about the manner in which the affair was being conducted, and by the mid-1620s Crokey's problem—as with some participants in religious disputations—was that people might object not just to his claims but also to his style.[60]

Crokey's situation became more challenging because he chose to promote his cause even more vigorously, with a substantial printed pamphlet about 'so many' vexatious suits 'wrongfully prosecuted against him'. Dated 1 June 1625, this

[58] GA, D9125/1/12008, pp. 64–5; TNA, STAC 8/107/7.

[59] PA, HL/PO/JO/10/1/24; HL/PO/JO/10/1/26; GA, D9125/1/12008, p. 65; Crokey, *Sacred Maiestie*, sig. A2. For the hospitals and free schools bill: *LJ*, iii. 532.

[60] See: Peter Lake, *The Boxmaker's Revenge: 'Orthodoxy', 'Heterodoxy' and the Politics of the Parish in Early Stuart London* (Manchester, 2009).

offered 'a true relation of the strange passages in divers suits twelve years together', and narrated Smyth's attempts to 'supplant' the school and secure lands worth £300 *per annum*. Crokey hoped to get his bill considered, to secure a parliamentary inquiry, and to ensure that the findings of the 1621 commission were 'maintained and prosecuted', and also to have the 1623 decree 'made void'. He wanted the school to be 'reduced according to the meaning of the founders', but also to secure compensation, 'in respect of his long and great expense'—£2,200—for 'rectifying of the said school', 'to the utter neglect of all his own affairs, being before a merchant of good credit and trading'. Crokey referred to the 'great labour and toil both of his body and mind', and to 'the wasting and consuming of his vital spirits in bearing the assaults and insufferable wrongs of Smyth's impiety and improbiety in the preservation of the said school'.[61] In the end, Crokey's chances of presenting his pamphlet and pursuing his case were stymied, not by Smyth but by the plague, which interrupted parliamentary proceedings (11 July). He was evidently unable to travel to the Oxford session before Parliament was finally dissolved on 12 August.[62]

Producing a lengthy pamphlet was a risky gambit, which reflected Crokey's frustration. He returned to Westminster with another petition in March 1626, and then presented his pamphlet the following May, but the upshot involved renewed proceedings against him in Star Chamber, brought by Smyth and Edward Cowper (Michaelmas 1626—Case 8).[63] However, in a measure of how far things had shifted from substantive legal issues to wrangling over behaviour, the charge on this occasion was libel. Smyth—like other members of the elite—now strove to defend his reputation, stressing that he had 'laboured for the welfare, and advancement of the said school', and for 'increasing... the revenue thereof', and that he had secured funds for 'one scholar more' with 'allowance and maintenance'. This was a libel case with a difference, however, and Smyth claimed that while 'all libels... are severely to be punished', severity was more important when accusations were framed not just 'against a private person', but also 'printed and exposed to public view and sale', and when they 'impudently, falsely and audaciously attempt to wound the reverend and honourable public ministers of justice, being your majesty's lieutenants who is the fountain of justice'. Crokey was accused of revisiting an issue that had been settled, and of attacking someone whose 'well deservings' to the school were 'oftentimes mentioned', and who faced 'disgrace, obloquy and ignominy', 'perpetual scandal, defamation and reproach'. Like other libellers, however, he was also prosecuted for besmirching the 'extraordinary, pious and religious care and travail' of officials, who were charged with

[61] Crokey, *Sacred Maiestie*, sigs Av, A2, H3–4.

[62] See also: PA, HL/PO/JO/10/1/32 (Peter Watson).

[63] PA, HL/PO/JO/10/1/29. Crokey's petition was logged on 16 March 1626, but no response was recorded: HL/PO/JO/10/1/30.

'connivance', 'partiality', and 'palpable injustice', and for taking his case into the public domain. Libels like this were 'hainous' and 'odious'; they tended to provoke 'impatience and contentions', and to disturb the 'peaceable government' and 'tranquility of the kingdom'. They were 'the occasions, motives and causes' of duels and 'deadly feuds', 'bloodshed and murder', 'insurrections and rebellions'. They were 'not to be suffered in a Christian and well governed commonwealth', and ought to be 'suppressed by the severity of an exemplary punishment'.[64]

Hereafter, Smyth pursued Crokey with a zeal that resulted in considerable frustration of his own, because Crokey had not yet exhausted all avenues for relief. Smyth was probably responsible for orders—on 7 and 13 February, 25 April and 8 May 1627—by which Crokey was kept 'close prisoner' in the Fleet, with the prospect of being proceeded against *pro confesso*, prompting him to submit what Smyth called a 'frivolous short' demurrer, which was immediately overruled, and then a more substantial response, to which Smyth 'immediately replied'. Things proceeded slowly, however, and having aimed for a trial in the summer of 1627, witnesses were still being examined in Michaelmas term.[65] A hearing into this 'most lewd and scandalous libel' was eventually scheduled for 28 January 1629, the first day of Hilary term, but by then Crokey had submitted an 'untrue' petition to the House of Lords, which halted legal proceedings until a committee 'should report their opinions'.[66]

Crokey's petition from the Fleet—where he had been incarcerated since 1621—confirmed that his best hopes remained with Parliament. His request—to end Smyth's Star Chamber proceedings—was read on 22 January, and resulted in a writ of *habeas corpus*, and although Smyth pleaded to keep his legal proceedings on track (26 January), he was unable to avoid being summoned—alongside Crokey—to a hearing the following day. Indeed, when Crokey submitted what he called 'good proofs', to substantiate the allegations in his pamphlet, a debate resulted in his trial being stayed and his draft bill being referred to the Committee for Petitions, the recommendations of which prompted the appointment of 'a new commission' (31 January). Although subsequent petitions—at least one of which was printed—bemoaned the challenges facing prisoners who sought to get matters heard in Parliament, peers proved remarkably receptive. Having sanctioned a new inquiry, they also accepted Crokey's suggestions that the job should be given to men 'who dwell out[side] of the said county', and that he should be released to attend the hearing. Crokey also insisted that Smyth and his tenants should 'produce all their evidences... upon oath', and successfully requested that, having

[64] GA, D9125/1/12008, pp. 83–9. See: Alastair Bellany, '"Rayling rymes and vaunting verse": libellous politics in early Stuart England, 1603–1628', in Kevin Sharpe and Peter Lake, eds, *Culture and Politics in Early Stuart England* (London, 1994), p. 294.

[65] GA, D9125/1/12008, pp. 91–2.

[66] GA, D9125/1/12003, 12008, pp. 91–2; Crokey, *Complaint*, sig. B4.

'consumed his estate' in defending the school, all expenses should be borne by Smyth once his claims were substantiated (5 February).[67]

By now, Crokey was probably sanguine about the chances of making real progress. Buoyed by parliamentary support he certainly made another attempt to 'tax' Smyth for legal costs awarded 'ten years since', only to find that the court did not think this 'fit', after 'so long time and after so many orders made to the contrary'.[68] More worryingly, his hard-won commission was not a great success. Smyth, his servant Archard, and their tenants were summoned to Arthur Bew's tavern in Wotton (2–3 April), but the commissioners concluded that 'expert and skilful' surveyors would not be able to complete their work before Trinity term (June 1629). Participants had 'other employment' ('the business of the county'), while Crokey—who attended with prison 'keepers' and contributed effectively—'must of necessity be at London the first day of the next term'. Crokey's surveyors—Richard Hathway and William Staples—resumed work in September, but the commissioners claimed 'no sufficient warrant' to proceed. No agreement was reached on the survey, and Hathway hinted that too much land was recorded by 'direction of Mr Crokey', although a suspicious Smyth confessed that his own survey did not 'differ much'.[69]

An abortive inquiry left Crokey facing the renewal of Star Chamber proceedings (Case 8), not least when Smyth successfully petitioned Lord Keeper Coventry for a hearing in Easter term.[70] Crokey made one final attempt to secure relief, and on 15 February 1630 Smyth was ordered to demonstrate why £52 costs—awarded to him in 1624—should not be remitted, on the grounds that they were awarded—'erroneously'—merely through Crokey 'not answering a bill in this court'. With Crokey incarcerated, the task of delivering this order fell to his 28-year-old daughter, Sarah, which she was eventually able to do on 6 May, once Smyth had returned to London from the country. When Smyth failed to 'show cause', Crokey was 'enlarged' from 'his long imprisonment' (28 June), although he was expected to 'yield himself again' by Christmas.[71]

Crokey might have been free, but he could not delay the judgment of Star Chamber, following a hearing on 14 June 1631.[72] The judges 'much disliked' Crokey's printed pamphlet, which involved 'a course utterly unlawful', and found him guilty of 'a very great offence' in getting this 'contrived, printed and published, being an odious libel . . . framed falsely and mischievously'. Crokey was ordered to return to the Fleet and pay £200, and a declaration was prepared for the

[67] PA, HL/PO/JO/10/1/37; *LJ*, iv. 9–10, 12, 17–18; Crokey, *Complaint*, sig. B4; GA, D9125/1/6694 (Crokey, *To the King's Most Excellent Matie and the Lords Spirituall and Temporall . . . the Humble Petition of Beniamin Crokey . . . 31 Jan. 1628/9*); S379/2/3/1/1; D733/3/1; D9125/1/13612/14.

[68] GA, D8887/6/103.

[69] GA, D9125/1/12022–3; Crokey, *Complaint*, sig. B4v. For the survey, see: GA, D733/3/2.

[70] GA, D9125/1/12023. [71] GA, D8887/6/102, 105.

[72] GA, D9125/1/12008, pp. 91–2; Gardiner, *Reports*, pp. 38–9. For Bridgewater's annotated copy of the 'cause list': HEH, EL7910.

'full and absolute clearing' of Smyth's reputation, 'to the end no blemish or spot may remain'. This was to be read at the Gloucestershire assizes, as copies of the pamphlet were 'publicly burned', and Crokey was required to make 'humble acknowledgement' of the 'wrong done to the plaintiff', and to beg Smyth's forgiveness.[73]

VIII

The Star Chamber ruling brought litigation to an end but did not bring closure to the dispute. Nevertheless, subsequent events largely involved Crokey's fruitless attempts to revive his fortunes, mostly by non-legal means. Reconstructing this final phase completes the narrative arc of the affair. It demonstrates the challenges involved in pursuing grievances through the Privy Council and Parliament; sheds light upon the approaches taken by both protagonists; and indicates how disputation passed to yet another generation before fizzling out.

Crokey was not present to hear the Star Chamber ruling in June 1631, and he escaped the ignominy of being forced—'if he can be apprehended'—to make a humiliating admission of guilt. As Smyth quickly recognised, he 'fled into Ireland' as a 'renegade', perhaps as soon as he had 'gotten out of prison' in 1630, thereby making it impossible to secure the costs awarded.[74] This exile lasted for eight years, 'upon his own charge of livelihood', which meant participating in 'the famous design called the Flax business'. This involved Crokey becoming a 'projector' and seeking official support—and financial backers—for a scheme to employ poor men 'for the raising of flax, hemp, yarn and linen cloth'. This design—for which Crokey lobbied the earl of Strafford and the Irish Privy Council—was eventually adopted; by late 1636 he was overseeing its enforcement as Strafford's agent, and he later claimed to have been fêted in Dublin as 'the best commonwealthsman that ever came for Ireland'. He certainly travelled to the Low Countries to secure supplies of flax seed, and to bring expert workmen 'to teach the Irish'.[75] Nevertheless, his situation remained perilous, and ongoing attempts to extricate himself from such difficulties eventually provoked the final skirmishes in this most protracted of disputes.

Crokey first returned to England—briefly—in the summer of 1636, asking Charles I to 'hear all differences' between himself and Smyth, and although an outbreak of the plague prevented a hearing, his petition was referred to Archbishop Laud, Lord Keeper Coventry, Lord Treasurer Juxon, and Sir Francis

[73] GA, D9125/1/12008, pp. 92–6; S379/2/3/1/3.

[74] GA, D9125/1/12008, pp. 92–7; S379/2/3/1/3; Crokey, *Complaint*, sigs B4v–C; Smyth, *Lives*, iii. 402.

[75] Crokey, *Complaint*, sigs B2–v; Jansson, *Proceedings*, iii. 301; GA, D9125/1/12028, p. 9. For Crokey's petition and brief: Sheffield Archives, WWM/StrP/24-5/340-1.

Cottington (17 July), who summoned Smyth to appear on 17 December. By then, however, Crokey had returned to Ireland, 'for the good of His Majesty and commonwealth', enabling Smyth's son—John Smyth junior—to get the matter discharged (4 December).[76] Councillors decreed that the volume of earlier cases, as well as 'agitation' in Parliament, rendered further deliberation unnecessary, adding that Crokey 'deserved to be punished' for a 'causeless and scandalous' petition, and for trying to 'rip up a business... so long depending, and so long since quieted'.[77] This did not stop Crokey from securing a new hearing—scheduled for 23 November 1638—alongside an order protecting him from arrest and imprisonment, which he handed to Smyth in person (5 August). However, Smyth was accused of using 'false suggestions' to escape scrutiny in early September, and to secure an order that Crokey would be punished if he should 'stir any more in the school business'. Smyth then managed to 'fetch up Crokey from Bristol' and have him committed close prisoner in the Fleet once more.[78]

Having prepared his will on 1 December 1640, Smyth perhaps went to his grave hoping that the Warrens Court affair was finally over. Rings were inscribed with the words 'be faithful' and given to friends and 'alliesmen', alongside a plea to use 'all possible means to prevent suits in law'. Smyth thanked God that he had 'never suffered adversary... to prevail against me'. He died—on 24 February 1641—days after issuing new legal instructions to John Smyth junior, and was buried at Nibley three days later.[79]

Crokey had other ideas, and like so many aggrieved contemporaries he hoped that the end of the 'personal rule' would provide opportunities for relief. He approached Parliament with another petition and another draft bill, and after testifying that Strafford exploited the flax project for personal benefit (1 April 1641), he was decreed to be a prisoner 'for no cause shown'. Crokey was released 'forthwith', and allowed to 'follow his cause' before the Committee of Petitions (25 May 1641).[80] Nothing more was heard of his case until February 1646, as he joined the ranks of supplicants whose grievances lost out to weightier matters during the civil wars. In August 1644, he was living in St Giles in the Fields, where his wife was buried, although when he resurfaced—as the king's surrender of Oxford loomed—he was an impoverished resident of Bowling Alley in Westminster, a stone's throw from the law courts.[81] Predictably, he returned to Parliament, to petition

[76] Crokey, *Complaint*, sig. C; TNA, PC 2/47, p. 11.

[77] Crokey, *Complaint*, sigs B3v, C; GA, S379/2/3/1/3; D733/3/3; TNA, PC 2/47, p. 11.

[78] Crokey, *Complaint*, sigs C-Cv; Smyth, *Lives*, iii. 402.

[79] TNA, PROB 11/187, fo. 239; GA, D8887/5/38; D8887/9/110; W. P. W. Phillimore and G. S. Fry, eds, *Abstracts of Gloucestershire Inquisitiones Post Mortem* (London, 1893–9), p. 168; Irvine Gray, 'Smith of Nibley's will', *TBGAS*, 78 (1959), 129.

[80] Crokey, *Complaint*, sigs A, Cv; *LJ*, iv. 204, 256; Crokey, *Contents*, sig. A2; GA, D9125/1/12028, sig. A; PA, HL/PO/JO/10/1/274; *The Tryal of Thomas Earl of Strafford* (London, 1680), pp. 67, 417–18; Jansson, *Proceedings*, iii. 295–6, 300–1.

[81] LMA, P82/GIS/A/04; WCA, SMW/E47/1581–2; SMW/E161.

about having spent thirty-three years—and £4,000—battling with Smyth, and to complain about two decades of imprisonment and injustice at the hands of Lord Chancellors Egerton, Bacon, and Cottington, Lord Keepers Williams and Coventry, and judges like Hobart and Chamberlain, as well as Lord Treasurer Juxon and Archbishop Laud. As was his wont, Crokey used a printed pamphlet to plead for a 'speedy hearing' of matters which were still 'depending before the Committee of Petitions'. Claiming that he was 'ready to perish', Crokey also sought £100 from John Smyth junior for 'present relief', in order to 'follow his business for settling of the school'.[82]

This attempt to revive an ancient dispute convinced another of John Smyth's sons, Thomas, that his brother was now 'entangled at London through the means of Crokey' (June 1646), although the matter dropped off the parliamentary radar yet again, until a petition from Sarah Crokey was read in the Lords on 5 October 1648. This was doubtless provoked by the grant of a new lease of Warrens Court in 1647, and it noted that matters had been delayed by 'weightier affairs' during 'these distracted times', and that key protagonists were now dead.[83] These now included Benjamin Crokey, who died intestate in November 1647, leaving his daughter as 'a poor orphan' who needed to oversee her father's funeral at St Margaret's Westminster.[84] John Smyth junior and others were ordered to respond to Sarah Crokey's petition by 5 November 1648, a deadline subsequently extended to 12 February 1649. By then, Charles I had been executed, and the House of Lords, although not quite abolished, had ceased to sit.[85]

The revolution might have killed the matter forever, had it not been for the persistence of Crokey's daughter, who prolonged the Warrens Court dispute even further. Sarah responded to her new predicament by getting married—aged 46, and presumably for financial reasons—to a 60-year-old widower called Roger Calcott (*d.*1652) of St Andrew's Holborn, after whose death she moved across London to Coleman Street.[86] She then revived the dispute once the turmoil of the Interregnum had passed, with a petition to the House of Lords, rehearsing the dispute's history, repeating allegations about 'oppression' (of her father) and 'suppression' (of the school), and reiterating complaints about the 'corrupt' practices of Caroline officials (July 1660). She claimed that Crokey spent £3,000 fighting for the school, that the original lease expired 'many years ago' (in 1633), and that the school was 'nothing advantaged' since 1624. Like other

[82] PA, HL/PO/JO/10/1/274; Crokey, *Contents*, sigs A-A2v.

[83] PA, HL/PO/JO/10/1/274. See: GA, D9125/1/12030/30.

[84] GA, D8887/6/106; *LJ*, x. 529; *HMC 7th Report* (London, 1879), p. 55; PA, HL/PO/JO/10/1/274; Arthur Meredyth Burke, ed., *Memorials of St Margaret's* (London, 1914), p. 617. See: TNA, PROB 6/22, fo. 148.

[85] GA, D8887/6/107–8; *LJ*, x. 529, 580; *HMC 7th Report*, p. 61; PA, HL/PO/JO/10/1/277.

[86] LMA, DL/A/D/002/MS10091/024; Joseph Lemuel Chester and George J. Armytage, *Allegations for Marriage Licenses* (London, 1887), p. 282; LMA, P69/TRI2/A/005/MS09241/001, fo. 107; Burke, ed., *Memorials*, p. 631.

contemporaries, she bemoaned that little progress had been made since 1640, 'in respect of those distracted times and the weightier affairs of the public', begged for relief as someone 'despoiled of all means of subsistence by power and oppression', and sought a final settlement for the school. As supplications flooded in to the restored Stuart regime, this particular plea went unanswered, and the dispute appeared to sink without trace. Sarah died, childless, in December 1662 or January 1663, and her 'little estate' was distributed by a London embroiderer called Edward Gosnall.[87]

IX

This chapter, when coupled with its predecessor, might be accused of offering a dizzying chronicle, but this difficult journey—with one damned thing after another—demonstrates the benefits that arise from pursuing a single dispute across time, in various guises, and in legal and extra-legal settings. Part One has established the affair's narrative arc, revealing the vivid story that lurks within its maze of technicalities, and while the contest over Warrens Court involved lots of twists and turns, significant movement between courts, and diverse claims and allegations, it also changed over time. Litigation was iterative, and the basis on which disputes were contested did not remain static. This is true in terms of the issues in dispute—the legal terrain—and in terms of mounting frustration, tension, and anger. Although an analytical approach might very easily have dwelt upon the fact—and likelihood—of Smyth's victory, reading the dispute forwards by examining specific legal moves and their outcomes indicates that both men had reasons to feel confident, and reasons to continue with litigation. To them, it did not necessarily seem 'perennially hopeless'.

Extending this analysis beyond 1615 brings the conclusions of Chapter One into sharper focus. Smyth and Crokey continued with contestation because they encountered indeterminate verdicts, confronted new circumstances, and faced new protagonists, and because they found new things to fight about. Disputation could involve substantive issues as well as procedural matters, not least relating to protagonists' decisions and actions, and as litigants navigated obstacles and setbacks they were incentivised to adopt new approaches and introduce new issues, which made contestation much more complex. As disputants adapted and disputes developed it was likely that bigger issues would arise, and that more people would become involved, thereby generating public interest, heightened anxiety, and official intervention. Smyth's estate management raised

[87] *HMC 7th Report*, p. 120; PA, HL/PO/JO/10/1/296; TNA, PROB 11/310, fo. 21v. For private business getting lost amid 'weighty affairs': PA, HL/PO/JO/10/1/32 (Peter Watson); HL/PO/JO/10/1/34 (Robert Lane).

questions about the 'intermingling' of Warrens Court with other property; novel claims emerged about the concealment of chantry lands; and doubts arose about the misappropriation of charitable funds. As such, a long legal dispute came to focus upon the treatment of Wotton school, and upon Crokey's insistence that the school was being suppressed, that measures were needed to secure its future, and that he was its zealous champion.

In terms of processes, the course of disputation demonstrated that substantive legal issues were not the only ones in play. At any one point, those who appeared to be on the front foot legally might find themselves undermined procedurally; legal progress did not always ensure success within the wider context of disputation, and it proved possible to offset legal losses with procedural gains. In a world where legal rules and procedural outcomes could pull in opposite directions, few legal victories were uncomplicated, and few defeats unmitigated. Over time, new and much more weighty complaints emerged about how the case was being contested, and about the kinds of move being made. Here, a phenomenon like litigation by proxy—involving Thomas Baddam and Edward Bishopp—provides a good example of how the need to adapt made the Warrens Court dispute much more contentious.

Legally, this affair suggests that litigation could operate like a ratchet, with logical legal decisions having unintended consequences, locking protagonists into an increasingly acrimonious mode of contestation. Once attention became focused upon Wotton school, the stakes were raised emphatically, and it became much more likely—if perhaps not inevitable—that people would resort to escalatory behaviour. This was made easier—and the dispute much worse—because the period after 1615 witnessed not just legal complexity and uncertainty, 'forum shopping', and Crokey's faltering fortunes, but also greater willingness to appeal beyond the courts, and greater opportunities to do so, even to the point of introducing draft legislation and engaging in parliamentary lobbying. This involved appeals to higher authorities, and provides evidence about the relative utility of different avenues. Crokey was capable of securing favourable verdicts in court, but was much more likely to find favour with petitions, most obviously to the House of Lords, and once parliamentary channels were successfully invoked the problem no longer involved indeterminate legal verdicts. Now, even a setback like the 1623 Chancery decree left Crokey hoping for, and expecting, better luck in Parliament. However, when disputes were taken to the higher authorities audiences also became wider, and claims became more serious, particularly when this involved the medium of print, even with breviates and weighty technical pamphlets.

Finally, grievances about legal and political processes became more evident and more acute, and were expressed in more controversial ways. For Crokey, mounting frustration reflected the threat posed by legal technicalities and procedural hiccups, but also the sense that verdicts, judgments, and decrees were problematic, and emblematic of corruption. Ultimately, there was a danger that new and much more sensitive issues, together with procedural grievances and more aggressive appeals to higher and wider audiences, would become intertwined with allegations about the abuse of legal and political processes. It was this cocktail of circumstances that emerged during the 1620s, which helps to explain the production of Crokey's printed texts, the libellous nature of which eventually resulted in him being prosecuted in Star Chamber. Put another way, these chapters have highlighted how, over time, there emerged a potent conjuncture in which it was logical to continue the dispute and to raise the stakes, and in which substantive and procedural issues became more stark and more controversial. However, a full appreciation of this situation requires a closer examination of how Crokey and Smyth approached their respective campaigns: of the claims that they made about each other; of their explanations regarding success and failure; and of their expectations of the law.

PART TWO
STRATEGIES

> Life is a campaign against malice. Shrewdness fights by strategically using such intentions . . . It passes over declared intentions, and waits for the real ones that lie beneath, and even the ones beneath those.
>
> *Baltasar Gracian* (1647)

Introduction

When John Smyth composed his will, he mused that 'concord increaseth small things' while 'discord consumeth great things', almost certainly reflecting his dispute with Benjamin Crokey. Smyth blamed litigation for 'wasting more treasure and time' than the Wars of the Roses, adding that it was 'one of the main causes why my neighbours grow poor with more, when their fathers grew rich with less'. However, Smyth also stated that God 'never suffered adversary . . . to prevail against me, though many of divers humours and to divers ends have risen up against m.'[1] His papers also demonstrate a sophisticated understanding of how litigants behaved. Men, he said, were 'no angels', precisely because it was possible to 'fall by the law', through unreliable attorneys and the 'practise' of adversaries, in terms of perjury and forgery, the suborning of witnesses and jurors, and 'affection, inclination or corruption in the judge'. Legal culture incentivised bad behaviour, something he knew by 'experience'. Analysing local tensions, Smyth also noted how law suits—'as a fiery comet draws her tail'—generated litigation that could drag on for years, and that might ultimately be determined by 'practice and greatness'.[2]

These statements set up the issues that dominate Part Two: how litigants understood and reflected upon legal processes. Smyth understood that litigation was not an ideal pursuit, which could be costly and troublesome, but he was proud of being good at it, appreciated that courts could be used to pursue one's interests, and recognised that success did not necessarily involve having the best case.

[1] TNA, PROB 11/187, fo. 239; Smyth, *Lives*, i. 242.

[2] Smyth, *Lives*, ii. 312–14, 316.

Smyth's comments thus throw into relief the moral sayings he selected to decorate the wainscot of his house in Nibley. These included predictable *sententiae* about 'virtue' and 'vice', 'truth' and 'lying', 'temperance' and 'continence', but they also included maxims that Smyth probably found testing. He knew that 'to forget injuries is true magnanimity', and that 'a covetous man is an infidel, for his gold is his God'; he 'liveth in continual fear, least he should lose what he hath got'. He recognised the value of not being 'proud in prosperity' and of behaving liberally towards those 'wanting money', and the need to 'forgive all, but especially him that is sorry for his offence'. He appreciated that it was desirable to 'look mildly on thy inferiors'. To Crokey, such sayings probably seemed hypocritical. Smyth avowed that a proud man would become 'the food of worms and serpents', while 'he that exalteth the humble and meek throweth down the mighty from his seat'. He apparently knew that it was wrong 'to deride a simple man who [ought] rather to be pitied', that it was good to 'spare a weaker [man] . . . that hath offended thee', and that it was necessary to 'bear mildly injurious words, loss of goods and sudden blows', since to do so revealed 'the virtue of a patient mind'. Smyth professed to believe that to 'thirst after revenge . . . is the beginning and entrance into madness.'[3] Putting such ideas into practice was another thing; he also understood the difference between 'goodness' and 'greatness', noting that 'according to that choice, of being good or great, each man doth frame the practice of his life.' He understood that life was a matter of 'might' as well as 'right', and that 'he that wreaks himself at every wrong, shall never sing the rich man's song.'[4]

Such sayings introduce the issue of how Smyth—and indeed Crokey—behaved, and what such behaviour reveals. This section argues that understanding why both men pursued such a lengthy dispute involves analysing how they acted and thought about their decisions; how they reflected on success and failure, and reacted to the behaviour to which they were exposed. The methodology involved has broader relevance for the study of early modern litigation, demonstrating what can be gleaned by exploring protagonists' experiences and perceptions of disputation, particularly regarding protracted contests. Historians have sometimes explored the narrative strategies of those who found themselves in court; the possibility that litigants told stories with 'great art', and that testimonies revealed 'cultural truth' even if they were 'fictions'.[5] Here, the aim is to discern attitudes to disputation and the law, by examining explicit statements about specific contests ('vocabularies' of litigation, and 'pleading strategies'), as well as litigants' behaviour; their strategies, tactics, and decision-making, and their handling of risks and opportunities. This means analysing the rationality behind litigation, the logic of

[3] GA, D9125/1/13619. See also: Smyth, *Lives*, ii. 150, 155. [4] Smyth, *Lives*, ii. 150, iii. 22–3.

[5] Natalie Zemon Davis, *Fiction in the Archives* (Cambridge, 1988); Thomas V. Cohen and Elizabeth S. Cohen, *Words and Deeds in Renaissance Rome* (Toronto, 2000), p. 10. See: Frances Dolan, *True Relations: Reading, Literature and Evidence in Seventeenth-Century England* (Philadelphia, 2013).

litigants' actions, interactions, and reactions, the strength of their feelings, and their expectations and ideas about legal processes. Working out what they wanted to achieve, and how they went about it, provides a bridge between the legal logic behind litigants' decisions, and the fascination that the dispute had for contemporaries, suggesting that in disputes like this there was much more at stake than merely money or 'winning'.[6]

Pursuing these lines of inquiry involves being guided by anthropologists who emphasise the importance of everyday, situational, and strategic behaviour, and explore the relationship between norms and observable behaviour, not least by focusing upon inventive practice. Rather than privileging institutions, customs, and moral rules, these scholars concentrate upon how people respond to constraints that affect thinking and action; how they behave pragmatically and instrumentally in the pursuit of goals; and how they react to 'moves' made by others. They analyse how people assess their options using strategic thinking; how they respond to the 'rules of the game', perhaps with gamesmanship (winning without cheating), or by blind-siding the referee (cheating without being disqualified). This means studying 'calculated breaches' of normative rules, and the inventiveness that is incentivised by competitive situations. It also means recognising that disputation is an inevitable rather than pathological activity, which needs to be understood in the broader context of cultural and social relations. Disputes involve actors comprehending and explaining their behaviour, strategising in the course of transactions, and making decisions in the face of normative constraints.[7] Observing how people negotiate the boundaries of acceptable behaviour reveals the power of norms, different interpretations of the rules, and how expectations change over time, drawing attention to the conditions—including ignorance—in which rules are broken, to situations in which relationships are deemed 'moral' rather than 'transactional', and to circumstances in which individuals behave ideologically rather than like profit-maximising entrepreneurs.[8]

Such ideas have underpinned anthropological approaches to law that focus upon 'processes' rather than the implementation of 'rules', and that view litigation as the 'everyday' activity of 'intelligent and determined antagonists'. This means analysing litigants' experiences of, and perspectives on, dispute resolution, and recognising that they might have goals other than 'winning' or reaching a settlement, from airing grievances to demonstrating status and humiliating opponents,

[6] See: Laura Flannigan, 'Litigants and the English 'Court of Poor Men's Causes,' or Court of Requests, 1515–25', *Law and History Review*, 38.2 (2020), 309; Stretton, *Women*, p. 178.

[7] Fredrik Barth, *Process and Form in Social Life* (London, 1981), pp. 2–30; Bruce Kapferer, ed., *Transaction and Meaning* (Philadelphia, 1976), pp. 2–19; Erving Goffman, *Strategic Interaction* (Philadelphia, 1969), pp. 100–1, 145; F. G. Bailey, *Stratagems and Spoils* (Oxford, 1969), pp. xiii, 1–6, 109, 113; Victor Turner, *Schism and Continuity in an African Society* (Manchester, 1957), p. 129; Fredrik Barth, *Models of Social Organisation* (London, 1966), pp. 1–22.

[8] Bailey, *Stratagems*, pp. 39, 113, 116; Victor Turner, *Dramas, Fields and Metaphors* (London, 1974), pp. 140–1.

or giving unscrupulous behaviour an air of legitimacy. It means identifying short-term aims as well as long-term goals, and concentrating upon disputants' practices, their methods (whether conventional or novel), and their willingness to transform 'rules' into 'resources'.[9] And it means assessing the impact of inequalities, in terms of power, resources, and skill, as part of a process of discerning incompatible senses of what cases are about, variant notions of rights and entitlements, and conflicting norms, values, and beliefs. Ultimately, focusing upon litigants' thinking makes it possible to recognise discrepancies between the underlying causes of disputation and the ostensible issues being contested, or between the 'trouble' and the 'case'.[10] In such situations legal judgments might not bring disputation to an end; courts might become frustrated by litigants who are perceived to be illogical, naive, or obstinate, and litigants might reveal distinctive expectations—realistic or otherwise—about the legal system, and become frustrated by perceptions of 'corruption', and by the failure to secure 'justice'. There is even scope to recover the logic of a 'powerless style', including 'strategic displays of passion'.[11]

Anthropological approaches have proved useful for historical analysis. Medievalists have explored how litigants grappled with behavioural norms, engaged in decision making, and strategised, demonstrating how litigation brought private disputes into the public domain, drew attention to animosities, and provided opportunities for revenge. They have examined expectations of the legal system, recognising that legal processes and judgments sometimes proved divisive, thereby ensuring that disputes were prolonged and exacerbated.[12] Such work reveals the propensity for legal *cases* to generate long-running *disputes*, which resembled 'untamed' feuding because the uses of litigation were various,

[9] Marc J. Swartz, Victor W. Turner and Arthur Tuden, 'Introduction', in Swartz, Turner and Tuden, eds, *Political Anthropology* (Chicago, 1966), p. 8. The literature is vast, but see: June Starr and Jane F. Collier, *History and Power in the Study of the Law* (Ithaca, 1989), pp. 4–12; Sally Falk Moore, *Social Facts and Fabrications* (Cambridge, 1986); Laura Nader and Harry F. Todd, eds, *The Disputing Process* (New York, 1978); Sally Falk Moore, *Law as Process* (London, 1978); John L. Comaroff and Simon Roberts, *Rules and Processes* (London, 1981); Simon Roberts, *Order and Dispute* (Harmondsworth, 1979); John M. Conley and William M. O'Barr, *Rules versus Relationships* (London, 1990); Laura Nader, *Harmony Ideology* (Stanford, 1990); Sally Engle Merry, *Getting Justice and Getting Even* (Chicago, 1990).

[10] David Sabean, *Power in the Blood* (Cambridge, 1987), p. 27; Elizabeth Colson, 'The contentiousness of disputes', in Pat Caplan, ed., *Understanding Disputes* (Oxford, 1995), p. 77.

[11] Conley and O'Barr, *Rules versus Relationships*, p. 173; Sally Falk Moore, 'Imperfect communication', in Caplan, ed., *Understanding Disputes*, p. 17; Patricia Ewick and Susan S. Silbey, *The Common Place of Law* (Chicago, 1998).

[12] For example: Chris Wickham, *Courts and Conflict in Twelfth Century Tuscany* (Oxford, 2003); Wendy Davies and Paul Fouracre, eds, *The Settlement of Disputes in Early Medieval Europe* (Cambridge, 1986); Daniel Lord Smail, 'Telling tales in Angevin courts', *French Historical Studies*, 20.2 (1997), 183–215; Daniel Lord Smail, *The Consumption of Justice* (Ithaca, 2013); Thomas V. Cohen, *Love and Death in Renaissance Italy* (Chicago, 2004); Thomas Kuehn, *Law, Family and Women* (London, 1991); Ian W. Miller, *Bloodtaking and Peacemaking* (Chicago, 1990); Stephen D. White, *Feuding and Peace-Making in Eleventh-Century France* (Aldershot, 2005); William M. Bowsky, *Piety and Property in Medieval Florence* (Milan, 1990).

because litigants recognised possibilities for tying opponents up in knots, and because the 'rules of the game' were imprecise. Attempts have thus been made to scrutinise litigants' goals and behaviour, tactical experimentation, and the risks of scandal, retaliation, and violence.[13] Less explicitly, such approaches have also informed early modern scholars, amid concerns about the relationship between decision-making, 'strategical negotiations', and dispute resolution.[14] It is recognised that the legal system was not merely a tool of the elite, that contemporaries interpreted it in different ways, and that it became 'a medium within which other social conflicts' were 'fought out'. Law was one of the 'weapons of the weak', and a participatory forum in which 'domination' was negotiated.[15] Attempts have occasionally been made to examine how contemporaries interacted with the law in precise contexts, made choices amid 'endless rounds of micro-litigation', and navigated pathways through systems and institutions that both constrained and empowered them.[16] Most importantly, scholars have grappled with evidence about 'strategic litigators'; 'suitors' with 'crafty minds' who engaged in 'nimble and sinister tricks and shifts' to 'pervert the plain and direct courses of courts'. These were people who engaged in what Ned Ward called 'the cunning part of the law'.[17] This has involved analysing 'procedural skirmishes', and claims about vexatious litigation and sharp practice, which tested the boundaries of acceptable behaviour, and which sometimes provoked attempts to escalate cases through the legal and political system.[18]

However, this remains an underdeveloped field of scholarship. Scholars have analysed how Parliament responded to problems with the legal system, but less attention has been paid to complaints about litigants' behaviour, and while

[13] Richard L. Kagan, *Lawsuits and Litigants in Castile, 1500–1700* (Chapel Hill, 1981) p. 48; Richard L. Kagan, 'A golden age of litigation: Castile, 1500–1700, in Bossy, *Disputes*, p. 156; Paul R. Hyams, *Rancor and Reconciliation in Medieval England* (Ithaca, 2003).

[14] David Sabean, *Property, Production and Family in Neckarhausen, 1700–1870* (Cambridge, 1990), p. 87. See: Stuart Carroll, 'The peace in the feud in sixteenth- and seventeenth-century France', *P&P*, 178 (2003), 74–115; Stephen Cummins and Laura Kounine, eds, *Cultures of Conflict Resolution in Early Modern Europe* (Farnham, 2016).

[15] E. P. Thompson, *Whigs and Hunters* (London, 1975), p. 208; John Walter, 'Public transcripts, popular agency and the politics of subsistence in early modern England', in Michael J. Braddick and John Walter, eds, *Negotiating Power in Early Stuart Society* (Cambridge, 2001), pp. 123–48.

[16] Julie Hardwick, *Family Business* (Oxford, 2009), p. 3. See: Giovanni Levi, *Inheriting Power* (Chicago, 1988), pp. xv–xvi, 120; Giovanni Levi, 'On microhistory', in Peter Burke, ed., *New Perspectives on Historical Writing* (Cambridge, 1991), pp. 94, 104.

[17] Hardwick, *Family Business*, pp. 74, 76, Francis Bacon, *The Major Works*, ed. Brian Vickers (Oxford, 2002), pp. 437–8, 448; Ned Ward, *The London Spy*, ed. Paul Hyland (East Lansing, 1993), p. 147.

[18] Thomas Barnes, 'Due process and slow process in the late Elizabethan-early Stuart Star Chamber', *AJLH*, 6 (1962), 232. See: Stretton, *Women*, pp. 11, 83, 86; J. A. Sharpe, '"Such disagreement betwyx neighbours": litigation and human relations in early modern England', in Bossy, *Disputes*, pp. 170, 177; Craig Muldrew, 'The culture of reconciliation: community and the settlement of economic disputes in early modern England', *HJ*, 39.4 (1996), 916; Thomas G. Barnes, 'Star Chamber litigants and their counsel, 1596–1641', in J. H. Baker, *Legal Records and the Historian* (London, 1978), pp. 7, 15; Prest, *Barristers*, pp. 27, 47, 58, 62, 70, 81, 266–7, 272.

scholars appreciate that the print revolution facilitated a 'commoning' of the law, the nature and desirability of which was much debated, insufficient work has been done on 'consumer oriented' approaches to litigation.[19] Little has been done on disputants' expectations of the legal system, on reactions to the processes they encountered, and on whether litigants became tactically adept through *experience*. This is despite the fact that dubious 'practices' were explicitly addressed by commentators, and by 'textbooks' like *The Attourneys Academy*, which highlighted possibilities for testing the perseverance and resources of opponents, for ensuring that disputes became 'immortal', and for indulging in 'grudge fights'.[20] This neglect of 'experiential' approaches to litigation reflects the fact that, as Christine Churches demonstrated, they involve piecing together voluminous but fragmentary evidence, and significant 'local knowledge' about families and communities affected by litigation.[21] Here, the Warrens Court dispute provides a rare opportunity to supplement scrutiny of formal legal records with analysis into 'the practices, conceptions and emotions of disputing individuals', and to test claims about litigants' 'emotional investment' in the legal system. It provides an opportunity to intervene in the debate about whether litigation integrated individuals into a functioning and participatory system for resolving problems, or else reveals societal dysfunction, and a means for 'continuing and expanding' conflicts rather than 'bringing them to an end'.[22]

Section Two analyses cross-generational disputation by exploring how Smyth, Crokey, and other protagonists approached litigation; how they reflected upon their experiences, upon each other, and upon the tactics and practices they encountered.[23] This means approaching the dispute from different directions, and moving beyond legal issues and arguments, by using surviving sources to examine the mechanics of litigation, the money and effort involved, and the tactics and strategies employed. It also means comparing—and attempting to triangulate—different perspectives on specific cases, and scrutinising the rhetoric with which the dispute was surrounded, in terms of claims and counterclaims, protestations and denials, brags and boasts, all of which survive in profusion. These competing—and incompatible—perceptions and depictions of the dispute, and of each side's actions, will be difficult to reconcile, although the aim here is not

[19] Richard J. Ross, 'Commoning of the Common Law', *University of Pennsylvania Law Review*, 146.2 (1998), 323–461; Hart, *Justice*, 17–19.

[20] George Norburie, 'The abuses and remedies of Chancery', in Francis Hargrave, ed., *A Collection of Tracts* (London, 1787), i. 444; Thomas Powell, *The Attourneys Academy* (1623), sigs A2, B3–4, C3, N3.

[21] Churches, 'Business at law'; Churches, 'False friends'; Churches, 'Equity'; Steve Hindle, 'The micro-spatial dynamics of litigation: the Chilvers-Coton tithe dispute, Barrows vs Archer (1657)', in Michael Lobban, Joanne Begiato, and Adrian Green, eds, *Law, Lawyers and Litigants in Early Modern England* (Cambridge, 2019), pp. 142, 159.

[22] Muldrew, 'Culture of reconciliation', p. 918; Prest, *Barristers*, pp. 299–300.

[23] Carroll, 'Peace in the feud', p. 79.

to arbitrate between rival accounts, but rather to distil different understandings of, and approaches to, litigation.[24]

These competing claims and interpretations can be introduced fairly succinctly with a resigned but defiant letter that Richard Moore wrote to 'brother Smyth' from the Fleet prison in June 1604. Moore's ostensible aim was to demand a small sum—25*s.*—that had earlier been awarded to him, but he took the opportunity to rehearse grievances about 'frivolous' suits and motions, old unresolved disputes, and 'fraudulent' or 'forged' deeds. He grumbled about judges being 'untruly informed' with false claims, about proceedings undertaken 'without my privity', and about hearings he missed by being imprisoned 'at your suit', and he protested about being 'beguiled' by Smyth, 'to my utter undoing'. Moore threatened Smyth with a new 'action . . . upon the statute of deceit', and with being 'committed' to prison, and warned him 'not to be so mad [as] to run into further dangers of the law', while also offering to meet in person, and to make 'a reasonable offer' by way of settlement, 'because I will buy my peace'.[25] Such talk of frivolous, fraudulent, and malicious behaviour, alongside confidence about how to litigate and the possibility of arbitration, encapsulates many of the issues with which this section grapples, and Smyth's reply supplies the remaining dimensions. Writing a few days later, Smyth offered a very different perspective on the dispute, and felt no need to compromise, having 'often . . . had experience of your like courses'. Smyth 'marvelled' that Moore was trying to claim money that had already been paid, 'as both you and mine attorneys well yet remember', insisting that Moore should 'leave these old practices and learn more honesty', and pay the 'great sums'—relating to 'costs, contempts, dismissions and judgments'—for which he had been imprisoned. Moore's letter was dismissed as 'idle, false, [and] scandalous to magistrates of great place in the commonwealth'.[26]

Such evidence leaves significant room for interpretation—between what litigants said and thought, and between rival accounts. However, such reflections also demonstrate that theories of dispute resolution need to be supplemented with evidence about the reality of litigation, and that wrestling with the Warrens Court saga involves the history of 'practice'. This sometimes involves focusing upon constrained 'agency' in an 'everyday' world of tacit norms, and routinised ways of thinking and behaving, and sometimes involves analysing 'technique' and 'strategy', and how contingent shifts in habitual modes of behaviour had ramifications for political, cultural, or social systems.[27] Here, it involves arguing that studying

[24] Thomas Kuehn, 'Reading microhistory', *JMH*, 61.3 (1989), 530, Tim Stretton, 'Social historians and the records of litigation', in Solvi Sogner, ed., *Fact, Fiction and Forensic Evidence* (Oslo, 1997), pp. 26–7, 31–2.

[25] GA, D8887/6/39. [26] GA, D8887/6/40.

[27] Pierre Bourdieu, *Outline of a Theory of Practice* (Cambridge, 1977). See: Noah Millstone, *Manuscript Circulation and the Invention of Politics in Early Modern England* (Cambridge, 2016), pp. 15–16, 323–4; Nicholas Popper, 'An information state in Elizabethan England', *JMH*, 90 (2018), 503–35; William H. Sewell, *Logics of History* (London, 2005), ch. 4, and pp. 161–72.

litigants' practices—the actions they chose to undertake—reveals their thinking, their zeal, and how carefully they reflected upon tactics and strategies. As George, 1st earl of Berkeley, explained, 'if many of us were judged by our practices, many abominable principles would be laid at our charge.'[28] Practices make it possible to analyse the thought processes of people who did not necessarily leave explicit statements about their ideas; they provide a chance to scrutinise the strategising of those whose thinking was demonstrated as much as described, through both conventional and experimental behaviour.

However, this is also a study of 'practice' in another sense, in terms of the negative connotations associated with 'practices', and rhetorical claims made about the methods and approaches that litigants witnessed. The language of 'practices' has already been shown to have suffused the dispute over Warrens Court. Smyth understood—and claimed to be the victim of—'wily devices' and 'practices', and Crokey made incessant references to Smyth's 'powerfulness' and 'indirect practices', as well as to 'cunning', 'subtlety', and 'false suggestions', suggesting that Smyth resorted to 'force and friendship', and indeed 'corruption'. For Crokey, such tactics reflected Smyth's 'greatness', but they were also 'vile', 'sinister', 'unconscionable', and 'unlawful'.[29] Crokey thus made claims not just about Smyth's aims—'to suppress the said school', and put it to 'his own use, contrary to the founder's meaning'—but also about his methods.[30]

Such language pervaded the dispute, and was certainly deployed by Richard Moore, but it might also be problematic, and goes to the heart of historiographical debates about whether litigation had a stabilising or destabilising effect. It might be thought to involve commonplace, formulaic, or even strategic rhetoric, and contemporary petitions and Star Chamber indictments abound with complaints about 'plots, practices, conspiracies, riots, routs, violent and unlawful assaults and other offences', and about 'corruption'.[31] According to Penry Williams, this was 'the usual attorney's jargon . . . and it would not be wise to take it too seriously'.[32] With Crokey, however, such accusations were substantive rather than rhetorical. They were discussed in detailed ways, and although they are often hard to validate they are sometimes verifiable, and were occasionally endorsed—or

[28] George Berkeley, *Historical Applications* (1670), p. 69.

[29] Crokey, *Sacred Maiestie*, sigs C2, C3, Fv, H3v–4; TNA, STAC 8/107/7; *LJ*, iii. 170–1; *LJ*, iv. 17–18; HL/PO/JO/10/1/24; HL/PO/JO/10/1/37; HL/PO/JO/10/1/274; HL/PO/JO/10/1/296; Crokey, *Contents*, sig. Av; Crokey, *Petition*, sig. A; Crokey, *Complaint*, sig. B4; GA, D9125/1/11996; Smyth, *Lives*, ii. 307, 311, 320, iii. 346.

[30] Crokey, *Complaint*, sig. B4; PA, HL/PO/JO/10/1/37; Crokey, *Petition*, p. 2.

[31] HEH, EL2735–6, EL2759, EL2762, EL2765, EL2771–2, EL2777–80, EL2792–4, EL2799, EL7882–5; PA, HL/PO/JO/10/1/25 (Nicholas Botiller); HL/PO/JO/10/1/26 (Alice Fowler); HL/PO/JO/10/1/29 (John Moigne). For Moore's rhetoric: TNA, STAC 5/M15/20; STAC 5/M13/19; GA, D9125/1/11989/4; D8887/6/17.

[32] P. H. Williams, 'The Star Chamber and the Council of the Marches of Wales, 1558–1603', *Bulletin of the Board of Celtic Studies*, 16.4 (1956), 289.

'discovered'—by the authorities, such that 'the whole house of Parliament' took notice of Smyth's 'powerfulness and practice in wronging... the school'.[33]

This language relates to the distinction between practice-as-convention and practice-as-innovation, and innovation of a dubious or questionable nature. For contemporaries, 'practice' sometimes meant the scheming, manipulative, and malevolent trickery of opponents, attempts to delude and deceive, conspiratorial endeavours, and the abuse of power, and even if such claims were ritualistic they also reveal conflicting ideas about the 'rules of the game'.[34] Perceptions of 'sharp' behaviour became motivating factors, stiffened litigants' resolve, and contributed to ideas about the proper and improper working of the law, and this section argues that contemporary reflections on 'practice' help to explain the longevity of the Warrens Court dispute, and why protagonists were determined to press on, not least by highlighting reasons for litigating that *emerged from* disputation. Such reflections demonstrate that modes of behaviour exacerbated tensions, and that contestation could be cumulative, and explain why litigants engaged in escalatory tactics and new modes of thinking.[35]

The aim is to demonstrate the serious and dogged way in which Crokey and Smyth contested their dispute: that they were capable of behaving in strategic and tactical ways; that they sharpened their techniques and refined their tactics; and that their thinking was evident even when it was not made explicit. Ultimately, the reflections of Smyth and Crokey provide fresh perspectives on what was happening, and indicate what they made of, and expected from, the law. The two men reached very different conclusions about the law being waged, about what constituted success and failure, and about how to be effective, and each man's perspective betrayed a certain logic. The incompatibility of their respective expectations—about the law and the dispute's meaning—helps to explain the nature and longevity of a dispute that bore more than a passing resemblance to a vendetta.[36] In short, this section argues that long-running disputes were driven not just by legal logic, or even by material interests and the desire to win, but also by conflicts that arose over how to behave and what to expect from the law.

[33] Crokey, *Complaint*, sig. B4; PA, HL/PO/JO/10/1/24; HL/PO/JO/10/1/274; HL/PO/JO/10/1/296.
[34] Barnes, 'Due Process', p. 232.
[35] Michael Sonenscher, *Work and Wages* (Cambridge, 1989), pp. 278–9.
[36] See: Edward Muir, *Mad Blood Rising* (London, 1998).

3

'A Lawyer by Practice'

John Smyth of Nibley as Litigant

When John Smyth reached London on 7 October 1622, he might not have realised that he was in for a long, challenging, and expensive winter. He perhaps expected to stay for the duration of Michaelmas term, but if so he was in for a nasty shock. He immediately set about work, paying £5 to a raft of lawyers—Serjeant Francis Harvey, George Evelyn, John Bridgman, and Richard Brownlow—to deal with Crokey's motions in Common Pleas. By early November, however, he was in prison, and needed to pay Harvey £1 'to move for my liberty', and the fee for a recognizance regarding his appearance in court the following term. Compelled to remain in the capital over Christmas, Smyth prepared for a winter campaign. He acquired law books (£3), but also made mundane purchases, recognising that London's winters could be cold, as the previous year's Frost Fair had demonstrated. He bought boots, woollen stockings, and cut-finger gloves, so that he could write even if his lodgings were freezing, and he secured a supply of cinnamon water to fend off colds. Back in the courts, he prepared a Star Chamber order against Crokey, which Bridgman moved on 3 December, while a week later Attorney General Coventry made a motion to have Smyth's case heard in Chancery. These two manoeuvres cost Smyth £6 12*s*., and from this point on his papers reveal a whirl of activity. He trekked around town on legal errands, paying for journeys by water, visits to the archives, and a trip to see Crokey. He copied relevant documents, including court orders and Crokey's bills of complaint, and paid to secure affidavits, enter motions in Common Pleas, and deal with Crokey's claim for costs. He also paid significant legal bills, to men like Coventry, Serjeant Randolph Crew, John Bridgman, Heneage Finch, Sir John Walter, Mr Gerrard, Francis Harvey, Mr Edwards, and Edward Trotman, and paid retainers to lawyers like Serjeant William Jones, even if there was 'nothing done' all term. He paid small fees to a range of less significant figures, including doorkeepers and a 'breviate bearer', not to mention assorted clerks and servants, who received gratuities 'in reward'. Finally, he paid for working dinners, fuelled by significant quantities of oysters, and it was only after the last round of such engagements in late February that

The Madman and the Churchrobber: Law and Conflict in Early Modern England. Jason Peacey, Oxford University Press.
 DOI: 10.1093/oso/9780192897138.003.0004

Smyth made the eighty-four-mile journey back to Nibley. His legal costs alone during this four-month period exceeded £65.[1]

Such detail indicates how Smyth approached the business of waging law, making it possible to use his behaviour to access his thinking. The Warrens Court dispute provides vivid evidence about the mechanics of litigation, and in addition to formal legal records there survive piles of writs and affidavits, some correspondence, and rich financial accounts, not to mention Smyth's extraordinary 'remembrances' (Fig. 3). The latter are particularly unusual, because they record Smyth's detailed plans—'to do' lists—for visits to London, which he not only composed and preserved, but also annotated, by crossing through entries for things that had been achieved, while still rendering them legible (Fig. 4). Such sources are by no means complete—they survive patchily across different archives, often as loose leaves—but in the absence of documentation in which Smyth explicitly set out his goals, they provide an intriguing way of recovering his thoughts. This is particularly important when set alongside Crokey's own interpretations and allegations regarding Smyth's strategies, not least because these accusations sometimes prompted Smyth—like others before him—to defend and

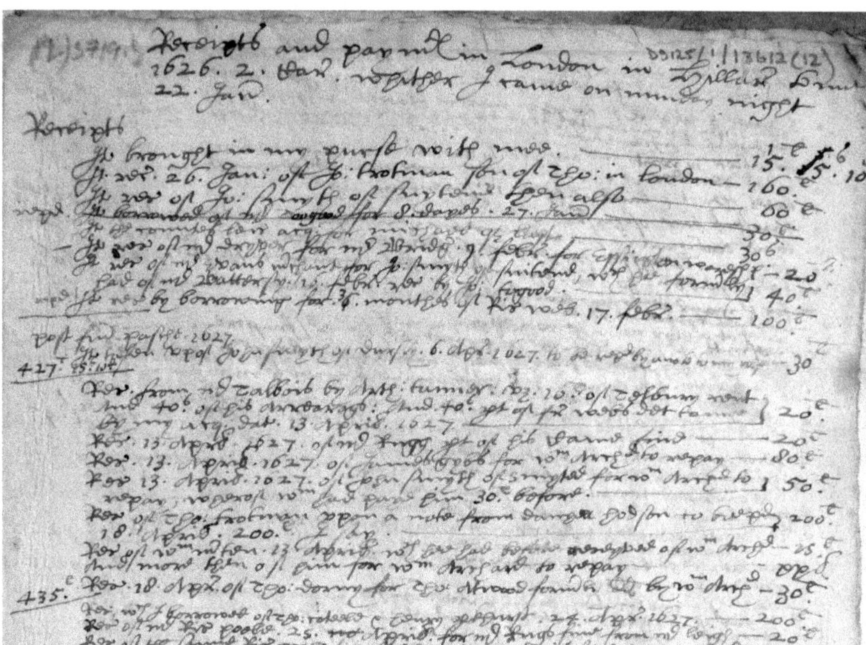

Fig. 3. 'Receipts and paym[en]ts in London in Hillar[y] terme 1626'. Gloucestershire Archives, D9125/1/13612(12). Reproduced by permission of Gloucestershire Archives.

[1] GA, D9125/1/13608/49, 52–3.

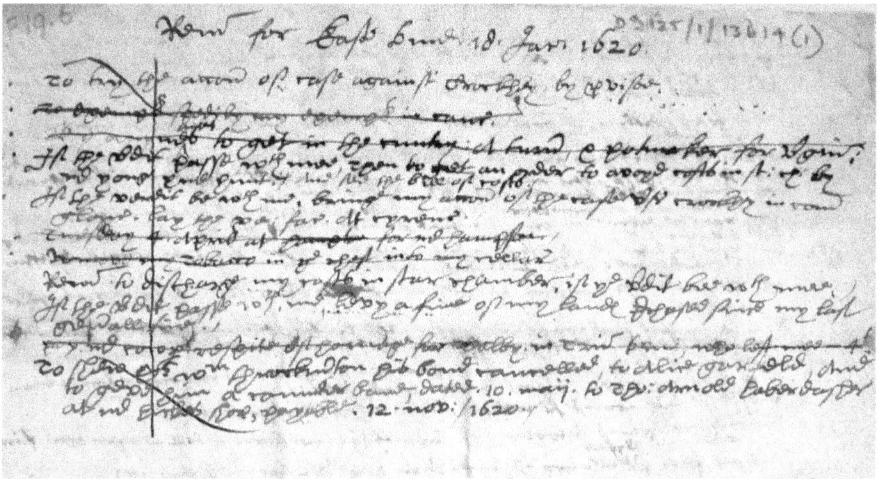

Fig. 4. ‘Rem[embrances] for East[er] terme 18 Jac. 1620’. Gloucestershire Archives, D9125/1/13614(1). Reproduced by permission of Gloucestershire Archives.

explain himself.[2] Irreconcilable though rival accounts might be, they provide insights into the mental world of litigants that are too important to ignore.

This chapter does not seek to arbitrate between rival accounts of what was happening, although there is scope to assess certain claims by both sides. Rather, it monitors Smyth’s aims and expectations, to enhance our understanding of why he pursued the dispute so doggedly. What emerges is that Smyth invested eye-watering amounts of time, energy, and money into this contest; that his determination increased over time; and that his tactical skills were refined. For Smyth the purpose of litigation was not always to win, and occasionally he seemed—perhaps only *seemed*—willing to compromise. In 1597, Richard Moore thought it possible that a commission ‘here in the country’ might resolve the matter outside the courts, that tension could be defused, and that Smyth was not taking the matter too seriously. According to Moore, Smyth was ‘very peremptory till he saw my bill’.[3]

Smyth also differed fairly clearly from Crokey, in terms of how he expected legal processes would and should work, and how they could and should be used. Key here is Crokey’s assertion that Smyth was ‘a lawyer by practice’ and ‘a man learned in the laws’, because Smyth made a somewhat disingenuous denial about his legal training—that he left the Middle Temple and ‘betook’ himself ‘to a ploughman’s life’—and because he was ‘a lawyer, alias a lawless man’.[4] Such

[2] See: TNA, STAC 5/M13/19; GA, D9125/1/11989/1, 4, 9–10; D8887/6/9, 13, 17, 26, 32, 34, 44–5; D9125/1/11994, 11996, 11997, 12002, 12008, pp. 11–13, 20–1, 32; D8887/4/107.

[3] GA, D8887/6/23.

[4] Crokey, *Contents*, sig. A; TNA, STAC 8/107/7; GA, D9125/1/12008, p. 73; Crokey, *Complaint*, sig. A.

language was not unprecedented, and whatever the truth of Crokey's allegations, competing interpretations of his behaviour were plausible, even if what Crokey found objectionable was what Smyth believed made him successful.[5] This chapter demonstrates how the ability to grapple with a litigant's thoughts and practices makes it possible to delve into the nature of early modern litigation; into how it was viewed by those involved, as well as by onlookers, not least within a wider context of similar claims.

I

The most challenging possibility is that Smyth engaged in blatant fraud and deceit.[6] Some such allegations had been evident since the 1590s, but they were inflammatory and difficult to prove. Richard Moore accused John and Grace Drew—together with their lawyer, George Snigge—of 'indirect practices', and of having 'practiced' and 'conspired' to get a lease from his mother, Alice, which was corrupted when Grace's name was 'razed and put out', thereby becoming void and necessitating a new lease. Moore detected a 'false and wicked' move, to 'frame, devise, contrive, forge and counterfeit' a new lease in Alice's name, which was 'published' in various courts and facilitated erroneous judgments. Moore also asserted that perjury had been committed, 'purposely to defraud', insisting that documents had been 'razed and defaced', and that disingenuous claims had been made that the 'blotting' of the 1584 lease happened 'by chance', when Snigge 'let a drop of ink fall out of his pen'.[7] Such accusations were colourful but ineffective, and by insisting that a 'somewhat blotted' document was still legible, and amended merely to become 'plain', it proved possible to deny that it had been 'forged', 'falsified or corrupted'. Moore, however, went to his grave insisting that courts had been 'abused' and 'beguiled... to my utter undoing', and claims about forged, 'razed', and 'blotted' documentation were certainly not uncommon at the time.[8]

Crokey's claims about fraud were equally problematic, and while his rhetoric was powerful his arguments were thin. Crokey regularly deployed a language familiar from contemporary petitions, bewailing Smyth's 'false' and 'untrue suggestions', and peppering documents with claims about legal processes being perverted by 'some slight... to the abuse of the court', for the 'maintenance and strengthening' of 'bad titles'.[9] Smyth, he said, had 'shadowed the matter' with a 'false' history of Warrens Court, and with 'pretended' titles, insisting that judges

[5] See: PA, HL/PO/JO/10/1/25 (John Chapman). [6] See: Brooks, *Law*, p. 316.

[7] TNA, STAC 5/M15/20; STAC 5/M13/19; GA, D9125/1/11989/4; D8887/6/17.

[8] TNA, STAC 5/M13/19. See: TNA, STAC 5/M50/37; GA, D8887/6/39; PA, HL/PO/JO/10/1/30 (John Wall); HL/PO/JO/10/1/34 (Robert Lane).

[9] Crokey, *Sacred Maiestie*, sigs A3–v, C, D3v, E, H2; Crokey, *Briefe*; BL, Harl. MS 6803, fos 56v–7. See: PA, HL/PO/JO/10/1/36 (John Horseley).

had been abused, and commissions of inquiry 'perverted', with 'untrue matters' and 'false reports'.[10] Payment of legal costs was evaded by 'surmising false matters', a phrase repeated in claims that the King and Privy Council had been misled. Such protests were invariably vague, and Crokey tended to offer little evidence to support claims that leading officials had been 'abused' by 'false suggestions', as a result of which they had become 'incensed' against him.[11]

When Crokey's claims were more specific they were difficult to substantiate and open to challenge. Smyth was described as a gold-digger, who married an 'old bed-ridden widow'—Grace Drew—to gain the disputed lands, being 'then of little or no value or estate'. Grace was said to be 'decrepid, sick in her bed, and likely to die', only able to participate in the ceremony in her chamber, 'held up by two maids'.[12] The wedding was said to have been followed by Smyth 'prying into the estate of the said school', by 'pretence of the said marriage'.[13] Here, Smyth insisted that, while Grace had indeed been sick, she was not yet forty-five and had recovered by the time of the wedding, and 'met me at her gate', as more than forty guests could testify.[14] She also lived for another twelve years.

Smyth also challenged claims that he exploited his marriage to acquire a landed estate. Crokey alleged that Smyth used 'cunning and untrue suggestions' to get the 'original lease' out of Chancery; that he 'practiced' with the Duport family to get their 'pretended' claims to the lands; and that he 'swallowed up' title deeds. He claimed that Smyth appointed Edward Cowper as schoolmaster 'unduly', caused him to convey school lands to Smyth's father-in-law, John Browning, and then took them himself, such that his titles were 'fraudulent' and 'forged'. He then insisted that Smyth carved up the estate through leases and sales, which 'plucked up the meads and bounds of the school lands', making their true extent difficult to discern and impossible to restore.[15] Smyth denied having anything to hide. He admitting responding to Moore's death by asking Grace to reconstruct the history of the estate, by unearthing documents, trawling her memory, and reflecting on her 'unkind brother'.[16] However, he claimed to have acted in good faith, having been persuaded that the Duport titles were sound, and that the courts had handed him the 'original lease', adding that he was entitled to grant new leases. He accused Crokey of being the only person who questioned his claim, noting his tendency to 'reprove at pleasure' with 'general' words about imprecise 'crimes'.[17]

[10] Crokey, *Sacred Maiestie*, sigs A4–v, B4v, D, E; GA, D9125/1/11996–7; PA, HL/PO/JO/10/1/37.
[11] Crokey, *Sacred Maiestie*, sigs A3, A4–v, C2v; Crokey, *Complaint*, sigs C–v; Crokey, *Contents*, sig. A2.
[12] Crokey, *Sacred Maiestie*, sig. A2v; Crokey, *Petition*, p. 2; Crokey, *Complaint*, sigs Av–A2; GA, D8887/6/68.
[13] PA, HL/PO/JO/10/1/274. See also: HL/PO/JO/10/1/296; Crokey, *Petition*, p. 2.
[14] GA, D9125/1/12008, pp. 76–7; Smyth, *Lives*, ii. 319–20. For Grace's illness: Bodl. MS Eng.Misc. e.6, fos 44–8.
[15] Crokey, *Sacred Maiestie*, sigs A3, B3–v; Crokey, *Contents*, sig. A; Crokey, *Complaint*, sig. A4v; Crokey, *Petition*, p. 2; PA, HL/PO/JO/10/1/37; HL/PO/JO/10/1/296; HL/PO/JO/10/1/274.
[16] GA, D8887/5/43. [17] GA, D9125/1/12008, pp. 16–18, 37–9.

Equally problematic were Crokey's claims about Smyth's duplicitous intentions regarding Wotton school, involving 'false shows . . . of a pious intent'. Crokey argued that Cowper 'never exercised' the place of schoolmaster, leaving the school in the hands of unqualified deputies, and that Smyth misled Chancery about increasing his financial contribution from 40*s*. to £12 *per annum*, insisting that the income had previously been £23 'until Smyth began his practices to supplant it'. Smyth re-founded the school, Crokey protested, 'for his own glory', to 'outface and blindfold the world, that his former practices for supplanting thereof might not be seen'. Mocking Smyth's 'dissembled piety and bounty', Crokey refused to accept that the school would receive £47 *per annum*, 'as Smyth would have it'.[18] Here too, Smyth simply contradicted Crokey, denying any plan to 'overthrow, impeach or hurt' the school, and insisting that he 'laboured' for its 'welfare and advancement', increasing its funding and recruiting additional pupils.[19]

Occasionally, Smyth's bluster covered his blushes, not least regarding Edward Bishopp's case about concealed lands. Smyth denied prior knowledge of such claims, protesting that he acquired the Duport property in good faith, and that he was 'ignorant of the crown's title' until being informed about it by Thomas Adams of Wotton.[20] Nevertheless, he admitted that the Duports knew about such allegations, and that this was probably 'the cause of their sales to him'. The issue was clearly mentioned in Duport family correspondence, and featured in Smyth's letters to them *before* Bishopp's case began. In 1616, James Duport expressed surprise 'that there should be any question made concerning those lands', and denied having concealed anything from Smyth, grumbling about 'the declining . . . days of the world, which now setteth shifting fellows on work, to whet their whits, to dive into every man's estate, to see if they can catch never so little . . . to work upon, that they may draw some money from other men'. Duport concluded that, while people might 'bark' about 'idle' claims, there was little chance of them 'biting', but admitted that similar claims surfaced repeatedly, and recommended that Smyth should 'confer' with John Staunton, former vicar of Wotton and tutor at the school, who knew all about them.[21] Unfortunately, it is unclear precisely when Smyth spent 'much money' to compile archival evidence about these earlier claims, about the grant made to Charles Badghot and Bartholemew Yardley (in 1589), and about how this claim passed to Bishopp, but it seems likely that he was aware of claims about concealed lands as early as 1608.[22]

Smyth's version of events was tendentious, and Crokey got close to exposing him. Smyth claimed that such evidence only emerged with Bishopp's complaint, and that upon 'advice of counsel' he 'bought in all the estates'. His accounts

[18] Crokey, *Sacred Maiestie*, sigs A3v, A4v, Bv, B3v, C4v–D, H2; Crokey, *Petition*, p. 7.

[19] GA, D9125/1/12008, pp. 18, 84–5.

[20] GA, D9125/1/11996, 12008, pp. 19–20.

[21] GA, D9125/1/11989/14, 11990.

[22] GA, D8887/6/96; D9125/1/11989/14, 11996, 12002, 12008, pp. 19–20. See: GA, D8887/3/105; TNA, PROB 11/83, fo. 8v. See below, p. C7.P43–C7.P45.

nevertheless reveal attempts to compound with one claimant 'for the schoolhouse lands' in July 1616, at a cost of 66*s*., after which he spent £250 for a grant of the lands upon the commission of 'defective titles' (December 1617). Such 'cost and trouble' was apparently incurred for 'the better quieting of his own possession', to protect tenants from 'vexation and trouble', and to ensure 'the final settling and preservation of the school'.[23] Crokey, however, suggested that Smyth, 'fearing his title to be weak', 'practised' to get the lands deemed 'concealed', and 'procured' a spurious challenge from Bishopp, his 'chamber fellow in the Inner Temple'. Smyth then pretended to respond, 'had the carriage' of the subsequent inquiry, and 'produced' witnesses to 'prove the plaintiff's bill', paying their expenses, and playing host to Bishopp in Nibley. He was accused of being 'both plaintiff and defendant', and such claims are palpably supported by Smyth's accounts. For Crokey, Smyth secured the lands using 'indirect and fraudulent practices', making it possible to get the school 'suppressed'.[24]

Crokey's account is interesting. This is because it received official endorsement, with reference being made to 'indirect practices', and because Smyth's response was economical with the truth.[25] He denied any link with Bishopp by insisting that he had never been a member of the *Inner* Temple, even though Crokey had merely mistaken the *Inner* for the *Middle* Temple. In fact, Smyth and Bishopp had been part of a tight network at the Middle Temple, involving shared chambers and reciprocal acts of patronage, and including their children as well as Richard Daston, Smyth's legal advisor on this case, and Anthony Gulson, Smyth's half-brother. Gulson was paid 'maintenance' by Smyth during this period, and was a beneficiary of the crown's grant of the lands, as Crokey recognised.[26]

However, such episodes are intriguing less for the possibility of discerning who was telling the truth than for the tone of the dispute, and the chance of identifying the subtle tactics and strategies—'practices'—that Smyth perfected as a litigant.

II

As demonstrated already, Smyth's legal activity can be observed through his meticulous financial accounts, revealing the challenges that London posed, the lifestyle that a litigant might lead, and the zeal with which Crokey was pursued, as

[23] GA, D8887/6/96; D9125/1/11989/14, 11996, 12008, pp. 19–20; Bodl. MS Eng.Misc.e.6, fo. 106v.

[24] Crokey, *Sacred Maiestie*, sigs A3v, C–Cv, E; GA, D9125/1/11996–7; TNA, STAC 8/107/7; PA, HL/PO/JO/10/1/296; Crokey, *Briefe*; BL, Harl. 6803, fos 56v–7. See: Bodl. MS Eng.Misc.e.6, fos 106v, 109.

[25] GA, D9125/1/11989/14.

[26] GA, D9125/1/12008, p. 47. See: *Admissions MT*, i. 91, 95; Hopwood, *MT Recs*, i. 327, 391, ii. 493, 503, 528, 539, 598–9, 617, 629, 631, 650, 722–3, 732. For 'maintenance' to Gulson: Bodl. MS Eng.Misc.e.6, fos 90v, 98v, 111v, 120v.

well as the time and money devoted to this one cause.[27] Knowing what litigants invested in litigation is central to any account of what they expected from the legal system.

First, we get a clear sense of how much time Smyth spent in the capital, since he recorded the precise dates when he set off 'towards London' and 'rode towards Nibley'. He was there from 4 May until 4 June 1620, and having arrived in town on 17 May 1632 he stayed for six weeks and three days. Not every trip was recorded so precisely, and sometimes we only learn of particular days he was in town, such as 7 November 1611, when he purchased four books, or 9 November 1609, when he rewarded a man who brought news 'the day that my wife died'. Nevertheless, once the dispute with Crokey really got going, Smyth spent almost the entirety of each legal term in London, and sometimes stayed much longer. He was there from 2 October 1617 to 28 February 1618, beyond the length of both Michaelmas and Hilary terms, and although a subsequent visit—from 19 December 1620 until 'my departure homewards' on 2 July 1621—reflected membership of the 1621 Parliament, Smyth stayed much longer than service in the Commons required. Having noted that he 'came to London' on 7 October 1622, Smyth stayed until August 1623, and upon leaving the capital on 11 June 1627 noted having been there since 22 January. These trips mostly revolved around litigation, and although Smyth was occasionally accompanied by his wife, not least for family christenings, he mostly travelled alone or with one servant. Such behaviour largely stopped with the Star Chamber ruling against Crokey in 1631.[28]

Secondly, Smyth's accounts offer remarkable clarity about the life of London's temporary residents, indicating that extended visits were hugely expensive, perhaps involving £8 and £11 *per* term, even without legal fees. Travelling between Nibley and London could take three to five days, and even if Smyth was not forced to visit blacksmiths and saddlers *en route*, such journeys could cost £7 each way, particularly if he hired a coach, and if snow and frost descended. Using a coach could reflect inclement weather, but also the need to carry papers and books back and forth, and to do so in anticipation of hearings that might never happen. In Trinity term 1627, Smyth recorded the expense of travelling to London to prosecute Crokey, '*expecting* his answer the first sitting of this term'. In October 1629, he carried two trunks—weighing 200*lb*—from Nibley, including legal papers and 'my statute book', and Smyth once reminded

[27] See also: GA, D9125/1/13608/2; Berkeley, BB107, fos 14v, 94; BB108, fos 11–v, 28–9v, 34, 58, 90v, 135v.

[28] Bodl. MS Eng.Misc.e.6, fos 26v, 30v, 33, 41v, 48, 61v, 82, 86v, 88, 92, 110v, 112, 117v, 123, 124v, 126v; GA, D9125/1/13612/1, 4–5, 8, 13–14; D9125/1/13608/41, 45, 49, 52–4, 67, 70–v, 72, 86–8v; D9125/1/13615/3; D8887/2/32; Smyth, *Lives*, iii. 42.

himself to 'bring a note of such books' as were in his London chambers, 'except law books'.[29]

Getting to and from London was only part of the story, and Smyth's accounts record conspicuous consumption—books for the Berkeleys; girdles, garters, and slippers for his wife; a demicastor for himself, not to mention 'frivolous use money'—as well as unavoidable expenses.[30] He needed socks and gloves, boots and shoes, shoestrings and shoehorns, as well as stockings, linen nightstraps, and a satin nightcap, not to mention hairwax and a brush, a penknife and an earpick, and combs (with case) and toothpicks (also with case). He paid the barber 'for trimming me', and the seamstress for mending worn clothes. Although Smyth occasionally dined out, and saw plays like *The World Goes Round*, he mostly worked on his papers. He made frequent trips to and from Westminster, Southwark, and Greenwich, paying between 6*d.* and 4*s.*6*d.* per journey, and his workload explains the frequent acquisition of spectacles, and ream after ream of paper, as well as ink, pens, and wax.[31]

Even less avoidable were costs associated with board and lodgings. Smyth usually stayed with his former attorney, Michael Moseley, where correspondents knew to find him, although occasionally he was forced to look elsewhere.[32] Moseley charged 4*s.* per week for lodging, while weekly diet and laundry cost around 14*s.*, excluding rewards to the maid. Smyth sometimes paid for six months (40*s.*) or even a year at a time. Living 'charges' for a ten-day trip during Hilary term 1629 were £2, and if he stayed an entire term he might expect to pay £5–10 over four to six weeks. During a four-month trip between October 1614 and January 1615, the cost of chamber, fire, and 'commons' ran to £21 16*s.*, and from Michaelmas 1614 to Midsummer 1615 Smyth spent almost £63 on diet. When he stayed from October 1617 to February 1618, his riding charges and diet came to £28, and the cost of diet in London during 1618 ran to £48 17*s.*[33] Such sums exclude the cost of postage and portage, of lamprey pies, and of red herrings by the hundred, not to mention supplies of nutmegs, cinnamon, cloves, mace, and ginger, as well as oranges, lemons, and chestnuts. If Smyth dined

[29] Bodl. MS Eng.Misc.e.6, fos 24v, 61v, 83v, 86v, 88, 98v, 102v, 111, 126v; GA, D9125/1/13611/11; D9125/1/13612/1–4, 6, 8–15; D9125/1/13615/3; D8887/6/104; D9125/1/13608/50, 53–4, 65–7, 76; D8887/5/12, 15; D8887/10/118. In 1605, the Wotton carrier charged Smyth 7*s.*6*d.* to take a trunk to London, at 3 farthings per pound: Bodl. MS Eng.Misc.e.6, fo. 24v.

[30] Bodl. MS Eng.Misc.e.6, fos 41v, 61v, 75v, 77, 82, 83v, 89, 91v–2, 105v, 111, 114v, 121v, 123; GA, D9125/1/13612/1, 3, 6–15; D8887/6/104; D8887/5/12, 32; D9125/1/13608/27, 29, 32–3, 67, 70–v, 72, 76v, 86-88v; D9125/1/13611/3, 11, 19, 21, 23v.

[31] GA, D9125/1/13612/1–4, 6, 7–15; D9125/1/13608/29, 32–3, 50, 53, 65–7, 76, 70–v; D9125/1/13611/11, 19; D9125/1/13612/8; D8887/5/15; D8887/6/104; Bodl. MS Eng.Misc.e.6, fos 126v, 128, 131.

[32] Chicago UL, MS 1465, folder 3; GA, D8887/1/72; D8887/9/, 70, 77, 83, 107; D8887/6/102; Berkeley, GPL 1017; Kingsbury, *Virginia*, iii. 289, 291, 401; Bodl. MS Eng.Misc.e.6, fo. 92. Moseley occasionally loaned Smyth money: GA, D9125/1/13612/10.

[33] GA, D9125/1/13612/12; D8887/6/104; D9125/1/13608/70–v; Bodl. MS Eng.Misc.e.6, fos 82v, 87, 92–v, 98, 102v, 105, 110v, 113, 118, 124v, 126v, 130v.

'abroad'—normally on business—expenses were much higher, and it is tempting to think that his wine bill—which rose from a few shillings to a few pounds per term—increased in direct proportion to the complexity and longevity of his legal travails.[34]

Thirdly, Smyth's accounts reveal that visits to London were dominated by litigation with Crokey. Of course, as a servant of the Berkeleys he sometimes travelled to their houses in Cranford and Clerkenwell, Redcross Street and the Barbican, and oversaw their business.[35] His own affairs also involved other legal battles, which ensured that legal expenses could be as high as £81 per term, and in 1618 reached £136.[36] Nevertheless, the Warrens Court dispute was Smyth's biggest concern, and he generally noted travelling 'to prosecute cause against Crokey', dealing with '*the* bill' or '*the* hearing', and prosecuting '*the cause*' or '*this* cause', as well as the need to 'bring *him* to answer'.[37] The specificity of his accounts indicates how expensive this one dispute became, as litigation ranged across courts, and as Smyth encountered the frightening consequences of delays and setbacks. In 1614, he spent £6 on the matter in Gloucester and Bristol, while 'law charges' in London during Hilary term 1615 ran to £15 7*s*.6*d*. (excluding costs associated with the Thornbury inquiry), and Star Chamber expenses during the following two terms came to £39 4*s*.4*d*. Not every year was this expensive, but the dispute became more costly over time. The Bishopp case cost £38 16*s*.8*d*. (1617–18); during the first eight months of 1617 costs involving Crokey ran to £30 7*s*.; and in the year to October 1617 cases with Crokey cost £52 10*s*.2*d*. The following year was even more expensive—over £70—because of fees for a royal grant of the school lands, and in Hilary term 1627 Smyth spent £23 5*s*.2*d*. even though nothing much happened.[38] As far as we know, Smyth never tallied his overall expenditure on the dispute, but it certainly involved many hundreds of pounds.[39]

Such costs reflected the scale and complexity of Smyth's litigation, and the imposing team of lawyers he mustered. This meant clerks like John Chadwick and Mr Hoopil, with whom he worked repeatedly, and who received anything from a few shillings to £18.[40] It also meant eminent attorneys like Richard Brownlow and

[34] GA, D9125/1/13612/1, 3–4, 6, 8–15; D8887/5/12, 15; D9125/1/13608/50, 53, 67, 76.

[35] GA, D9125/1/13612/1, 4, 8–15; D9125/1/13608/50v; Berkeley, BB108, fo. 212; GA, D8887/1/97; D8887/2/20–4, 28, 57–9, 65, 79; D8887/3/13; D8887/5/2; Chicago UL, MS 1465, folder 3; Berkeley, GPL 222, 843, 1076, 1158. See: *CD 1621*, i. 70–3.

[36] Bodl. MS Eng.Misc.e.6, fos 75, 78, 82–v, 83v, 86v, 88, 92–3, 98v, 102v, 111; GA, D9125/1/13612/4; D9125/1/13617; D8887/2/19–20; D9125/1/12016–18.

[37] GA, D9125/1/13612/12; D8887/6/104 (emphasis added).

[38] Bodl. MS Eng.Misc.e.6, fos 89v, 92–3, 100v–1, 105v, 106v, 111, 113, 114v, 117v–18v, 119v–20v, 122, 125, 126v–7, 131; GA, D9125/1/13612/2.

[39] GA, D8887/6/94; S379/2/3/2/7.

[40] GA, D9125/1/13612/1–2, 4; D9125/1/13608/27, 29, 32–3. Hoopil had worked for Berkeley: Berkeley, BB110, fo. 39v.

George Evelyn, whose fees might be as high as 50*s*.[41] Some advisers—Mr Edwards, Mr Gayre, and Mr Gerrard—appeared only occasionally, and some were specialists, like William Hudson, to whom Smyth paid over £16 for Star Chamber business between 1627 and 1629.[42] More striking is evidence about lawyers employed over protracted periods, many from the highest echelons of the profession. Some trusted counsellors were local men, to whom Smyth was related by marriage, like Edward Trotman of Cam and the Inner Temple. Other stalwarts who commanded similar fees—£1–2—were players at a national level, including William Jones, 'my attorney'.[43] Smyth increasingly relied upon the most successful lawyers of the age, including Leonard Bawtry, Thomas Atto, and Francis Harvey, whom he knew from his work for Lord Berkeley, as well as Francis Moore, solicitor to Queen Anne and favourite of Lord Chancellor Ellesmere.[44] Others were men 'near whom I dwelt', like John Bridgman, just before he became Chief Justice of Chester, and Thomas Chamberlain, retained lawyer for the Berkeleys since the 1590s, who was on the verge of being knighted and becoming a judge.[45] More important still was Sir Randolph Crew, another Ellesmere protégé with ties to the Berkeley family, Speaker of the Commons in 1614, and a future Chief Justice.[46] Such men were not just eminent—they commanded fees of £1 to £5—but also well-connected rising stars, Smyth boasting that one was 'now a judge'.[47] It clearly mattered to him to be able to hire such men, and he may have been particularly happy to retain the services of Sir John Walter, Attorney General to the Prince of Wales, and Sir Heneage Finch, Recorder of London and prominent MP.[48] For their services, like those of the Attorney General, Sir Thomas Coventry, he paid a hefty premium, which meant £5 for every motion made.[49] Smyth's

[41] GA, D9125/1/13612/2; D9125/1/13608/50–v, 52. See: Brooks, *Pettyfoggers*, pp. 230–33; TNA, E 215/629.

[42] GA, D9125/1/13612/2, 5–8, 12–14; D9125/1/13608/49–50v, 65–6; D8887/5/12. See: Thomas G. Barnes, 'Mr Hudson's Star Chamber', in DeLloyd J. Guth and J. W. McKenna, eds, *Tudor Rule and Revolution* (Cambridge, Mass., 1982), pp. 285–308.

[43] GA, D8887/8/6; D9125/1/13608/27, 30, 45, 49, 50–v, 59, 65–6; D9125/1/13612/2–3, 5–9, 12–14; D8887/6/94; D9125/1/12008, p. 60. See TNA, STAC 8/107/7. See: Prest, *Barristers*, pp. 374, 398; *ODNB*.

[44] GA, D9125/1/13608/29, 32–3, 49, 52; D9125/1/13612/2–4, 7–8; D9125/1/12008, pp. 48–9. See: Berkeley, BB110, fo. 167; Prest, *Barristers*, 341, 343, 367, 380; *ODNB*.

[45] GA, D9125/1/13612/5, 6, 7, 8; D9125/1/13608/49, 52v, 54–v; D9125/1/12008, p. 60. See: STAC 8/107/7. See: Berkeley, BB107, fo. 99v; BB108, fos 149v, 206; BB109, fos. 27–8; Smyth, *Lives*, ii. 343; Prest, *Barristers*, pp. 347, 349; *ODNB*; TNA, PROB 11/176, fo. 234.

[46] GA, D9125/1/13612/2, 4; D9125/1/13608/49; D8887/6/55; D9125/1/11989/8, 12008, p. 41. See: Berkeley, BB107, fos 19v, 66, 103; Prest, *Barristers*, p. 353.

[47] GA, D9125/1/12008/18. See: Prest, *Barristers*, pp. 27, 47, 58, 62, 70, 81; HEH, EL452; Francis Bacon, *The Major Works*, ed., Brian Vickers (Oxford, 2002), pp. 447–8; William Lambarde, *The Iust Lawyer* (1631), sig. A2v, pp. 5, 8.

[48] GA, D9125/1/13608/49; D9125/1/13612/5, 14; D8887/6/94. See: *ODNB*.

[49] GA, D9125/1/13612/8; D9125/1/13608/52v–3. In 1626, Smyth also used the new attorney general, Robert Heath: GA, D8887/6/94.

willingness and ability to pay such sums speaks volumes about his determination, and created a roster of counsellors with which Crokey could not compete.

III

Surviving accounts also reveal the kinds of work—specific actions and moves—for which lawyers were employed, and the granularity of Smyth's accounts highlights his intimate involvement in managing, and making decisions about, litigation.[50] Evidence about how men like Smyth approached disputes contributes to our understanding of the degree to which litigants' 'voices' can be detected in legal cases, and informs our appreciation of what they hoped and expected to achieve.[51]

One way of assessing Smyth's care in overseeing the Warrens Court dispute involves reflecting on the time and money he devoted to clerical dimensions of contestation. Like all litigants, Smyth needed to navigate complex legal and administrative bureaucracies, such that every word written, matter handled, and document signed incurred fees, and he generally recorded the cost of every piece of work done—no matter how trivial and formulaic—with meticulous monotony. Occasionally, these 'charges' involved aggregations of legal and clerical fees, as with the 'exemplification' of proceedings in one Chancery suit (over £13), the process of attaching the great seal to the letters patent for Wotton School (over £10), and the business of incorporating the school (£14).[52] Mostly, however, Smyth documented the complexity and cost of simple clerical procedures; paying an undersheriff 10*s*.4*d*. for a 'distress' against Crokey (1614), or getting Star Chamber costs discharged, which involved 22*s*. in legal fees, 3*s*. for the order to be 'fair written', and 2*s*. for the clerk's services (1623).[53] The 'briefs' and 'breviates' given to counsel also needed to be sourced, and although Mr Gerrard's clerk charged 5*s*. for 'five short' briefs, longer documents were much more expensive. Smyth once paid an unnamed clerk £2 for fair writing four breviates for 'several learned counsel'.[54] Most clerks charged 8*d*. *per* sheet for such business, but even scriveners demand 6*d*. per sheet, and long documents—like the 240 'close written' sheets required on one occasion—could cost up to £6.[55] Ultimately, Smyth paid for copying almost every document the dispute generated, including those submitted by, or sent to, Crokey, from court orders to demurrers, affidavits, and

[50] Churches, 'Business at law', p. 950.

[51] Joanne Bailey, 'Voices in court: lawyers' or litigants'?', *HR*, 74.186 (2001), 392–408; Deborah Youngs, '"A besy woman... and full of law": female litigants in early Tudor Star Chamber', *JBS*, 58 (2019), 735–50; Tim Stretton, 'Women, legal records, and the problem of the lawyer's hand', *JBS*, 58 (2019), 684–700; Alexandra Shepard, 'Worthless witnesses? Marginal voices and women's legal agency in early modern England', *JBS*, 58 (2019), 717–34.

[52] GA, D9125/1/13612/6; D9125/1/13608/54–v.

[53] Bodl. MS Eng.Misc.e.6, fo. 88v; GA, D9125/1/13608/50–v.

[54] GA, D9125/1/113612/2–3; D8887/6/104; D8887/5/2.

[55] GA, D9125/1/13608/29, 32–3.

petitions. Individually, these might cost a few shillings, but longer documents could easily cost £1, and Smyth's copy of the 1631 Star Chamber decree cost 36*s*. Anything written on parchment cost 26*s*.8*d*. *per* skin.[56] Parliamentary officials commanded even higher fees, with individual orders costing between 2*s*. and 16*s*., while a copy of Crokey's draft legislation set Smyth back £1 5*s*. During 1629 Smyth racked up costs of £3 to the clerk, Henry Elsynge, and 20*s*.3*d*. to his under-clerks, excluding the copy of Crokey's re-submitted bill (46*s*.), as well as various petitions and orders (19*s*.).[57] Such costs really rocketed when Smyth sought copies of witness statements, which might cost 11*s*. apiece.[58] That Smyth's copying charges came to £20 in *one term* in 1628 reflected his acquisition of 183 sheets of depositions, and £9 spent on statements at one commission of inquiry.[59]

Litigation was also eye-wateringly expensive because individual moves and motions involved a succession of fees, and payments or gratuities to everyone encountered along the route that documents took from conception to submission and entry into official records. Smyth's papers abound with evidence about fees for 'entering' documents, 'expediting' orders, and 'filing' recognizances, and for 'cryers' who called counsel to court. He greased the palms of Sir Henry Yelverton's 'doorkeeper', of Heneage Finch's 'man', and of the 'bag bearer' and 'breviate bearer', for their 'pains' or 'in reward'. Each transaction was small, perhaps a few pence, but perhaps a few shillings, and they mounted up.[60] In June 1624, when settling the account of Mr Yonge for an 'exemplification' regarding Wotton school, Smyth itemised Mr Henley's fee for writing on six vellum skins (£8), fees at the Hanaper (23*s*.), and fees to Masters in Chancery and the Master of the Rolls (24*s*. and 7*s*. respectively), as well as fees for the vellum (19*s*.), for the docquet and 'expedition' (3*s*.), and for the 'sealer' and the 'chasewax' (2*s*.), not to mention the fee to Yonge himself (20*s*.), and to his clerk (6*s*.). Dealing with byzantine legal processes was a regular, laborious occurrence, and a significant financial burden.[61]

Such evidence sheds light upon litigants' choices, and while administrative fees were unavoidable they also reflected the moves litigants made, indicating the zeal—even ruthlessness—with which disputes were pursued, and tactical decisions. Smyth's accounts highlight the frequency and impact of legal delays—including those caused deliberately by opponents—as orders and motions needed to be renewed, setting off new cycles of fee-paying.[62] The legal instruments—warrants, writs, and affidavits—that Smyth acquired were intrinsically cheap, but

[56] GA, D9125/1/13608/45, 49–50v, 54, 65–7, 70v; D9125/1/13612/3, 5–6; D8887/6/38, 104.

[57] GA, D9125/1/13612/5, 14. See: Elizabeth Read Foster, *The House of Lords, 1603–1649* (Chapel Hill, 1983), pp. 56–7, 59, 93.

[58] GA, D9125/1/13612/2, 7; D8887/6/104.

[59] GA, D8887/5/12; D8887/6/104.

[60] GA, D9125/1/13612/3, 5–9, 13; D9125/1/13608/8, 49, 50–v, 52, 65–6; D8887/6/38, 94, 104; D8887/5/12.

[61] GA, D8887/6/92; D9125/1/13608/50–v.

[62] GA, D9125/1/13612/10.

the expense involved was dependent upon a litigant's behaviour.[63] Smyth paid between 1*s*. and 6*s*. *per* subpoena, but racked up a hefty bill in 1616 because he chose to call twenty-one witnesses, and since it made strategic sense to ensure that servants like William Archard 'make affidavit' that Crokey had been served 'with the injunction', it became necessary to spend even more money, and to pay 3*s*. to ensure that each document was entered upon the official record. Small payments thus reveal tactical decisions, about which of Crokey's associates to chase as hearings approached, about which issues to pursue, and about which evidence to marshal.[64]

The most obvious way in which clerical fees signal Smyth's zeal involves the interrogation of witnesses. He not only made copies of evidence, but also paid for the entire process by which people were examined; preparing interrogatories (4*d*.), purchasing parchment (9*d*.), and paying the clerks who recorded statements (25*d*.), and then engrossing the depositions.[65] Here too, procedural actions reveal strategic choices, because Smyth also paid witnesses' expenses. In 1627 he paid for the diet and horsemeat of witnesses and commissioners for five days, in two locations, at a cost of £16, and then issued subpoenas to fifteen witnesses (20*s*.), spent £3 for these to be served in London, Middlesex, Dorset, and Gloucestershire, and paid 35*s*. to record evidence. He then forked out £6 to cover the charges witnesses incurred travelling to court, £6 'for their attendance before they could be examined', and £6 'in their return home'.[66]

Smyth also interacted with members of his legal team. He regularly recorded traditional fees—3*s*.4*d*. per term—to attorneys, as well as trips 'out of the country . . . to take advice' on issues like 'framing the bill', and he itemised work that lawyers undertook preparing cases and making motions, both substantive and procedural.[67] Smyth felt compelled to pay counsellors to be in court when things *might* happen, or were *expected* to happen, and his use of retainers reflected a determination to be in readiness 'against'—i.e. ahead of—anticipated hearings.[68] Smyth's accounts thus bear witness to the meticulous nature of legal preparations, as lawyers were paid for drafting bills, 'framing' petitions, 'penning' interrogations, and 'drawing' motions, as well as for 'entering' recognizances.[69] Smyth repeatedly paid 'learned counsel' £1–2 for 'opinions', to 'peruse all their books', and to 'frame a perfect breviate', but also paid for documents to be 'perused'—at additional expense—by senior lawyers. Indeed, lawyers often worked from draft

[63] GA, D8887/6/38, 104.

[64] GA, D9125/1/13612/2, 9–10, 13; D8887/6/38, 104; D8887/5/12; D9125/1/13608/70v; D9125/1/13611/8; D8887/8/6.

[65] GA, D9125/1/13612/4, 13.

[66] GA, D8887/6/104.

[67] GA, D8887/5/12, 15; D8887/6/38, 104; D8887/8/58; D9125/1/13612/4, 9.

[68] GA, D9125/1/13612/3–7, 12, 14; D9125/1/13608/29, 32–3, 45, 49, 50–v, 52–v, 54–v, 65–6; D8887/6/104.

[69] GA, D8887/5/12, 15; D8887/6/38, 94, 104; D9125/1/13608/50v, 53; D9125/1/13612/1–3, 8, 12, 15.

bills, or 'heads', that Smyth prepared, and from written 'instructions'. As such, 'instructing' counsel was for Smyth a literal rather than a figurative business.[70]

Occasionally, documents that Smyth prepared for his lawyers survive. These include 'instructions' for Mr Nye (1601), tracing the story of suits back to 1597, and bringing him up to speed with the dispute at the moment when Smyth moved—'on Friday last'—to have Richard Moore committed close prisoner.[71] More intriguing are documents that combine information provided by Smyth, the 'opinions' for which advisers were paid, and questions he posed to lawyers.[72] Once, he traced the early history of the dispute, outlined queries about transactions that had been contested, and noted the answers he received. Smyth then took these opinions and considered hypothetical objections to make his case watertight.[73] Two such 'opinions'—regarding Bishopp's suit (Case 6)—also reveal Smyth's thinking. His half-brother, Anthony Gulson, confirmed the importance of the Chantry Act, identified a parallel case recently contested in Common Pleas, and concluded that Lady Katherine Berkeley's intentions had been 'intermingled with superstition and prayers for the dead'. He advised that the land belonged to the crown because 'there must be a priest or no school'.[74] Gulson reiterated such views in additional 'observations' when Crokey secured an inquiry at Gloucester (September 1617), and his view—based upon the example of Thetford school—was that it was wrong to 'intermeddle' in the running of the school, and that both patron and schoolmaster were entitled to lease its lands.[75] The views of Richard Daston—another lawyer Smyth had known since the 1590s—related to the process for appointing schoolmasters, their duties—including praying 'for the souls of the founder'—and management of the estate. Here we can infer the questions Smyth posed about the impact of earlier legislation, and the clarification he sought about the advice he received, not least about whether grants made by Elizabeth I were 'good'.[76]

IV

Evidence about Smyth questioning his lawyers, and then clarifying and testing their opinions, indicates a willingness to micro-manage the Warrens Court dispute, and a determination not just to finance legal cases, but also to oversee their preparation and execution. Key here was research, and attempts to monitor

70 GA, D9125/1/13612/1–4, 6–8, 13; D8887/6/94, 104; D9125/1/13608/27, 29, 32–3, 49, 50–v, 52.

71 GA, D8887/6/36.

72 GA, D9125/1/12004. See: GA, D9125/1/13611/19v.

73 GA, D8887/6/45.

74 GA, D8887/6/57. See: GA, D8887/5/101.

75 GA, D8887/6/69. For Thetford school: John Herne, *The Lawe of Charitable Uses* (1663), sigs K8v–Lv.

76 GA, D8887/6/56. For Daston: Berkeley, BB108, fos 174, 198v, 213v; BB109, fos 76, 115v; BB110, fo. 1.

the progress of a legal battle waged on many fronts simultaneously, and whether or not such involvement in legal proceedings was normal, Smyth's behaviour indicates how much litigants could have invested in the legal system, and how active it was possible to be in disputation.

In terms of research, Smyth purchased law books—Coke's reports, Rastall and Poulton, Dalton and Littleton, as well as statutes—and delved into the archives for new documents and ancient records.[77] His 'searches' began at the moment Crokey became involved in the dispute, and were crucial to understanding the underlying issues, not least his opinion that school lands had been used for superstitious purposes. They can also be documented fairly precisely.[78] In 1614 and 1615, Smyth paid his 'man' to 'examine books' at London and Gloucester 'in all things ... against Crokey', and he sought a range of relevant documents 'by all means'.[79] In 1616 he paid 2*s*.6*d*. for Edwardian evidence in the 'Beds Office' and the Augmentation Office, and subsequent searches were undertaken in the Petty Bag office, amongst the Close Rolls, and in King's Bench, normally for a few shillings each time.[80] Although some such research related to Smyth's historical interests, he also sought documents about Wotton school dating back to the fourteenth century, and about Crokey. The former involved a search regarding the grant made to Charles Badghot (11*s*.8*d*.), while the latter involved specific cases, motions, and rulings, as well as a petition whereby Crokey asked to proceed '*in forma pauperis*'.[81] Surviving evidence also reveals how Smyth went about such tasks. He paid Mr Clopton for a 'view of Crokey's deed now brought in', and wined and dined Mr Hathway to get another 'view' of the same document. He made a note 'to speak to the clerk that read evidence in the Exchequer', and to get 'full sight of many crabbed deeds'.[82] The fruits of such research are scattered throughout his papers: notes about Wotton school, and about masses conducted by its schoolmasters; genealogies for people involved in the dispute; leases of the school lands; and evidence about how profits from the estate supported the school's 'necessary' functions and 'the maintenance of a priest'.[83]

Smyth clearly knew what evidence he wanted, where to find it, and the uses to which it would be put, and he often noted the precise locations of material he wanted to see, and that would be useful to lawyers. In 1623 he paid 1*s*. to find a copy of an earlier judgment regarding chantry lands, noting that it survived in

[77] Bodl. MS Eng.Misc.e.6, fos 51, 56v, 61v, 83v; D9125/1/13612/1, 14; D9125/1/13608/53; D9125/1/13611/9; D8887/5/6, 18; BL, Add. MS 33588, fo. 63. See also: Chicago UL, MS 1465, folder 2/5.

[78] GA, D9125/1/13608/49; D9125/1/12008, pp. 19–20.

[79] Bodl. MS Eng.Misc.e.6, fo. 89; GA, D8887/8/6; D9125/1/13611/23v; D2957/216/17.

[80] GA, D9125/1/13608/33, 45.

[81] Bodl. MS Eng.Misc.e.6, fo. 113; GA, D9125/1/13612/7–8, 12, 14; D9125/1/13611/19, 23v; D9125/1/13608/46, 65–6; D9125/1/13614; D8887/3/105.

[82] GA, D9125/1/13612/3; D9125/1/13611/23v.

[83] GA, D8887/6/96; D9125/1/11996; D9125/1/13611/7; D4431/2/128/4; D9125/1/13608/70v.

'Mich.12 Jac.Rot.3604'.[84] In 1613 he noted in a 'remembrance' specific records he sought to peruse, and in 1639 gave his son precise instructions about King's Bench records to examine, to see if they would be 'good for me'.[85] Frequent trips to the Tower of London and the Rolls Chapel involved searches to help Thomas Chamberlain construct one particular case, while a 'remembrance' from 1639 records Smyth's desire to take copies of the inquisition 'I like best out of my breviate'.[86] Elsewhere, Smyth referred to the need to 'prove' that he had a 'true copy' of one Exchequer commission, 'and to insert in my brief', and noted the need to 'mend', 'finish', and 'make perfect' his notes; to demonstrate 'what witnesses will depose', and to 'sort the deeds and lay them in order... as they successively follow in the breviate'.[87]

Once cases were prepared and lawyers briefed, Smyth also worked laboriously to ensure things were managed according to his wishes. He scuttled around London, visiting the Three Cups Inn in Bread Street to collect documents sent from Nibley, travelling by water 'about Crokey', and even visiting his adversary in prison. He called at lawyers' chambers 'about Crokey's rule', travelled with Randolph Crew to Whitehall, and dined with lawyers before and during trials.[88] He once doorstepped the Attorney General, Sir Edward Coke, tipping the man who 'kept the door' of Temple Garden, and 'tarrying' Coke *en route* to his chamber, to brief him about particular issues and developments.[89] In 1618, he was so anxious to learn the outcome of an inquiry in Gloucester that he went 'divers times' to the Exchequer office for news. As soon as it arrived, he obtained a copy, retained counsel, and formulated a response.[90] Repeatedly, Smyth made small payments—to Crew's clerk and the Attorney General's doorkeeper and 'bookbearer'—to 'remember' their masters about 'my breviates', 'my decree with Crokey', and the need to secure letters patent for Wotton school.[91]

Occasionally, Smyth prepared an 'estate of my own suits in law', as an *aide memoire*, complete with the names of lawyers and details of cases that 'continueth', as well as of outstanding business. These could be updated each term, even when there was 'nothing done' for terms on end, and Smyth noted bills 'exhibited', actions brought, and pleas submitted, as well as writs despatched, demurrers entered, and writs of errors presented. He also noted decisions reached, from the 'verdict passed with me' at Bristol's assizes to a 'dismission' in Star Chamber, and the judgment for which Richard Moore 'lieth in execution in the Fleet'. Smyth also recorded the occasion when Moore 'arrested me' in Westminster Hall,

[84] GA, D9125/1/13612/3, 8; D8887/5/15.
[85] GA, D9125/1/13611/5, 23–v. See also: GA, D9125/1/13614.
[86] GA, D9125/1/13612/9–10, 12; D9125/1/13611/19v, 23; D9125/1/13608/65–6. See: TNA, SP 14/200, fos 117v, 120–3, 129v, 133, 136v. I am grateful to Nick Popper for this reference.
[87] GA, D8887/8/6; D9125/1/13611/7v, 12, 23–v, 24v; D9125/1/12016.
[88] GA, D9125/1/13612/3–4, 8–9; D9125/1/13608/49–50v.
[89] Berkeley, BB110, fo. 32v.
[90] GA, D9125/1/12008, p. 60.
[91] GA, D9125/1/13612/3, 8; D9125/1/13608/50.

'whereunto I appeared by Mr Gibbs my attorney'.[92] Another such document noted that one King's Bench case was delayed repeatedly from 1600 to 1603, 'and so ever after', and recorded the precise location of records relevant to each case.[93] Smyth's 'remembrances', meanwhile, included notes to chase up specific cases, to decide what to do about 'the concealed rents for Wotton school', and to discover 'what is become of Crokey, if in Fleet', and 'what is become of Ben Crokey'.[94] When matters were delayed, Smyth thought ahead, recording when he was 'expecting the cause to have been heard', when his business was listed 'in the paper of causes', and when matters were due 'to be heard first sitting'.[95]

Smyth's planning reveals that, much as he felt dependent upon legal advice, he was also involved in day-to-day manoeuvres. He was determined 'to show Mr [Henry] Yelverton his old brief' about things 'he intended to give... in evidence'; 'to speak with Mr Clench about readying our evidences'; and 'to see what answer may be framed to the bill and deposition'.[96] Once, Smyth resolved 'to be with Mr Solicitor' (Yelverton) ahead of a Common Pleas hearing, while also noting the need to prepare paperwork 'for divers witnesses'.[97] Elsewhere, Smyth made a note to enquire 'whether we may challenge any juror', and gave precise instructions about using aggressive lines of argument 'in the entrance to his evidence'. He made sure to 'advertise' lawyers about records he had 'taken copies of', and planned 'to distribute into parts each portion of my breviates to my several counsel at a conference on Friday'.[98]

V

Evidence about active participation in all aspects of litigation makes it possible to revisit specific episodes, to observe Smyth assessing his options, and to analyse his tactical thinking. Since this involves dealing with the allegations that his behaviour provoked, it will ultimately be possible to test historiographical claims about the nature and rhetoric of the law in early modern England.

Like Moore before him, Crokey bemoaned being 'crossed' by Smyth's 'practices'—'shifts and delays', 'devices and sleights'—including the repeated and tactical use of injunctions, motions, and demurrers.[99] Smyth was accused of 'surmising false matter' in court to evade rulings and 'stay judgments', of using

[92] GA, D8887/7/21. [93] GA, D8887/6/44.

[94] GA, D9125/1/13611/14–15, 21; D9125/1/13614/2. [95] GA, D8887/6/104.

[96] GA, D9125/1/12008, p. 20; D9125/1/13611/5. For Yelverton: Berkeley, BB107, fos 13v–14, 68v, 70, 103–v; BB108, fos 7v, 10, 17, 33, 39, 58, 145, 187, 198, 206; BB109, fos 27–8, 91v–2, 126; BB110, fo. 23.

[97] GA, D8887/8/6. [98] GA, D9125/1/13611/23v, 24v.

[99] GA, D8887/6/39; Crokey, *Sacred Maiestie*, sigs A2v–3v, B, D2; PA, HL/PO/JO/10/1/24; HL/PO/JO/10/1/37; HL/PO/JO/10/1/274; HL/PO/JO/10/1/296; GA, D9125/1/11996; Crokey, *Contents*, sig. A2; TNA, STAC 8/107/7; Crokey, *Complaint*, sig. B4v.

'indirect dealing' to spin out business, and of having 'earnestly laboured' to avoid trials, and he allegedly sought to 'seduce' plaintiffs and witnesses, and to prolong hearings for hours on end.[100] Claims were repeatedly made that Smyth, knowing Crokey's straightened circumstances, deliberately pursued 'causeless' suits; cases 'wrongfully prosecuted' to 'weary' and 'oppress' him.[101] It was even said that Smyth—like other litigants—*promised* to tire his opponent out with 'vexatious suits in law', and to 'lay' him up 'in prison', with the boast that Crokey 'should remove a mountain' as soon as eject Smyth from Warrens Court.[102] Ultimately, it was said that Smyth showed contempt for 'decrees, orders, rules, [and] verdicts', by declining to withdraw one Chancery suit in the face of an express order to do so, and by refusing to yield possession of land 'according to several rules in court made'. Crokey insisted that such behaviour was recognised and condemned by the authorities, even to the point where it was possible to have him 'committed' to prison 'until he yielded possession'.[103]

This language of vexation and 'oppression'—of attempts to weary opponents and weaken them financially—was entirely familiar, and might easily be regarded as formulaic. However, it is worth observing Smyth's attempts to refute such inflammatory allegations, and evidence that his behaviour could indeed be subtle and tactically thoughtful.[104] Smyth acknowledged that litigants could vary their 'pleadings' in line with 'present advantages', and understood that possibilities existed to speed up or slow down cases.[105] His notes regarding Richard Moore referred to evidence and writs being kept 'in my hands to file *when need shall be* hereafter', and to how he sometimes refrained from pressing home an advantage: 'I did forbear to *non-suit* him'; 'I... *might* have *non-suited* him'. Doing so increased the chances of tying adversaries up in hopeless suits 'ever after'.[106] Occasionally, Smyth can be observed thinking through his options and making contingency plans. He stressed the importance of digging out old breviates in case lawyers were able to 'withstand' moves by Crokey, and one 'remembrance' recorded that 'I think best first to demurr', but also the need to muster evidence '*if* I must answer.' Smyth also appreciated potential difficulties, and wondered whether to 'set forth' the backstory of disputation, whether to pursue the matter 'at the common law', and whether to use a local forum rather than a Westminster court.[107]

[100] Crokey, *Sacred Maiestie*, sigs A4–v, D2; Crokey, *Petition*, p. 3. See: TNA, STAC 5/M52/22.

[101] PA, HL/PO/JO/10/1/37; Crokey, *Sacred Maiestie*, sigs Av, A3; Crokey, *Petition*, pp. 3, 6; Crokey, *Briefe*. See: TNA, C 2/Eliz.M3/53.

[102] GA, D8887/6/67–8; Crokey, *Complaint*, sig. A2v; PA, HL/PO/JO/10/1/296; Crokey, *Petition*, p. 7; Crokey, *Briefe*. See also: GA, D9125/1/12008, p. 78. See: Jones, *Chancery*, p. 349; PA, HL/PO/JO/10/1/36 (John Horseley).

[103] Crokey, *Sacred Maiestie*, sig. B; Crokey, *Contents*, sig. Av.

[104] See: PA: HL/PO/JO/10/1/10 (Richard Vaughan); HL/PO/JO/10/1/24 (Gricell Rogers, Susan Dancye); HL/PO/JO/10/1/31 (Edmund Laysinby); HL/PO/JO/10/1/35 (John Randall).

[105] GA, D9125/1/12008, pp. 14, 78.

[106] GA, D8887/7/21; D8887/6/44.

[107] GA, D9125/1/13611/3–4, 23–v.

Smyth thus demonstrated a capacity to exploit his understanding of different legal avenues, and it is understandable that he was thought to have demonstrated a ruthless streak, and to have pushed the boundaries of acceptable behaviour. He allegedly brought one case—an 'action of trespass'—'without Crokey's privity', such that the matter 'passed by default', not least because Smyth ignored 'an order in Chancery' to halt proceedings.[108] He considered prosecuting Crokey 'for words' (slander), repeatedly noting plans to 'try the action . . . against Crokey' for 'rayling' speeches, and even prepared a King's Bench motion, which he ultimately declined to deploy.[109] He also tried to persuade officials to let him deploy old depositions, even though 'such witnesses . . . are dead', and then mused on the advantages of introducing motions 'the first day of term'.[110] He applied pressure to expedite cases Crokey had begun, but that were 'drooping', using John Bridgman to secure an order forcing Crokey to 'call in' those 'he would have to answer', and then proceed 'termly with effect' (1622). After repeated motions Smyth eventually got the case dismissed, on the grounds that Crokey had 'done nothing to the knowledge of the defendants', and was guilty of 'neglect of prosecution' (June 1624).[111] On other occasions, Smyth used blocking tactics, in ways that reflected contemporary concerns about ruthless litigants.[112] In 1620, he was accused of responding to the Attorney General's case not just with 'untrue suggestions', but also with an injunction—which 'Smyth himself served'—that prevented new proceedings from being instigated by Crokey, whose 'endeavours' for the school were 'utterly defeated' as a result.[113] Such strategies involved guile or legitimate tactics, depending upon one's perspective. Smyth evaded a Privy Council hearing in 1636 by exploiting his knowledge that Crokey needed to return to Ireland, and by sending his son to Windsor to get matters discharged. The same trick was repeated in 1638, his son being accused of making 'false suggestions' before the Court at Oatlands.[114]

What also emerges is more complex strategising. Smyth sometimes sought to postpone hearings in cases he himself initiated, noting in 1615 that, having begun proceedings against Crokey and Joyce Cotterell for maintenance and champerty, he needed to *avoid* a 'trial at law . . . by all means', and that it was his opponents who sought a formal hearing.[115] This provoked claims of vexation, and the possibility emerges that Smyth, recognising his case to be weak, used litigation to respond to Crokey's ongoing Chancery proceedings. On other occasions Smyth responded to legal setbacks—including the rejection of his claims by a

108 Crokey, *Sacred Maiestie*, sig. B4.
109 GA, D9125/1/13614; D9125/1/13612/4, 8; D8887/6/71.
110 GA, D9125/1/13611/23–v.
111 GA, D9125/1/13612/7, 9; D9125/1/12008, p. 64; D9125/1/13608/50–v, 52v.
112 PA, HL/PO/JO/10/1/18 (William Smyth); HL/PO/JO/10/1/30 (Edmund Felton).
113 GA, D9125/1/11996; Crokey, *Sacred Maiestie*, sig. E.
114 Crokey, *Complaint*, sigs B3v, C; GA, S379/2/3/1/3. See: GA, D9125/1/13611/19.
115 GA, D8887/8/6.

Gloucestershire jury (1615)—by *appearing* to be conciliatory. He 'entreated' Crokey to 'take composition', enter arbitration, and accept 'a piece of money', at least while pursuing a 'dismission' of Crokey's Chancery case, and until commencing new suits in Chancery and Star Chamber (Cases 3–4).[116]

Such evidence highlights a disjunction between the perspectives of the two combatants. Crokey claimed that such behaviour involved 'indirect practices', as well as 'vexations and delays', because Smyth's suits revived in new settings the 'self-same' claims that had been dismissed elsewhere. He accused Smyth of suggesting that his deed of assignment from Joyce Cotterell was 'forged', despite it being 'proved' a 'true and sufficient deed... in Chancery and Common Pleas'.[117] Crokey feared that Smyth was forum-shopping, but Smyth dismissed such claims as 'hyperbole', insisting that his tactics were legitimate, not least because Chancery cases could involve fact-finding missions—'to have a deed out of your hands'—rather than trials. Having secured the information he needed, Smyth 'rested satisfied and the suit proceeded no further'.[118] Crokey nevertheless felt that Smyth could not be trusted to deal fairly, suspecting that apparently conciliatory moves were disingenuous. He was thus inclined to reject offers of arbitration that might actually have been genuine, and when Smyth obeyed a court decision to provide a copy of the 'original lease', Crokey refused to accept either the copy or sight of the original, even at a meeting in Thornbury attended by representatives of both sides (January 1615).[119]

VI

Smyth highlights the zeal with which litigants might pursue disputation, and their capacity for strategic thinking. Occasionally, it is also possible to scrutinise claims about the distortion of accepted processes, at least as men like Crokey understood them, and Smyth's behaviour reveals four striking things with wider implications for our understanding of legal processes.

First, Smyth demonstrated a sophisticated appreciation of the entire legal landscape—the terrain of litigation—and strategised individual cases accordingly. He understood what can only rarely be observed from formal legal papers: that apparently separate cases overlapped and interlinked. This is evident from the machinations surrounding Crokey's attempt—via Thomas Baddam (Case 5)—to secure Smyth's 'ejection' from Warrens Court. Smyth's response involved a determination to pursue unfinished suits, pointing out that his own Star

[116] GA, D8887/6/67; D9125/1/13608/54v. See: Jones, *Chancery*, p. 271.

[117] Crokey, *Sacred Maiestie*, sigs B4v–C2, E; GA, D9125/1/11996–7; D8887/6/67. See: Jones, *Chancery*, pp. 438–9.

[118] GA, D9125/1/12008, p. 47. See: Jones, *Chancery*, pp. 214, 455; GA, D9125/1/13611/7.

[119] GA, D8887/6/51–3.

Chamber case against Crokey and Joyce Cotterell was ongoing (Case 4). He was still taking careful steps to pursue this action, by seeking opinions on the 'heads' of a bill, reflecting on possible motions, preparing counsel for expected hearings, and making plans to interrogate Crokey's associate, William Porter, while also considering whether to 'go to commission with . . . Crokey'.[120] Subsequently, Smyth made plans for the moment 'when Crokey's deed is brought into the Star Chamber', resolving to 'examine it' and question other witnesses, including Anthony Hathway, 'as he cometh to sell clothes' (Spring 1617). He sought affidavits to prove that an injunction was issued demanding this document, and that one of Crokey's relatives, Thomas Tempest, had offered to 'bring . . . the deed', so that he could 'obtain an order . . . against Joyce'. Menacingly, Smyth added that he sought a 'legal course', rather than to 'come by the deed . . . suspiciously'.[121]

It was this ongoing activity, and Smyth's sense that Star Chamber proceedings might yet be concluded, which underpinned his determination—noted in his 'remembrance' for Hilary term 1617—to '*fail not* an injunction against Crokey', something he duly secured (15 February).[122] His legal rationale was that Crokey had pursued litigation—'three bills in Chancery' and one in Common Pleas—despite rulings against him, as well as that a Common Pleas ruling would 'prejudicate' Star Chamber 'by a verdict at common law'. Smyth's move—which capitalised upon an important recent decision defending equity courts—infuriated Crokey, who apparently 'never . . . had any notice to show cause why the injunction should be granted'. As such, he spent four years, £400, and 'great vexation and trouble', trying to get it 'dissolved'. As others claimed in similar situations, this involved being 'enforced to attend that court every term with counsel', without success, even though he 'procured four several . . . orders' for hearings into the matter.[123] Crokey grumbled that he struggled to get 'the said cause to be heard', or the injunction 'dissolved', accusing Smyth of wriggling out of court orders and of keeping the injunction 'afoot', to 'weary out this examinant'. Here was a familiar kind of claim: that Smyth chose certain courses of action knowing that Crokey was 'a very poor man and worn out of all his means by the delays and multiplicity of suits'.[124]

Smyth not only worked hard to sustain his injunction, in order to block Baddam's case, but also undertook contingency planning. In 1617 he instructed

[120] GA, D9125/1/13612/2; D9125/1/13608/29, 32–3; D9125/1/13611/7. For Porter, of Bristol and the Middle Temple: Hopwood, *MT Recs*, ii. 495, 600, 642, 669, 676, 714, 733, 743, 745, 755, 767, 799; TNA, PROB 6/16, fo. 146v.

[121] GA, D9125/1/13611/7v–8. For Tempest (*d.*1632): TNA, PROB 11/162, fo. 186v.

[122] GA, D9125/1/13611/7v.

[123] GA, D8887/6/64, 68; D9125/1/11989/13–14, 11994; D9125/1/12008, pp. 48–9; Crokey, *Sacred Maiestie*, sigs Cv–C2. See: PA, HL/PO/JO/10/1/36 (John Horseley); J. H. Baker, 'The common lawyers and the Chancery: 1616', in J. H. Baker, *The Legal Profession and the Common Law* (London, 1986), pp. 205–29.

[124] GA, D8887/6/68. See: PA, HL/PO/JO/10/1/36 (John Horseley).

'Mr [William] Jones to answer any of Crokey's motions', and to 'see the deed brought in', subsequently asking Harvey to respond '*if* Crokey should move to dissolve my injunction'.[125] Smyth was perhaps smoothing the passage of his own litigation, but Crokey was able to offer an alternative explanation of his behaviour. In 1618, when claiming that Smyth had 'impoverished' him with 'causeless suits', Crokey insisted that Smyth's Star Chamber bill involved claims that had already been dismissed, that his own case could not come to 'execution of trial', being 'locked up by an injunction', and that Smyth used 'all the delays he can'.[126] Subsequently, Crokey accused Smyth of deliberately running down the clock, fully aware that Baddam's lease had 'almost expired', and having boasted 'that he would weary him out in suits of law'. Crokey also pointed out that he had 'divers times fee'd his counsel', incurring 'great charges to bring up many witnesses almost 100 miles for a trial', only to find that 'the jury did not all appear'. Smyth's determination to delay, Crokey believed, also involved exploiting a 'frivolous error' in the paperwork; the 'mere suggestion' that the name of a juror, Mr Tippets, had been mis-recorded as *Trippets*.[127]

Crokey's eventual success—in securing sympathy from judges about Smyth's 'sinister practices', and getting the injunction overturned—merely convinced him that Smyth had engaged in sharp practice.[128] Smyth's determination not to let his Star Chamber case be derailed by Baddam's case certainly opened him up to criticism. He was accused of ensuring that even a verdict in Baddam's favour (in 1620) had no meaningful impact, and Crokey complained about being 'delayed in the judgment and altogether defeated'. This reflected Smyth's decision—recorded in his accounts—to submit a motion to 'stay judgment' (Easter 1620), using what Crokey called 'false suggestions', and fully aware that Baddam's five-year lease had 'well-nigh expired'. It was for 'further vexation', Crokey alleged, that Smyth got the matter referred to judges in Common Pleas, ostensibly for 'composing of the differences between them'. He thus gave the impression that he was 'conformable' to the idea of a settlement, to accepting their ruling, and to compensating Crokey if his case was withdrawn. Smyth submitted an affidavit to demonstrate his willingness to 'perform their order and abitrement' (July 1620). However, while the king's order for further meetings with the judges brought renewed hope, Crokey insisted that Smyth's attempt to 'press' for a 'composition' was made in the knowledge that he would refuse, and that such manoeuvring delayed final judgment until after the expiration of Baddam's lease. As such, Crokey 'obtained judgment but no possession'.[129]

125 GA, D9125/1/13611/8; D9125/1/13612/3; D8887/6/64–5.

126 GA, D8887/6/67.

127 GA, D8887/6/68; D9125/1/11996; Crokey, *Sacred Maiestie*, sigs C2v, D3, D4v.

128 Crokey, *Sacred Maiestie*, sigs C, E; GA, D9125/1/11996–7.

129 GA, D8887/6/65, 86; D9125/1/12008, pp. 51, 54; D9125/1/11996–7; D9125/1/13608/49, 52–v; D9125/1/13612/4; Crokey, *Sacred Maiestie*, sigs C2v, D2v–D3v, D4v, E; Crokey, *Petition*, pp. 3–4; Crokey, *Briefe*.

The second thing to emerge from Smyth's behaviour is evidence of blocking and delaying tactics, another area where contemporary allegations involved more than just inflamed rhetoric.[130] Following the dismissal of his Star Chamber case in 1619 (Case 4), Smyth allegedly 'practiced and wrought' so that Crokey could not get costs 'taxed', despite 'orders in open court', not least that costs should be *increased* because of Smyth's delays.[131] Here too, Smyth's papers verify such claims. His 'remembrance' for Michaelmas 1620 included a note to 'have a care about the costs in the Star Chamber int. Crokey', while accounts reveal that Edward Trotman was repeatedly instructed to 'attend' to Crokey's motions for 'taxing of costs in Star Chamber'. That Smyth wanted this to be done on the 'last day of term'—in Michaelmas 1621, Hilary 1622, and Hilary 1623—suggests a determination to cause maximum delay.[132] Here too, Crokey sensed sharp practice, and the last of these moves—which cost Smyth £5, excluding the fee for copying the discharge—prompted an accusation that Smyth used 'untrue informations' and 'false suggestions and practices'. Smyth petitioned Lord Keeper Williams to get costs waived, claiming that his Star Chamber suit was dismissed because Crokey had a Common Pleas case pending, not because of 'the merits of the cause'. Crokey insisted that the decision to discharge Smyth was made without his 'privity', and without informing his lawyers, and when such claims 'incensed' the Lord Keeper, Crokey grumbled about Williams being 'abused'.[133] Moreover, while Smyth could not always evade 'costs', this was not for want of trying, and the whole business proved time-consuming and expensive for all concerned. Smyth delayed paying costs of £6 awarded to Crokey in 1615, following the failure of the Common Pleas suit regarding champerty (Case 2), until November 1623, after a last ditch attempt to get a reprieve.[134] More often, Smyth's delays—which hampered a poor opponent's ability to litigate—obliged Crokey to make regular motions in the hope of forcing Smyth's hand, only for his hopes to be dashed by the very delays that Smyth caused. In May 1629, Crokey's counsel (Mr Brierley) asked that he should 'now be admitted to prefer a bill of costs', regarding the dismissal of Star Chamber proceedings 'ten years since', only to discover that judges 'did not hold fit after so long time, and after so many orders made to the contrary'.[135]

Obstruction was also evident in other ways, giving Crokey grounds to claim that 'practices' had undermined various inquiries into 'charitable uses'. Crokey apparently worked hard to muster witnesses and jurors, only for hearings to be

[130] See: PA, HL/PO/JO/10/1/16 (Thomas Fuller); HL/PO/JO/10/1/24 (Edward Osbaldeston); HL/PO/JO/10/1/25 (Anthony Maine).

[131] Crokey, *Sacred Maiestie*, sigs C2–v.

[132] GA, D9125/1/13614; D9125/1/13608/45, 49; D9125/1/13612/6; D9125/1/12008, p. 51.

[133] FLS, Z.e.1(27); GA, D9125/1/13608/49–50v; D9125/1/12008, pp. 52–3, 58; Crokey, *Sacred Maiestie*, sigs C2–v.

[134] GA, D9125/1/13612/8.

[135] GA, D8887/6/103.

'interrupted' repeatedly, such that commissions were 'lost', along with 'all his labour and charge'.[136] In 1618 Crokey blamed Smyth for the fact that, of four commissions appointed only one was 'executed', noting that his opponent 'brought never a witness to be examined'.[137] He also complained that, having 'paid the charge' for yet another inquiry, Smyth used similar 'practices' to delay matters for months.[138] Such claims were plausible because Smyth admitted that, following an abortive hearing in Gloucester (September 1617), he delayed the next hearing until December, by insisting that 'necessary employments' would keep him 'out of the county till the end of Michaelmas term'. Smyth subsequently protested that he could not attend the 1619 commission at Thornbury, having only received the warrant—dated 22 March—on 1 April, the day before hearings were due to commence. This meant he was unable to be 'present and prepared with counsel or evidence'.[139]

More often, evidence lends credence to Crokey's allegations about Smyth's tactics. In 1618, when Smyth secured a commission into 'concealed lands', Crokey turned up at Thornbury on 20 April with one of the commissioners he had chosen—John Dowle of Over—only to find that Smyth 'came not', having declined to examine witnesses or nominate commissioners 'on his part'. Crokey also claimed that Smyth sought yet another commission, 'of purpose to delay this examinant and the rest of the defendants'.[140] When Crokey responded to the failed Thornbury hearing by pressing Lord Chancellor Bacon for a new inquiry (June 1619), Smyth's lawyer Anthony Gulson persuaded the court to deny Crokey's request. He insisted that a new inquiry was unnecessary, given the findings of earlier investigations, and prompted Crokey's censure by persuading judges that he had admitted under oath that the lands were 'concealed'.[141]

Smyth's delaying tactics also became evident when Crokey's desperation led him to get matters referred to Archbishop Abbot and the bishops of London and Winchester (June 1619), who summoned Smyth to answer 'matters . . . exhibited' and then 'certified' his 'practices to suppress the school'.[142] Smyth allegedly refused to appear at Lambeth until 'four several warrants' had been issued, knowing that 'many witnesses' had been 'brought up to London' to Crokey's 'great trouble and charge', and that lawyers had been paid 'divers times' ahead of the scheduled hearing.[143] Here too Smyth blamed pressing business, and sought 'dispensation for a few days', but his professed willingness to attend a later hearing—insisting that 'no subject liveth' more ready to 'acquit' himself 'of this

[136] Crokey, *Sacred Maiestie*, sigs C2v–3. See: Christine Churches, '"The most unconvincing testimony": the genesis and historical usefulness of the country depositions in Chancery', *Seventeenth Century*, 11.2 (1996), 209–27.

[137] GA, D8887/6/67. [138] Crokey, *Sacred Maiestie*, sigs C3–v.

[139] GA, D9125/1/12008, pp. 65–7. [140] GA, D8887/6/66.

[141] GA, D8887/6/74–5; Crokey, *Sacred Maiestie*, sigs D–Dv; GA, D9125/1/12008, pp. 58–9, 68.

[142] GA, D9125/1/11996. [143] Crokey, *Sacred Maiestie*, sig. Dv.

malicious accusation'—was accompanied by a request to delay matters until his own case against Crokey—'now to be heard . . . in the Star Chamber'—was underway (Case 4).[144]

Smyth's willingness to block official investigations also emerged following the decision to establish another commission of charitable uses (November 1620). Perhaps sensing trouble, Smyth instructed John Bridgman to hasten the completion of the Attorney General's case against both himself and Crokey, claiming that Crokey 'doth not endeavour to bring the cause to a speedy hearing'. Smyth was once again successful, and it was ordered that this vital case should be 'heard the next term upon one of his lordship's days'.[145] Finally, Smyth was accused of delaying the outcome of the commission—under the bishops of Worcester, Bristol and Gloucester—granted to Crokey in June 1621.[146] This was the inquiry, Crokey insisted, which 'discovered and certified' Smyth's 'practices in the suppression of the school', decreed that the estate was 'misemployed', and resolved that lands should be restored to the school's use, 'according to the true meaning of the donor', even if it referred matters to Parliament for final adjudication (September 1621). Smyth responded—'for further delay' said Crokey—by getting permission to submit 'exceptions' (December 1621), something he had considered doing during the inquiry itself, before deciding to 'waive and relinquish them'. Doing so *after* findings became clear forced Crokey to submit a reply, to which Smyth was able to offer a 'replication' in early 1622. This ensured that Smyth's day of reckoning—a hearing where Lord Keeper Williams and Judge Hutton declared his exceptions 'idle and frivolous', and proposed to 're-establish' Wotton school—was deferred until July 1622.[147] Smyth then secured another commission to survey the lands, and when this produced more favourable results he paid Attorney General Coventry to move for a new hearing (December 1622).[148]

A third key aspect of Smyth's behaviour involved successful 'practices' becoming pervasive features of legal culture. Similar excuses and explanations were employed by his descendants—and those with whom they were accused of conspiring—when the business was taken up in Parliament by Sarah Crokey. Responding to a summons to appear before the Lords—dated 5 October 1648—John Smyth junior insisted that he only received the order on 21 October, that the petition was 'very long', and that matters had been contested in 'all the courts' for 'more than three score years', before being settled in 1623. He denied being a party to the contest, and protested about the need to 'peruse very great numbers of

[144] GA, D8887/6/77–9.

[145] Crokey, *Sacred Maiestie*, sigs E–v; GA, D9125/1/11996, 12002, 12008, pp. 23–4.

[146] GA, D8887/6/85; Crokey, *Sacred Maiestie*, sig. Ev.

[147] GA, D9125/1/12008, p. 68; D9125/1/13612/6; *LJ*, iii. 170–1, 173–4; Crokey, *Sacred Maiestie*, sigs B, E2v–4v; GA, D8887/6/87; PA, HL/PO/JO/10/1/24; HL/PO/JO/10/1/37; TNA, C 93/8/21. See: GA, D2957/354/8.

[148] GA, D9125/1/13608/52v; PA, HL/PO/JO/10/1/26.

deeds, writings, and ... records', many of which were 'dispersed', before submitting a 'full answer'. Smyth even bemoaned living 'near 100 miles distance from Westminster', claiming that witnesses were 'not able to travel without apparent danger of their lives'.[149] Similar pleas were made by his associates, Thomas and Aldworth Elbridge, and Nathaniel Cole, who insisted that 'much time' would be required to prepare their case.[150]

Fourthly, Smyth's behaviour suggests that, in the world of early modern litigation, tactics and practices were sometimes more sinister, involving entrapment and conspiracy. Crokey perceived that, having 'practised' to obtain a ruling that Warrens Court consisted of 'concealed' lands, Smyth tried to 'intrap' him, so that he might 'forbear' further activity 'on behalf of the school'. He allegedly 'confederated' with two men—Sir John Poyntz and Henry Minors—who had been empowered to hunt for concealed lands, and 'so handled' the matter that they were appointed to an Exchequer commission at Tetbury (August 1618). After delaying proceedings—when Crokey presented the opinions of Attorney General Yelverton and Solicitor General Coventry that the lands were 'free from superstitious uses' and not liable to pass to the crown—Poyntz and Minors apparently 'laboured' to 'draw' Crokey towards a 'composition'. Crokey 'utterly refused', but they did not give up, renewing their offer at the Wickwar inquiry, 'by the procurement of Smyth' (October 1618). Crokey later protested that, 'not meaning to defraud the school', he resisted such pressure and defended the school 'in all he might', only for jurors to declare the lands 'concealed' through Smyth's 'indirect and unlawful' pressure, against their 'precise knowledge'.[151] It was in the wake of this hearing that Crokey apparently made the fateful decision to accept the offer to compound, something he later regretted. The idea was to grant him 'a fee farm of the ... lands in Nibley' (52 acres, with rent of 40*s. per annum*), as 'recompense for his pains and testimony', in return for accepting the inquiry's findings. Crokey later claimed that Poyntz and Minors exploited his difficult position—'knowing your poor subject to be the only opponent therein'—in order to 'draw him from defending the school ... by Smyth's plot and practice'.[152]

At this point evidence about the Wickwar hearing becomes murky, because Smyth and Crokey *both* claimed credit for overturning the inquiry's findings. For Crokey, this revealed Smyth's 'craft in dawbing', and deluding the court into recording that this decision was effected by his lawyers, rather than by Crokey's counsel. Crokey claimed that Smyth 'foisted' this falsehood upon the court and 'the country', and only 'began to make a show of a pious intent'—by

149 GA, D8887/6/108; *LJ*, x. 580; PA, HL/PO/JO/10/1/277; GA, D9125/1/12008, p. 63.
150 GA, D8887/6/107.
151 Crokey, *Sacred Maiestie*, sigs A3v, C3v–4; GA, D9125/1/11996. See: *CSPD 1611–18*, p. 499; *CD 1621*, vii. 343–4.
152 GA, D9125/1/11996; Crokey, *Sacred Maiestie*, sigs C4–v; GA, D9125/1/12002; TNA, STAC 8/107/7. See: GA, D9125/1/12008, p. 55; D8887/6/61.

re-establishing the school—upon recognising that his 'plot' with Poyntz and Minors 'would not take'.[153] Moreover, while Smyth agreed that Crokey had entered into an agreement with Poyntz and Minors, he denied being a 'practiser' with them, denied 'foisting' his lawyer's name into the official record, and denied orchestrating the Tetbury inquiry. Smyth claimed to have missed the hearing 'in regard of my harvest works', and was apparently in London during proceedings at Wickwar ('eighty miles from that place'), professing to know 'as little or less of that meeting'. He insisted that Crokey was 'the only person to submit evidence', that he only heard about the verdict during a chance meeting with Poyntz, and that his lawyers quickly deemed it 'insufficient', whereupon he devoted 'labour' and 'charges' to overturning it with 'several motions . . . at the Exchequer bar'. Smyth dismissed Crokey's claims in trenchant style, describing his account as 'counterfeit bastardly stuff', and asking 'Fye, Mr Crokey, fye for shame, can anything more impudently be spoken?'[154]

Smyth's forthright rhetoric once again masked a complex reality. He insisted that he could produce the order which declared the inquiry void (citing 'manifest imperfections'), and that Yelverton would testify that it was his lawyer, Bridgman, who caused this to happen. However, he conceded that Crokey was present on that occasion, and evidence from a friend suggests that Smyth distanced himself from the Wickwar hearing disingenuously.[155] Reporting upon the hearing, Henry Townshend noted that Poyntz was one of the commissioners, that Smyth was represented by his servant, William Archard, and that 'the jury found for the king', expressing satisfaction precisely because 'some friends of mine' who 'served in that jury . . . told me *you had made sure work* beforehand, or else they should have had no verdict'.[156]

VII

Townshend's letter provides a useful point at which to reflect upon Smyth's approach to disputation, and upon early modern litigation. This chapter has argued that, in the absence of explicit statements about aims and ambitions, Smyth's day-to-day behaviour—recorded in financial accounts, 'remembrances', notes, and correspondence—reveals his zeal for the dispute with Crokey, as well as his strategic thinking and tactical skill. The extraordinary expense of time and money—upon a powerful legal team—entailed a huge commitment, as did his involvement in every aspect of each suit, and his monitoring of proceedings financially and logistically. In micro-managing litigation, Smyth grappled with the complexities involved in interlocking and overlapping suits, and with the

153 Crokey, *Sacred Maiestie*, sig. C4v.
154 GA, D9125/1/12008, pp. 56, 59–63; D8887/6/77–9.
155 GA, D9125/1/12008, pp. 60–2.
156 GA, D8887/6/72 (emphasis added).

pressures and risks involved, reflecting tactically upon options and how best to proceed, making choices and reflecting upon success and failure. By moving beyond the ostensible causes and claims that emerge from formal records, observing how litigants engaged in disputation, and deducing how they thought about individual suits and the legal terrain, it is possible to understand not just why disputes became protracted, but also how litigation was viewed by those involved.

What also becomes clear is that Smyth's tactics, like those of other litigants, were controversial. Reconstructing how he and Crokey reflected on specific incidents involves complex twists and turns, and contradictory claims, and there is no easy way to distinguish between fraud, sharp practice, and legitimate manoeuvring. Nevertheless, such analysis helps to reveal how litigation was understood, and why men like Smyth and Crokey pursued their dispute for so long.[157] While the aim has not been to assess the truth of rival claims, it has been suggested that Crokey and Smyth had reasons to do what they did, could rationalise their actions, and felt justified in criticising each other. Here too, a deeper understanding of what litigation meant for contemporaries, how it was approached, and what might be expected from it, requires situating individual cases within the wider context of disputation, and treating the claims litigants made as something other than mere rhetoric.

As such, this chapter has demonstrated that protagonists sometimes had clear and distinct perspectives on the law being waged, and on how disputation was being conducted, and viewpoints that were more or less incompatible with those of their adversaries. To the extent that such perspectives can be recovered and comprehended, it is possible to discern distinct visions and expectations of the legal system, and to understand why litigants became so exercised and frustrated. On this occasion, what Crokey considered to be vexatious behaviour, or at least sharp practice, was what Smyth considered to be legally legitimate. What Crokey considered to be 'indirect practice' was what Smyth considered to be tactical skill. Here, it is notable that Smyth commended as 'prudent' the activities with which Lord Berkeley 'blindfolded the eyes' of judges and lawyers, and which affirmed that 'necessity makes men skilful artists who never meant to have practised.'[158] Such differences of opinion related not just to the substance of the dispute but also to the manner in which it was conducted, and contrasting perceptions about the processes and practices of litigation served to increase tension, and to animate, prolong, and deepen the dispute. To the extent that Townshend's letter revealed Smyth's willingness to make 'sure work' of influencing juries, it also provides the launchpad for an investigation not just of Smyth's 'practices', but also his 'powerfulness'.

[157] Jones, *Chancery*, pp. 432–3.

[158] Smyth, *Lives*, ii. 167–8, 190. See also: ibid., 192, 245, 330.

4

'Power and wicked practices'

Influence, Intimidation, and Imprisonment

On 2 September 1586, Richard Moore was ejected from Warrens Court by George and Giles Veyners and John Garlicke. According to the ensuing lawsuit, this was done—at the behest of John Drew—through 'riotous means', which involved breaking a window with 'weapons invasive and defensive', in 'warlike manner', such that Moore was dispossessed 'forcibly and violently'. Moore described Garlicke and the Veyners as men of undesirable 'behaviour and conversation', who had stolen a silver cup from the Horse Head tavern in Bristol, and committed 'robbery by the highway side'. The defendants denied such claims, insisting that they acted in accordance with a Chancery decree, and that Drew's agents merely 'pulled out a loose combe of a window and so entered'.[1] What followed, however, was more complicated. Moore secured an indictment at the quarter sessions (April 1587), and planned to return to Nibley, only to find that John and Grace Drew, having 'intelligence' of his plan, 'assembled...in most riotous manner'. Alongside 'disordered persons', and armed with guns, swords, bows, and arrows, they chose to 'forcibly and violently... resist' a delegation led by the deputy sheriff, using 'malicious and contemptuous words', and threatening to 'kill and murder' anyone who helped Moore. Drew apparently stood guard, 'with a rapier or sword drawn', exclaiming he would 'kill or be killed' rather than yield possession, while Grace issued orders to 'throw out scalding water and stones'. Moore was allegedly 'hurt in the head with an arrow shot out of the house', and was in 'great peril and despair of his life'. The result was yet another legal case, in which John, Grace and others were interrogated about what weapons had been used, about who had fired at Moore, and about who had given the order to do so. Such language—of riot, and of weapons offensive and defensive—is often said to be formulaic, involving things that needed to be said to justify a Star Chamber hearing, but on this occasion it was verifiable and justifiable. Drew, who felt threatened by 'the subtle and sinister devices then and long before daily practised', admitted enlisting men to 'make fast the doors'. Grace admitted resisting the sheriff's men, at her husband's command, with 'small ordinary weapons'. She even admitted that Moore was injured by an

[1] TNA, STAC 5/M13/19.

The Madman and the Churchrobber: Law and Conflict in Early Modern England. Jason Peacey, Oxford University Press.
 DOI: 10.1093/oso/9780192897138.003.0005

arrow 'shot from the house', and that stones and scalding water were cast at people 'breaking into the house'.[2]

This dramatic episode introduces the issues addressed by this chapter, which involve allegations not just about 'indirect practices', but also about the 'powerfulness' of Drew and Smyth.[3] Complaining about an adversary who was 'potent both in purse and friends' was a frequent theme for Crokey, as it was for other aggrieved litigants, but it also involved allegations that were accepted by the authorities. For Crokey, Smyth's 'practices' were not just sharp but also 'vile', 'foul', and 'impious', and Smyth reputedly left nothing 'unattempted to keep down and ruinate' him, even to the point of trying 'to have his life'.[4] This chapter explores how Smyth's campaign was said to have involved ruthlessness, the abuse of power and influence, and corruption, as well as the use of intimidation, imprisonment, and force. It also examines how such allegations—relating to behaviour with which Smyth was familiar—informed litigants' perceptions of their dispute and each other.[5]

As with the discussion of 'indirect' practices, analysis of 'vile' and 'foul' behaviour involves methodological and historiographical challenges. This chapter questions the idea that common claims about bad behaviour involved mere rhetoric, uncovers evidence that they could be based in fact, and moves beyond simply focusing upon violence and 'corruption'. The latter is a problematic term for legal and political historians, given 'difficulties of fact and interpretation' and the problem of recovering contemporary norms, and debates have arguably become bogged down in discussions about the 'severity' of dysfunctional behaviour, and the polarised perspectives of 'optimists' and 'pessimists'. Here it is argued that well-documented episodes like the Warrens Court dispute make it possible to reflect upon contemporary standards of conduct, and upon a broader discourse of 'power' and 'powerfulness', of which violence and corruption were specific manifestations. This chapter identifies disagreements about how men like Smyth wielded 'undue' influence within local communities, manipulated legal processes, and 'confederated' with allies and associates, and also behaved in intimidatory ways. It argues that interrogating the perceptions and realities of 'power' provides insights into the minds of Smyth and Crokey—the latter of whom might easily be regarded as one of those disappointed and disgruntled litigants who 'tended . . . to

[2] TNA, STAC 5/M5/23; STAC 5/M50/37; STAC 5/M52/22.

[3] See: Churches, 'Putting women', p. 54; Churches, 'Equity', p. 75; Churches, 'Business at law', p. 942; Churches, 'False friends', p. 63.

[4] Crokey, *Sacred Maiestie*, sigs A2, D2, E, Fv, G4v, H3; GA, D9125/1/11996–7, 11989/14; PA, HL/PO/JO/10/1/24; HL/PO/JO/10/1/274; Crokey, *Contents*, sigs Av, A2v; Crokey, *Complaint*, sigs B4, Cv; Crokey, *Petition*, pp. 7, 12. See: PA, HL/PO/JO/10/1/17A (Sir Ralph Hansby); HL/PO/JO/10/1/25 (John Chapman); HL/PO/JO/10/1/26 (Alice Fowler); William Cole, *A Rod for the Lawyers* (1659), p. 10.

[5] See: Smyth, *Lives*, ii. 314.

blame their legal misfortunes on . . . bias or corruption'—and into more widespread contestation over acceptable and unacceptable behaviour.[6]

I

The place to begin is not with allegations of force and violence, but with suggestions that Smyth's mobilised, and exploited his influence with, friends and neighbours, including people over whom he exercised power. Such claims featured frequently in contemporary petitions, and notice has already been paid to the accusation that Smyth procured Bishopp—'a friend' and 'chamber fellow'—to bring a case that served his interests (Case 6).[7] This is indicative of a wider pattern, in terms of getting men to attend hearings, and taking informal advice from neighbours and kinsmen, and although such behaviour was integral to early modern life it could also be regarded as problematic.[8]

Key here were servants like William Archard, upon whom Smyth relied heavily for many years. Archard was in charge of Smyth's affairs in Gloucester during 'my absence' in London, and delivered warrants and subpoenas to the people Smyth planned to interrogate or prosecute. According to an affidavit submitted in April 1619, Archard visited Crokey and the bed-ridden Joyce Cotterell on Easter Eve, to deliver a writ summoning them both to a Star Chamber hearing on 23 April.[9] Archard also spent time in London, sometimes armed with Smyth's 'remembrances', and his expenses reveal how assiduous he was in promoting litigation. Archard examined a Star Chamber decree regarding Wotton school (1623), and was responsible for 'orders, searches and attachments', for which he earned 20*s.* (1627). He was clearly a loyal factotum.[10]

More controversial was Peter Bird, sometime undersheriff of Gloucester and examiner in the Council of the Marches. He was one of Smyth's tenants, and was described by Crokey as one of the 'practicers' in 'designs for supplanting the school'; one of 'his instruments always ready to execute any evil act'.[11] Complaints

[6] Wilfrid Prest, 'Judicial corruption in early modern England', *P&P*, 133 (1991), 69, 72, 77–8. See also: Christine Carpenter, 'Law, justice and landowners in Late Medieval England', *Law and History Review*, 1 (1983), 205–37; Mark Knights, 'Anticorruption in seventeenth- and eighteenth-century Britain', in Ronald Kroeze et al., eds, *Anti-Corruption in History* (Oxford, 2017), pp. 1–34. See also: Laura Flannigan, 'Litigants and the English 'Court of Poor Men's Causes,' or Court of Requests, 1515–25', *Law and History Review*, 38.2 (2020), 303–37.

[7] Crokey, *Sacred Maiestie*, sig. Cv. See: PA, HL/PO/JO/10/1/31 (Thomas Chambers); 10/1/37 (Nicholas Cayford).

[8] GA, D9125/1/13611/23v; D9125/1/12008, p. 77.

[9] Bodl. MS Eng.Misc.e.6, fos 94, 106, 107, 117, 125; GA, D9125/1/13612/15; D8887/6/81, 93; D9125/1/12008, p. 65. For Archard: TNA, PROB 11/187, fo. 239.

[10] GA, D9125/1/13611/11v–12, 15, 18, 21, 23; D9125/1/13612/3, 8, 12–13; D9125/1/13608/76v.

[11] Crokey, *Sacred Maiestie*, sigs E2, H3v; *HMC Thirteenth Report, Appendix 4* (London, 1892), pp. 251–2.

about adversaries 'practising' with officials were not uncommon, and although Smyth professed amazement about allegations against such a 'worthy gentleman', Bird certainly provided invaluable assistance, liaising with lawyers, checking documents, and collecting 'schoolhouse money'. Smyth made notes about the need 'to confer with Peter Bird', sometimes described as his 'attorney'; Bird was paid for his services, drank and dined with Smyth, and accompanied him on business trips.[12] Crokey's concern was that Bird was working for Smyth while also being a local official, and that he engaged in dubious activities.[13] Bird attended the 1615 Thornbury hearing, where Crokey suspected an attempt to trick him over the 'original lease', and did so on Smyth's behalf. When he reported back, Bird explained that he had planned to deliver 'your letter', *if* a sufficient number of commissioners had turned up.[14] Bird also represented Smyth at the controversial Wickwar hearing about concealed lands (alongside other allies like Robert Smyth (mayor of Wotton), John Garlicke, and William Archard), reporting how one commissioner, Sir John Stafford, 'departed . . . before the verdict was given', and indicating that nobody provided evidence, 'saving . . . Benjamin Crokey'.[15]

Crokey also worried that Smyth was 'powerful in the county', a view shared by the bishops who commented upon the 'powerfulness' that stemmed from 'his employment under the lord Berkeley'.[16] In the 1590s, John Drew had called upon the support of local powerbrokers, including a JP and sometime MP, Matthew Poyntz, and Smyth acknowledged his reliance upon men like Thomas Adams of Wotton, who alerted him to claims that Warrens Court consisted of concealed lands. Crokey insisted that such relationships rested upon Smyth's 'power'.[17] He claimed that 'the chief of the town' in Wotton, and in 'the country' thereabouts, wanted to testify to Smyth's 'vile practices in abuse of the school', but that 'none of them . . . durst show themselves' because Smyth was 'so powerful'.[18] Such power, he feared, made it difficult to get a fair hearing, and any local jury that ruled in his favour—like the one which declared his assignment from Joyce Cotterell a 'true and sufficient deed'—was said to have done so *despite* being made up of Berkeley's tenants and Smyth's neighbours.[19] Here too, the bishops who investigated the dispute recognised the importance of a new commission having a 'sufficient' jury.[20]

[12] GA, D9125/1/12008, pp. 58–9, 12018; D9125/1/13608/24, 27, 41, 45, 49; D9125/1/13612/4, 8–9, 11–12, 14–15; D8887/6/6, 58; D8887/8/6. See: PA, HL/PO/JO/10/1/24 (Susan Dancye).

[13] GA, D9125/1/13612/1. [14] GA, D8887/6/51–3.

[15] GA, D9125/1/12008, p. 55; D8887/6/70, 72.

[16] PA, HL/PO/JO/10/1/24; HL/PO/JO/10/1/296; GA, D9125/1/11989/14; TNA, STAC 8/107/7; Crokey, *Petition*, p. 6.

[17] GA, D8887/6/15; D9125/1/12008, p. 19.

[18] Crokey, *Petition*, p. 2; BL, Harl. MS 6803, fos 56v–7.

[19] Crokey, *Sacred Maiestie*, sig. C; GA, D8887/6/67; D9125/1/11994; TNA, STAC 8/274/8.

[20] GA, D9125/1/11989/14.

Such suspicions also fuelled Crokey's doubts about the school's management after its re-foundation. Smyth insisted that upon advice from the bishop of Gloucester (Dr Smith), his chancellor (Dr Seaman), and the authorities in Wotton—as well as 'the better part of the inhabitants... in Nibley'—he entrusted the lands to twenty-five 'principal inhabitants', to generate funds for the master, the poor, and local tradesmen, as well as for binding their children as apprentices. This was central to Smyth's claim that he sought 'the final settling and preservation of the school'.[21] Crokey mocked the new arrangements precisely because of Smyth's local eminence, claiming that the school was established 'in his own name, and for his own glory'. He likened the appointment of trustees, and the endowment of scholarships, to 'dissembled piety and bounty', referring to Smyth's 'false foundation of the school'.[22]

If Smyth was—and was perceived to be—'powerful', then this was an image he cultivated. Crokey noted that Smyth 'caused 300 little pamphlets to be printed', containing prayers to be 'used daily by the schoolmaster', complaining these were prayers *for* Smyth, as 'the only preserver of the said school', which were 'published' and 'dispersed... over the whole country' (Fig. 5).[23] Smyth's papers confirm this claim, and Smyth told Crokey that he should not 'reprehend their poetry or flattery too censoriously, nor me of ambition or vain glory, for avowing the same as *due unto me*'.[24] He also produced a substantial tract about the dispute, which was begun in 1626 (when he paid 2*s*.6*d*. for paper 'to write my answer to Crokey's libelling book'), but which was not completed until the early 1630s (Fig. 6).[25] This was carefully calibrated, and while Smyth was not averse to inflamed rhetoric—some allegations were dismissed as 'beggarly trash'—it was mostly restrained. It seems only to have been intended for scribal circulation, within a discreet community of readers, and its tone was measured. Smyth begged 'pardon for adventuring upon this paper course', which he 'disliked', but sought to rescue a reputation 'insufferably traduced' and 'exposed to ignominy and reproach', hoping that this apologetical tone would lead readers to 'favourably accept his just defence'. Smyth's style was mostly careful, as befitted a scholar: he reproduced, and made precise references to, judgments, decrees, certificates, and court orders, 'which you may read' in 'the register's office'. Smyth intended his account to be verifiable.[26]

Smyth's book is suggestive of a determined but methodical approach, and of his willingness and ability to influence people. He wined and dined key individuals,

[21] GA, D9125/1/12008, pp. 20–1; S379/2/2/1/3.
[22] Crokey, *Sacred Maiestie*, sig. D. See also: GA, D9125/1/12008, p. 35.
[23] Crokey, *Complaint*, sig. A4v; Crokey, *Petition*, p. 7. The printed version does not survive, although Smyth's papers contain a manuscript: GA, D9125/1/12006. For their printing and distribution, see: GA, D9125/1/12008, p. 36; D9125/1/12024, 13612/1.
[24] GA, D9125/1/12008, p. 36 (emphasis added).
[25] GA, D9125/1/12008, 13612/104; D8887/6/104.
[26] GA, D9125/1/12008, pp. 1, 33–4, 42, 53–4.

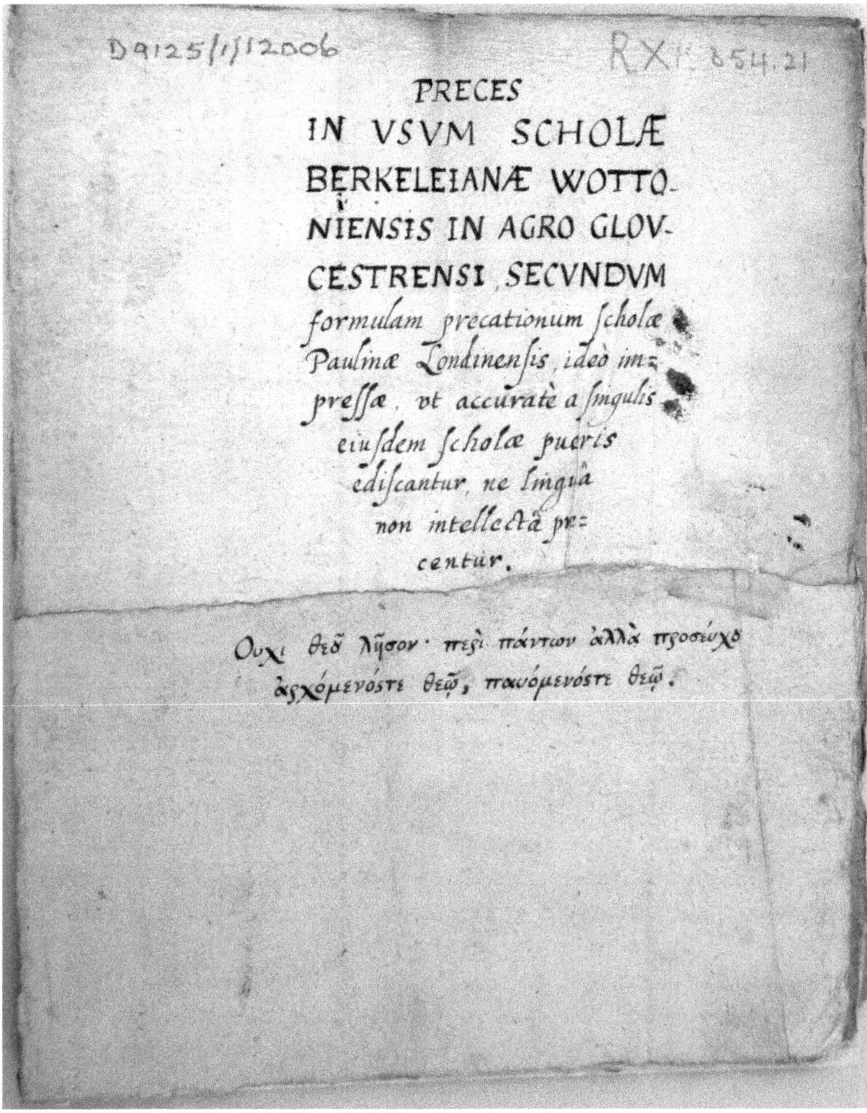

Fig. 5. 'Preces in usum scholae Berkeleianae Wottoniensis' (*c.*1624). Gloucestershire Archives, D9125/1/12006. Reproduced by permission of Gloucestershire Archives.

and presented them with gifts. It has already been noted how he entertained Anthony Hathway, to get sight of Crokey's deed with Joyce Cotterell, and ingratiated himself with archivists, but his accounts suggest a more general trend. One gift was made to the Warden of the Fleet, for unspecified reasons (1617), but more transparent were other presents: pies to judges 'in all things' in 1621 (28*s.*), lambs and lampreys to judges in 1627 (22*s.*6*d.*), and two lambs, two carps, and two jacks,

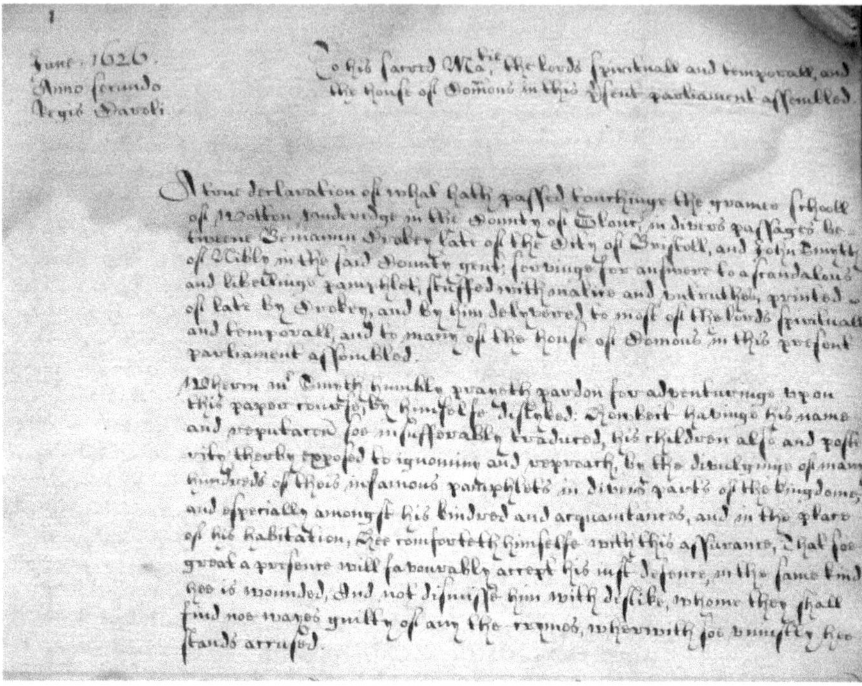
June 1626.
Anno secundo
Regis Caroli

To his sacred Ma[jes]tie, the lords spirituall and temporall, and
the House of Commons in this present parliament assembled.

Fig. 6. John Smyth, 'To his sacred Ma[jes]tie, the lords spirituall and temporall, and the House of Commons' (1626). Gloucestershire Archives, D9125/1/12008. Reproduced by permission of Gloucestershire Archives.

as well as six lamprey pies, to Sir John Finch, Speaker of the 1628 Parliament (29*s*.2*d*.).[27] Another lawyer, Francis Harvey, was given one of Smyth's scholarly works, alongside repeated gifts of tobacco, while another, Gerrard, received a sugar loaf.[28] Such gifts were obviously conventional, and to the extent that contemporaries thought them compatible with legal impartiality they were not intrinsically problematic. Nevertheless, they prompted concern, and Crokey was not alone in worrying what they meant, not least in 1621, when the issue received considerable parliamentary attention.[29] They certainly reveal Smyth's willingness to capitalise upon his financial resources by cultivating relationships, and contemporary notions of 'corruption' extended beyond 'bribery'—a common complaint—to encompass the 'favour' shown by friends and contacts, involving

[27] GA, D9125/1/13612/3; D9125/1/13608/41, 65v; D8887/2/29.

[28] GA, D9125/1/13612/7–8, 15; D9125/1/13608/52v.

[29] PA, HL/PO/JO/10/1/25 (Philip Smith). See: Robert Zaller, *The Parliament of 1621* (Berkeley, 1971), pp. 75–84, 97–9; Stephen D. White, *Sir Edward Coke and the Grievances of the Commonwealth* (Manchester, 1979), pp. 49–50, 53.

conflicts of interest and 'corrupt partiality'.[30] In his accounts as steward to the Berkeleys, Smyth recorded payments (70*s.*) for 'friendly intelligence' about adversaries, and repeatedly paid people for their 'favour'. He referred to one lawyer being employed as the 'favourite' of Sir Lawrence Tanfield, a judge in King's Bench, and once paid Dr Carew 'to be friendly' in a legal case, and it was from Lord Berkeley that Smyth learned that gift-giving 'reaped both honour and profit, an hundred times more than the charge'.[31]

Such practices almost certainly helped Smyth—an *arriviste*—to exploit the credit he accumulated with friends in high places. The best example of this involved his election to Parliament, as MP for Midhurst. This might have been effected through Berkeley connections—the family owned an estate at nearby Bosham, with which Smyth was heavily involved—but it more likely reflected local contacts, not least with powerbrokers like Richard Lewkenor, with whom Smyth had studied at the Middle Temple.[32] In assessing Smyth's motivation for securing a Commons seat it is worth noting that he was an assiduous MP, who paid his fees, bought the book in which he recorded his diary, and paid for frequent trips to Westminster 'by water', as well as for numerous dinners. However, he almost certainly sought the immunity from prosecution that came with parliamentary 'privilege'.[33] Crokey insisted that Smyth '*procured* himself to be made a burgess', mocking him as a carpetbagger in getting elected for a borough '130 miles distant from his residence', and explaining that Smyth sought 'to delay Crokey and... countenance his unjust dealings'. Smyth's election occurred—the return was dated 2 January 1621—just as Crokey was preparing a new Star Chamber suit, and Crokey served him with a subpoena—which he managed to avoid—just before Parliament assembled. Equally important was Crokey's suspicion that Smyth's membership of the Commons prevented his parliamentary bill from being read for six months.[34] Moreover, while Crokey breached the December 1620 order against litigation during the parliamentary session, Smyth was quick to protest that this involved a breach of privilege.[35]

II

Whatever the suspicions about Smyth's local power, his attempts to woo powerbrokers, and his motives for securing election, Crokey eventually concluded that

[30] Brooks, *Law*, p. 290; Prest, *Barristers*, pp. 304–6, 308, 311; Brooks, *Pettyfoggers*, p. 92; Prest, 'Corruption', pp. 67–95; Linda Levy Peck, *Court Patronage and Corruption in Early Stuart England* (London, 1993), pp. 162, 164, 180, 184, 187–8. See: William Lambarde, *The Iust Lawyer* (1631), sig. A2v, p. 18; PA, HL/PO/JO/10/1/42 (Nicholas Cayford); HL/PO/JO/10/1/43 (William Fearnall).

[31] Berkeley, BB110, fos 13, 39v, 58v, 59v; Smyth, *Lives*, ii. 287.

[32] *Commons 1604–1629*, ii. 415–16. [33] GA, D9125/1/13608/41, 45.

[34] Crokey, *Sacred Maiestie*, sigs A4, Ev, F2; Crokey, *Briefe*; Crokey, *Complaint*, sigs A3–v.

[35] GA, D8887/6/97.

his own 'endeavours' were fruitless, and that 'no good effect' could be achieved 'in ordinary courts of justice', implicating Smyth in more straightforward corruption. Such claims featured regularly in litigants' complaints, as well as in contemporary reflections upon the fate of the poor 'honest suitor' whose 'just cause' lost out to people who were rich and 'well assisted'.[36] Smyth could allegedly 'cross' commissions of inquiry, obtain orders preventing litigation, and ensure that Crokey was 'disgraced'. He could also secure orders promising severe punishment 'if he should stir any more in the school business'. Crokey observed Smyth 'speak in arrest of judgment' during Baddam's suit (Case 5), and secure hearings at which he was persuaded to reach a settlement, and he eventually went beyond arguing that Smyth 'abused and deluded' the courts with 'false suggestions'. Since Smyth seemed to get things done 'upon a mere suggestion', Crokey sensed that Smyth's 'oppression and potency' involved undue influence being exerted over powerful officials.[37]

The spectre of 'corruption' had been raised in the 1590s, when Richard Moore accused the lawyer, George Snigge, of publishing a 'false deed' for financial reward, and Grace Drew of procuring writs illicitly. Moore also accused Edward Willan—a clerk in the Crown Office—of 'confederacy, combination, forgery, [and] counterfeiting', for producing 'false writs'.[38] Crokey made similar claims, suggesting that, to circumvent the Common Pleas 'rules' to which both men agreed, Smyth 'practiced with one Gayre'—one of Richard Brownlow's clerks—to alter the official record, 'by razing and interlining' documents. Gayre apparently confessed to this charge, 'upon proof made', prompting Judge Hobart to commit Smyth to prison.[39] As has already been shown, Crokey also accused Smyth of manipulating the official record about who was responsible for overturning the findings of the Wickwar inquiry, in order to credit Smyth with being the chief and only 'opposer'. Smyth was untroubled by such accusations, but his response regarding Wickwar fell short of an outright denial. Elsewhere, he merely resorted to mockery regarding notions about 'the court's dalliance with you, the favour it reached to me, and wrong to yourself'.[40]

More obviously—if imprecisely—Crokey highlighted subtle ways in which Smyth exerted 'potent power ... with the higher powers of judicature', and with Hobart, Attorney General Coventry, and Lord Keeper Williams. The latter became a target for many frustrated litigants, some of whose complaints were

[36] PA, HL/PO/JO/10/1/274; Lambarde, *Iust Lawyer*, sig. A2v, pp. 8, 10, 16. See: HEH, EL2672; PA, HL/PO/JO/10/1/24 (George White); 10/1/25 (John Freeman, Isott Bidwell).

[37] PA, HL/PO/JO/10/1/274; Crokey, *Sacred Maiestie*, sigs A4v, Dv, D2v–D3v, D4v; Crokey, *Contents*, sig. A2.

[38] TNA, STAC 5/M13/19; STAC 5M50/37.

[39] Crokey, *Sacred Maiestie*, sigs A4, D4v. For Gayre in Smyth's accounts, see: GA, D9125/1/13608/49, 52v.

[40] Crokey, *Sacred Maiestie*, sig. C4v; GA, D9125/1/12008, pp. 61, 70.

deemed credible by Parliament.[41] Time and again, Crokey accused Smyth of 'scandalising' his reputation, and of persuading officials about his 'double-dealing', adding that he 'left no practice unattempted to keep down and defame the petitioner to the higher powers'.[42] This was perhaps how Smyth secured the revocation—on 20 June 1621—of a 'protection' that Crokey received from Lord Stafford, thereby making it possible to effect his arrest, and Stafford apparently protested about being 'abused' in rescinding this protection, thereby enabling Crokey to get out of prison.[43] As someone who found himself arrested following litigation and petitioning, and detained despite thinking himself 'privileged', Crokey was not alone, not least in relation to Lord Stafford.[44] Meanwhile, when Crokey reflected on the abuse of courts through 'false reports', he referred to Smyth's 'power' over grandees.[45] His language was often vague, and Smyth mocked the idea that he had 'wound' himself 'into the good opinions of all, especially those in authority'. Nevertheless, Smyth's 'remembrances' reveal attempts 'to *solicit* the barons and judges Jones and B[erkeley]', and Crokey's claims were sometimes more specific and credible.[46]

First, Crokey made consistent claims about the help Smyth received. He noted how Smyth asked for their dispute to be referred to the judges in Common Pleas; that Hobart acted 'in favour of Smyth' and 'perverted' the process of settling the school; and that when Smyth was arrested he 'got out of prison' through 'the power he had with . . . Lord Hobart'. Similar language was used about others, Crokey claiming that Smyth secured a 1631 hearing by 'being powerful with . . . Lord Keeper Coventry'.[47] More obviously, Crokey focused upon Smyth's relationship with Williams. It was said that Smyth got out of prison a second time 'by the power he had with the Lord Keeper', and the same phrase was used to explain why Crokey failed to secure £300 'costs'.[48] Williams was also blamed for the dubious process by which Smyth's 'exceptions' to the Gloucester inquiry were considered (1621). This involved Crokey securing a hearing before Williams and Sir Richard Hutton, only to find that the latter was replaced—through Smyth's 'practices'—by Justice Thomas Chamberlain, the new husband of Lady Berkeley, and 'Smyth's

[41] Crokey, *Petition*, p. 6. For Williams, see: PA, HL/PO/JO/10/1/25 (Thomas Smethwicke); HL/PO/JO/10/1/26 (Thomas Morley); HL/PO/JO/10/1/34 (Anthony Lamplugh); HL/PO/JO/10/1/37 (John Freeman). See also: Hart, *Justice*, p. 38.

[42] PA, HL/PO/JO/10/1/274; Crokey, *Sacred Maiestie*, sig. A4v; Crokey, *Contents*, sigs A2–v.

[43] *LJ*, iii. 170–1, 173–4; Crokey, *Complaint*, sigs A3–v; Crokey, *Sacred Maiestie*, sigs E2v–4v; PA, HO/PO/JO/10/14/4, item 3363; GA, D8887/6/87. For Stafford and protections, see: HL/PO/JO/10/1/19; *LJ*, iii. 170–3; Elizabeth Read Foster, *The House of Lords, 1603–1649* (Chapel Hill, 1983), p. 142.

[44] PA, HL/PO/JO/10/1/17 (Sir Henry Fynes; Francis Brode); HL/PO/JO/10/1/26 (Mathew Head); HL/PO/JO/10/1/37 (Robert Hewett). For Stafford: PA, HL/PO/JO/10/1/15 (Roger Harris); HL/PO/JO/10/13/4; HL/PO/JO/14/4/3362.

[45] Crokey, *Sacred Maiestie*, sig. A4v; Crokey, *Complaint*, sig. A3.

[46] GA, D9125/1/12008, p. 33; D9125/1/13611/23.

[47] GA, D9125/1/11996; Crokey, *Complaint*, sigs B4v–C.

[48] Crokey, *Contents*, sig. Av; Crokey, *Petition*, pp. 3–4; PA, HL/PO/JO/10/1/274; HL/PO/JO/10/1/296.

master'. The result, according to Crokey, was that while Smyth's 'exceptions' were deemed 'frivolous', Williams and Chamberlain refused to uphold the commissioners' decision, and instead granted Smyth another inquiry, 'as he desired'.[49]

Williams was also central to the boldest claim that Crokey made about corruption. This involved allegations that Smyth actually 'caused' the suit that was brought against both men by Attorney General Coventry (1620), and that Williams and Chamberlain issued a ruling favourable to Smyth through 'corrupt and oppressive means'. The result, according to Crokey, was that Smyth secured the lands 'at a third part of their value', and 'upon little or no . . . enhancement of rent', which was 'against justice and equity'. Crokey marvelled that Smyth secured such a favourable verdict, even though the court recognised that the lands 'belong to the school, and that all his titles . . . were nought'; that Smyth sought to 'ruin' the school, and that he 'ingrossed all the revenues . . . unto his own hands'.[50] Smyth's ability to rely upon Williams at this stage seems clear from the fact that, immediately after the decree to re-establish the school was passed, he applied pressure upon the Lord Keeper regarding issues that were referred to him for 'further direction'. As a result, matters were quickly referred to Chamberlain, Jones, and Coventry (18 February 1623), with instructions to perfect the decree 'with all speed', prompting Crokey to complain that the new foundation emerged 'as Smyth would have it'.[51]

III

Claims about Williams and Chamberlain highlight another dimension of Crokey's discourse of corruption: Smyth's influence over how new commissions were approved and undertaken. Crokey claimed that Smyth secured a 'charitable uses' inquiry in 1621 by using 'untrue suggestions', with help from John Hunt, 'my Lord Chancellor's man', and suggested that when Williams and Chamberlain granted a new investigation in 1622—on the basis of 'false informations'—'divers of Smyth's friends were made commissioners'. Crokey claimed that these men had a track record of undermining the school, and of failing to execute earlier commissions obtained by Crokey, and he insisted that, having 'laboured both by petition and motion' to amend the commission, he 'could not prevail therein'. According to Crokey, Smyth 'managed' such business 'at his pleasure, not permitting any material witnesses for the school to be . . . examined', such that the lands were undervalued, 'to his own profit'.[52]

[49] Crokey, *Petition*, pp. 6–7; Crokey, *Complaint*, sig. A4; Crokey, *Sacred Maiestie*, sigs E4v–F.
[50] PA, HL/PO/JO/10/1/274; HL/PO/JO/10/1/296.
[51] GA, D9125/1/12008, pp. 33–4, 83–5; Crokey, *Petition*, p. 7.
[52] BL, Harl. MS 6803, fos 56v–7; Crokey, *Sacred Maiestie*, sigs A4v, E4v–F; PA, HL/PO/JO/10/1/24; HL/PO/JO/10/1/37.

Such accusations became a common theme, based upon understandable if not always certifiable doubts about official transparency. Crokey was probably as surprised as he was pleased that a Gloucestershire jury deemed his 'deed of assignment' from Joyce Cotterell 'true and sufficient', given that it was largely comprised of Berkeley's tenants and Smyth's neighbours. Usually he argued that Smyth exerted undue influence over such proceedings.[53] He alleged that, having secured a commission to examine Bishopp's claims about 'concealed lands' (1616), Smyth selected the commissioners, tried to 'solicit' witnesses, and 'defrayed the whole charge'.[54] Crokey also complained about the process whereby Sir John Poyntz and Henry Minors were made commissioners at another hearing, even though they were concealment-hunters who had selfish reasons for finding that the lands belonged to the crown. For Crokey, this involved a clear conflict of interest, and he suspected the 'procurement and confederacy' of Smyth, who was loading the dice in favour of his preferred verdict, and who 'so handled the matter' that he secured a jury 'of simple men'—'special friends and kinsmen'. Peter Bird, who had 'often been employed' as undersheriff, was accused of arguing that the lands were concealed, contrary to his 'precise knowledge', and Crokey complained about the 'unlawful labouring' of a 'simple jury' at Wickwar (1618), in terms of 'solicitation' and 'untrue evidences'. (One juror was evidently removed for 'going to tables' with the chairman, Sir John Stafford.) It was also said that Smyth 'practised', 'combined', and 'confederated' with 'special friends'—Sir George Huntley, Sir William Guise, Jasper Selwyn, and Arthur Kemys—to 'hinder' Crokey's inquiry into 'charitable uses'. They acted 'in contempt' by refusing to serve, having been offered 'great sums of money' and 'other rewards', and Kemys apparently absented himself 'wilfully, willingly and corruptly' as a result of Smyth's 'bribes'.[55] Here was a familiar claim: that witnesses, and potential witnesses, could be bought off.[56]

Crokey believed that almost every commission succumbed to Smyth's power. When Crokey was awarded a second charitable uses inquiry—at Thornbury in 1619—it was alleged that Smyth 'practiced' to delay its execution, and altered the list of commissioners to get friends nominated, and then ensured that 'there did come to the place... but three commissioners of seven that had signed the warrant'. As such 'it could not proceed', and 'all Crokey's labours and charges [were] lost'.[57] Having failed to prevent Crokey from securing yet another commission (June 1619), Smyth purportedly petitioned Lord Chancellor Bacon

[53] Crokey, *Sacred Maiestie*, sigs C, C3; GA, D8887/6/67; D9125/1/11994; TNA, STAC 8/274/8.

[54] TNA, STAC 8/107/7.

[55] TNA, STAC 8/107/7; GA, D9125/1/11996; Crokey, *Sacred Maiestie*, sigs C3v–4. See: HEH, EL2785. For the corrupt juror, see: GA, D8887/6/70.

[56] PA, HL/PO/JO/10/1/18 (William Smyth); HL/PO/JO/10/1/30 (Edmund Felton); HL/PO/JO/10/1/43 (William Fearnall).

[57] Crokey, *Sacred Maiestie*, sigs A4v, C3–v; GA, D8887/6/74–5; D9125/1/12008, p. 67.

against the nominees, 'scandalised' them with 'false suggestions', and got them replaced by his own 'friends', at least until Crokey got the list 'altered' again.[58] Here, Crokey joined a significant body of people who condemned Bacon, both before and after his fall from grace in 1621.[59] Finally, Crokey claimed that the process of surveying the lands in 1623 was nobbled, that those present 'were only such as Smyth would have there', and that the surveyors were 'neighbours and friends' who had 'some dependency' upon him, and also that no 'depositions or examinations' were taken 'upon oath'.[60]

Such claims are difficult to verify, but Smyth recognised that juries were susceptible to 'packing and plots', and allegations about manipulated commissions were certainly plausible.[61] The Thornbury inquiry in 1615 was ineffective, according to Peter Bird, because 'there met not a complete number of commissioners', such that the jury 'returned as they came', at a cost to Crokey of £5. Whether or not Smyth was responsible, he certainly hoped to influence proceedings. He prepared a letter for Bird to deliver at the hearing, and may also have relied upon tenants, two of whom—John Bull and the mayor of Wotton—turned up 'out of love to you'.[62] A similar problem undermined Crokey's first commission of charitable uses (1617), when the warrant to return a jury was signed by only three commissioners, rather than the four required.[63] At the re-scheduled meeting, meanwhile, commissioners concluded that the school lands were 'excepted out of the statute', and that they 'had not any power to examine' the issues.[64] Finally, Henry Townshend's letter to Smyth after the Wickwar hearing hinted that the process of selecting a jury was manipulated. Townshend, a former friend of Crokey, expressed surprise at being overlooked, and noted that Crokey was 'very sorry I was not of the jury'.[65]

Crokey's claims might be regarded as problematic, but he persuaded 'the whole House of Parliament' that Smyth's 'powerfulness and practice' meant that care would be needed when establishing *any* new commissions. In January 1629, when Crokey lobbied for another inquiry, the matter was referred to the Committee for Petitions, and a report not only criticised Smyth's 'cunning practices' but also recognised that he should be prevented from overpowering proceedings. Crokey thus needed to 'have the carriage' of an inquiry, to counteract 'the power of the said John Smyth', although Crokey worried that the cost would be 'far beyond' his ability. Like other petitioners he referred to having 'consumed his estate' (i.e. 'in the defence of the school for sixteen years'), and to having 'grown very poor',

[58] GA, D9125/1/11996, 12008, pp. 58–9; D8887/6/74–5; Crokey, *Sacred Maiestie*, sigs D–Dv.

[59] For example: PA, HL/PO/JO/10/1/17A (Ralph Hansby); HL/PO/JO/10/1/24 (George White). See: Jonathan L. Marwil, *The Trials of Counsel: Francis Bacon in 1621* (Detroit, 1976), pp. 43–50.

[60] Crokey, *Sacred Maiestie*, sigs F3v–4.

[61] Smyth, *Lives*, ii. 306–8.

[62] GA, D8887/6/51–3.

[63] Crokey, *Sacred Maiestie*, sig. C3; GA, D9125/1/12008, pp. 65–6; D8887/6/58a.

[64] GA, D9125/1/12008, p. 66.

[65] GA, D8887/6/72. This was Henry Townshend of Oldbury: *Men and Armour*, p. 228.

noting that friends were 'afraid to relieve' him because of Smyth's power and the threat of lawsuits. As such, he asked that Smyth should repay the cost of the commission, as and when his 'assertions' were vindicated, and that steps should be taken to prevent 'waste or spoil upon the premises', in order to sustain his claim that school lands were 'sold and exchanged', their boundaries 'taken away', and new tenements erected. As with other cases, Crokey persuaded peers that commissioners should come from *outside* Gloucestershire, and was satisfied that those nominated had 'great worth and integrity', even if their 'occasions and remoteness' might 'hinder their presence'.[66]

Even these precautions proved insufficient, and Crokey insisted that Smyth 'crossed the said commission'.[67] According to the commissioners, 'the most part' of Smyth's tenants appeared, but while Crokey nominated 'expert and skilful men' to survey the lands, they were forced to suspend proceedings because of 'other employment', and because Crokey—whose presence was 'useful for the better execution of that service'—needed to return to prison. When work was resumed, only 'some' of Smyth's tenants turned up, and it proved impossible to certify the survey undertaken by William Staples and Richard Hathway, which only involved 'most' of the estate.[68]

On this occasion, Smyth certainly *sought* to influence the proceedings. Days before the survey began, he wrote to his friend Sir William Guise, grumbling that Crokey—'out of his idle, restless spirit'—had secured a new survey by alleging that the previous investigation was 'corruptly and partially executed', and expressing outrage at the suggestion 'that no better justice might be expected from gentlemen of this county'. Smyth sought to ensure that the surveyors employed in 1623 should reappear, and hoped that Guise, a commissioner on that occasion, would offer assistance. Thus, although he left it to Guise's 'wisdom and direction, what you will do', the implication was that Smyth wanted to meddle in a process purposely designed to prevent his friends from interfering.[69]

IV

Crokey's allegations were often vague, but they were plausible and deemed credible by contemporaries, and can sometimes be substantiated. Indeed, claims about the abuse of power were viable because of Smyth's proven ability to muster witnesses. This meant identifying and mobilising people who could give evidence,

[66] Crokey, *Complaint*, sig. B4; PA, HL/PO/JO/10/1/37; *LJ*, iv. 10, 12, 13, 17–18; GA, S379/2/3/1/1. For claims about poverty, and friends being discouraged: PA, HL/PO/JO/10/1/19 (Bryan Griffin); HL/PO/JO/10/1/26 (Mary Brocas). For the need to appoint neutral men: PA, HL/PO/JO/10/1/44 (Henry Fynes).

[67] Crokey, *Complaint*, sig. B4v; Crokey, *Petition*, p. 9. For the summons: GA, D9125/1/12022.

[68] GA, D9125/1/12023; S379/2/3/1/2.

[69] GA, D9125/1/12021.

with help from local men like 'Mr Oldisworth', and then putting Crokey's allies under pressure.[70] What emerges is that Smyth's energetic approach to the Warrens Court dispute involved not just time and money, but also influence.

The doggedness with which Smyth gathered witnesses emerges in relation to Crokey's first lawsuit (Case 1). Between October 1614 and January 1615, he compiled a ninety-page dossier of evidence from people who knew Crokey and Joyce Cotterell, about a host of relatives and associates, and about Richard Moore (Fig. 7). He sought to understand kinship ties, the status of Moore's 'apprentices', and the role of Crokey's servant, Mr Lemon. Witnesses were asked about tenancy arrangements, and required to cast their minds back many years to provide information about wills, legacies, and debts, and about the history of Warren's Court. Pointed questions were asked about the will Grace Drew prepared before marrying Smyth, about agreements made thereafter, and about the Cotterells, as well as about how the school was run and how Smyth 'intermingled' its lands with other property. Witnesses were also asked about Crokey's deal with Joyce Cotterell, in terms of who prepared the documentation, acted as counsel, and served as witnesses, and about whether Crokey offered to pay Joyce £10 *per annum*.[71]

Such interrogations enabled Smyth to develop a detailed picture about this episode, upon which to base his legal defence. First, he identified the *dramatis*

Fig. 7. Examination of witnesses for John Smyth in Exchequer case against Benjamin Crokey (1615). Gloucestershire Archives, D9125/1/11992. Reproduced by permission of Gloucestershire Archives.

[70] GA, D8887/8/6; D9125/1/13611/24v.

[71] GA, D9125/1/11992, fos 70–89.

personae and how they were connected. Crokey's 'natural sister', the widow Anne Tempest of Bristol (aged 54), confirmed that Margaret Olyver—wife of Wotton's mayor—was Crokey's cousin. Joyce Cotterell—'very near four-score years of age'—was Crokey's aunt, while John Cotterell was Joyce's step-son. These details were confirmed by Joyce's husband, John Cotterell, who also added that Jane Moore was Crokey's cousin. Tempest confirmed that Crokey had a servant called William, although she was unsure if this was Lemon, and deposed that Moore's apprentices had occupied Warrens Court nearly three decades earlier. William Porter of Bristol admitted to being Crokey's attorney, but only vaguely recalled being involved in this business.[72]

Secondly, an impressive range of witnesses professed to have knowledge about key deeds, having seen them, read them, or been 'credibly informed' about them, or indeed having witnessed (and benefitted) from them. William Archard—who 'dwelled' as Smyth's 'servant in-house' for many years—claimed to have 'seen the bills and accounts', while another servant, Gyles Parsons, who now worked as a scrivener in St Michael Bassishaw, London, claimed to have been 'privy' to Grace's land deals. More interesting, in terms of Smyth's 'power', was the collation of evidence from a wide range of local people, including an aged yeoman, William Williams of Wotton, as well as John Thomas of Stinchcombe (the great nephew of William Thomas), not to mention tenants like John Bolton of Berkeley, a former trustee of Grace Drew, and Thomas Trotman, a clothier from Stinchcombe who claimed to know Warrens Court because 'he dwelleth three bows shot of it.'[73]

Thirdly, Smyth's local influence made it possible to follow leads as evidence accumulated. William Williams remembered that fifty years earlier a Dursley clothier called John Smallwood occupied some of the lands, and Smyth confirmed this with Smallwood's son, a yeoman from Newton Bagpath. Alexander Williams, a victualler from St Mary Savoy in the Strand, professed to having 'heard much' about the land, and said that Grace made a will during a period of sickness before marrying Smyth, and also admitted being one of the witnesses. He told Smyth that Grace disposed of certain lands to Richard Thomas, 'in respect of kindred... friendship and love', and Smyth tracked down Thomas's son, who claimed that the will named his father as executor, and was designed to prevent Joyce Cotterell from securing the lease. He added that Joyce 'did importune her to alter her will', although Grace 'would by no means yield thereunto'.[74]

In the summer of 1616, Smyth also interrogated witnesses at the inquiry into Edward Bishopp's claims. He managed to call upon many humble villagers who may have been dependent upon him, and who would certainly have seen him as an imposing figure. Smyth posed questions about things known, or 'credibly

[72] GA, D9125/1/11992, fos 1–3, 5–6, 8–12, 53–4.
[73] GA, D9125/1/11992, fos 15–16, 31–2, 38–44, 50, 55–6, 58–9, 65–9.
[74] GA, D9125/1/11992, fos 4–5, 17–23, 24–30, 52–3.

heard', regarding the school's 'mass priest', and about earlier claims that the lands were concealed, and tracked down the very elderly people who subsequently gave evidence. These included an 83-year old weaver called Edward Dawe, who put Smyth in contact with 'old William Phelps', estate steward as far back as the time of Robert Coldwell, the schoolmaster whose 1545 lease was the original source of the dispute.[75] Such witnesses testified that Smyth purchased lands worth around £4,000, which were 'intermingled' with the school lands, and which were improved—at the expense of some £800—by the addition of barns, stables, walks, outhouses, fishpools, gardens, and mills, as well as a hopyard, not to mention orchards planted with thousands of trees. They also confirmed that Smyth maintained 'a common school and a schoolmaster', who was 'a preacher' and a 'master of arts', and that this was done 'out of the profits of the said old lease'.[76]

Smyth's ability to exploit his local influence was even clearer during his own Star Chamber suit (Case 4), when Archard and Parsons once again helped to pursue claims about maintenance and champerty with evidence regarding Crokey's family network. Some new witnesses seem to have been Smyth's tenants and former tenants, or else their kinsmen, including John Curnock, a yeoman then living in St Giles Cripplegate, London. Smyth tracked down Crokey's relatives, including Jane Moore of Bristol, who was present when the lands were assigned by Joyce Cotterell, and he also pursued associates like William Lemon, Thomas Rogers, and William Beale, not to mention Anthony Hathway, a wine porter from St Martin Vintry, London, and Hugh Deinton, a weaver who was 'born and ever-dwelling in North Nibley'. This process—tracing and taking statements from a substantial cast of characters—was protracted, lasting from 1615 to 1618, and perhaps suggests a willingness to prolong proceedings. Crokey certainly claimed that Smyth failed to attend hearings, and failed to examine witnesses, and yet he went to great lengths to gather evidence, and did so in ways that may have been intimidating. Smyth identified new witnesses, like Alby Muston of the Middle Temple, and visited certain people—Hathway, Cotterell, Deinton, John Thomas, Thomas Trotman, John Price, and Jane Moore—more than once, cross-referencing notes made upon their testimonies, and trying to spot inconsistences.[77] Whether or not Smyth sought to intimidate them, he certainly drew attention—'mark this Mr Crokey'—to Crokey's relatives who provided evidence with which to sustain a claim about 'maintenance and champerty'. It was from these people that Smyth claimed to know that Joyce Cotterell would get

[75] TNA, E 134/14Jas1/Mich28. [76] GA, D9125/1/11992, fos 33–8, 45–9, 59–63.

[77] GA, D8887/6/62, 66, 99; D9125/1/11989/11–14, 11994; TNA, STAC 8/274/8. See: LB, MS 3549/165.

£10 *per annum* for assigning the lands, even if this also reflected 'natural affection', and Crokey's 'pains taken . . . on her business'.[78]

That Smyth was willing to pressurise witnesses seems clear. During 1617 and 1618 he sought a sworn statement from Crokey's nephew, Thomas Tempest, whose letters reveal a determination to *avoid* being interrogated, resulting in noticeable tension. Tempest insisted that he had been away from Bristol, and that he planned to be away again, indicating that he would only be available for brief periods, and that, at a push, he could meet in Sodbury or Tetbury.[79] Tempest promised to be 'honest and plain', but also protested that Smyth treated him with 'scorn', and that as a result he would 'scorn' Smyth's 'proffer': 'speak with me you shall not, for tomorrow in the evening I am to depart from Bristol'. To Archard, meanwhile, Tempest said that he would only answer questions if Smyth promised—upon 'a bond of £100'—not to indict him.[80] The subtext of these letters is that Tempest was afraid of Smyth, who clearly sensed an opportunity to exploit 'a quarrel that arose' between the young man and Crokey. Smyth even prepared an affidavit for Tempest to sign, which referred to 'bitter words' and his desire to be 'revenged', and to an offer he made to produce Crokey's forged deed 'out of a chest in Bristol . . . in return for £20'. This was blatantly intimidatory, indicating the lengths to which Smyth went to get such an important document, and his willingness to capitalise upon the weakness—and rash words—of certain witnesses, not least by threatening to accuse them of bribery. On this occasion, Smyth's gambit failed, and by June 1618 he had concluded that 'no possible labour' could get Tempest to testify, 'being since reconciled to his uncle Crokey'.[81] However, Smyth was himself accused of using bribery to get what he wanted. One witness, John Bolton of Berkeley, alleged that Smyth had visited Joyce Cotterell shortly before the death of her husband, offering to give her 'a chain of gold worth £20'. Smyth apparently professed that he did so to recognise 'the love which had formerly been between her and Grace', and 'not for any interest she had in the lease'.[82]

The clearest evidence of the thinking behind such behaviour is an extraordinary letter written to Smyth by the minister at Nibley, John Ham (April 1638). This related to an apparent disagreement between Smyth and a tenant, Thomas Dorney, which involved at least the possibility of litigation, and Ham's letter outlined the tactics that Smyth should adopt to achieve success. Ham explained that he had made Dorney aware of Smyth's 'displeasure', in 'most truculent and terrible forms', hoping that 'his mind being possessed with some perturbation . . . his fear would be the more fatal, and himself the more flexible' when a writ was eventually served. Ham boasted that this strategy worked, and that when the writ

78 GA, D9125/1/12008, p. 15. 79 GA, D8887/8/21. 80 GA, D8887/8/27.
81 GA, D9125/1/11994; TNA, STAC 8/274/8; GA, D8887/6/59.
82 GA, D9125/1/11992, fos 66–7, 68–9.

was issued, Dorney 'repaired to me the next morning, to request me to present my entreaty to you for... composing the matter', and to beg that Smyth would be 'propitious to a yielding adversary'. Ham clearly understood Smyth's methods, because on this occasion he advised restraint, urging Smyth to 'prosecute' the matter 'no further against a submitting man, who defyeth the very thought of opposing his weakness against your strength'. Ham reminded Smyth that it was 'a policy in war to undermine those walls that cannot be scaled', but in doing so he revealed both men's awareness that Smyth had power and was willing to use it.[83]

V

For Crokey, attempts to interrogate and intimidate ultimately involved ruthless efforts to weaken the bonds that held his network together, and to undermine his ability to sustain a protracted campaign of litigation, not least by crippling him financially.

In part this was said to involve Smyth trying to 'defame' Crokey, not just to the 'higher powers' but also to his 'most intimate friends', such that he was 'made a scorn to his wife and children and best friends'.[84] In recounting attempts to undermine the case brought by Baddam (Case 5), Crokey alleged that Smyth 'laboured to seduce the said Baddam, Crokey's lessee'.[85] In 1621, Smyth was accused of 'confederating' with Giles Elbridge, Crokey's 'intimate bosom friend' and an apprentice to Robert Aldworth, 'the greatest eminent merchant in Bristol'. Smyth apparently drove a wedge between Crokey and his family—the 'aged and weak' Aldworth, as well as Crokey's wife—for twenty years, by getting Elbridge to 'enrage' them with 'scandal and false report'. Such 'vile practices' supposedly robbed Crokey of his inheritance, thereby undermining him financially, because the childless Aldworth—with whom Crokey's wife lived as his 'only joy and comfort'—reneged on a promise to pay an annuity of £50 and then make him heir to an estate worth £20,000. Elbridge allegedly ingratiated himself with Aldworth, moved into his house, and become his executor, such that 'Crokey's brother's help was drawn from him', and after Aldworth's death in 1634 Elbridge reputedly tried to 'starve' his former friend.[86] Crokey was clearly animated by the loss of a substantial inheritance, later complaining that Elbridge 'ploughed with the petitioner's heifer twenty-four years together'.[87]

[83] D9125/1/12025. [84] Crokey, *Contents*, sigs A2–v.

[85] Crokey, *Sacred Maiestie*, sig. D2.

[86] Crokey, *Complaint*, sig. Bv; PA, HL/PO/JO/10/1/274; Crokey, *Petition*, pp. 8–9. See also: PA, HL/PO/JO/10/1/274. Robert Aldworth left an annuity of £50 to Elizabeth Crokey, and £30 to Sarah Crokey: TNA, PROB 11/167, fo. 21.

[87] Crokey, *Contents*, sigs A2–v.

Crokey thus accused Elbridge and Smyth of making common cause against him, and of helping each other by undermining someone who represented an obstacle to both of them. This conspiracy was then said to have continued after Crokey moved to Ireland, and was 'in a very hopeful way to raise his fortunes'. Elbridge apparently called Crokey to a meeting in Bristol, and threatened to 'bring him out of favour with . . . Lord Deputy Wentworth, whatsoever it cost him'. Working alongside Smyth and his 'familiars', Elbridge 'wrought' with Wentworth's steward—Josias Carpenter, who was 'very powerful with his lordship'—to blacken Crokey's reputation and set workmen against him. They ensured that Wentworth 'converted' the Flax venture 'to his own use', and that Crokey was 'turned out' of his 'design and employments, without cause, reward or recompense'.[88] In ways similar to other petitioners, Crokey claimed that Smyth, Elbridge, and their 'agents' had 'impiously outfaced and deluded' the authorities 'in the administration of justice'. He claimed to have been 'undone'—a common term—'by impostures, practises, plotters and deceivers, that bend their minds and endeavours wholly to injury and oppression, without any regard of whom they deluded and abused for their own impious ends, seeming not to dread any punishment either in this life or in the life to come'.[89] Such language was wild, but it involved problems and tendencies that were recognisable to legal commentators like William Lambarde.[90]

A related and equally nefarious practice, according to Crokey, involved Smyth conspiring with other people to whom Crokey was connected. Central here was the accusation that Smyth 'dealt underhand' with—i.e. suborned—Crokey's creditors, such that debts were assigned to Smyth or his 'agents and confederates', thereby putting Crokey under greater financial pressure.[91] Similar claims were made by many litigants, and for Crokey a case in point involved a Somerset clothier, Augustine Harvey, with whom he once 'lived in good credit and reputation'. Harvey had been one of Crokey's suppliers in his mercantile days, and someone to whom he became indebted when pirates brought about his 'undoing'. Initially sympathetic to Crokey's plight, Harvey eventually lost patience and arrested him for defaulting on a bond, but Crokey soon discovered that the original debt had been assigned to one Ashman, and then to a merchant called Arthur Fisher, whereupon he became embroiled in a byzantine world of debt, imprisonment, and litigation in the late 1610s and early 1620s. The significance of these tribulations only makes sense within the context of the Warrens Court affair, and Fisher will reappear in the story. Crokey was sued by Harvey, and responded with a Chancery suit of his own; he obtained an injunction against Harvey's case,

[88] Croeky, *Complaint*, sigs B2v–3; Crokey, *Petition*, p. 9.

[89] Crokey, *Petition*, p. 12; Crokey, *Contents*, sig. A2v. For being 'undone' by misled judges: PA, HL/PO/JO/10/1/18 (George Geldarde); HL/PO/JO/10/1/25 (Ann Pike, John Freeman); HL/PO/JO/10/1/30 (Mary Sole).

[90] Lambarde, *Iust Lawyer*, pp. 8–9.

[91] Crokey, *Sacred Maiestie*, sig. A4.

which Harvey got overturned; and he secured an official hearing that Harvey ignored in favour of further litigation, despite an injunction from the Court of Requests. Meanwhile, Arthur Fisher got Crokey arrested, on 24 June 1621, allegedly through 'bribes' and 'rewards' to Thomas Audley, serjeant-at-mace.[92]

By this stage Crokey was 'entangled', and he detected Smyth's handiwork. This was because such manoeuvres were perfectly timed to undermine the commission of inquiry appointed by the 1621 Parliament, to his 'utter undoing', and because he remained in prison even when friends offered to settle his debts. Apparently, 'no penny would be accepted', Harvey proclaiming he would rather see Crokey 'rot in prison' than accept money from his friends. Crokey's suspicions also reflected the fact that a letter of protection from Lord Stafford, which was supposed to ensure privileged status as the 'servant' of a peer, was revoked—using 'untrue suggestions and false information'—four days before his arrest. Crokey was re-arrested—'on a sabbath . . . on his way to a sermon at St Paul's Cross'—and sent to Poultry Compter. Crokey quickly got a transfer to King's Bench prison, hoping that this would make it easier to secure a *habeas corpus* and attend the commission, but his efforts proved fruitless, and he remained in prison for five months, 'until the Parliament sat again'. Eventually, Parliament released Crokey, and investigated the revocation of Stafford's protection (November 1621), discovering that the peer had been 'abused' by Crokey's enemies. Those responsible only evaded justice, Crokey claimed, because Parliament was dissolved (January 1622).[93]

This was a complicated business—an 'intricacy'—and it did not end there. Harvey and Fisher allegedly worked together to cause 'further vexation' in 1622, entering a demurrer to Crokey's Chancery bill, commencing a new suit against him, and getting him re-arrested, with Audley's assistance. Having 'laid him in the . . . Compter', they kept Crokey prisoner 'in miserable and pitiful manner . . . utterly denying any composition'. For Crokey, however, this all reflected the 'practices and procurement' of Smyth, who 'ever sought' his 'overthrow', precisely because of his 'charitable prosecution for the said school'. Crokey protested that such 'extremities' would ensure his 'utter undoing' and hinder him from working 'on the school's behalf', noting that the latter was to be discussed in court 'this term', as 'Smyth well knoweth and . . . praticeth to restrain'. Harvey was summoned to appear before one of the Lord Chief Justices, but refused to appear. Crokey's Chancery case was referred to Sir James Hussey, who decreed that Fisher should accept payment for the debt, although Fisher refused to 'conform',

[92] TNA, C 3/338/8. This cannot be confirmed with Court of Requests papers: TNA, REQ 1/29–30, 54–5. For similar claims: PA, HL/PO/JO/10/1/26 (Timothy Pinckney).

[93] TNA, C 3/338/8; *LJ*, iii. 170–1, 173–4; Crokey, *Sacred Maiestie*, sigs E2v–4; GA, D8887/6/87; Crokey, *Complaint*, sigs A3–v.

apparently explaining that he 'would have the extremity of the law against Crokey', and 'that he cared not for his debt... for he would make dice of Crokey's bones'.

It was Smyth, however, that Crokey blamed, referring to 'sinister practices', and suggesting that he 'set his agents' to effect an arrest, to 'weary' him and 'hinder' the inquiry. According to Crokey, Smyth 'had his hand in all these matters', using 'practices', 'procurement', and 'insinuation', as well as 'agents and confederates'. The latter included not just Harvey and Fisher, but also Mr Farrer, a Chancery clerk, as well as William Archard and Peter Bird, 'whom Smyth hath long used and employed in his affairs'. Archard and Bird were apparently present when Crokey was arrested in 1621—Bird would be questioned for arresting other privileged people—and Smyth was said to be 'inquisitive' about the litigation with which such men were involved, as well as instrumental in persuading Stafford to revoke Crokey's protection. For Crokey, this was all designed to render him less effective at key moments, and he grumbled that his efforts for the school had cost £1,200, 'to his utter impoverishment and decaying of his estate'.[94]

Crokey's claims about Smyth's ruthlessness are obviously hard to substantiate, predicated as they were upon the idea that strings were being pulled behind the scenes. However, tempting as it is to suggest that Crokey had a paranoid imagination, it makes sense to acknowledge the possibility that he was the victim of conspiratorial behaviour, and of Smyth's 'power'. Smyth had certainly assigned debts—like those of Richard Moore—to other men so that they could be recovered, and evidence reveals a pattern of claims regarding the handling of Crokey's debts.[95] After Smyth's death, his two sons, John Smyth junior and Edward Smyth, allegedly conspired with Thomas Thomas—to whom Crokey owed £4 10*s*. for rent—in a similar fashion. This involved the transferral of a debt, payment being declined, and attempts—'privately' and 'without any warrant'—to sequester a 'cartload' of Crokey's 'household stuff', not to mention 'writings of record'. When confronted about this, Edward Smyth claimed to have had 'nothing to do in it', but Crokey sensed another 'confederacy' to restrict his ability to wage law. The seized papers, he said, offered 'proof of his great oppression', and being 'kept... from all his goods and writing' hindered attempts to 'make good his complaint in Parliament', a point also made by other frustrated litigants. Crokey sensed another attempt to ensure that he was 'kept down in great want and distress', without 'means... to right himself in course of law or equity'.[96] Such language—about the absence of effective legal channels—was fairly common, but Crokey's fears may also have been justified by Smyth's response to

[94] Crokey, *Complaint*, sigs A3–v; Crokey, *Briefe*; PA, HL/PO/JO/10/1/37; Crokey, *Sacred Maiestie*, sigs A4, Ev–E2v, F–v; TNA, C 3/338/8; STAC 8/107/7. For Bird making arrests, see: *LJ*, iii. 183, 198.
[95] GA, D8887/6/44; D8887/7/21.
[96] Crokey, *Petition*, p. 10. See: PA, HL/PO/JO/10/1/32 (Rose Payne).

claims about his power and ruthlessness, and by evidence about his willingness to imprison opponents.[97]

VI

Given Smyth's willingness to produce detailed statements about his dispute with Crokey, it is tempting to suggest that the accusations about which he said the *least* involved issues where he had most to hide. In dealing with claims about Harvey, Ashman, and Fisher, Smyth offered only a brief aside about Crokey's attempt to 'lay an army of plots, devices and practices to my charge, making me the contriver and plotter of all your misery', before calling him a 'lying fellow'. Later, Smyth made an evasive claim about not having caused Crokey to be imprisoned in 1621, referring to an oath—sworn before Judge Hobart—that he 'neither knew the parties at whose suit he was... arrested', nor was 'any way privy thereto'.[98] However, surviving evidence suggests that Smyth had a fairly ruthless propensity to see adversaries imprisoned, and perhaps even to use other forms of intimidation.[99] By the 1640s, Crokey's complaint that 'no vile practices' had been left 'unattempted' to ruin him and 'have his life' involved claims that Smyth used 'power and wicked practices' to get him 'wrongfully' imprisoned four times, for a total of twenty years.[100]

Smyth's notes reveal the zeal with which he pursued Richard Moore, regarding financial 'costs' awarded during the dispute. Writs were issued to seize portions of Moore's estate, which could then be acquired through intermediaries, aided by the sheriff of Gloucester, George Huntley of Frocester, and the under-sheriff, one Peter Bird. Even when Smyth resolved on 'not meddling' with costs that could be recovered, he reserved the right 'to levy as I may', to hound Moore for such debts 'till his death', and to have Moore imprisoned until costs were paid.[101] When Moore wrote to Smyth about being 'in execution in the Fleet at your suit' (June 1604), he protested that this was done so that legal cases could be pursued without his 'privity', and in the knowledge that he would be unable to attend hearings in Gloucester. Moore admitted being forced to 'buy my peace'. Smyth pursued the matter even after noting that Moore was 'dead in the Fleet', obtaining a copy of Moore's inventory, presumably with a view to pursuing the matter with his heirs.[102] Subsequently, Smyth considered having Crokey committed to prison as

[97] See: PA, HL/PO/JO/10/1/25 (John Freeman); HL/PO/JO/10/1/26 (Alice Fowler); HL/PO/JO/10/1/30 (Edmund Felton); HL/PO/JO/10/1/32 (Peter Watson); HL/PO/JO/10/1/34 (William Inman); HL/PO/JO/10/1/35 (Nicholas Hooker).

[98] GA, D9125/1/12008, p. 69; PA/HL/PO/JO/10/1/37.

[99] GA, D9125/1/13611/12; D9125/1/13612/10.

[100] PA, HL/PO/JO/10/1/274; Crokey, *Contents*, sigs A2–v.

[101] GA, D8887/6/44; D8887/7/21.

[102] GA, D8887/6/39, 41, 43, 46.

early as Easter 1617, and issued overt threats in 1626, pointing out that in his disputes with Richard Moore he had not been content merely 'to ward his blows', but sometimes saw cause to strike, 'as I have done with you'. He asked Crokey whether Moore could 'ever prevail', and boasted about not desisting until Moore 'died in the Fleet... for non-payment of costs', adding 'I wish you better fortune than to die in your uncle's bed.'[103]

Crokey had good reason to think that Smyth might effect his imprisonment for tactical reasons.[104] When he petitioned Parliament from the Fleet to demand a new commission (January 1629), Crokey insisted that it was the award of a new commission on 4 June 1621 that prompted his arrest a couple of weeks later; that while this was *effected* by Arthur Fisher, it was *caused* by Smyth's 'sinister practices'; and that it was done 'purposely' to 'hinder... the said commission'. He also blamed Smyth for the fact that, having been released after five months in prison, the dissolution of Parliament made it possible to get him detained again, 'by the said Smyth's means'. Crokey claimed to have 'ever since been kept in prison', 'lying groaning under the great oppressions of his adversary', and unable to get his case heard. This was why he needed—and got—a *habeas corpus* even just to make his case before Parliament, and why he sought permission to attend the now commission, even if only in the company of 'keepers', and even if he was compelled to return to London for the start of Trinity term.[105]

Smyth clearly capitalised upon opportunities to imprison Crokey, in ways that undermined his opponent's ability to litigate and prosecute commissions of inquiry. This was evident in relation to the costs—£52—awarded to Smyth in June 1624. Crokey claimed that such money had been 'erroneously awarded', although Smyth argued that it resulted from 'a vexatious suit', and he instructed William Archard to deliver a subpoena to Crokey, and then complained when Crokey refused to pay.[106] However, Smyth also seemed content with a situation in which he did not expect to recover the money, given Crokey's straightened circumstances, precisely because this—like the Sword of Damocles—made it possible to insist on his being kept 'close prisoner', in ways that curtailed litigation.[107] The debt was still hanging over Crokey in February 1630, when he secured a Star Chamber order requiring Smyth to demonstrate why it should not be rescinded. Sarah Crokey then swore an affidavit that Smyth's departure from London prevented her from delivering this order to Smyth until 6 May, and Smyth's decision to ignore successive demands for him to respond eventually

[103] Crokey, *Complaint*, sig. A2v; GA, D9125/1/13612/3; D9125/1/12008, pp. 13–14.
[104] Crokey, *Complaint*, sig. A2v.
[105] PA, HL/PO/JO/10/1/37; *LJ*, iv. 10, 12–13, 17–18; GA, S379/2/3/1/1; D9125/1/12023; Crokey, *Complaint*, sigs B4–v; Crokey, *Petition*, p. 9.
[106] Crokey, *Sacred Maiestie*, sig. B; GA, D8887/6/93, 105; D9125/1/12008, p. 65; PA, HL/PO/JO/10/1/37.
[107] PA, HL/PO/JO/10/1/37; GA, D9125/1/12008, p. 65.

led to Crokey being awarded a temporary reprieve. Crokey was released from what officials called his 'long imprisonment' (30 June), and Smyth was given until the end of the year to demonstrate why the debt should not be discharged completely.

Thus, Smyth secured Crokey's incarceration over costs that had been awarded, and was more interested in keeping Crokey prisoner than in recovering the money, not least while litigation was in hand.[108] Although he failed to ensure that Crokey remained in prison until the completion of libel proceedings in 1631, he persisted in using 'costs' as a stick with which to beat his opponent. Crokey claimed that, when he returned to England to 'right himself' (July 1638), Smyth not only used 'false suggestions' to defy a Privy Council summons, but also got him arrested. Smyth's son apparently hired 'one of the warden's men of the Fleet to fetch up Crokey from Bristol', even though he was theoretically protected from Smyth's 'abuses'. Crokey claimed to have been kept prisoner until the summoning of the Long Parliament, and this was one charge that Smyth willingly acknowledged: his 'remembrance' for late 1638—'about Ben Crokey'—explicitly mentioned plans to 'charge' his opponent with 'old' costs.[109]

Only news of a new Parliament in late 1639 may have prompted Smyth to change tack. On Crokey's account, Smyth and Elbridge 'consulted together' before sending delegates—Elbridge's son, Robert, and Smyth's nephew, Edward Turner, the schoolmaster—to visit Crokey in the Fleet. Their mission apparently involved 'labouring' a suggestion that he could get out of prison by accepting a settlement worth £2,000, while reminding him about the power his adversaries possessed. Perhaps sensing that Smyth now feared the impact of a new Parliament, such offers were apparently 'slighted' and 'utterly refused'.[110]

VII

This tortuous set of events prompted allegations that Smyth, his family, and his associates resorted to even more forceful behaviour, and although this element of Crokey's case seems fantastical, it might contain elements of truth, and certainly proves revealing about how the dispute was perceived and portrayed.

Occasionally, Crokey's accusations—like those of so many others—involved intimidation and threats of violence.[111] In referring to the confederacy between John Smyth junior and Thomas Thomas, Crokey claimed that his goods and papers were taken away 'violently and forceably', and similar claims emerged

[108] GA, D8887/6/102, 105.

[109] Crokey, *Complaint*, sigs B2v–Cv; Crokey, *Petition*, pp. 9–10; Smyth, *Lives*, iii. 402; GA, D9125/1/13611/19.

[110] Crokey, *Complaint*, sig. Cv.

[111] See: PA, HL/PO/JO/10/1/16 (Thomas Fuller); HL/PO/JO/10/1/24 (Gricell Rogers); HL/PO/JO/10/1/33 (John Harman); HL/PO/JO/10/1/37 (George Hudson).

regarding subsequent events.[112] Recognising that Crokey was 'ready to perish', Smyth and his associates—Thomas Elbridge and Nathaniel Cole—apparently reiterated their offer to 'compound' in ways that would have rewarded Crokey financially, while also engaging in 'practise and underhand dealing' (November 1645). This allegedly involved getting Philip Beast—who was 'familiar' with Crokey—to 'importune' him about the need to accept such an offer, but it also involved Beast becoming angry when such 'persuasion' failed, telling Crokey 'plainly' that 'one time or another' he would be 'privately knocked on the head'.[113]

Even wilder claims were made about Giles Elbridge, who was not only said to have seized 'divers goods and writings of import' from Crokey—'of purpose to keep him down'—but also to have kept Crokey's wife from him 'forcibly' and 'with a strong hand' after Robert Aldworth's death.[114] Crokey claimed that Elbridge engaged in 'wicked practice' by keeping his wife in 'awe and fear . . . as a child may be kept in fear of a rod', and that in 1638 he 'caused his man George Payne with a multitude of poor people' to 'violently take Crokey's wife from him a second time', while they were walking 'peaceably together in Bristol'. Crokey claimed that he only 'obtained his wife' again in 1641, adding that after living with him for three years 'in their extremities' she was 'starved' to death for want of her inheritance.[115]

As on other occasions these stories are difficult to substantiate, although Elizabeth Crokey certainly died in 1644, and was buried on 25 August at St Giles in the Fields.[116] However, Crokey's claims about violence only generated evasive responses. The most obvious involved Robert Pritchard, sometime tutor at Wotton school, who allegedly incurred Smyth's wrath in 1617 because he 'inclined to Crokey', and planned to assist him by testifying about the mis-management of school lands. According to Crokey, Smyth recognised his own 'guiltiness', and that his 'wrongs and practices' for suppressing the school would be 'discovered', and thus ensured that Pritchard was 'misused and evilly treated'. This involved him being 'set upon' with 'high and threatening speeches', and offered 'money and other rewards' if he would 'forbear his testimony', before being threatened with removal from his post as a 'professed maintainer' of the school 'against Smyth'. Upon Pritchard 'slighting' such threats, Smyth allegedly conspired with local men—Robert Smyth, Peter Bird, William Archard, Sir John Poyntz, Sir George Huntley, and Sir William Guise, as well as three score 'riotous persons'—to deal with Pritchard. Such men were 'armed and arrayed' with pikes and staves, swords and daggers, guns and pistols, and other weapons 'invasive as defensive', and they entered Pritchard's lands in a 'riotous . . . and unlawful manner', intending 'bodily hurt' and threatening 'to set fire upon his house'. Pritchard was said to have been in 'great terror' as a result, as was his wife, 'then in child bed', and Crokey

[112] Crokey, *Petition*, p. 8. [113] Crokey, *Petition*, pp. 9–10.
[114] Crokey, *Complaint*, sigs B2–v; Crokey, *Petition*, pp. 8–9; PA, HL/PO/JO/10/1/274.
[115] Crokey, *Complaint*, sig. B2; Crokey, *Petition*, p. 9. [116] LMA, P82/GIS/A/04.

concluded that such behaviour would discourage witnesses from testifying in support of his claims, to his 'wrong and oppression'.[117]

This story is fascinating because Smyth's response involved something less than a straightforward rebuttal. Rather than denying that Pritchard faced strong words, intimidation, and even force, Smyth insisted that this 'riot' involved the mayor of Wotton (Robert Smyth), a local constable, and members of the court leet 'holden that day', including feoffees of the school lands. He relied, in short, upon the improbability that upstanding members of the local community would behave in such a manner, reflecting that Pritchard's 'ignorance made him err', that he showed 'no thanks for nine years breeding and feeding', and that he was probably 'sorrowful' for his actions.[118]

VIII

In pursuing his claim about Smyth's 'powerfulness', Crokey made colourful allegations about his opponent's capacity for exploiting wealth and family connections to manipulate courts and commissions. These accusations ranged from the inevitable effects of being a prominent landlord, with many local dependents, to the exploitation of powerful contacts at a national level; the kinds of elite behaviour that historians have at least occasionally acknowledged.[119] Such suggestions involved his willingness to engage in ruthless, intimidatory, and even violent behaviour, rather than just 'corruption'. Crokey's suits, petitions, and pamphlets contained vivid stories about slanderous words and physical fights, and about imprisonment and kidnap, some of which were undertaken by associates and proxies, but all of which were used to weaken him financially and physically, to hinder his efforts at litigation, and to hamper commissions of inquiry, and to prevent him from mobilising parliamentary support.

Such claims are challenging, and difficult to verify, and Wilfrid Prest suggested that defeated litigants 'found a convenient excuse in professional conspiracy, partiality and venality'.[120] Nevertheless, Smyth did not always respond clearly, and Crokey occasionally persuaded powerful people about the veracity of his accusations, and about behaviour that demonstrably characterised the dispute. Crokey's claims might have been exaggerated, but they did not simply involve conventional rhetoric, of a kind that is sometimes said to have been *de rigueur* in early modern litigation. They thus provide plausible insights into Smyth's willingness to pursue the dispute in an energetic and determined fashion, and his

[117] TNA, STAC 8/107/7; Crokey, *Sacred Maiestie*, sigs A3v, D.
[118] TNA, STAC 8/107/7; GA, D9125/1/12008, p. 65.
[119] Jones, *Chancery*, p. 477; Brooks, *Law*, pp. 288, 290; Brooks, *Pettyfoggers*, p. 92.
[120] Prest, *Barristers*, p. 311.

ability to exploit resources and social capital. They suggest that 'sharp practice' extended to more aggressive behaviour. Just as importantly, Crokey's depictions of the dispute matter because his understanding of what was happening helps to explain why—and how—he opposed Smyth so doggedly. It was Smyth's alleged *conduct*—not least depriving his opponent of a massive inheritance from Aldworth—that inspired Crokey, rather than just legal arguments.

This issue of perceptions is central to the wider significance of the evidence presented here. This chapter has argued that, while claims about violence and 'corruption' obviously require cautious treatment, they should not be dismissed too quickly. Crokey's allegations were often vague, but they could also be specific, and a richly documented case study permits tentative steps towards substantiating them. This requires being attentive to the responses that allegations elicited, and to evidence from the wider landscape of litigation and disputation, not least apparently unrelated lawsuits. It means recognising that the most dramatic claims—about bribery and physical force—were set in a wider context of tactics and bad behaviour. Disputants made wild and formulaic assertions not just to get matters heard in court, but also to develop a rounded discourse of 'power' and its abuse, even if this was not rigorously conceptualised. It involved more than just predictable complaints by unsuccessful litigants, not least because it sometimes received official endorsement, and it highlights fairly profound differences of opinion about what constituted acceptable standards of behaviour, particularly during legal disputation. Crokey's claims about Smyth's 'powerfulness' provide a window into contemporary debates about norms and standards of conduct that have received insufficient scholarly attention, and that revolved not just around specific acts but also around pervasive moral traits.[121]

The implications of this line of argument are significant, because they make it possible to draw connections between experiences of litigation and what Linda Levy Peck called an 'ideology' of corruption, which will be relevant in subsequent chapters. For Crokey, Smyth was not all that he seemed to be, which was why he made sure to draw attention to an ill-tempered outburst in court during proceedings regarding Thomas Baddam. Crokey claimed that Smyth, perceiving that 'the trial must needs pass against him, and thereby all his practices come to light, and be brought to naught to his utter disgrace and infamy', cried out 'with a loud voice in most earnest and pitiful manner... that he was undone if they would not have compassion on him'. That this tactical outburst apparently worked, such that the judges sought to effect an accommodation, probably confirmed Crokey's worst fears about the legal system.[122] It suggests that the dispute involved something

[121] Peck, *Court Patronage*, pp. 158–9, 161, 171. See: G. W. Bernard, '"A water-spout springing from the neck of freedom"? Corruption in sixteenth- and seventeenth-century England', in R. Kroeze et al., *Anti-Corruption in History* (Oxford, 2017), pp. 125–38.

[122] Crokey, *Sacred Maiestie*, sig. D2v.

other than Crokey's powerlessness when confronted by John Smyth, in the sense that he remained hopeful about making some kind of progress, and that he was dealing with an opponent who was wealthy and influential, more or less powerful, more or less ruthless, and more or less successful. Developing this line of argument requires turning from Smyth's tactics and strategies to those of Crokey himself, in terms of how he behaved as a litigant, and what he believed about the legal system.

5

'A huntsman after broken titles'

Benjamin Crokey as Litigant

On 24 October 1618, when Henry Townshend wrote to John Smyth about the Wickwar hearing, he explained that Crokey 'pleaded very hard' that thirty-six tenements owned by Wotton school should be declared for charitable uses. This was done to 'put you by', although Crokey 'could not prevail'. However, as proceedings drew to a close, Townshend 'singled out' Crokey to 'renovate' their 'former acquaintance', which Crokey 'kindly accepted'. He encouraged Crokey to 'accept of a peace', saying that Smyth had 'skill and knowledge in the law', and that the power of his 'friends' was 'so great' that Crokey 'would hardly prevail'. Crokey acknowledged that Townshend 'spoke truth', while pointing out that he originally tried to 'end the controversy' amicably, an offer Smyth rejected 'in most scornful manner'. Since then, Crokey continued, Smyth had 'so much disgraced him in all places, and made him spend so much time and money' that he would 'never give it over', adding that Smyth sought to 'quell him by force and friendship'. Crokey grumbled that he could now 'have no proceedings' against Smyth, and that he failed to persuade Sir Henry Yelverton and Sir Thomas Coventry to 'put their hands to the cause now in question' until Archbishop Abbot threatened to 'complain to the king'. This resulted in the award of a new commission, which had 'such force' as to 'compel the jury . . . to give a verdict'. Townshend apparently professed satisfaction that Crokey 'had such good friends', whereupon Crokey confirmed that he did indeed have 'good friends', including Abbot and 'other bishops', and he invited Townshend to Bristol to 'know all his proceedings'. Finally, Crokey added a defiant comment—'to use his very words'—that he 'would not excuse your ears for £20,000', and that he would prevail despite Smyth's 'cunning'.[1]

Townshend's letter highlights Crokey's sense of how Smyth operated—through 'power' and 'practices'—as well as his own attitude. Acknowledging the possibility of compromise and arbitration, he also recognised that other issues—pride and trust—militated against harmonious forms of dispute resolution, and that he faced significant difficulties in pursuing litigation, in terms of skill and power. Such problems were offset, however, by a sense that ways could be found to strengthen

[1] GA, D8887/6/72.

The Madman and the Churchrobber: Law and Conflict in Early Modern England. Jason Peacey, Oxford University Press.
© Jason Peacey 2022. DOI: 10.1093/oso/9780192897138.003.0006

his position. This chapter examines surviving evidence about Crokey's behaviour, attitude, and strategies, and questions whether his methods were as illogical—and his chances as slim—as Smyth thought. In 1626, Smyth advised Crokey to 'submit' to authority, 'obey' the courts, and 'revile not' magistrates and 'private persons'. He implored Crokey to 'suspect' his knowledge and ability, and not to be the cause of his own 'want and poverty', suggesting that it was better to take care of 'wife, children and liberty' than to pursue other ambitions, and adding that Crokey was unlikely to achieve success 'at my hands'.[2]

What emerges is that, while Crokey's thinking is less well documented than Smyth's, he pursued a logical strategy, making up for a lack of legal acumen by pursuing innovative and aggressive tactics, as petitioner, lobbyist, and pamphleteer, and by reflecting upon judicial and political systems. He demonstrates how litigation generated thinking about legal strategies, fostering rival depictions of what constituted rational and acceptable behaviour, and incompatible ideas about the legal system. This chapter argues that an extended case study brings such things to light, by assessing protagonists' claims, using their behaviour to recover their strategies, and reflecting upon legal as well as non-legal rationalities. It suggests that such strategising revealed the importance of navigating the courts, other institutions, and wider publics, and of reflecting upon more profound issues, including the likelihood of achieving justice.

I

Smyth's take on Crokey was powerfully expressed and extremely dismissive. This is evident from his unpublished reply to Crokey's 1625 pamphlet, which was probably intended to dissuade people from taking Crokey seriously, even as it was addressed—rhetorically—to Crokey himself. Smyth rejected Crokey's allegations as 'hyperbole', 'foulness', 'prattle', and 'smut', and dismissed his pamphlet as a 'tragical catastrophe', a 'fable', and an 'idle and ignorant invective'. It belonged, he said, 'either in Sir Thomas More's *Utopia*, or in no other country'.[3] Crokey was derided for his 'passionate demeanour' and his 'contentious' and 'troublesome disposition', and Smyth saw him as someone whose 'natural talent' involved being a 'rayler, overcharged with spiteful invectives'.[4] Smyth mocked Crokey as a 'fool' for abandoning an 'honest' trade to become a 'huntsman after broken titles', pursuing 'this new monopoly or sole prosecution of suits against me' despite the financial cost.[5]

[2] GA, D9125/1/12008, p. 80. [3] GA, D9125/1/12008, pp. 4, 10, 47, 50, 55, 59, 65, 71, 73–4, 76.
[4] TNA, STAC 8/107/7; GA, D9125/1/12008, pp. 14, 60, 67, 79; D9125/1/11989/8, 11994.
[5] GA, D9125/1/12008, pp. 16, 77.

Smyth portrayed Crokey as someone who was fighting a lost cause, who knew it, and who had 'given out' that he would continue to sue Smyth upon his 'pretended title'.[6] He questioned whether Crokey was 'an honest and sober man', even to the point of doubting his sanity. He referred to 'old tales and circular fooleries, which no man that hath *mentem sanam in corpore sano* would have vented in print', and to 'a fardle of afflictive terms and spiteful invectives, offending every modest ear'. Crokey, he suggested, had been schooled in prison, by 'all the foaming discontented wits'. The result was a pamphlet involving 'empty clouds without rain, saltness or moisture, no piece of proofs, more than idle and childish words', and something even Crokey's well-wishers regarded as having been 'penned in Bedlam . . . either by a brother of that corporation, or by some cousin of the half-blood of that fraternity'. Ominously, Smyth exclaimed that it was for such 'madman like behaviour' that Crokey was 'shortly like to yield account'.[7]

Substantiating such rhetoric involved a series of claims. First, Smyth insisted that Crokey was motivated by the 'advancement' of his 'own ends', mocking 'reiterated proclamations' about 'the common good of the school', and protesting that for a long time 'there was no speech, nor rumour, nor complaint . . . of any wrong by me done.' He concluded that 'simulata sanctitas duplex iniquitas' [a simulated sanctity is a twofold iniquity], adding 'blush, Mr Crokey, blush to see these things thus retorted upon you'. Secondly, Smyth criticised Crokey's tendency to make unsubstantiated claims: 'your words are general as almost all the crimes in your book are.' He contrasted Crokey's style—'vain and idle words, without proof'—with his own, involving precise citations of 'judgments, decrees, orders of courts and judges certificates'. When Crokey accused Smyth of corrupting the official record—regarding the Wickwar hearing—Smyth retorted that this was 'not well done', and that Crokey should have 'delivered the name of such counsel as you retained, or that spake in the cause'. Claims about Smyth's conspiracy with Harvey and Fisher were said to involve an unproven 'army of plots, devices and practices', and Smyth mocked vague claims about Crokey being able to back up his statements with certificates and sworn statements. He referred to 'frivolous' affidavits, 'kept to this day from sight in the darkness of your pocket', and to 'pocket affidavits, wherewith you abound', insisting that 'you should have given us a clearer knowledge by whom that affidavit was sworn, to whom spoken'. Smyth also replied to Crokey's claim about having secured certificates from local ministers regarding nefarious 'practices', asking to see them, and insisting that allegations would be 'publicly disclaimed'. Crokey was 'much to blame' for

[6] GA, D9125/1/11989/8, 11994, 12008, p. 14.

[7] GA, D9125/1/12008, pp. 32–3, 67, 73, 81. See: Richard Bell, 'Dens of tyranny and oppression: the politics of imprisonment for debt in seventeenth-century London' (Stanford University PhD, 2017). Smyth's Latin phrase translates as 'a healthy mind in a healthy body'.

devising things that 'never were in deed nor words', and for which he had no proof, and for providing marginal references to documents 'wherein is no such matter, nor resemblance of any such matter'. Smyth felt no need to answer 'such... beggarly trash', accusing Crokey of having 'out-paced' Ovid's 'fable'.[8] Having apparently got Crokey imprisoned, Smyth chided his opponent for failing to cite the very documents to which his access had thus become restricted.

Thirdly, Smyth attacked Crokey for 'ill-advised allegations' and 'false pretences', which had been 'unmasked and reproved', and which contained 'as many untruths as lines'. He decried a 'scandalous and libelling pamphlet', stuffed with 'malice and untruths', 'cunning and dissembled hypocrisy', and 'bastardly stuff'. Crokey's suits were 'not much unlike a libel', involving lies told 'so often' that he now believed them 'for truths'. For Smyth, Crokey's account was partial at best and dissembling at worst, and he claimed to have identified forty-seven untruths, seventeen material things omitted, and eight points where Crokey contradicted statements made under oath. He told Crokey not to 'outface... the world nor matters of record', without actually itemising such faults, claiming that 'your study and mine are more filled with the papers and exemplifications... than with better furniture.'[9]

Fourthly, Smyth cited Crokey's unstable and volatile behaviour, including three episodes from 1617. He referred to a hearing before Sir Richard Hutton, when Crokey 'secretly conveyed' Smyth's breviate 'out of his chamber', provoking a 'reproof from that reverend judge'. He cited the inquiry into concealed lands, where Crokey 'snatched up' the commission 'lying open' on a table, 'with the great reprehension of... the commissioners'. And he claimed that Crokey uttered 'contemptuous and reviling speeches' in response to one unfavourable decree, resulting in his imprisonment in Fleet.[10] Following the Wickwar hearing, Smyth gathered evidence about an episode at the Three Cups inn in Bread Street, London (3 November 1618), when a fireside conversation involving Henry Townshend, Maurice Andrewes, and Albane Saunders saw Crokey insult his adversary 'most maliciously'. Smyth was labelled 'a churchrobber' and a 'jesuitical fellow', who had 'a black conscience', and Crokey apparently promised to 'rail upon me in all places wherever he came', and 'never leave me free from suits'.[11] Similarly, while Smyth apparently resolved to 'reverence and obey' the 1623 decree regarding Wotton school, Crokey 'fretted more like a madman than a sober subject and temperate Christian', and 'fell upon' officials with 'rude and unseemly words', to the point where some wanted to 'cast' him 'over the bar'. Smyth insisted that many people—'besides your own counsel, who could not contain you'—witnessed this 'vent' of

[8] GA, D9125/1/12008, p. 16, 37, 42, 48, 50, 53–4, 55, 57, 61, 63, 69, 78.
[9] GA, D9125/1/12008, pp. 1, 12, 47, 49, 62, 63, 68, 69, 72.
[10] GA, D9125/1/12008, pp. 12–13, 49, 66–7. See also: GA, D9125/1/11989/4.
[11] GA, D8887/6/71.

'distempered humours'.[12] Peter Bird, who reported on the behaviour of 'the idiot Crokey' more than once, claimed to have witnessed 'contention and altercation' between Crokey and his lawyer—George Peters—at Wickwar.[13]

Fifthly, references to lawyers struggling to control their client fuelled allegations that Crokey misunderstood the legal and political system. Smyth thought it a 'special piece of controversy' to bemoan his election for a constituency far removed from Nibley, insisting that Crokey should have 'inquired after the precedents of that honourable assembly'. He denied that anyone regarded his judicial manoeuvres as illegal, 'save you, Mr Crokey, who reprove at pleasure'. Smyth detected 'malicious misconstructions' of his behaviour 'in the courts of justice', telling Archbishop Abbot that Crokey was less interested in legal rights than in 'his often reiterated oaths and protestations not to leave his restless courses against me whilst he liveth or is worth one shilling'. For Smyth, this warped sense of purpose generated unfathomable legal manoeuvres, and Crokey was accused of changing his case to suit his 'present advantage', of concealing evidence from counsellors, and of behaving with 'wilfull . . . obstinacy'.[14] This ensured that courts grew frustrated with his behaviour, and Smyth cited an occasion when one of Attorney General Coventry's servants made a fruitless visit to Crokey in King's Bench prison, to make inquiries 'for the benefit of the . . . school'.[15] Similar bemusement arose from Crokey's behaviour at hearings before Judges Hutton and Hobart, when a potential agreement was apparently stymied by Crokey, who 'signified to them that he would not stand thereunto'.[16]

Crokey was allegedly incapable of understanding—let alone accepting—legal decrees, and Smyth accused him of having 'clipped and washed that coin, which you should sincerely have delivered in your book'. He was particularly vexed by Crokey not knowing about—or refusing to acknowledge—ordinances and letters patent passed following the 1623 decree, and feared that his adversary 'willingly' blinded his eyes to reality, least he should 'see the truth, and speak like an honest man'. For Smyth, it was ignorance or wilfulness that caused Crokey's 'madness and passion', his refusal to accept anything 'distasteful', and his propensity to undermine his own reputation, 'more . . . than I desired you should have done'. Such orders were 'as bitter as Coloquintida in your taste, and therefore you have spit them out of your book'.[17]

Ultimately, Smyth cited unfavourable comments made about Crokey in court. Lawyers apparently dismissed him as someone who 'careth not what he speaketh nor of whom', and described him as 'a lying fellow', while judges like Hutton and Hobart deemed him 'unconformable, as neither understanding his own cause nor willing to be ruled by his counsel'. This was indicative, Smyth thought, of

[12] GA, D9125/1/12008, pp. 32, 55. [13] GA, D8887/6/52, 70.
[14] GA, D9125/1/12008, pp. 14, 18, 53, 54, 70, 72; D8887/6/77–9. [15] GA, D8887/6/89.
[16] GA, D8887/6/65. [17] GA, D9125/1/12008, pp. 23, 37, 42.

'Crokey's anatomy' or 'constitution', and he reported lawyers 'misliking' Crokey's 'troublesome and contentious disposition', in 'troubling' courts for 'matters settled and determined'.[18] Lord Keeper Williams was said to have exclaimed that Crokey deserved to have his ears 'cropped', something Smyth found 'half prophetical in a future contingency'.[19]

Such claims are intriguing because Crokey *acknowledged* that this was his reputation within the legal profession, and while Smyth produced a damning indictment of his opponent's behaviour and attitude, Crokey saw things differently. Smyth's allegations probably reinforced Crokey's sense that the odds were stacked against him; that his own expectations of the legal system differed radically from those of his adversary; and that he needed alternative strategies to overcome such problems. Crokey's self-description differed markedly different from Smyth's depiction. As already noted, Crokey reflected upon his misfortunes in trade by insisting that Smyth, knowing him to be a 'poor man', commenced 'divers causeless suits' to 'oppress' and 'weary him out'. He bemoaned being 'impoverished' by cases across numerous courts, which he struggled to contest and bring to 'execution of trial', and protested about being 'locked up' by injunctions, imprisoned, and hamstrung by Smyth using 'all the delays he can'.[20] Crokey admitted seeking 'lawful title' to Warrens Court for the residue of the original lease ('thirteen or fourteen years to come'), and felt vindicated by Smyth's failure to challenge this claim in court. Nevertheless, he was determined to correct 'manifest wrongs' done to Wotton school ('to the subversion of good literature' and 'the grievance of all well-disposed persons'), insisting that he became its 'agent' and 'solicitor' out of a 'charitable disposition'.[21] This explained the 'labour and toil' of 'body and mind . . . with the wasting and consuming of his vital spirits in bearing the assaults and insufferable wrongs of Smyth's impiety', and Crokey saw no incompatibility between promoting 'his own right' and seeking the 'preservation of the school'.[22]

II

Such professions of zeal provide reasons for looking closely at Smyth's claims and Crokey's behaviour. This means contextualising contemporary comments and rulings, and establishing the reasons—other than hopeful signs about an imminent legal victory—why Crokey pursued the dispute in the face of overwhelming

[18] GA, D9125/1/12008, pp. 43, 51, 53, 54, 70; D8887/6/65.

[19] GA, D9125/1/12008, p. 53. See: Crokey, *Sacred Maiestie*, sigs C2–v.

[20] GA, D9125/1/11994; D8887/6/67; TNA, C 3/338/8.

[21] Crokey, *Sacred Maiestie*, sigs C3–v, E, G4; GA, D9125/1/11996–7; TNA, C 3/338/8. For Crokey as 'solicitor': BL, Harl. MS 6803, fos 56v–7.

[22] Crokey, *Sacred Maiestie*, sigs B4v, H3v–4; Crokey, *Contents*, A2v; Crokey, *Petition*, p. 4.

odds. It means recognising that, while his behaviour perplexed contemporaries, its logic can be appreciated.

Crokey's obstinacy was far from unique and can be comprehended. In noting that Richard Moore persisted with unsuccessful litigation, Smyth insisted that his adversary misunderstood the legal basis on which transactions had been undertaken, while another onlooker argued that his willingness to 'vex' opponents with 'suits and actions' involved desperation and foolishness, since these would 'impoverish a richer man than we do take him to have been'. John Drew suggested that Moore's refusal to submit to unfavourable rulings revealed 'subtle and sinister devices', and felt emboldened to take possession of Warrens Court, 'make fast the doors', and prevent Moore from regaining control.[23] Moore's determination was undeniable. He persisted with litigation even when it was ruled that he unfairly 'interrupted' Grace's possession of the lands, when his claim to the administration of her estates was 'utterly confuted', and when his 'busy speaking' was 'checked' by judges.[24] He even put pressure on opponents from the Fleet, corresponding with 'poor widow' Baston about 'household stuff' she had provided when he occupied Warrens Court, and demanding that 'brother Drew' should return it, since he had 'no title to it'.[25] More perplexing is his thinking, although correspondence with John Cotterell demonstrates that he expected to bring lawsuits 'to some perfection', and that he was animated by Smyth's 'peremptory' manner.[26] He spurned ideas about a negotiated settlement by saying he would 'never leave' the matter alone while 'the sun and moon went about', and 'never give over suing and vexing' opponents, carrying over such threats from Drew to the widowed Grace, and then to Smyth.[27]

Crokey's apparently obsessive behaviour, in relation to causes that seemed fruitless, is also telling. An example involves the difficulties he encountered in obtaining the 'good costs' awarded in 1619, following Smyth's unsuccessful Star Chamber suit (Case 4). As noted already, Crokey's pursuit of this issue reflected frustration at Smyth's 'practices', but it also reveals incomprehension regarding the legal system, and what he regarded as flawed judgments. Having moved the court 'divers times', Crokey secured additional awards (to almost £300), but found Smyth unyielding. Smyth insisted that the award was 'stayed' (December 1620), and that his suit was dismissed because Crokey's Common Pleas case was 'depending', rather than because of its 'merits'.[28] Crokey was unwilling to accept this scenario, to the point where he infringed Smyth's constitutional privilege by pursuing matters during the 1621 Parliament.[29] He struggled to see why

[23] GA, D9125/1/12008, pp. 13–14; TNA, STAC 5/M50/37; GA, D8887/6/15.

[24] GA, D8887/6/13.

[25] GA, D8887/6/42.

[26] GA, D8887/6/23. Moore also asked for papers, £10 to help with expenses, and a 'petycote... to keep me warm this winter'.

[27] GA, D9125/1/11989/4.

[28] Crokey, *Sacred Maiestie*, sigs C2–v; GA, D9125/1/12008, pp. 51–2, 58.

[29] GA, D8887/6/97.

injunctions were awarded against him, and why Smyth secured a discharge 'about the taxation of the said costs', merely by insisting that Crokey had put him to 'extreme trouble' (February 1623).[30] Subsequent episodes proved equally perplexing. A petition to Lord Keeper Williams provoked the suggestion that Crokey 'deserved to have his ears cropped' (May 1623), as well as an order 'remitting all the said costs', and a decree 'misliking' his 'troublesome and contentious disposition', and his pursuit of matters 'settled and determined'. Suspicions that Smyth had deceived the courts with 'untrue informations' were compounded by the decision to award costs of £52 to Smyth, and by Smyth's determination to claim such money until the late 1630s. This apparent inconsistency left Crokey feeling mistreated: he refused to pay, saying he would answer Smyth 'by leisure', and claiming his own 'bill of costs'. To make matters worse, Star Chamber ruled that his demand was not 'fit', after 'so long time and... so many orders made to the contrary' (1629).[31]

Beyond rationalising Crokey's obstinacy, it is also possible to scrutinise Smyth's most serious claims, regarding fraud and conspiracy. Such allegations had been prevalent for a long time, and Smyth described Richard Moore's attempt to secure administration of various estates as 'fraudulent and subtle'; 'maliciously intended' to 'defraud' John and Grace Drew of their 'good and lawful title'.[32] Crokey was accused of being party to 'combinations, confederacies and conspiracies', working with Joyce Cotterell, Anne Tempest, and the attorney William Porter, as well as Porter's servant John Price, to produce the illegal deed—dated 27 December 1613—which generated his claim to Warrens Court.[33]

First, Smyth challenged the 'secret entry' that Crokey made onto his land in January 1614. He insisted that Crokey and Price travelled from Bristol 'in vaunting, boasting and forcible manner', to sign the deed within the boundaries of Warrens Court, such that having 'dug a turf' he could claim possession and serve Smyth with a subpoena.[34] Unfortunately, the document was signed—by Anthony Hathway, Thomas Rogers, and William Lemon, as well as a local weaver, Hugh Deinton—'upon a stone wall' in Long Close, near a style leading 'out of the common street'. This was 'no part of the land in question'; Crokey had apparently been misled by an aged farmer! Smyth produced hand-drawn maps, as well as testimony from William Archard, to prove an error 'notoriously known to all that neighbourhood', insisting that Hathway and Deinton should have known better. Both were 'born and ever-dwelling in North Nibley', knew 'the names of both closes', and were skilled at 'writing and reading'.[35]

[30] GA, D9125/1/12008, pp. 51–2, 58.
[31] Crokey, *Sacred Maiestie*, sigs C2–v; GA, D8887/6/93, 103; D9125/1/12008, pp. 52–3, 65.
[32] TNA, C 2/Eliz/M3/53; STAC 5/M50/37; GA, D8887/6/62. [33] GA, D9125/1/11989/8.
[34] GA, D9125/1/11994, 11989/8–10; TNA, STAC 8/274/8.
[35] GA, D9125/1/11989/12, 11994; D8887/6/62, 99; TNA, STAC 8/274/8; GA, D9125/1/12008, p. 45.

For Smyth, this farcical scene resulted in illegality. He suggested that, upon realising the mistake, Crokey forged a revised version of the deed, shifting the action to Home Mead, which was 'indeed parcel of the lands in question', even if Smyth pointed out that this field lacked 'a style nor gate leading into it out of the common street'. His point was that Crokey's Chancery proceedings relied upon a fraudulent document, which is why he went to such lengths to find it, and why he interrogated Crokey's associates about whether they could verify their signatures. Hathway was apparently unable to do so, pointing out that the 'great letter' of both his names was not his style, and that 'he doth not make his H with a tail drawn down below the line'. Deinton was less certain, saying he tended to 'turn up' the final 'n' of his surname 'with a knot', while confessing that the signature was 'very like unto his own handwriting'.[36] Nevertheless, Smyth was emboldened to petition the king, complaining that the document was 'counterfeited and forged' (and that Crokey repeatedly chose to 'publish' it 'as a true and good deed'), insisting he had been 'molested, vexed and troubled', and demanding 'exemplary punishment' (May 1615).[37] Whether or not Crokey believed this deed to be any more problematic than the 'blotted' deed about which Richard Moore complained, he was probably fortunate that the matter was dropped with the (procedural) dismissal of Smyth's Star Chamber suit in 1619 (Case 4).

Smyth's most explosive claim—about 'maintenance' and the 'unlawful selling and buying of pretended rights'—proved more difficult to substantiate. According to Smyth, Joyce Cotterell showed scant regard for 'good and just laws', used 'undue and unlawful means to... stir up and maintain suits and controversies', and sought to 'trouble, oppress and disinherit' him, insisting that she conveyed her claim to Warrens Court in return for £10 *per annum* from Crokey.[38] Smyth's problem was Cotterell's protestation that the transaction reflected 'natural love' and 'affection' towards her nephew, and involved compensation for his 'pains' during her legal 'troubles', and he heard contradictory stories from her niece, Jane Moore, about whether money changed hands.[39] Smyth also struggled to get a clear account from Crokey's nephew, Thomas Tempest. Tempest claimed that Joyce possessed two versions of the deed—only one of which referred to payments—but only after a 'quarrel' with Crokey, and in return for a 'reward' from Smyth. When the two men were reconciled Tempest withdrew his offer, leaving Smyth without hard evidence.[40]

Here too, allegations about conspiracy and illegality were plausible but hard to prove, while behaviour that seemed obstructive and incomprehensible could involve logical strategising amid frustrating circumstances, thereby revealing energy and

[36] GA, D9125/1/11989/12, 11994; D8887/6/62, 99; TNA, STAC 8/274/8.
[37] GA, D9125/1/11989/8.
[38] GA, D9125/1/11994, 11996, 11989/8, 12008, p. 14; TNA, STAC 8/274/8.
[39] GA, D8887/6/62, 99; D9125/1/11989/12.
[40] GA, D9125/1/11994; TNA, STAC 8/274/8.

effectiveness. During the 1623 survey, Crokey 'pressed' commissioners that only a handful of the school's thirty-nine tenants appeared, and identified those who were missing, but his protestations were ignored, making him 'discontented'.[41] On other occasions, Crokey produced credible witnesses. In February 1620 he mustered John Harte, John Strachey, and Richard Alder [Aldworth?], and in the following May a local jury agreed that Smyth sought to 'subvert' and 'convert' the school, provoking Smyth to suggest that jurymen were 'misled' by Crokey's 'false pretences'.[42]

Crokey's refusal to compromise with Smyth was also logical. His apparently bewildering refusal to accept sight of the 'original' lease in 1615—after Smyth was ordered to make it available—probably reflected the fact that Chancery proceedings were ongoing (Case 1), and an expectation that Smyth's Common Pleas case would fail (Case 2).[43] Crokey's refusal to 'compound' probably reflected a belief that Smyth only made offers when he faced defeat in court (April 1615).[44] Since Smyth was 'non-suited' almost immediately, Crokey perhaps concluded that officials who promoted such deals favoured his opponent, and that he should reject other proposals. With Baddam's suit ongoing in June 1620 (Case 5), Crokey may have felt confident, and his ability to get Smyth imprisoned 'until he yielded possession' of the estate made it natural to decline a composition. Crokey later described this as the moment when—his 'back being at wall', and 'his plots and devices . . . discovered'—Smyth tried to 'save his reputation' by making 'show of innocency', using 'some compromise to take off Crokey from further prosecution for the school'.[45]

It might even be possible to make sense of Crokey's behaviour during one of the dispute's murkiest episodes: the Wickwar inquiry into concealed lands (1618). Smyth's allegation, *apparently* based on Peter Bird's report, was that Crokey 'brought all the evidence' that the land belonged to the crown, with certified copies of ancient deeds 'from the bishop's records of Worcester'.[46] Smyth repeatedly claimed—in a letter to Archbishop Abbot, in legal cases, and in his tract—that Crokey 'caused the said lands to be found concealed'.[47] Crokey, meanwhile, insisted that Smyth 'practiced' to get this outcome, and despite his own 'defence of the school' at the Tetbury hearing (August 1618), armed with a statement from Attorney General Yelverton and Solicitor General Coventry that the lands were 'free from superstitious uses' and should *not* pass to the crown.[48] Crokey also protested about defending the school 'in all he might' at Wickwar, blaming Smyth's 'unlawful labouring of the jury' for the decision that the lands were

[41] Crokey, *Sacred Maiestie*, sigs F3v–4.
[42] LB, MS 3549/175; Crokey, *Sacred Maiestie*, sig. C2v; GA, D9125/1/11996, 11989/9.
[43] GA, D8887/6/51–3. [44] Crokey, *Sacred Maiestie*, sig. C; GA, D8887/6/67; D9125/1/11994.
[45] Crokey, *Sacred Maiestie*, sigs D3v–4v, G2v; GA, D9125/1/12028, p. 4; Crokey, *Contents*, sig. Av.
[46] GA, D8887/6/70. [47] GA, D9125/1/11996, 12008, p. 63; D8887/6/77–9.
[48] Crokey, *Sacred Maiestie*, sigs A3v, C3v–4; GA, D9125/1/11996.

concealed.[49] This version of events was actually supported by Henry Townshend and Peter Bird, who affirmed that Crokey supplied evidence while also noting that he submitted the opinion of Yelverton and Coventry, insisted on the need to put the lands to 'charitable uses', and 'could *not* prevail'.[50]

Smyth's ability to tinker with this narrative reflected Crokey's subsequent decision—already noted—to accept a financial settlement from Sir John Poyntz and Henry Minors. Smyth alleged that this deal was struck *before* the Tetbury hearing, at the Three Cups inn and at a meeting with Sir Richard Hill, and that it revealed selfish motives.[51] Crokey admitted that the decision to 'compound' was a mistake, but protested that he faced pressure to reach a settlement precisely because he *refused* to accept that the lands were concealed, insisting that Poyntz and Minors 'laboured' with him 'earnestly' *after* the Tetbury hearing and *before* the Wickwar inquiry, as their 'only opponent'. Crokey 'utterly refused' their offer, 'not meaning to defraud the school', but confessed that he relented after failing to convince the jury, while contending that he accepted their offer tactically, and 'in good policy'. He recognised that Poyntz and Minors sought to 'intrap' him, and 'draw him from defending the school', but hoped they might 'intrap *themselves*', by demonstrating that as commissioners and concealment hunters they were judging their own cause. Crokey also felt that they might implicate Smyth, and aimed to secure 'some advantage', professing to know of 'no other, or better way for discovery of their practices'.[52]

As such, Crokey insisted that he worked with Archbishop Abbot to reverse the 'undue proceedings' at Wickwar. Having alerted Abbot to Smyth's 'practices against the school', he followed the 'direction' of an Exchequer judge (Sir Lawrence Tanfield), by getting Poyntz and Minors summoned to a hearing. On Crokey's telling it was their failure to disprove allegations about 'indirect courses' that caused the Wickwar inquiry to be 'made void', at which point Smyth tried to claim credit for overturning the verdict, by getting his own lawyer's name 'foisted' into the official record. As such Smyth deluded court and country about his 'pious intent' towards the school.[53]

III

Crokey made unwise decisions, and laid himself open to serious allegations, but also demonstrated strategic thinking, and his obstinacy reflected a sense of what was *right*, and frustration that legal rulings failed to produce justice. His refusal to

[49] GA, D9125/1/11996, 12002, 12008, p. 55; Crokey, *Sacred Maiestie*, sigs C4–v; TNA, STAC 8/107/7.
[50] GA, D8887/6/70, 72. [51] GA, D9125/1/11996, 12008, pp. 55–6, 62; D8887/6/77–9.
[52] GA, D9125/1/11996, 12002, 12008, p. 55; Crokey, *Sacred Maiestie*, sigs A3v, C3v–4v; TNA, STAC 8/107/7.
[53] Crokey, *Sacred Maiestie*, sigs C4v–D, E; GA, D9125/1/11996–7; TNA, STAC 8/107/7.

'compound' reflected a belief that he might yet prove successful in court, and that Smyth could not be trusted to deal honestly, only seeking arbitration when confronted by the prospect of defeat. Whatever the accuracy of Crokey's claims, there was a perfectly reasonable logic behind the approach he claimed to have pursued. Indeed, by examining the people with whom he worked, and the tactics he devised, it can be shown that he was not entirely at sea within the legal system.

First, Crokey secured the services of a legal team, and while many of his counsellors—Mr Benn (or Bennet), Edward Rogers, Humphrey Peter, George Peters, Thomas Grosvenor, Mr Brierley, and Thomas Farewell—were fairly obscure, others were more eminent, including Serjeant Robert Hitchman, Sir Lawrence Hyde, and Thomas Richardson, Speaker of the Commons in 1621. It seems to have been Hyde who helped Crokey to navigate the Tower of London archive and access the school's charters, and who assisted with his most important cases, including the Attorney General's suit.[54] As he boasted to Henry Townshend, Crokey was also supported by Archbishop Abbot, 'who had well informed himself of the cause on the behalf of the school', and to whom attention will return.[55]

Secondly, Crokey—like Moore—understood the possibility of tactical legal manoeuvres and aggressive tactics. Moore was accused of instigating vexatious suits, and of serving Grace with subpoenas 'as she was following her former husband's body to his funeral', and on the day she married Smyth, as evidence of what Smyth called the 'trouble I was like to enter into if I married with her'.[56] In 1589, Moore *excommunicated* Grace for failing to attend a hearing, excluding her from the benefits of 'society' and making it impossible to litigate.[57] As he languished in the Fleet, Moore admitted that Smyth had shown 'more love and kindness' than his 'contentious suits ... deserved', reflected upon pursuing litigation 'fruitlessly' for two decades 'in all or most of His Majesty's courts', and promised to 'desist all my life henceforth'.[58] He hoped to discuss things in a 'gentle manner', without the 'foul words' and 'railing speeches' used in the past, and hoped that Smyth could 'put aside all former unkindness'.[59]

Although Crokey claimed to have played with a straight bat, he was shrewd and demonstrated a ruthless streak. He professed to have honoured the injunction against further litigation (1620), even though this ensured that 'endeavours' for the school—'faithfully and zealously followed'—were 'utterly defeated'. Nevertheless, he tried to recover costs awarded to him, ignored Smyth's parliamentary privilege, and saw value in pursuing cases—like his 1614 Chancery suit

[54] GA, D9125/1/12008, pp. 41, 52, 58–9, 62, 68; D8887/6/55, 74–5, 103; Crokey, *Sacred Maiestie*, sigs C2–v, G3v; Crokey, *Complaint*, sigs A–v. Rogers was attorney to the corporation in Bristol, and an under-sheriff: BA, M/BCC/CCP/1/1/, p. 32; F/AU/1/16, pp. 156–7. For Hitchman, Hyde and Richardson, see: Prest, *Barristers*, pp. 369, 371, 388; *ODNB*.

[55] Crokey, *Sacred Maiestie*, sig. F2. Abbot had undertaken the episcopal visitation at Gloucester in 1612: Fincham, *Prelate*, pp. 199, 202–3, 207.

[56] GA, D8887/6/15; D9125/1/12008, pp. 76–7.

[57] GA, D8887/6/14, 32.

[58] GA, D8887/6/109.

[59] GA, D8887/6/41.

(Case 1)—that did not look hopeful. Smyth regarded this move as peculiar, given that the claims had been answered on previous occasions, but Crokey probably felt justified when judges decreed that Smyth, who had been allowed to keep the 'original lease', should let Crokey see it. That Crokey declined to take up this opportunity may not have been the point.[60] The aim may simply have been to put Smyth under pressure. This may also have involved providing minimal notice about hearings, something that Smyth called a 'poor practice'. Smyth allegedly only received 'sudden and short warning' about Crokey's inquiry into charitable uses—scheduled for 1 April 1619—with a warrant dated 22 March, such that 'it was not possible... to be present and prepared with counsel or evidence'. Crokey—like Moore—also got Smyth imprisoned, persuading judges to send him to the Fleet in 1620 or 1621, for 'not yielding possession' of Warrens Court, and detaining him a second time when he effected a quick release. This reflected Crokey's sense that Smyth was evading the 'rules' which bound both men to abide by a Common Pleas verdict in Baddam's case (Case 5), and trying to alter those rules when the verdict proved unfavourable.[61] Smyth was imprisoned again in early 1623, and although he quickly secured a Common Pleas order 'discharging my commitment', he was back in prison before the end of the year, making a note to move for his liberty in Michaelmas term.[62]

If Crokey behaved ruthlessly, he was also capable of subtle legal manoeuvres. He appreciated the utility of delaying tactics, pursuing an order to halt Smyth's proceedings in 1614 because they were instigated without his knowledge, even if Smyth 'in contempt went to trial' (Case 2).[63] He allegedly 'delayed' Smyth's Star Chamber case 'for seven terms' before it could be 'brought to examination' in early 1617 (Case 3), and declined to attend two meetings—scheduled for December 1620—to choose commissioners for a charitable uses inquiry. Crokey claimed that this commission was aborted because a new Parliament was 'at hand'; Smyth insisted that Crokey saw an opportunity to pursue 'other courses'.[64]

Crokey may also have hindered Smyth by using lawsuits as blocking devices. Smyth saw this as the motive for Baddam's case, instigated just as his own Star Chamber case was due to be heard (Case 4), and he justified getting an injunction to halt Baddam's suit lest it should 'prejudicate' the ruling in a different court. Smyth complained that Crokey sought to use 'a verdict at common law' against a judgment in Star Chamber, bracketing this with other attempts to use 'many delays'.[65] Smyth's counsel, Edward Trotman, later reflected that this Star Chamber case was dismissed—in Michaelmas 1619—not upon its 'merits', but because an

[60] Crokey, *Sacred Maiestie*, sig. B4, E; GA, D8887/6/23, 55; D9125/1/12008, p. 41.
[61] GA, D9125/1/12028, pp. 4, 67; D8887/7/21; Crokey, *Sacred Maiestie*, sigs B, D4v–E.
[62] GA, D8887/6/90; D9125/1/13608/52v.
[63] Crokey, *Sacred Maiestie*, sig. B4.
[64] GA, D9125/1/11996, 11989/13–14, 12002; Crokey, *Sacred Maiestie*, sigs E–v.
[65] GA, D9125/1/11898/13–14, 11994; D8887/6/63–4, 68; Crokey, *Sacred Maiestie*, sig. C2.

'action'—Baddam's case—was depending in Common Pleas.[66] This reading of Crokey's tactics would explain his determination to get Smyth's injunction lifted, and the rhetoric used in making this request—that he never received an explanation 'why the said injunction should be granted'—probably involved a legal rationale for a strategic move. Crokey's claim that Smyth sought to 'keep the injunction a foot' to 'weary' a 'poor man' may also have been disingenuous; Smyth had good cause to prevent a legal action that obstructed his own strategic move.[67]

In exploring what Smyth called a pattern of non-cooperation, interesting things emerge about Crokey's attitudes and abilities. With the case brought against both men by Attorney General Coventry, Smyth's lawyers accused Crokey of preventing 'a speedy hearing' (December 1620), prompting an order to speed things up, and in the summer of 1624 Crokey was accused of running a 'drooping prosecution', by moving slowly to interrogate witnesses regarding Star Chamber proceedings instigated three years earlier, in February 1621 (Case 7). This tardiness had apparently continued despite instructions to call 'all those that he would have to answer and proceed against', and to proceed 'termly with effect' (December 1622). Crokey's failure to speed things up eventually led to a dismissal (June 1624). Why things reached this stage is unclear. Perhaps Crokey was distracted by imprisonment and the Attorney General's case; perhaps he misjudged the possibility of using delaying tactics to pressurise Smyth; perhaps he had a poor working relationship with lawyers. One counsellor confessed he had 'not heard from his client' for twelve months. The outcome, however, was important: Smyth was awarded the costs– £52—that caused Crokey such problems in later years (February 1625).[68]

Finally, allegations about Crokey's methods provide evidence about his strategic thinking. Smyth claimed that Crokey 'oftentimes had three, four, or five chases on foot at once', and his lawyers detected evidence of 'forum shopping'.[69] Anthony Gulson argued that, having failed in Chancery and at common law, Crokey sought a charitable uses commission to make Smyth produce the 'original lease' (1618).[70] This involved Crokey taking matters out of the courts and into a different setting, and a willingness to look beyond his lawyers for advice. In instigating Star Chamber proceedings in January 1621 (Case 7)—noted in an account of 'Crokey's courses since December 1620'—he claimed to have been encouraged by 'a most reverend and worthy prelate', Archbishop Abbot, and although Smyth dismissed this as a suggestion made 'audaciously' and 'impudently', he provided no evidence that it was untrue.[71]

[66] GA, D9125/1/12008, pp. 51–2, 58.
[67] GA, D9125/1/11989/13–14, 11994, 12008, pp. 48–9; D8887/6/63–4, 68.
[68] GA, D9125/1/12008, pp. 23–4, 64–5. [69] GA, D9125/1/12008, p. 80.
[70] GA, D8887/6/69. [71] GA, D8887/6/84; D9125/1/12008, p. 63.

IV

Whether or not Crokey heeded good advice, he had competent advisors, appreciated legal guile, and demonstrated ruthlessness, thereby making his arguments, behaviour, and reflections on disputation fascinating and challenging. He also responded to difficulties like an entrepreneur, escalating matters out of the courts, to the higher authorities and into different settings.

His most obvious tactic involved petitions. Crokey approached James I when his first commission proved abortive in September 1617, requesting 'a speedier day' for a hearing after Smyth re-scheduled the inquiry to the following December. Following the Wickwar inquiry, Crokey submitted petitions to the Lord Chancellor, the Lord Chief Baron, and the Archbishop of Canterbury, the last upon the recommendation of Mr Proctor, chaplain to Archbishop Toby Matthew.[72] When another commission was denied in June 1619, a plea to the king was referred to Abbot and the bishops of London and Winchester, prompting both an inquiry and a statement about Smyth's 'practices', even if Smyth proved reluctant to appear in person.[73] Likewise, as Baddam's case dragged on Crokey asked the king for 'direction to the judges' in Common Pleas, triggering an order for effective action (September 1620).[74] Finally, as 'prosecutor' on the school's behalf, Crokey petitioned Lord Keeper Williams in March 1622, complaining about Smyth's 'indirect means', about commissions pursued at his 'own charge', and about £1,200 spent 'to his great impoverishment'. Here too, Crokey was effective: Williams scheduled a hearing and summoned Smyth to attend, at least once Crokey drew attention to his arrival in town.[75]

Petitioning was a commonplace activity, but Crokey probably sensed that it offered a more promising route than the courts, and his solicitation of Parliament is even more striking. He attempted to claim privilege, and immunity from prosecution, and upon being arrested—on 24 June 1621—presented a letter of protection as a 'servant' of Lord Stafford, unaware that this had been revoked four days earlier, thereby making it possible to despatch him to the Poultry Compter. Having protested that Stafford was 'abused'—in order to block a commission and effect his 'undoing'—Crokey was called to appear before the House of Lords, upon a writ of *habeas corpus* sent to the warden of the Marshalsea (November 1621), even if the adjournment and dissolution of Parliament—so often a problem for petitioners—delayed his formal release.[76]

[72] GA, D9125/1/12008, pp. 65–6; D8887/6/58a, 71; Crokey, *Sacred Maiestie*, sig. C3. See: GA, D2404/3–4; R. W. Hoyle, 'Fountains of Justice: James I, Charles I and equity', in Michael Lobban, Joanne Begiato, and Adrian Green, eds, *Law, Lawyers and Litigants in Early Modern England* (Cambridge, 2019), pp. 79–113.

[73] GA, D9125/1/11996; Crokey, *Sacred Maiestie*, sig. Dv; Crokey, *Briefe*.

[74] Crokey, *Sacred Maiestie*, sigs D2v–D3v.

[75] GA, D8887/6/87–8.

[76] TNA, C 3/338/8; *LJ*, iii. 170–1, 173–4; Crokey, *Complaint*, sigs A3–v; Crokey, *Sacred Maiestie*, sigs E2v–4v; PA, HO/PO/JO/10/14/4, item 3363; GA, D8887/6/87. See: PA, HO/PO/JO/10/1/30 (Edmund Felton); HO/PO/JO/10/1/33 (Meredith Madey); HO/PO/JO/10/1/34 (Sir John Savage); HO/PO/JO/10/1/37 (Robert Lane).

Much more innovative was Crokey's parliamentary bill, 'for the establishment of the school' and 'recompences' for himself. Smyth noted that Crokey 'betook himself to petitions to Parliament', and echoed other litigants by referring to 'scandalous' supplications rejected by the Commons because they sought to 'disgrace' a sitting MP, before being directed to the Lords, 'where . . . he exhibited a bill'.[77] The petition and printed 'brief' of Crokey's bill valued the school estate at £300 *per annum*, and noted that the 'original lease' had fourteen years left to run. It complained about 'indirect practices' and 'powerfulness', a 'multiplicity of unjust suits', and sales of school lands, as well as Bishopp's machinations and the 'subversion of the school'.[78] Crokey spent £23 submitting the bill to the Commons, where it languished for six months, and then to the Lords, where its reading prompted an order for a new commission, under the bishops of Worcester, Bristol, and Gloucester, as well as their chancellors and men 'of good rank' (4 June).[79] Although Crokey encountered further problems, he placed considerable faith in Parliament; he returned with another petition in April 1624, complaining about £1,600 spent pursuing his 'charitable disposition' towards the school, to his 'utter undoing', and about Smyth undermining several commissions. He alleged that inquiries which 'found for the school'—that 'mis-employed' lands should be 'restored' according to the donor's 'true meaning'—were subverted, while Smyth secured a new commission from the Attorney General, even though the Lord Keeper had resolved to re-establish the school. Crokey's aim was not to rehearse such grievances but to get his bill reconsidered, without additional fees.[80]

Like others who valued Parliament, Crokey returned to Westminster repeatedly, in 1625, 1626, and 1629, as he languished in the Fleet.[81] His petition in 1629 protested about his initial detention, his re-arrest after the 1621 Parliament, and his imprisonment ever since, and about how consideration of his case was stymied by the session 'breaking up' in 1626. By this stage, Crokey judged his expenditure to have reached £2,300, not least because of 'vexatious' suits. He lauded the 'accustomed goodness' of peers in being willing to 'relieve the distressed', and Parliament once again effected his release. This prompted a flurry of similar petitions in which Crokey reiterated that he was 'groaning under the great oppressions of his adversary', requested a new commission, and protested about the undue influence of Sir Thomas Chamberlain. He also complained about how the commission that Smyth secured from Bishop Williams was executed by 'friends'. Parliament referred his case to the Committee of Petitions

[77] GA, D9125/1/11996; Crokey, *Sacred Maiestie*, sig. Ev; GA, D8887/6/84; D9125/1/12008, p. 68. See: PA, HO/PO/JO/10/1/25 (Great Tewe, Philip Smith, Isott Bidwell, John Freeman). See: Hart, *Justice*, pp. 37–8.

[78] BL, Harl. MS 6803, fos 56v–7; Crokey, *Briefe*.

[79] Crokey, *Complaint*, sigs A3–v; GA, D8887/6/85; Crokey, *Sacred Maiestie*, sig. Ev.

[80] PA, HL/PO/JO/10/1/24.

[81] See: PA, HL/PO/JO/10/1/13 (Mary Sole).

(27 January), which debated the issues in the presence of both disputants. Smyth's legal proceedings were halted, and Crokey's bill—'so long depending'—was finally read.[82] Crokey submitted even more petitions once a new commission was granted (31 January), insisting that Smyth's 'power' made it imperative he should be allowed out of prison to 'have the carriage' of proceedings; that commissioners should come from outside Gloucestershire to examine all the school's tenants; and that expenses should be borne by Smyth, since Crokey's estate had been 'consumed'. All of these conditions were met.[83]

Crokey continued to solicit the higher powers during the 'personal rule', when Parliament did not meet. As noted already, he petitioned Charles I in June 1636, and his 'differences' with Smyth were referred to Archbishop Laud, Lord Keeper Coventry, Lord Treasurer Juxon, and Sir Francis Cottington, and then, following an outbreak of the plague, secured a warrant for Smyth to appear at the council board in December. It was this hearing that Smyth evaded by insisting that previous 'agitation' made it redundant, prompting a resolution to punish Crokey for submitting a 'scandalous' petition and trying to 'rip up a business... so long depending, and so long since quieted' (4 December).[84] Even so, Crokey was given another chance to 'right himself', and was protected from Smyth's 'abuses' (July 1638), even if he was outmanoeuvred once again, as Smyth dodged the summons delivered on 5 August—using 'false suggestions'—and got him returned to prison.[85]

In such circumstances, Crokey inevitably turned to Parliament in 1640. He complained that the legal and political system had been 'deluded and abused' by 'practises'—by 'plotters and deceivers' bent on 'injury', 'oppression', and 'impious ends'—and attached his bill for re-establishing Wotton school.[86] As on previous occasions, Parliament looked kindly upon Crokey, releasing him from prison to pursue his legislative goals (May 1641). Here too, however, Crokey became the victim of circumstance, as his business was lost amid weightier matters. It was only in February 1646, as the first civil war drew to a close, that Crokey renewed his plea for help, seeking £100 from John Smyth junior (as someone 'ready to perish, as by affidavit appeareth'), as well as 'a speedy hearing'.[87] However, it was only as the Second Civil War approached its *denouement*, and after Crokey's death, that the Long Parliament took action. This involved responding to a petition from Sarah Crokey, which complained about ongoing 'vexation' linked

[82] PA, HL/PO/JO/10/1/29 (Catalogue of petitions, 23 Feb.–23 Mar. 1626); HL/PO/JO/10/1/30 (Catalogue of petitions, 16 Mar. 1626); HL/PO/JO/10/1/31 (catalogue of petitions, 18 Apr. 1626); HL/PO/JO/10/1/37; Crokey, *Complaint*, sig. B4.

[83] PA, HL/PO/JO/10/1/37; *LJ*, iv. 18; GA, S379/2/3/1/1.

[84] Crokey, *Complaint*, sigs B3v, C; GA, S379/2/3/1/3. See: Hart, *Justice*, pp. 33–4; John P. Dawson, 'The Privy Council and private law in the Tudor and Stuart period', *Michigan Law Review*, 48 (1950), 393–428, 627–56.

[85] Crokey, *Complaint*, sigs C–v.

[86] Crokey, *Complaint*, sigs A, Cv.

[87] D9125/1/12028, sig. A; Crokey, *Contents*, sigs A-A2v.

to 'these distracted times', and about the behaviour of John Smyth junior and the heirs of Giles Elbridge (Thomas Elbridge, Aldworth Elbridge, and Nathaniel Cole), and which sought relief for herself and action for the school.[88] Yet again this petition was successful, even if there then emerged an equally familiar story, whereby an order that defendants should submit a formal response—on 2 November 1648—was evaded for long enough that new and extremely weighty matters of national importance got in the way.[89]

V

That Crokey was so successful in the parliamentary domain reflected his most innovative tactic, and the most obvious way he escalated his case. This involved becoming what Smyth called 'a printed actor', who brought matters to 'a trial on the stage' by cultivating support in dramatic ways.[90]

This began in 1621, when Crokey printed 'divers hundreds' of the breviate about his parliamentary bill. Smyth derided this as 'full of lies and scandal', and as 'much differing' from Crokey's legal bills and responses, and he complained that it was distributed to 'many of the members of both the said Houses' and 'sundry other persons' in London, Bristol, and 'the country where Smyth dwelleth'.[91] This was a novel tactic at the time, and Smyth was appalled at Crokey's 'face of brass... to rail upon me... by a new precedent and fashion in print', and at being portrayed 'in so black a character as I think is unparalleled since pens and ink did first meet together'.[92] For Crokey, however, this was an essential means to overcome weakness in the courts and Smyth's power in Gloucestershire. The aim was to attract attention in both Parliament and the locality, where attempts to garner signatures for a complaint against Smyth were ongoing in the summer of 1620, shortly before Parliament assembled.[93] Indeed, Crokey submitted his 1621 petition alongside Wotton's mayor and burgesses and numerous local preachers.[94]

Crokey's next printed venture—the pamphlet dated 1 June 1625—was the most striking, for its nature, its rationale, and its impact. It was extraordinary for its scale and bitterness, even if it was toned down and made less libellous at the last minute, as will become clear. Crokey's complaints ranged over sixty-four quarto pages, and even he recognised that it was too long. A prefatory note apologised for its 'tediousness', while protesting that 'a more brief' account was impossible given the complexity of the dispute, and 'so many... vexatious suits wrongfully

[88] PA, HL/PO/JO/10/1/274. [89] GA, D8887/6/107–8.
[90] GA, D9125/1/12008, p. 80. See: Churches, 'Business at law', p. 950; Churches, 'False friends', p. 62.
[91] Crokey, *Sacred Maiestie*, sig. Ev; GA, D8887/6/84; D9125/1/11996, 12008, p. 68.
[92] GA, D9125/1/12008, p. 46.
[93] Crokey, *Complaint*, sigs A–v; Crokey, *Briefe*; GA, D8887/6/83.
[94] BL, Harl. MS 6803, fos 56v–7.

prosecuted against him'. A hand-written note recommended that peers should 'leave the reading thereof to your secretaries' (Fig. 8). Any reader not put off by such warnings encountered a fascinating but problematic tract. Crokey narrated the dispute, damned Smyth's 'foul and impious practices', and cast himself as a martyr for 'defence of the school' (rather than 'his own title'); someone who was imprisoned four times, whose 'vital spirits' were wasted, and who was 'decayed in his estate'. Unfortunately, the tract was badly organised; it ranged back and forth across time, and although specific issues were dealt with at length—discussion of

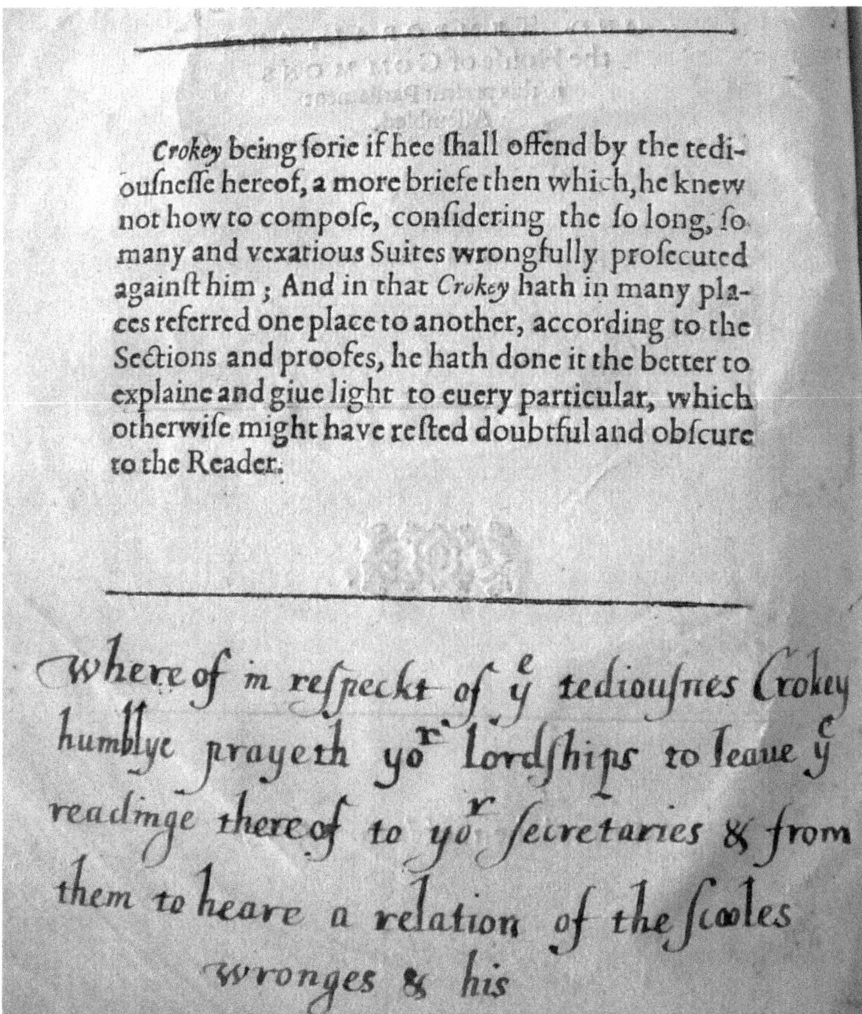

Crokey being ſorie if hee ſhall offend by the tedi-
ouſneſſe hereof, a more briefe then which, he knew
not how to compoſe, conſidering the ſo long, ſo
many and vexatious Suites wrongfully proſecuted
againſt him; And in that *Crokey* hath in many pla-
ces referred one place to another, according to the
Sections and proofes, he hath done it the better to
explaine and giue light to euery particular, which
otherwiſe might have reſted doubtful and obſcure
to the Reader.

where of in reſpeckt of ye tediouſnes Crokey
humblye prayeth yor lordſhips to leave ye
readinge thereof to yor ſecretaries & from
them to heare a relation of the ſcooles
wronges & his

Fig. 8. Benjamin Crokey, *To his Sacred Maiestie, the lords spiritual, and temporal, and the House of Commons* ([London,] 1625), sig. Av. Gloucestershire Archives, D9125/1/12007. Reproduced by permission of Gloucestershire Archives.

the 1623 Chancery decree extended over sixteen pages—many claims were unsubstantiated. The margins directed readers towards 'proofs', but generally contained vague references to 'several records exemplified' and 'notes from the rolls'; to 'information', 'certificates', 'affidavit', or 'witnesses'. This was understandable given that a prisoner like Crokey lacked access to his papers, but insisting that claims were 'not to be denied' was not the same as proving them.[95]

The danger with Crokey's tone was clear. He risked libelling Smyth, who was accused of having 'abused and deluded' monarchs, archbishops, and judges, and 'most of His Majesty's courts at Westminster', and who used 'power', 'subtlety', and 'unconscionable practices'. Crokey also appeared to criticise the establishment. Mostly, he limited himself to carefully worded claims about officials being 'deluded and abused', although he openly accused clerks like Gayre and Ferrar of conspiracy and bribery. However, Crokey also claimed that the 1623 Chancery decree was 'contrary to' Parliament's commission, to the available evidence, and to the inquiry's findings, as well as to 'Crokey's particular right'.[96]

In explaining the tract's origins, Crokey admitted that it reflected his weakened position. He grumbled about lacking the resources to employ 'sufficient penmen', and in noting that it was intended to accompany draft legislation for the school—copies of which were 'presented to many of your lordships'—he admitted that it was hard to attract attention while 'groaning' as a prisoner 'under the great oppressions of his adversary'. The use of print was thus necessary, 'for the better understanding and expedition of the said cause', and Crokey sought to ensure that copies were given to the King and 'most of the lords', to encourage 'the calling of Crokey's bill'. This is why it was dated two weeks before the opening of Parliament, on 18 June 1625. In Crokey's position, print was crucial to get noticed, justify his claims, and secure an inquiry, as well as to revoke the 1623 Chancery decree. Without print, it would be impossible to get the school 'reduced' to 'the meaning of the founders', albeit with 'additions . . . meet and agreeable to the time', let alone to get compensation for the 'expense of his whole estate and more'.[97]

The predictable result of such lobbying was another Star Chamber case, instigated by Smyth and Wotton's schoolmaster, Edward Cowper (Case 8). Their bill defended the 'good government' of the school against a 'scandalous and libellous pamphlet', accusing Crokey of a 'contentious, malicious and unquiet spirit', and of casting 'foul aspersions' upon 'persons of eminent note and authority, both ecclesiastical and temporal'. These served to 'deprave the justice' of the legal system and 'the government of the realm'. Crokey was also accused of conspiring with John Dowle junior and two Bristol merchants, Ralph and Thomas Wright,

[95] Crokey, *Sacred Maiestie*, sigs Aiiv, Av–2, B2-4v, Cv–2, D, Ev, E2v–4v, Fv, F2v–H2.

[96] Crokey, *Sacred Maiestie*, sigs A2, A4–v, C2, Fv, F2v, H3. For Gayre: ibid., sigs A4, D4v. For Ferrar: ibid., sig. Fv.

[97] PA, HL/PO/JO/10/1/37; Crokey, *Sacred Maiestie*, sigs A2, H3v.

as well as with others 'yet unkown', so that 400 copies were 'published and divulged... both by sale and gift', to MPs, peers and people across the country, especially 'in and near' Wotton and Nibley. Smyth later claimed that 200 copies were sent to friends, 'to be published in the country' after Parliament was dissolved, such that his reputation was 'insufferably traduced' and his 'posterity... exposed to ignominy and reproach'.[98]

Crokey's experiment with printed lobbying was controversial, and eventually saw him sentenced in Star Chamber (1631), but rather than retreat from print he modified his tactics, to ensure that subsequent pamphlets were shorter and more aggressive. In 1640, he addressed a twenty-page *Humble Account* to Parliament, summarising the dispute and his grievances—as someone 'still tyrannised by his adversaries for his most charitable... endeavours'—and making vague references to 'witnesses' who could 'prove this'. Preaching to the choir in a reforming assembly, Crokey made overt references to Smyth's 'power' with leading officials, including his 'master' Sir Thomas Chamberlain, and to the deleterious effects upon 'the administration of justice by impostures practises, plotters and deceivers'.[99] In 1646, Crokey and his daughter distilled the message yet further, into a four-page tract—*The Contents and Short Briefe*—which reiterated complaints about 'crying oppressions', 'injustice', and 'defamations', summarised litigation that lasted 'threescore years' (and cost £4,000), and outlined new complaints about John Smyth junior and his allies (Fig. 9). They sought to revive a case that was buried in the Committee for Petitions, hoping that it 'might yet come to a speedy hearing', and that steps might be taken for 'the speedy rectifying of justice'.[100] Finally, in 1647, Crokey submitted the twelve-page *Humble Petition*, his most aggressive text yet (Fig. 10). This restated claims about 'vexatious suits', and about the vast cost of Crokey's campaign, and explained the 'confederacy' involving John Smyth junior, Thomas Thomas, and Philip Beast, but it was much more critical of Hobart, Williams, and Chamberlain, who abused their power by releasing Smyth from prison, 'perverted... the directions for settling of the school', and rejected the findings of official inquiries. Like other petitioners, Crokey also claimed that his adversary had ignored parliamentary orders, and was guilty of contempt.[101]

Crokey recognised the need for brevity, but failed to learn the lesson that printed lobbying would be controversial if its message was broadcast beyond Westminster. He ensured that copies of his 1646 petition reached Gloucestershire, and when John Smyth junior found himself 'entangled at London through the means of

98 GA, D9125/1/12008, pp. 1, 83–9; PA, HL/PO/JO/10/1/37.
99 Crokey, *Complaint*, sigs A, A3, A4, B2, Cv.
100 Crokey, *Contents*, sigs A–v, A2–v. See: GA, D9125/1/12027.
101 Crokey, *Petition*, pp. 2, 3, 4, 6, 7, 10, 12. See: GA, D125/1/12028; Crokey, *Sacred Maiestie*, sigs D4v–E. See: PA, HL/PO/JO/10/1/29 (Mary Brocas); HL/PO/JO/10/1/35 (Matthew Dale); HL/PO/JO/10/1/37 (Richard Stoddard).

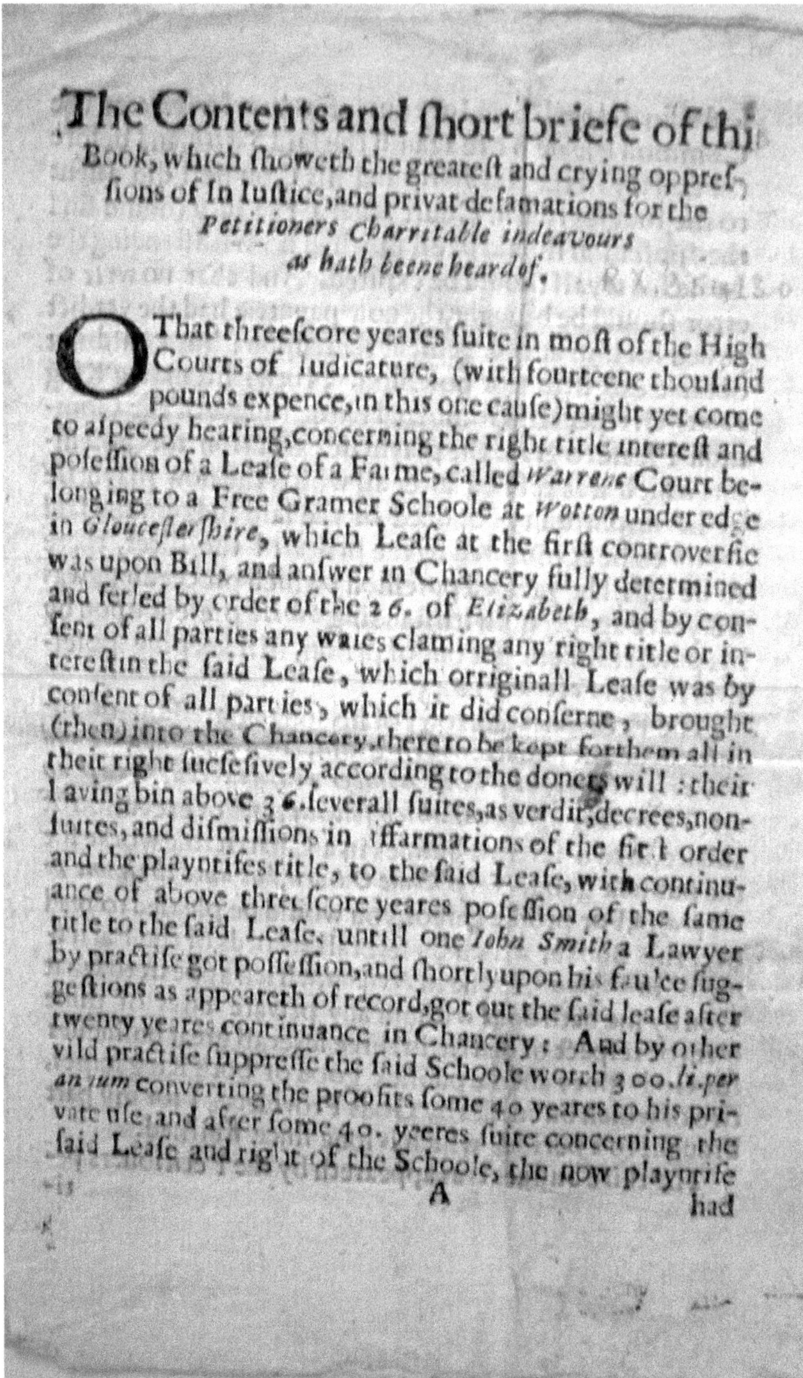

The Contents and ſhort briefe of thi
Book, which ſheweth the greateſt and crying oppreſ-
ſions of In Iuſtice, and privat defamations for the
Petitioners Charritable indeavours
as hath beene heard of.

O That threeſcore yeares ſuite in moſt of the High Courts of Iudicature, (with fourteene thouſand pounds expence, in this one cauſe) might yet come to a ſpeedy hearing, concerning the right title intereſt and poſeſſion of a Leaſe of a Farme, called *Warrens* Court belonging to a Free Gramer Schoole at *Wotton* under edge in *Glouceſterſhire*, which Leaſe at the firſt controverſie was upon Bill, and anſwer in Chancery fully determined and ſetled by order of the 26. of *Elizabeth*, and by conſent of all parties any waies claming any right title or intereſt in the ſaid Leaſe, which orriginall Leaſe was by conſent of all parties, which it did conſerne, brought (then) into the Chancery, there to be kept for them all in their right ſucſeſively according to the doners will: their having bin above 36. ſeverall ſuites, as verdit, decrees, nonſuites, and diſmiſſions in affarmations of the firſt order and the playntifes title, to the ſaid Leaſe, with continuance of above threeſcore yeares poſeſſion of the ſame title to the ſaid Leaſe, untill one *Iohn Smith* a Lawyer by practiſe got poſſeſſion, and ſhortly upon his faulce ſuggeſtions as appeareth of record, got out the ſaid leaſe after twenty yeares continuance in Chancery: And by other vild practiſe ſuppreſſe the ſaid Schoole worth 300. *li. per annum* converting the proofits ſome 40 yeares to his private uſe, and after ſome 40. yeeres ſuite concerning the ſaid Leaſe and right of the Schoole, the now playntiſe

A had

Fig. 9. Benjamin Crokey, *The Contents and short briefe* ([London,] 1646). Gloucestershire Archives, D9125/1/12027. Reproduced by permission of Gloucestershire Archives.

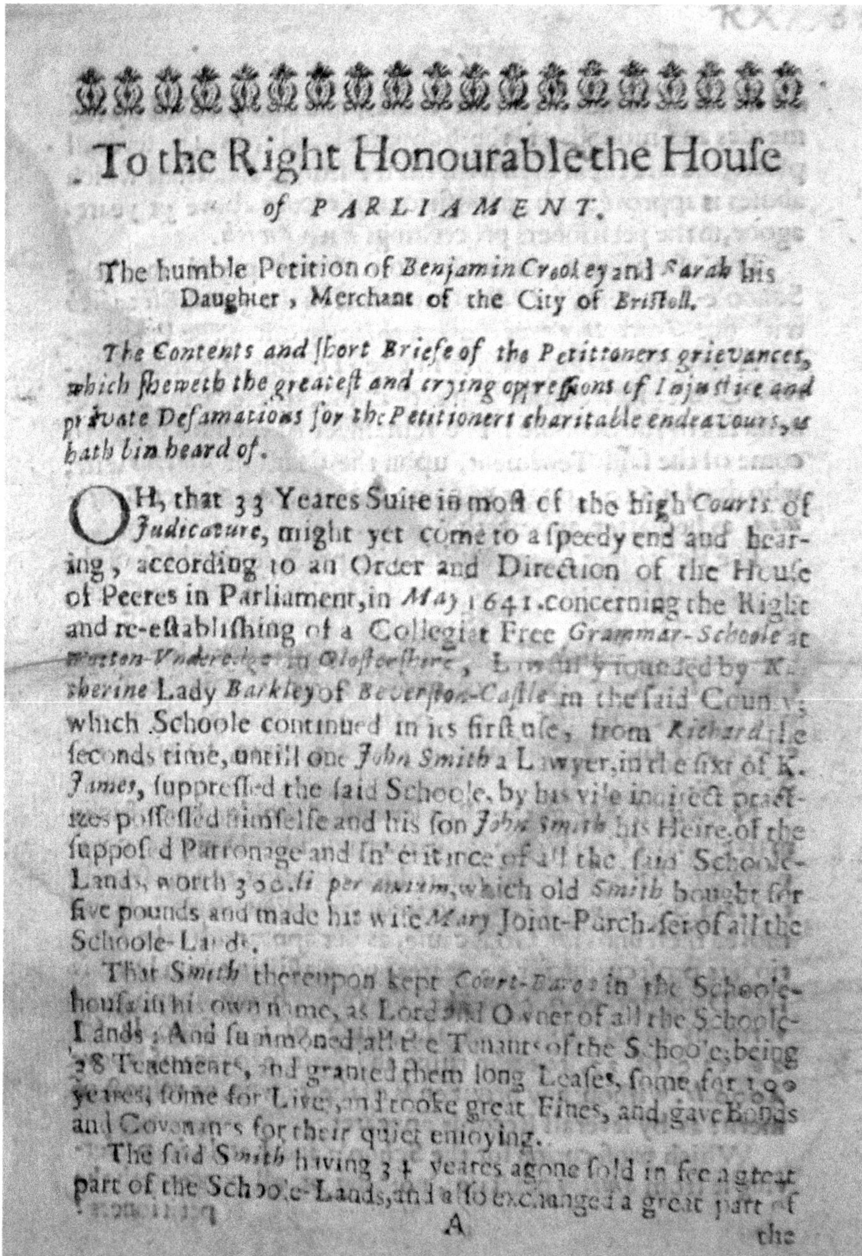

To the Right Honourable the House

of PARLIAMENT.

The humble Petition of *Benjamin Crookey* and *Sarah* his Daughter, Merchant of the City of *Bristoll*.

The Contents and short Briefe of the Petitioners grievances, which sheweth the greatest and crying oppressions of Injustice and private Defamations for the Petitioners charitable endeavours, as hath bin heard of.

OH, that 33 Yeares Suite in most of the high *Courts* of *Judicature*, might yet come to a speedy end and hearing, according to an Order and Direction of the House of Peeres in Parliament, in *May* 1641. concerning the Right and re-establishing of a Collegiate Free *Grammar-Schoole* at *Wotton-Vnderedge* in *Glocestershire*, Lawfully founded by *Katherine* Lady *Barkley* of *Beverston-Castle* in the said County, which Schoole continued in its first use, from *Richard* the seconds time, untill one *John Smith* a Lawyer, in the sixt of K. *James*, suppressed the said Schoole, by his vile indirect practises possessed himselfe and his son *John Smith* his Heire, of the supposed Patronage and Inheritance of all the said Schoole-Lands, worth 300.*li per annum*, which old *Smith* bought for five pounds and made his wife *Mary* Joint-Purchaser of all the Schoole-Lands.

That *Smith* thereupon kept *Court-Barons* in the Schoole-house in his owne name, as Lord and Owner of all the Schoole-Lands; And summoned all the Tenants of the Schoole, being 38 Tenements, and granted them long Leases, some for 100 yeares, some for Lives, and tooke great Fines, and gave Bonds and Covenants for their quiet enjoying.

The said *Smith* having 34 yeares agone sold in fee a great part of the Schoole-Lands, and also exchanged a great part of

A the

Fig. 10. Benjamin Crokey, *To the Right Honourable the House of Parliament. The Humble Petition of Benjamin Crookey and Sarah his Daughter* ([London,] 1647). Gloucestershire Archives, D9125/1/12028. Reproduced by permission of Gloucestershire Archives.

Crokey', his brother reflected that it was 'by reason of this printed paper'. One copy was apparently 'brought down' by a clothier called Dimery, 'and showed almost to every one', and Thomas Smyth noted that 'my brother [Christopher] Purnell chanced to meet with it at Tortworth'. He was thus able to send his brother the copy of Crokey's pamphlet that remains within the family's papers.[102]

VI

Crokey was perhaps a less skilled—and less wise—litigant than John Smyth, and he was sometimes out-manoeuvred. He may have been less well guided by, or less willing to follow, legal counsel, to their apparent frustration. Nevertheless, evidence indicates the need to look beyond contemporary claims that Crokey's behaviour was erratic and illogical, and that he was little better than mad. It is possible to recognise his ability, reconstruct his thinking, and comprehend why he pursued the Warrens Court dispute so doggedly, despite overwhelming odds and the cost to his family. Crokey's tactics were considered to be logical, by himself and others, and this logic can sometimes be recovered, even if only tentatively, and even if his moves were not necessarily successful. Crokey displayed a ruthless streak, in ways that reflected his experience as a litigant and made him similar to Smyth, and he behaved in an entrepreneurial fashion, by escalating matters from the courts to the higher authorities, and by adopting new modes of disputation. Crokey was a skilled petitioner, an early practitioner of printed lobbying, and an inveterate pamphleteer, and although this ultimately did him more harm than good, it would be unwise to overlook the good that it did him.

In teasing out Crokey's logic, it is important to grapple with Smyth's allegations, and with how Crokey explained himself, and it is fruitless to seek certainty about his thinking regarding every episode and action, let alone to arbitrate between rival interpretations. Nevertheless, while Crokey's claims might appear tendentious, he sometimes used legal and technical language to justify tactical decisions, and his rhetoric reveals how he thought about litigation and how it could and should be done. Crokey's behaviour reflected strategic thinking, and he developed a powerful sense of having been mistreated, and not just at the hands of Smyth. He came to believe that his 'endeavours' were more or less fruitless, and that 'no good effect' could be achieved 'in ordinary courts of justice', and he accused Smyth of 'impiously outfacing all justice and authority', and of behaving 'against justice and equity'.[103]

Historians sometimes reflect that such cravings for justice—and for proceedings that were accessible in English—led litigants to favour equity courts over the

[102] GA, D8887/6/106. [103] Crokey, *Petition*, p. 12; Hart, *Justice*, p. 30.

common law. These provided ways to prevent 'oppression' and enforce rights that might otherwise be neglected; to address litigants' moral qualities and secure definitive judgments; and to enforce abstract, natural, or religious principles, rather than strict liability.[104] Crokey perhaps shared these instincts; he certainly regarded himself as a victim of tyranny, oppression, and injustice, and of 'afflictions which so loudly cry for execution of justice'. As such, he joined many other litigants and petitioners who appealed for 'the speedy rectifying of injustice'.[105] Nevertheless, his response to the maladministration of justice, and to imprisonment, involved not just 'untoward words' but also logical attempts to escalate matters out of the courts, to Parliament, to Archbishop Abbot, and to the king and his council, and into the public domain, even if he risked being accused of libel.[106] Crokey persisted with the Warrens Court dispute because he saw signs of progress through legal channels—the eternal hope of struggling litigants—but also because he felt himself to be *right*, because his pride was dented by Smyth's behaviour, and because he could not trust Smyth or the courts to play fair or see justice done. He may thus have despaired about his libel trial, which involved the 'manner' rather than the 'matter' of his pamphlet, and ignored the 'truth' of his claims. At one point, Crokey made a telling comment about having 'so just a cause', which was 'more precious than life itself'.[107]

Herein lies the broader significance of Crokey's behaviour and thinking as a litigant. Crokey's actions—and Smyth's responses—indicate that it is less profitable to assess which man had the best case than to recognise the potential for litigation to result in incommensurable perspectives on disputation. This was not just a matter of legal strategies colliding, or of polemical attempts to describe an opponent's conduct as nefarious or illogical. Such things are evident, but so too are profound disagreements about what constituted logical contestation, and about whether protagonists' behaviour was reasonable. Litigation could generate incompatible visions—and expectations—of the legal system, and failures to comprehend opponents could be extremely damaging. Such incomprehension prolonged disputation, incentivised innovative and questionable behaviour, and exacerbated animosity. Crokey also highlights a 'powerless' style in early modern litigation; strategies and tactics devised more or less consciously in response to the 'powerfulness' of men like Smyth, which offered meaningful—and potentially

[104] Jones, *Chancery*, pp. 323, 420–1, 461–2; Brooks, *Law*, pp. 146–51, 314–15; Dennis R. Klinck, *Conscience, Equity and the Court of Chancery in Early Modern England* (Farnham, 2010); Mark Fortier, *The Culture of Equity in Early Modern England* (London, 2005); Laura Flannigan, '"Allowable or not?" John Stokseley, the court of requests and royal justice in sixteenth-century England', *HR*, 93.262 (2020), 621–37.

[105] Crokey, *Complaint*, sig. A; PA, HL/PO/JO/10/1/296; Crokey, *Contents*, sigs Av, A2v; Crokey, *Petition*, pp. 6, 12. See: PA, HL/PO/JO/10/1/30 (Mary Sole); HL/PO/JO/10/1/32 (Robert Lane); HL/PO/JO/10/1/34 (Anthony Lamplugh).

[106] Brooks, *Law*, pp. 289, 396; Hart, *Justice*, pp. 17, 38, 45.

[107] Debora K. Shuger, *Censorship and Cultural Sensibility* (Philadelphia, 2006), pp. 173–4; Crokey, *Sacred Maiestie*, sigs B4v, H3v–4.

successful—approaches to contestation, even if they might be considered illegitimate. He also reveals the propensity for litigation to provoke thinking, about how to succeed, what constituted success, and the chances of success being achieved. For Crokey this meant reflecting upon whether to trust his opponent, to put faith in the legal system, and to move beyond pure legal rationality.

For Crokey, litigation was—or became—connected with bigger issues, and he betrays what historians call 'eigensinn'; stubborn, wilful, and assertive behaviour that could be unruly and provoke tense encounters with structures of power. His complaints echo those of little-known petitioners—like Bernard Dakins, John Horseley, and Timothy Pinckney—who petitioned Parliament repeatedly after being 'undone' by vexatious, fruitless, and expensive litigation 'as long as the siege of Troy', and by 'oppression', 'conspiracy', and 'cruel and sinister practices', including the 'labouring' of creditors and the use of 'undue means' to corrupt judges like Bacon and Williams. Like them, Crokey complained about the perversion of justice, and about the 'potency' of opponents, who boasted and bragged about their ability, exploited their poverty, and caused imprisonment and impoverishment, and even resorted to force. Like them, Crokey made claims that sounded far-fetched while also being taken seriously by Parliament.[108] However, Crokey also resembles John Felton, the duke of Buckingham's assassin, a humbled and disgruntled figure who resented his treatment, and who highlights the fault lines within society and the dynamic of political life. However, before addressing what Crokey—and indeed Smyth—thought these bigger issues were, it is worth assessing what the fallout from Crokey's 1625 pamphlet reveals about both men's tactics and strategies.[109]

[108] PA, HL/PO/JO/10/1/26; HL/PO/JO/10/1/29; HL/PO/JO/10/1/30; HL/PO/JO/10/1/32; HL/PO/JO/10/1/35; HL/PO/JO/10/1/36.

[109] Paul Steege et al., 'The history of everyday life: a second chapter', *JMH*, 80 (2008), 373; Thomas Cogswell, 'John Felton, popular political culture, and the assassination of the duke of Buckingham', *HJ*, 49.2 (2006), 357–85.

6

'For your sake I sent this down'

The Battle over Crokey's Pamphlet, 1625–31

On 5 and 6 May 1626, Benjamin Crokey pulled off an audacious coup, and one relatively rare for the time, even if it involved behaviour that soon became more common. Despite being incarcerated within King's Bench prison, he travelled to Westminster and ensured that 200 copies of his printed pamphlet about the Warrens Court dispute were 'dispersed' among 'the lords of the high house of Parliament'. This was risky, given that prison officers 'laid in wait for him', and he did not act alone. He allegedly 'hired' someone to join him in Westminster Hall, and sent another man to the Painted Chamber, to see if 'the spirit'—as yet another assistant was called—'did deliver them'. One accomplice 'did much repent' giving a copy to Lord Berkeley, John Smyth's employer, but Crokey 'rejoiced thereat', and having 'accomplished his design' returned to prison 'of his own accord'.[1]

This extraordinary incident is part of a dramatic story about the use to which Crokey's tract was put, and about the response it provoked. This can be recovered thanks to Smyth's determination to document the dispute, and his papers bring the abilities, approaches, and attitudes of both men into sharp focus. Smyth exploited an extensive network in London and the West Country, laboriously constructing the libel case that eventually convicted Crokey, and revealing his thought processes.[2] This reinforces the sense that he was ruthless and tactically aggressive, co-opting and coercing Crokey's friends, and intimidating witnesses. However, while it might be tempting to conclude that this phase of the dispute reveals Smyth's superior power and practices, it also highlights Crokey's well-developed sense of how to force Smyth onto the back foot, and perhaps snatch victory from the jaws of defeat with a calibrated print campaign. This involved not just his spectacular feat in May 1626, but also innovative forms of networking and agitation from within King's Bench and the Fleet. Making this clear requires examining Smyth's forensic investigation into Crokey's tract, Crokey's print campaign, and convoluted litigation and parliamentary agitation between 1626 and 1631.

Such analysis provides new perspectives on the 'print revolution' and the culture of London's prisons, in terms of how becoming 'a printed actor' could

[1] GA, D9125/1/12009, 12014. [2] GA, D9125/1/12013–14.

The Madman and the Churchrobber: Law and Conflict in Early Modern England. Jason Peacey, Oxford University Press.
 DOI: 10.1093/oso/9780192897138.003.0007

achieve specific results by reaching particular audiences. Scholars have developed a sophisticated understanding of different modes of 'public' discourse, of the contexts from which they emerged, and of texts being deployed in targeted ways within petitioning and lobbying campaigns.[3] However, it has been difficult to move beyond the texts themselves, and aside from religious disputations that spilled over into less restrained forms of polemic it has proved hard to analyse the issues and grievances that animated such strategies, the ways in which texts were deployed, and the impact they made.[4] Having demonstrated how and why the Warrens Court dispute became so protracted, and why it spilled over from the law courts into Parliament and the public domain, this chapter analyses the composition, production, distribution, and reception of printed texts. Such detail about Crokey's pamphlet complicates our understanding of the relationship between print and publicity, and provides new ways of gauging the anxiety provoked by new kinds of text and new modes of discourse.

I

'The first time' that Smyth 'heard any word' of Crokey's tract was in April 1626. His information came from Anthony Hungerford, who learned about it from a Bristol merchant, Thomas Colston, who in turn read it the previous February, 'before it was delivered in Parliament'. In early May, Smyth became aware of an encounter 'in the street', as Mr Dowdswell 'came from, or went to, Westminster', in which William Hill offered to 'show him his neighbour Mr Bird in print'. On 12 May, Benjamin Webb relayed information from an attorney, William May of Charfield, who was informed about Crokey's tract by Thomas Poyntz of Uley, and by this stage information was also reaching Smyth from Edward Slaughter, Richard Wakeman, and Mr Sturchy of Bloomsbury. On 22 May, George Raymond pointed out that Job Deighton in the Court of Wards had read the book, 'and hath one of them', and on 25 May Christopher Stokes reported seeing a copy in the chamber of Mr Chester near St Clement Danes, 'which he there read in part'. Chester, who also 'read it over', received it from Sir Robert Poyntz, MP for Gloucestershire. When William Archard arrived in London on 31 May, he relayed news from Richard Poole of Wortley that the mayor of Bristol, John Barker, received a copy around Easter, and that copies had reached Edward Olyver, the mayor of Wotton. Equally alarming was evidence about local responses to Crokey's text. Archard 'heard in Wotton' that the school was being 'overthrown,

[3] Chris R. Kyle, *Theater of State. Parliament and Political Culture in Early Stuart England* (Stanford, 2012), ch. 6; Jason Peacey, *Print and Public Politics in the English Revolution* (Cambridge, 2013), chs. 8–9.

[4] Peter Lake, *The Boxmaker's Revenge: 'Orthodoxy, 'Heterodoxy' and the Politics of the Parish in Early Stuart London* (Manchester, 2009).

and that there were books come down in print thereof', while William Hopton reported what Robert Baker overheard at Gloucester's Bell Inn: William Wright's exclamation that 'were it not for my lord Berkeley' Smyth was 'in as great danger as the Duke of Buckingham by reason of that book'.[5]

It is unclear whether such reports—and the idea that Parliament might *impeach* him—arrived unsolicited, but Smyth recognised the need to find out as much as possible about Crokey's pamphlet. By 14 May, Smyth had spoken to William May, and made a note to ask Thomas Poyntz how he knew about it, only to discover that Poyntz had gone 'out of London'. He noted that 'Mr Wakeman will find out one that shall inform me fully', and Wakeman advised him to print a response 'by all means', because he stood 'wounded, lying and dead'. On 11 June, Smyth met another man—John Leigh—who had encountered the tract, and on 16 June he met Nicholas Webb to learn more about the mayor of Bristol, and got an update from Peter Bird. This reveals that Smyth sent two men—Edward Prayle and Wotton's under-schoolmaster, Henry Rugge—to visit Edward Olyver in Wotton, who had *six* copies of the pamphlet, and who revealed that it was being discussed by students at Wotton school, one of whom heard about it from his father, Albane Saunders. On 20 June, Philip Langley told Smyth that his maidservant had a copy, and promised to 'learn me out who had these books'. Help also came from Mr Doughty of Bristol, a friend of Crokey's brother-in-law, Robert Aldworth, and from Richard Poole, who offered to ask Olyver who sent him the tract.[6]

Smyth's response to news of Crokey's tract was quick and effective, and involved an extensive network of friends and associates, but particularly impressive was the speed with which he tracked down those responsible for its creation and dissemination. Smyth sent people to see Crokey in King's Bench prison, who won his trust by pretending to sympathise with his cause. These included Smyth's cousin, William Hill, 'under colour of visiting Mr Nathaniel Tracy', another Gloucestershire inmate (20 June). Hill discovered that 400 copies had been printed, that half were given 'to the lords and others', and that the remainder were in Crokey's chamber, 'ready to be delivered abroad'. Crokey apparently boasted that he would have been released from prison if the 1626 Parliament had lasted 'but four days longer'. Unsuspected, Hill made more visits alongside Henry Morris, a servant of Sir Richard Tracy of Stanway. He reported that Crokey 'cared not' about the 'great' men mentioned in the tract; that he would 'take his course' against them; and that he would protect the identity of his printer (27 June). Hill was followed by other local men, like Richard Wakeman (29 June) and Morgan Ady (28 and 30 June), the latter of whom also pretended

[5] GA, D9125/1/12014. Articles of impeachment against the Duke of Buckingham were introduced on 8 May: *CJ*, i. 857.
[6] GA, D9125/1/12014.

to be visiting another prisoner, Edward Oldisworth of Lincoln's Inn, who was prosecuted by Smyth for 'setting his hand' to Crokey's legal bills. According to Ady, Crokey boasted about printing *1,000* copies of the tract, and that 'the great lords were all his friends', using 'high words' that Smyth would become 'the basest companion of the shire', unable to 'dwell in his country'. Smyth also noted being challenged to 'do my worst'.[7]

Smyth also targeted Crokey's associates, particularly a brewer's clerk, William Burford, who lived at the Black Griffin in St Giles in the Fields. Burford was identified—by Edward Slaughter and Mr Sturchy—as one of those who gave out pamphlets at Westminster, and he not only offered to lend Slaughter a copy—'he having no more'—but also boasted about their popularity. Burford claimed that 'he could take 5*s.* apiece for as many of them as he could get', because they 'revealed such briberies and knaveries as never were practised', adding that the tract was 'quoted like a sermon'. Smyth sent Peter Bird to visit the Burfords, and caught Burford's father 'reading of the book', at which point William's wife Susan 'snatched' it 'out of his hands' (21 June). She also boasted that her husband had 'a bundle' of them 'more than a foot high', and that they 'would be plenty enough shortly'. Later that day, Bird took Burford to visit Smyth at his chamber, where he admitted having 'dispersed fifty or sixty of them', not least to Henry Elsynge's clerks and Mr Short, servant to the earl of Arundel, before naming the others involved: Joseph Harding, James Ashby, a 'pot seller' from St Giles, and Mr Tuby, 'a gentleman towards a noble lord'.[8]

Smyth promptly subjected these men to closer scrutiny. On 22 June, two cousins, Samuel Trotman and Christopher Stokes, visited Burford, who sensed that his association with Crokey might cause 'trouble' and seemed willing to talk. This prompted another visit by Trotman, in the company of his brother—and Smyth's lawyer—Edward Trotman. It was on this occasion that Crokey's printed breviate was spotted, 'fixed like a ballad on the wall', at least until it was 'pulled down' by Susan Burford 'in a rage' (25 June). The Trotmans confirmed that James Ashby, who lived 'near St Giles's church', was 'a great publisher' of Crokey's pamphlets, and that Tuby was his tenant, although he was suspiciously well dressed in a cloak 'lined with velvet'. They too believed that 1,000 copies had been produced, and felt confident that Burford knew 'the house of the printer'.[9]

Smyth's response was extraordinary in terms of his ability to pursue leads, trace connections, and unearth witnesses during frantic weeks in the summer of 1626, and to capitalise upon their fear of prosecution. Smyth interviewed Sturchy and met with Sir William Guise (22 June), Richard Wakeman (29 June), and Gyles Bird of New Inn (4 and 6 July), the latter of whom recommended talking to a soldier, John Leigh. Smyth's attorney, Mr Jones, 'saw and read one of Crokey's

7 GA, D9125/1/12014. For Hill's letter: GA, D9125/1/12009.
8 GA, D9125/1/12014.
9 GA, D9125/1/12014.

books' at his 'place of dieting'. Other interviews were conducted by friends, including the grocer, Arthur Fisher, the man who arrested Crokey in 1621, thereby confirming Crokey's claim that his imprisonment was effected through Smyth's contacts. Fisher discovered that Sir George Reynell, the marshall of King's Bench prison, had a copy 'which he had read' (28 June), while one of the Trotman brothers questioned Christopher Eyre, who was afraid of being 'made a defendant', and who was promised leniency if he 'confessed the truth'. Smyth accompanied Stokes when he visited Mr Chester, and went with Mr Togood to see Mr Washer 'at his chamber by Clement's Well' on the Strand (23 June). Washer had been shown a copy by his 'bedfellow', a solicitor called Adams; he explained that the two men read the pamphlet together, and promised to put Smyth in contact with other men, including Job Deighton. Finally, Smyth went with Peter Bird to see James Ashby, who confirmed that Tuby lodged 'at his house', while insisting that he did not 'belong' to any lord, but was an 'agent of himself' (27 June). Ashby admitted distributing the pamphlets, but protested that he 'never meddled further' in the business. Upon being visited again the following day, Ashby confessed to having 'many of the books' in his house, but refused to hand them over.[10]

Smyth also pursued people who helped Crokey in other ways, in London, King's Bench, and the country. William Hill and Edward Wakeman reported meeting 'old Wright of Bristol', meaning Ralph Wright, who read Crokey's tract because his son Thomas had 'many' copies. William Archard was sent to interrogate Thomas Wright, armed with Smyth's questions.[11] It was also thanks to Hill that Smyth met a lawyer called Thomas Whatman, who recommended talking to Thomas Tempest—presumably Crokey's nephew—who lived at the Golden Calf in Thames Street (25 June). In following Burford's leads it proved possible to track down other lawyers: Mr Archibold of Lyon's Inn, with whom Smyth had a meeting in the Pope's Head tavern in Chancery Lane; Mr Farewell, who was threatened with prosecution in Star Chamber; and Edward Oldisworth, Crokey's 'bedfellow' in King's Bench, who was interviewed by Morgan Ady. Oldisworth's involvement probably worried Smyth, because he was the son of a Gloucestershire magnate—Arnold Oldisworth of Wotton, a clerk of the Hanaper and receiver of fines in King's Bench—and because he described Crokey as 'sober and discrete', and not 'mad' as Smyth reported him to be.[12]

Smyth's energetic approach to finding and interviewing Crokey's associates reflected the need to make progress before the end of term, when many people would leave London, although returning to Nibley made it possible to pursue other leads. These included Wotton's former schoolmaster, Robert Pritchard,

[10] GA, D9125/1/12014. This was John Washer (*d.*1653): TNA, PROB 6/30, fo. 93.

[11] GA, D9125/1/12011.

[12] GA, D9125/1/12014. For 1617 a bond involving Arnold Oldisworth, his son Edward and John Smyth: LB, MS 3549/166.

identified by Morgan Ady as 'a meddler in this business', and Edward Brinkworth, a Wotton tailor. Brinkworth was reluctant to talk, but Smyth visited him in the company of Peter Bird, who was 'powerful with him', and as the three men 'drank together' Brinkworth confirmed that Crokey's tract was in the possession of John Bridges of Combe, and spoke about copies being read by local people, including maidservants (20 July). Smyth then talked to other local men whose names had cropped up in earlier interviews, including Edward Olyver, Robert Smyth, Richard Poole, and William Player, who in turn identified witnesses like Edward Tanner. Henry Rugge, who noted that the 'first coming of the books' caused 'a notable bruit and wonderment', claimed that Thomas Hewitt of Ozleworth would be able to help, having received a copy from Pritchard, and advised that Edmund Grayle could provide valuable information about Edmund Olyver and Albane Saunders.[13]

From May 1626 onwards, Smyth worked hard to gather information from people who encountered Crokey's tract, and who helped him in some way. He called upon friends, relatives, servants, and lawyers, and capitalised upon the 'power' that he and others possessed. He loosened tongues with drink and pressured witnesses through repeated interrogations, pursuing leads, testing memories, and verifying stories. His papers reveal a rigorous investigative process, meticulously recorded in an extraordinary if scrappy dossier, and one that generated an alarming picture about the web of people who read Crokey's pamphlet (Fig. 11).

Fig. 11. 'What witnesses will swere' [statements collected by John Smyth] (1626). Reproduced by permission of Gloucestershire Archives.

[13] GA, D9125/1/12014.

II

A key aim behind such interviews was to discover how Crokey's books had been produced and financed, revealing Smyth's doggedness in pursuing his adversary, and the strengths and weaknesses of Crokey's strategy.[14]

What became clear was that, rather than hire people to distribute his pamphlet, Crokey utilised a network from St Giles that stretched all the way to Wotton. William Burford's wife—who snatched the book from her father-in-law's hands and tore down Crokey's breviate—had been a maid to Edward Trotman of Cam, and apparently promised a copy to his son, Samuel, the brother of Smyth's lawyer, Edward Trotman.[15] William Burford also came from the area; he knew Peter Bird, and moved 'from Sodbury to St Giles' in pursuit of trade. The Burfords knew Crokey through others with Gloucestershire roots. William Burford first met him at the house of Mr Hathaway in Bloomsbury, in the company of a lodger, Joseph Harding, who hailed from Cam and was 'a familiar friend of Crokey's', and who 'surely had a hand in the business'. This connection enabled Crokey to stay with Ashby, who considered him 'honest and civil' (April–May 1626), while Susan Burford helped to arrange lodgings and move supplies of the pamphlet around London.[16]

It also emerged that King's Bench prison was vital for composing Crokey's pamphlet. Smyth assumed that Crokey received help, questioning witnesses about 'who penned the book or was of counsel' with him. William Burford 'seemed . . . to infer' that a fellow prisoner, Edward Oldisworth, as well as Mr Farewell, had 'a great hand in penning this book', although Smyth registered a difference between what Burford 'thinketh' and 'knoweth'. When questioned by Morgan Ady, Oldisworth protested that he had 'not heard' of Crokey's book 'till within six or seven weeks last', and boasted 'extremely' about relying upon the 'favour' of his brother, Michael Oldisworth, MP and secretary to the earl of Pembroke.[17] Such threats might explain why Smyth declined to pursue Oldisworth, but Archard also identified other leads, discovering that the handwritten note 'in the book's beginning' was by James Ashby, and pursuing information that Crokey was assisted by 'young Mr Dowle', namely John Dowle of the Middle Temple, the son of John Dowle of Almondsbury.[18] More alarming were other stories. One was that a 'great agent' in 'penning' the tract was Mr Belman, 'an intelligent lawyer and statesman' employed by Lord Keeper Coventry or his predecessor, Lord Keeper Williams. Another suggested it was 'specially penned' by George Goodyear, servant to Sir Robert Naunton (a former Secretary of State), and one of 'two or three prisoners'

[14] GA, D9125/1/13612/5.
[15] GA, D9125/1/12014. For a letter from Edward Trotman to Smyth on 26 June 1626: GA, D8887/9, p. 7.
[16] GA, D9125/1/12014. For Harding's connections in Cam: TNA, PROB 11/163, fo. 233.
[17] GA, D9125/1/12014.
[18] GA, D9125/1/12011, 12013. For Ashby: GA, D9125/1/12014.

in King's Bench who assisted in its composition. It was Goodyear who would be mentioned, although not made a defendant, in Crokey's Star Chamber trial.[19]

Such evidence—uncertain but suggestive—indicates that Crokey had contacts, and perhaps powerful supporters, and equally tantalising evidence about the tract's printing indicates that he invested heavily in its production. Crokey protested to William Hill that he received no financial help from his brother-in-law, Robert Aldworth, although Ralph Wright apparently 'procured' a friend in London to lend £20. Crokey explained—'for certain'—that 'the books were printed in France', and Thomas Wright suggested Amsterdam, the venue for so much seditious printing, but Burford confessed—after 'absolutely' denying 'any knowledge of the printer'—that the work was done by 'Atkinson', a compositor in Whitecross Street. This was presumably John Atkinson, who completed his apprenticeship with Thomas Snodham in May 1625.[20] Crokey later admitted that printing cost £9, because the 'extraordinary' paper cost 5*s*. *per* ream, although since he told Hill that each of the 400 copies cost 12*d*. to produce, the total bill may have been £20, the amount of the loan Wright reputedly arranged.[21]

Crokey apparently navigated the task of producing his pamphlet with skill and some assistance, although Smyth discovered that the process was fraught, as the need to avoid prosecution caused serious delays. William Burford claimed the text was 'twelve times written over' before being printed, and Richard Wakeman affirmed that when Crokey showed him a copy at the Three Cups in Bread Street—June 1625—it did not contain a reference to Thomas Trotman, accused in the final version of using 'untrue suggestions' in court. This suggests that Crokey agonised over who to name and what claims to make, and that the text was subsequently 'reformed with an addition', so that printing was ongoing until at least late June.[22] Similar problems dogged the drafting of Crokey's legislation, something Smyth used to suggest that Crokey was unbalanced. During the Oxford parliamentary session, Crokey's nephew Thomas Tempest employed a lawyer, Whatman, who confessed to Archard and Hill that he was involved in 'drawing' Crokey's 'parliament bill' (for £2), only to become involved in furious arguments—during *forty* meetings—about the text. Things apparently reached such a pitch that Crokey and Tempest 'railed' against him 'intemperately'.[23]

[19] GA, D9125/1/12013–14; Gardiner, *Reports*, p. 39. See: Richard Bell, 'Dens of tyranny and oppression: the politics of imprisonment for debt in seventeenth-century London' (Stanford University PhD, 2017); W. J. Sheehan, 'Finding solace in eighteenth-century Newgate', in J. S. Cockburn, *Crime in England, 1550–1800* (London, 1977), pp. 236–8.

[20] GA, D9125/1/12011, 12014. For Atkinson and Snodham: D. F. McKenzie, *Stationers' Company Apprentices, 1605–1640* (Charlottesville, 1961), p. 26; R. B. McKerrow, *A Dictionary of Printers and Booksellers in England, Scotland and Ireland... 1557–1640* (London, 1910), pp. 250–1.

[21] Gardiner, *Reports*, p. 39; GA, D9125/1/12009.

[22] GA, D9125/1/12014. This was Thomas Whatman, Inner Temple bencher and MP: Prest, *Barristers*, pp. 401–2. For the claim about Trotman: Crokey, *Sacred Maiestie*, sig. C2v.

[23] GA, D9125/1/12014.

Such claims were perhaps embellished, but Crokey certainly deliberated at length, delaying the submission of the bill and the distribution of the book. The tract was dated 1 June *1625*, but Crokey told Hill it was not 'finished and printed' until after the first parliamentary session in mid-July, and although he planned to disperse copies during the Oxford session—which began on 1 August—this was prevented because the row with Whatman was ongoing as MPs reassembled. Things may have been ready shortly thereafter, only for Crokey to be 'disappointed' by the 'sudden dissolution' of Parliament (12 August). Having broken the bank to finance his lobbying, Crokey was left with a stock of useless pamphlets. He gave a copy to a mercantile acquaintance—Mr Ballow of St Lawrence Poultry—and 'would . . . have pawned many of them with him', but Ballow refused to dabble in so risky a business.[24]

Such problems explain why Crokey only distributed his pamphlets in *1626*, when another Parliament provided a chance to submit the bill and lobby members. Even then textual doubts remained, and the pamphlet was apparently 'censured' by Crokey's 'best friends, on whom he most relied'. Allegedly, these 'friends' distanced themselves from Crokey's 'jugglings', and the printed text was subjected to further emendation. Portions of text were pasted in, words were obliterated, and sentences were rephrased. Some changes were trivial, and it is unclear why a printed slip altered the opening line—'A true relation of the passages in divers suits'—to read '. . . *strange* suits'. Other modifications corrected typographical irregularities and factual errors, including the value of the school lands and the scale of Crokey's losses. Some tweaks were required because key officeholders had changed between 1625 and 1626, such that references to 'the Lord Keeper' needed to be changed—by hand—to 'late' Lord Keeper, following the replacement of Bishop Williams with Thomas Coventry (1 November 1625).[25]

More significant were changes that removed offensive phrases and hid the names of key players. The obliteration of words by pen makes some of these changes difficult to fathom, both others are clear. A reference to Smyth 'persecuting' was changed to 'prosecuting', and a sentence referring to leases that Smyth 'falsely made' was changed to read 'leases as Smyth had made are naught.' Crokey toned down references to Smyth's collusion with judges, and pulled back from saying that he 'suborned' or 'seduced' witnesses. More dramatically, Crokey tipped-in a half-page of printed text complaining about an unsatisfactory survey of the school lands—'without examination of any witnesses upon oath as the commission required'—and about decisions by Lord Keeper Williams that were 'repugnant' to Archbishop Abbot and Parliament (Fig. 12). He did so even though this made the next page begin mid-sentence. Finally—as his opponent

[24] GA, D9125/1/12009, 12014. This was John Ballow, formerly servant to Robert Aldworth: TNA, PROB 11/167, fo. 21.

[25] Crokey, *Sacred Maiestie*, sigs A2, C2, Ev, E4, F2v, F3, G3, H.

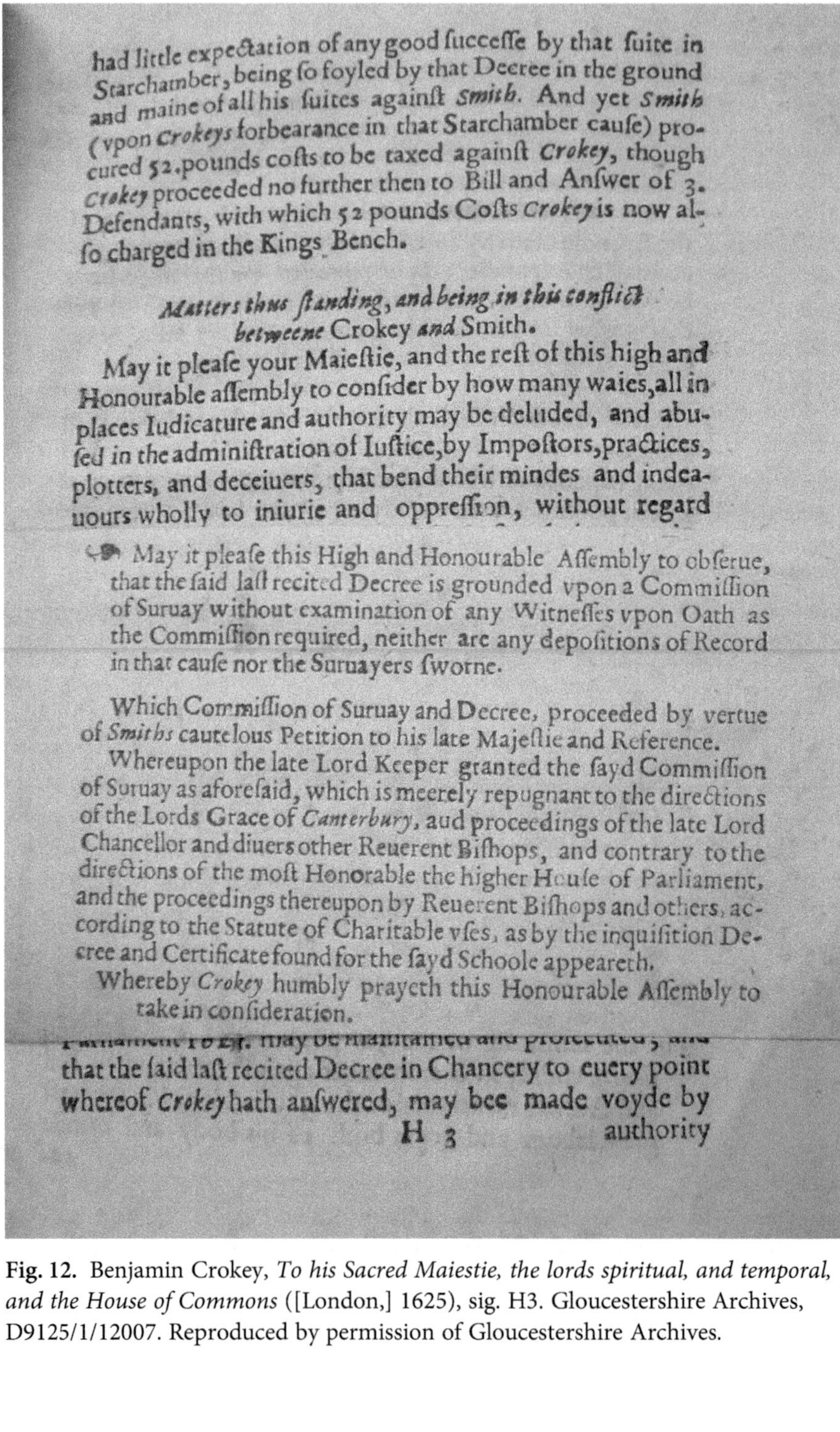

had little expectation of any good ſucceſſe by that ſuite in Starchamber, being ſo foyled by that Decree in the ground and maine of all his ſuites againſt *Smith*. And yet *Smith* (vpon *Crokeys* forbearance in that Starchamber cauſe) procured 52.pounds coſts to be taxed againſt *Crokey*, though *Crokey* proceeded no further then to Bill and Anſwer of 3. Defendants, with which 52 pounds Coſts *Crokey* is now alſo charged in the Kings Bench.

Matters thus ſtanding, and being in this conflict betweene Crokey *and* Smith.

May it pleaſe your Maieſtie, and the reſt of this high and Honourable aſſembly to conſider by how many waies, all in places Iudicature and authority may be deluded, and abuſed in the adminiſtration of Iuſtice, by Impoſtors, practices, plotters, and deceiuers, that bend their mindes and indeauours wholly to iniurie and oppreſſion, without regard

May it pleaſe this High and Honourable Aſſembly to obſerue, that the ſaid laſt recited Decree is grounded vpon a Commiſſion of Suruay without examination of any Witneſſes vpon Oath as the Commiſſion required, neither are any depoſitions of Record in that cauſe nor the Suruayers ſworne.

Which Commiſſion of Suruay and Decree, proceeded by vertue of *Smiths* cautelous Petition to his late Maieſtie and Reference.

Whereupon the late Lord Keeper granted the ſayd Commiſſion of Suruay as aforeſaid, which is meerely repugnant to the directions of the Lords Grace of *Canterbury*, aud proceedings of the late Lord Chancellor and diuers other Reuerent Biſhops, and contrary to the directions of the moſt Honorable the higher Houſe of Parliament, and the proceedings thereupon by Reuerent Biſhops and others, according to the Statute of Charitable vſes, as by the inquiſition Decree and Certificate found for the ſayd Schoole appeareth.

Whereby *Crokey* humbly prayeth this Honourable Aſſembly to take in conſideration.

that the ſaid laſt recited Decree in Chancery to euery point whereof *Crokey* hath anſwered, may bee made voyde by

H 3 authority

Fig. 12. Benjamin Crokey, *To his Sacred Maiestie, the lords spiritual, and temporal, and the House of Commons* ([London,] 1625), sig. H3. Gloucestershire Archives, D9125/1/12007. Reproduced by permission of Gloucestershire Archives.

noted—Crokey obliterated the name of one of Smyth's 'instruments' and 'practicers . . . in all or most of his designs for supplanting the school', even though the names of Peter Bird and Edward Cowper remained.[26] Archard asked witnesses 'whose name' had been 'stricken out in the end of the book', and although no answer surfaced William Hill suggested that this was done 'by the request of a very special friend', and involved someone Crokey 'would not have known'.[27]

Such changes seem trivial given the angry tone of what was left untouched. However, they indicate the challenges Crokey faced in framing his critique, not least in terms of who to put in the frame, and suggest an attempt to focus readers' attention upon Smyth and his closest allies. Careful calibration was also undertaken to make Crokey's parliamentary bill less inflammatory, and as the 1626 Parliament opened Tempest apparently 'railed' at Whatman 'basely and bitterly' for refusing to remove 'bitter and railing matter'. This led Crokey to suspect a 'confederacy' between Whatman and Smyth, and he went back to the drawing board. According to the attorney, Mr Archibold, the task was given to Mr Eyre, 'late a clerk to my Lord Chief Baron' (Sir John Walter), before being 'perused' by Serjeant Egremond Thynne. Thynne was also shown the pamphlet, and Archibold claimed to have been 'offered . . . one of the books', which he read 'in part' a few months 'before the bill was put in'.[28] Such claims explain why Crokey could only lobby Parliament in May 1626, three months after members assembled. He had discovered that getting the text right militated against getting it ready, and getting it read.

III

Upon recognising that Crokey's pamphlets were given out freely, Smyth felt compelled to understand how they were distributed, and by whom they were received. He may have attempted something similar in 1621, paying Mr Potts of the Three Cups inn in Bread Street to get Crokey's breviate, perhaps suspecting that this was the venue from which copies were despatched to Gloucestershire.[29] The picture that now emerged was as alarming for Smyth as it is instructive for historians, in terms of the efficiency with which Crokey distributed pamphlets in a non-commercial fashion, and Smyth's ability to subject Crokey's network to forensic examination.

[26] Crokey, *Sacred Maiestie*, sigs B3v, Cv, D2v–3, E, F2v–3, F4, H2v–3, H3v.

[27] GA, D9125/1/12011; D9125/1/12014. [28] GA, D9125/1/12014.

[29] GA, D9125/1/13612/5. The Three Cups was a hub for West Country folk; the base from which coaches and carriers left for and arrived from Gloucestershire, and for Bristol's MPs: W. Bruce Bannerman, ed., *The Registers of All Hallows, Bread Street* (London, 1913), pp. 162–3, 168, 173, 176, 182, 188, 191, 194; John Taylor, *The Carriers Cosmographie* (1637), sigs A4–v, Cv; McGrath, *Records*, pp. 9–11, 149, 204, 215.

Smyth's first concern was to establish whether copies had been sold by London's stationers, which would have been a serious offence, and here he encountered obfuscation and contradictory evidence. He was doubtless appalled to learn of the solicitor, Adams, telling colleagues about the 'strange book he had *bought*', at the bookshop by Lincoln's Inn gate, and while the owner—presumably Francis Parke—'denied the sale, or knowledge of any such book', Thomas Walkeley claimed that William Burford offered him copies for his shop in the New Bourse. This is intriguing because Walkeley's shop was a vital outlet for political and parliamentary texts, suggesting that Crokey recognised how best to reach one target audience. At this stage, however, Smyth could not prove that copies had been sold, and William Hill and John Leigh both reported that Crokey 'would take no money' for copies. Crokey made plain that he wanted the book to be read by 'friends' and *not* by people unknown to him.[30]

While Smyth interrogated witnesses about whether the books were available commercially, attention also focused on Crokey's bespoke audience. This meant exploring how copies passed from hand-to-hand within an extensive and socially diverse—but self-selecting—group in London, Westminster, Bristol, and Gloucestershire. It emerged that Crokey undertook a restrained publicity campaign, and did so in response to Smyth getting his own books 'printed and published to the country where the school is', which blackened Crokey's reputation with 'untrue scandals', and co-opted 'bosom friends' like Giles Elbridge.[31] At the same time, Crokey's campaign made a striking impact because of how individual readers behaved.

What troubled Smyth was evidence that Crokey's tract was mobile, as copies given to prominent individuals within London's administrative and legal community circulated more widely, although not indiscriminately. Whatever Crokey's intentions, Smyth recognised that copies given to MPs, peers, and parliamentary clerks could not be contained within Westminster, but were instead borrowed, lent, and discussed across the capital. Having discovered that Job Deighton, an auditor in the Court of Wards, 'read the book', Smyth learnt that this copy was lent to him by Adams, while another lawyer, Gyles Bird of New Inn, received a copy from someone who asked him 'whether he would read a piece of news'. Sharing Crokey's tract was also common amongst people of less exalted status. A wool 'factor' called Edward Tanner 'read the book in Blackwell Hall', the centre of the cloth trade, but confessed that it was something he 'heard with others, borrowed and read over', suggesting communal reading. Mr Sturchy of Bloomsbury claimed to have been shown a copy by Job Throckmorton, who worked for Henry Elsynge, 'clerk of the Parliament', to whom Burford gave

[30] GA, D98125/1/12014. See: McKerrow, *Dictionary*, p. 210; Henry R. Plomer, *A Dictionary of the Booksellers and Printers . . . 1641 to 1667* (London, 1907), p. 187; Kyle, *Theater of State*, pp. 155–6.

[31] Crokey, *Petition*, pp. 7–8; GA, D9125/1/12014.

'four or five' copies. Sir Robert Poyntz quickly passed his copy to Mr Chester, who 'read it over' before allowing it to be read by Christopher Stokes, who spotted it 'on his table'. It is noteworthy that many of these people had West Country connections. Gyles Bird was presumably approached as the son of Smyth's ally, Peter Bird, and kept the book because it had 'his father's name therein'. Within the Court of Wards, Deighton had particular responsibilities in Somerset, and settled in Gloucestershire, while Adams served as solicitor to John Poulett of Hinton St George in Somerset, MP and Deputy Lieutenant.[32] The cloth factor, Edward Tanner, came from Tetbury, and was well connected in Wotton, as other colleagues at Blackwell Hall would have been.[33]

What emerged was a concerted attempt to influence local opinion, and Smyth quickly recognised that copies of Crokey's tract were sent directly to selected individuals and found a socially diverse readership. Susan Burford promised one to her employer, Edward Trotman of Cam, and copies were seen and read by Thomas Poyntz of Uley, Benjamin Webb, and William May, the Charfield attorney. The mayor of Bristol, John Barker, received one in 'a letter ... from London', although from whom 'he knew not'. Henry Rugge, the schoolmaster, suggested that Edmund Grayle could shed light on discussions of the book involving two Wotton merchants, Edward Olyver and Albane Saunders, the latter of whose son talked about it with fellow pupils at Wotton school, and Rugge and Morgan Ady both intimated that Thomas Hewett of Ozleworth could 'speak of them'. A local tailor, Thomas Brinkworth, 'had a book' but would 'by no means ... acknowledge where he had it', while admitting that John Bridges had one, 'which he keepeth close'.[34]

Perhaps the most disturbing revelation was that Crokey sent 'many of the books' to Thomas Wright, a 'familiar acquaintance' and 'giddy young man', who operated a bookshop at the Black Moor's Head in Bristol's High Street. Smyth was warned by William Burford that Crokey had such a plan, and details emerged from an interview that William Hill and Edward Wakeman conducted with Wright's father ('old Wright'), and from Archard's meeting with Wright himself. Crokey had travelled to Bristol from prison in early 1626, held a 'conference' with Wright before departing 'towards London' in April, and then despatched 150 pamphlets by carrier.[35] The aim was to 'disperse' rather than sell them, and Wright delivered the books 'according to Crokey's direction', outlined in a letter dated 6 May. By the time Archard arrived few copies remained.[36] Wright was evasive, but a list of recipients was constructed, including local

[32] GA, D9125/1/12014. For Job Throckmorton: TNA, E 215/58D, p. 242. For Gyles Bird: Smyth, *Lives*, iii. 146; TNA, PROB 6/17, fo. 85v; Edward Alexander Fry, *Abstracts of Gloucestershire Inquisitiones Post Mortem ... Part III* (London, 1899), p. 3. For Deighton: TNA, PROB 11/300, fo. 373v.

[33] TNA, PROB 11/189, fo. 242; *Men and Armour*, p. 284.

[34] GA, D9125/1/12014.

[35] GA, D9125/1/12011, 12014.

[36] GA, D9125/1/12011, 12013.

worthies, clerics, and clothiers, as well as leading Bristol citizens, to all of whom attention will return. He admitted that one person 'had the greatest part of the books', although others received multiple copies for onward distribution, including Crokey's daughter, Elizabeth (four), and John Dowle (seventeen). Crokey's kinsman, Edward Olyver of Wotton, received copies 'to disperse in that country', and admitted to Edward Prayle and Henry Rugge that six were 'sent him' from Bristol, although confusingly he professed not to know 'by whom' they were sent *and* that he returned them 'from whence he had them'. Crokey evidently targeted associates, kinsmen, and power-brokers, including Robert Pritchard, sometime master of Wotton school, who was allegedly sacked for supporting his cause, and who was seen as a 'meddler in this business'.[37]

To make matters worse, pamphlets that Crokey directed to the West Country found multiple readers. Wright was probably the source of copies that reached William Player and John Bridges of Combe, the former of whom was offered it as 'a book of news', and Player lent one to a scrivener, George Hartwell, a friend of Ralph Wright, who passed it to a maidservant to show her master, Philip Langley, before returning it. The copy given to John Bridges passed to Brinkworth, and Smyth assumed that the one in the hands Thomas Hewett of Ozleworth came from his brother-in-law, Robert Pritchard, who allegedly had 'a hand in dispersing of the books'. Thomas Colston's copy was shown to Anthony Hungerford, while William Player gave the copy he saw to his father-in-law, Arthur Kemis.[38] Jeffrey Webb of Berkeley passed one to Edward Olyver, and Smyth was informed that Olyver allowed his maid to read it, and lent another copy to Edward Brinkworth, a tailor who worked for him. That one was lent to Francis Wright, who passed it to Rugge, from whom it reached Morgan Ady, Smyth's informant. Local people apparently knew that Olyver had a store of pamphlets, and Edward Prayle visited him in the hope of getting a copy.[39]

Crokey's pamphlet was promiscuous, and much discussed in local villages and the dormitories of Wotton school, and its distribution was orchestrated from within King's Bench prison, a vital hub in Crokey's network. Smyth discovered that copies were given to fellow inmates, and to the marshall (Sir George Reynell), and sent directly to Olyver and Barker, the mayors of Wotton and Bristol. Others were handed to Crokey's visitors, including men—Morgan Ady, Richard Wakeman, and Giles Elbridge—who turned out to be Smyth's agents, presumably to help with onward distribution. Crokey apparently boasted to William Hill about 'making... them ready to be delivered abroad', and gave him a copy, asking him 'to publish it' but 'take no money for it'. Ady told a similar story: Crokey

[37] GA, D9125/1/12011, 12013–14; Crokey, *Sacred Maiestie*, sig. D.

[38] GA, D9125/1/12013–14. Hartwell, or his son, a local attorney, witnessed Ralph Wright's will: TNA, PROB 11/184, fo. 296; McGrath, *Merchants*, p. 29.

[39] GA, D9125/1/12011, 12013–14.

'willed' him to 'disperse it' and to 'spare not for he would be his warrant and defend him', explaining that friends 'should not... be afraid to divulge them to all men', and that Smyth would become renowned as 'the basest companion of the shire'. A soldier who visited Crokey was also given a copy, 'desiring he would deliver it to his brother', Sir William Guise of Brockworth, and Guise claimed the tract was 'pressed' upon him, although Smyth also heard that it came from another prisoner, Lacy, 'the old parson's son of Tytherington'. Crucial in this regard was another soldier, John Leigh, who admitted visiting King's Bench more than once, collecting copies that were read in Blackwell Hall and given to Gyles Bird. Smyth regarded Leigh as someone whose 'common trade' was 'to fetch books' from Crokey.[40]

Crokey's strategic deployment of print, and the tendency for pamphlets to circulate within discrete communities, encouraged Smyth to *retrieve* as many copies as possible. This involved damage limitation, based upon forensic investigation. William Archard explained that John Barker would hand over his copy, albeit only after reading it, 'which yet he had not done'. During June 1626, John Leigh and Morgan Ady gave Smyth the copies seen by Lacy the minister's son, Henry Rugge, Francis Wright, Sir William Guise, and Gyles Bird, and by Thomas and Edward Brinkworth, although John Bridges was less forthcoming. Richard Wakeman handed over the copy 'he had from Crokey at King's Bench'. At the very least, Smyth sought to borrow or get sight of copies, noting that Sturchy and William Burford promised 'to lend me' them. This was useful because it revealed Crokey's methods. Smyth concluded that the copy Edward Olyver 'fetched me' originated with Thomas Wright, noting the instructions—on its brown paper wrapper—that it should be 'delivered unto Mr Rich. [sic] Olyver at Wotton', in return for a small payment (2*d*.). Smyth contended that this involved the 'selfsame hand' as 'a bill of Thomas Wright's writing', and that Wright should be examined 'specially' about 'to whom, by whom, and when' the books circulated. This lead prompted Wright's confession that he 'sent four books' to Olyver. Smyth also sought the letter that accompanied Crokey's parcel of tracts, suspecting that a note on the cover of one copy—'for your sake I sent this down'—was by Crokey himself. Proving the link between the two men convinced Smyth to 'make Thomas Wright a defendant', and was crucial for thinking about how to respond to Crokey's pamphleteering.[41]

IV

By late summer 1626, Smyth had unearthed troubling evidence about Crokey's confidence, ability, and support, and about damage to his own reputation far

[40] GA, D9125/1/12013–14. [41] GA, D9125/1/12011, 12014.

beyond a narrow political elite, amongst the gentlefolk and weavers of Gloucestershire, and into the lower orders of maidservants, pot-sellers, and brewers' clerks, and even schoolboys.[42] It was in this context that Smyth prepared his own strategy. This included a long manuscript pamphlet addressed to Crokey and Parliament, the first draft of which—in Archard's hand—was ready before the dissolution of Parliament (June 1626), only weeks after Crokey's tract appeared. How widely this circulated is unclear, but it was expanded over time, not least to record Smyth's more significant response: new and decisive legal proceedings, which shed more valuable light upon the strategising of both men.[43]

Smyth had new litigation in mind from the moment he began investigating Crokey's pamphlet, and he adopted a ruthless approach to those with whom he made contact. Smyth identified people who were 'ready to testify' (William Player of Wotton) and who would 'depose' (Richard Dowdswell), as well as those 'whom I make a witness' (Edward Brinkworth, Margaret Olyver), and who would be 'a good witness' (Edmund Grayle, Whatman). He also pinpointed those who would make 'a good defendant' (Thomas Brinkworth, Thomas Tempest). By the autumn Smyth had compiled a substantial list of witnesses, including people involved in writing the book (George Goodyear), and in its distribution (William Burford, James Ashby), and those who received copies from Thomas Wright. He also made notes about questions to ask them, regarding 'what became' of copies, and 'what persons' they 'acquainted with them'. More striking is Smyth's candour about those who felt threatened by frequent visits and persistent questioning. Edward Oldisworth was defiant in the face of Star Chamber indictments, but Smyth recognised that humbler characters—like William Burford and James Ashby—expected 'trouble' and felt 'threatened'. As noted already, Christopher Eyre was promised 'favour' if he 'confessed the truth', and when a prisoner like Edward Adisworth realised that he might be prosecuted, 'he begged pardon on his knees, crying', bemoaning Smyth's 'malice' and likening him to 'a toothdrawer'.[44]

Star Chamber proceedings against Crokey and Thomas Wright—for a 'libellous and defamatory printed book'—began in Michaelmas 1626, but they involved serious challenges and significant delays, and proved revealing about thinking on both sides. First, it is possible to observe Smyth's reasoning as he prepared the indictment. This involved 'questions to be asked of counsel touching Crokey's bill in Star Chamber', some of which were clearly dealt with by lawyers. Smyth wondered whether to cite Crokey's 'old railing words against me', and having initially decided 'no' he subsequently opted to deploy the evidence, even if only 'sparingly'. He considered how to handle 'aspersions' and 'aggravating' claims in both bill and pamphlet, which were 'heavy' but might complicate things unnecessarily. He pondered how to frame interrogatories covering 'the rest of his scandals,

[42] GA, D9125/1/12014. [43] GA, D9125/1/12008.
[44] GA, D9125/1/12013–14. See: GA, D9125/1/13611/15.

not mentioned in the bill', and how to deal with changes made to Crokey's text, not least the 'bitter' final sections so heavily modified. Smyth also reflected whether to examine Crokey 'upon each particular in the book', or pursue 'a general examination' into whether he caused it to be 'penned... printed and published'; whether to charge the printer, who perhaps only anticipated that copies would be given to MPs and peers; and whether to highlight Crokey's claims against other people. These last allegations were 'not pertinent' to the school, but sought to 'revile upon' Smyth's allies, and he eventually decided to let them rest, and also declined to 'seize Crokey's books', at least for the moment.[45]

Secondly, Smyth grappled with difficult decisions about who should join him as a plaintiff. Ultimately, he resolved to involve the schoolmaster, Edward Cowper, given that the book contained 'scandals' about someone who was a preacher and bachelor of divinity, while recognising that it might be necessary to explain 'why Mr Cowper becomes a plaintiff', and that it might be distracting to focus upon claims that did not feature in the draft legislation. On the other hand, Smyth eventually decided not to attach Lord Berkeley's name to the bill, even though he was 'patron' of the school 'by the new incorporation... which this libel tends to disinherit him of'. This reflected his lawyers' pragmatic advice: that Berkeley's involvement would 'take away damages from us'.[46]

Thirdly, lawyers were asked about two wider issues that Crokey's allegations raised. The first involved the school, and Smyth wondered whether to argue that Crokey's libel subverted the king's letters patent (and 'the incorporation of the school'), and whether it was necessary to 'fashion' his complaint so that 'the decree may be read in court', lest the judge might 'never understand the cause'. Smyth's lawyers evidently dealt with this question—crossed through on Smyth's sheet—even if their advice was not recorded. Smyth's second question was more profound: whether to include references to Crokey's argument about 'how *all* in places of judicature and authority may be deluded and abused in the administration of justice', by 'imposters', 'plotters', and 'deceivers'. Here the issue was whether to accuse Crokey of libelling the plaintiffs, or to claim that he also undermined the authority of the crown and its courts. This was central to the issue of how successfully Crokey had calibrated his attack, and the answer to Smyth's question soon became clear, if problematic.[47]

Smyth's bill of complaint referred back to the 1623 decree, the patent of 1624, and the ordinances 'for the good government' of the school, and both plaintiffs were depicted as its reputable guardians. It stressed that the affair was 'fully settled' after being 'controverted' for 'many years'; that the school was re-established and new leases made of its lands; and that they 'laboured' for its 'welfare and advancement', noting that 'one scholar more is already added'. The point here was that

[45] GA, D9125/1/12004. [46] GA, D9125/1/12004.
[47] GA, D9125/1/12004. See: Crokey, *Sacred Maiestie*, sig. H3.

Crokey had 'purposely omitted' such facts, in order to 'assume to himself a liberty to rail and defame', and Crokey was accused of trying to 'scandalise' opponents 'maliciously', with 'hateful defamations, reproaches and scandals'. Particular emphasis was placed upon claims about Smyth's 'foul practices' and 'fair pretences', his 'plots' and 'dissembled honesty', and it was said that 'no practise' was 'unattempted' to bring Smyth into 'disgrace, obloquy and ignominy'. Such 'defamations, scandals and reproaches' were all the more troubling for having been 'printed and divulged', 'at least' 400 copies of the pamphlet having been distributed, particularly 'in and near... Wotton-under-Edge and North Nibley where your subject John Smyth dwelleth'. The plaintiffs made the obvious point that the pamphlet breached regulations by omitting the printer's name, but also the more contentious claim that copies were 'dispersed, vented and published', both 'by sale and gift'. They insisted that the defendants were guilty of conspiracy, by working with 'the help, assistance and abetting' of John Dowle junior and Ralph Wright. All of them 'caused to be drawn and written a most scandalous and libellous pamphlet', and Smyth even hoped to be allowed to add the names of 'others as yet unknown', 'as they shall be found out and discovered'.

Finally, the plaintiffs insisted that Crokey—out of 'malignity' and a 'contentious, malicious and unquiet spirit'—had libelled officials, the courts of justice, 'and consequently... the government of the realm'. He had 'let fly' many 'scandalous and libellous defamations... aspersions and reproaches' against the 'directions' of the king's 'royal father', and had accused judges of 'connivance', 'partiality', and 'injustice'. They alleged that Crokey had, 'through the sides of your said subjects... fiercely assaulted... the honours, integrities, wisdoms, discretions and reputations' of people who had 'eminency in the commonwealth'. Smyth and Cowper stressed that, while 'all libels and defamatory writings'—even against 'a private person'—ought to be severely punished, more troubling were those 'printed and exposed to public view and sale', and those that 'impudently, falsely and audaciously' sought to 'wound... public ministers of justice, being your majesty's lieutenants, who is the fountain of justice'. Libels tended to provoke 'impatience and contentions', which disturbed 'the peaceable government and happy tranquility of the kingdom', leading to duels, 'deadly feuds amongst families', 'bloodshed and murder', 'insurrections and rebellions'. They were 'not to be suffered in a Christian and well governed commonwealth', and were to be 'suppressed by the severity of an exemplary punishment', including the public burning of Crokey's pamphlets. More prosaically, Smyth and Cowper insisted that 'no other course of justice' would put an end to Crokey's attempts to introduce legislation in Parliament.[48]

[48] GA, D9125/1/12008, pp. 83–9; S379/2/3/1/3; Gardiner, *Reports*, pp. 38–9.

V

No amount of preparation could guarantee judicial success, however, and Smyth's papers reveal a frustrating and expensive five-year period before the case was finally determined.[49] Taking advice from 'several learned counsel' in Michaelmas 1626 took three weeks and cost £12. Smyth recorded the expense involved in securing and delivering a warrant for Crokey's 'attachment' (8*s*.2*d*.), engrossing his bill of complaint (12*s*.), and preparing subpoenas, not to mention the fees to Edward Trotman, Lord Keeper Coventry, and Sir Heneage Finch, for perusing and adding their 'hand to the bill' (£4 14*s*.). Examining witnesses and defendants required further warrants, payments to William Hudson's clerk for 'engrossing the interrogatories' (7*s*.6*d*.), and a fee to 'Mr Evans the examiner' (24*s*.). Costs were incurred for copying their answers (£2 3*s*.8*d*.), and for sending a messenger to Bristol, merely to confirm that Thomas Wright was served with a subpoena (20*s*.).[50]

Prosecuting such a case was expensive but also perilous, in terms of how defendants might react. Thomas Wright was intimidated: upon hearing that he was 'served' in Star Chamber, he wrote to Smyth with a whiff of defiance—saying he had done no more than 'any servant of yours would a done'—but also with contrition. He pleaded with Smyth to 'trouble us not', promising that if the charges were dropped he would 'show... who had the books' and who 'may better give you answer than I can'.[51] Crokey reacted rather differently, and although Smyth secured a 'rule' for him to submit 'his answer' (12*d*.), calling him to court provoked the dispute's most extraordinary episode, and what Smyth referred to in an affidavit as 'abuse in serving process... in the King's Bench'.[52]

This 'abuse' involved Crokey's 'angry and fierce' response to the decision to send young William Ford—'Mr Moseley's man'—to serve him with a subpoena (25 October). On Ford's account, Crokey exclaimed: 'I will teach you to serve subpoenas in a prison.' He then took 'fast hold' of Ford's cloak, and sought assistance from other prisoners, crying out 'soho, soho, I am served with a subpoena.' This caused 'much ado', and inmates were prompted to seize Ford, accepting Crokey's demand to have him 'committed to the house'. He was carried to an impromptu 'court', where Crokey demanded that 'their lord chief justice'—the 'ancientest prisoner'—should 'give sentence of punishment'. Ford was subjected to a 'formal examination', and required to withdraw the writ, and upon refusing to do so was subjected to 'the punishment of the house'. He was thrown into a cellar, amid threats that he would have to 'eat the subpoena', and that prisoners would 'pump and shave him'. His cloak was pawned, and the proceeds were spent on beer and tobacco. He was only turned 'out of doors' two hours later,

[49] GA, D8887/6/104. [50] GA, D8887/6/94, 104. [51] GA, D9125/1/12010.
[52] GA, D8887/6/94, 104.

doubtless with the assistance of Smyth, who paid the tipstaves to 'fetch out' Ford and effect his 'rescue'.[53]

This desperate and angry move suggests that the dispute had reached a point of unprecedented bitterness, but it may also have been logical. It was inevitably exploited by Smyth's lawyers, although doing so may have been counterproductive. Hudson explained that it had been impossible to serve a writ, for fear of 'barbarous usage', and judges bemoaned the 'foulness' of Crokey's behaviour, and the 'affront of justice' involved (26 January 1627). Calls were made for 'punishment'—and for the 'reform' or 'better governing' of King's Bench—and Crokey was removed to the Fleet 'until he had answered and was examined in this cause'.[54] However, this generated delays and costs, as Crokey perhaps anticipated. Smyth's expenses for Hilary term 1627—which ran to £9 17*s*.4*d*.—show that he battled his way to London through 'frost and snow', and that fees to a large legal team were dominated by the fallout from Ford's kidnapping. Smyth paid to bring Crokey before Star Chamber (17*s*.), secured his removal to the Fleet (37*s*.), and paid the warden to receive his new inmate (21*s*.).[55]

Further delays occurred because Smyth was still marshalling evidence. Smyth met his accomplice, Arthur Fisher, who had encountered one of Crokey's fellow prisoners in Fleet Street (5 February), and dined with Archibold, the Lyon's Inn attorney, at the Pope's Head tavern in Chancery Lane (20 February). He also interviewed John Dowle, who had 'been with Crokey in the Fleet', and served him 'with process'.[56] Dowle responded by trying to prevent 'causeless suits', confessing that he and Crokey were old acquaintances, but insisting that he 'never ... endeavoured to hazard my credit on his behalf'. He claimed 'no hand' in penning the book, and knew no more than that 'a counsellor at law contrived the same', although he admitting receiving 'sixteen or seventeen copies', which he 'delivered according to a note' from Thomas Wright.[57] Smyth made Dowle submit a formal deposition, paying 28*s*. for copies of his evidence, at a rate of 12*d*. per sheet.[58] With stakes now so high, Smyth sought to construct the strongest possible case, but doing so involved significant costs in terms of both time and money.

A more significant obstacle to a speedy trial was Crokey, who frustrated Smyth's progress repeatedly. His reluctance to respond to the bill of complaint prompted Smyth's lawyer, Hudson, to try and 'bring him in to answer'. This involved a motion—on 7 February—that Crokey should submit an answer by the end of term, 'or ... be taken *pro confesso*' (20*s*.). Crokey waited until the very end of term before petitioning for more time, and while Smyth's lawyers ensured that he was given only eight more days—with the threat of being 'committed close

53 GA, D8887/6/94, 100; D9125/1/12008, pp. 89–90.
54 GA, D8887/6/100; D9125/1/12008, pp. 90–1.
55 GA, D9125/1/13612/12; D8887/6/104.
56 GA, D9125/1/12014; D9125/1/13612/12.
57 GA, D9125/1/12012.
58 GA, D9125/1/13612/12.

prisoner'—this motion cost £2 (excluding 11*s.* spent on copies for himself and Crokey). It also provoked another petition, in which Crokey pleaded poverty and successfully asked 'to be admitted *in forma pauperis*'. Such tactics involved desperate measures, but they brought costs to his opponent—a copy of this last petition cost 2*s.*—and were successful, ensuring that proceedings became protracted and frustrating.[59] Smyth spent Easter term—and £10—in London, trying in vain to make progress by renewing the motion for Crokey to submit his answer or risk 'close' imprisonment (13 April). Incessant demands were placed upon his purse, demonstrating how easily costs and delays could be exacerbated by an attentive and obstructive adversary. This ruling cost 20*s.*, but Smyth also needed to pay the man who delivered it 'to the hands of Crokey' in the Fleet (4*s.*4*d.*), wanted an affidavit to show that this was done (5*s.*), and needed another copy of the order when 'Crokey snatched the other away' (2*s.*6*d.*). Further costs were incurred for similar orders and threats at the end of Easter term, when Crokey responded—on the last day of term—with a demurrer. Smyth deemed this 'frivolous', but spent 3*s.* to get a copy, and although Hudson got the demurrer overturned, the new order for Crokey to 'make better answer'—passed on 8 May (20*s.*)—only set a deadline of 'the first sitting day of the next term'. Crokey was informed about this on 10 May (because Smyth paid 1*s.* to notify him), but may have been satisfied with his ability to cause another delay, and to annoy Smyth further by walking freely around Palace Yard and the Royal Exchange.[60]

Crokey's victories were small, but must have been frustrating. When Smyth returned to London in Trinity term 1627, he did so 'expecting' Crokey to answer, 'according to an order of 8 May', but quickly discovered that progress was slow and costly. Over a few short weeks he spent £28, including expenses for copying the answer that Crokey finally submitted (23*s.*), and for responding 'immediately'. He instructed Hudson to 'peruse' the pamphlet and 'frame interrogatories' (30*s.*), paid the examiner to visit Crokey in the Fleet (30*s.*), and got a copy of the examination (13*s.*). Taking evidence—'testifications in the country'—was even more costly, in terms of subpoenas, affidavits, and witnesses' expenses, which ran to £16. Smyth then *repeated* most of these exercises in Michaelmas term, at a cost of £31 for travel, accommodation, and legal bills, and then spent a further £21 in Hilary term 1628. This involved getting copies of depositions (£9), paying lawyers to 'peruse all their books' and 'frame a perfect breviat' (£4), and supplying briefs to barristers (£2). He was forced to agree that Crokey should have time to examine the witnesses, and although he resolved to 'move the Lord Keeper' for a hearing in Easter term, this did little good.[61] Smyth spent yet another term in London,

[59] GA, D9125/1/13612/12; D8887/6/104; D9125/1/12008, pp. 65, 91–2. For Crokey's writ 'forma pauperis' (27 February 1627): TNA, PRO 30/38/22, fo. 1.

[60] GA, D9125/1/13612/12; D8887/6/104; D9125/1/12015, 12008, pp. 91–2.

[61] GA, D8887/6/104; D9125/1/12008, pp. 91–2; D9125/1/13612/13; D8887/5/12.

anticipating a hearing on 23 May, but the £11 spent on personal expenses and legal fees produced little return, and the case effectively stalled. Smyth may not have bothered returning to the capital in Trinity term. He was probably consoled to get confirmation that Crokey's pamphlets were, after all, being sold. Dowdswell signed an affidavit that he 'did buy one of the books . . . at a bookseller's shop under the Six Clerks Office' (in Chancery Lane), and that 'more were there to be sold'. Archard was able to purchase Crokey's 'printed paper in folio' from 1621. The money—4*s*.6*d*.—for each of these affidavits was well spent, but Smyth's hopes of making progress were quickly dashed. He spent 'above a month' in London in Michaelmas term 1628, but £14 paid to lawyers was effectively wasted. The hearing—scheduled for 23 October—was postponed until 'the last sitting' of term, and then cancelled, despite 'several learned counsel' having 'attended at the bar'.[62]

It remains unclear how far Crokey and his lawyers were responsible for such delays, but the events of early 1629 demonstrate the trouble they were capable of causing. Once again, Smyth travelled to London in optimistic mood, and was probably happy to spend £11 instructing his legal team—Hudson, Finch, Trotman, and Jones—since the case had 'come so far' as to be included in 'the special paper for hearings', on the first day of Hilary term (28 January). Yet again, he returned home disappointed, ten days later and £4 worse off, once Crokey halted proceedings with 'false suggestions in Parliament'.[63] Only days before the hearing, Crokey petitioned from the Fleet, complaining about Smyth's 'sinister practices', justifying the production and distribution of 'diverse small books', and protesting that a 'vexatious' libel suit deterred friends from offering help. This well-timed intervention had the desired effect: peers 'stayed' the trial pending a report from one of its committees, thereby prompting a flurry of petitions from both men. Crokey complained about Smyth's 'strange and unusual proceedings to ensnare your petitioner'; Smyth was willing for him to be granted a *habeas corpus*, but pleaded that the Star Chamber hearing—scheduled for 'Wednesday next'—should be allowed to proceed. He reminded peers that Crokey 'sold' copies of his pamphlet, and distributed 200 copies to people 'in the country' who were 'no parliament men'. This was done to 'defame' him and scandalise the legal system, and he begged for the chance to defend his reputation, 'which is more dear unto me than my life'.[64]

Smyth's protests fell on deaf ears, and Crokey's appeal to Parliament proved timely and costly. Smyth's accounts reveal frenetic activity during these weeks. He secured copies of Crokey's petitions and the draft bill by which they were

[62] GA, D8887/6/104; D9125/1/13612/14. The bookseller was probably Samuel Albyn: McKerrow, *Dictionary*, p. 4. The London scrivener, Humfrey Dyson, purchased a copy for 4*d*.: All Souls College, Oxford, MS 117, unfol.

[63] GA, D9125/1/13612/14; D8887/6/104; D9125/1/12008, pp. 91–2; Crokey, *Complaint*, sig. B4.

[64] GA, D9125/1/12023; PA, HL/PO/JO/10/1/37; *LJ*, iv. 10, 12.

accompanied (the latter cost 46*s.*), gave £3 to Henry Elsynge, and paid Trotman £2 to attend 'the hearing before the committees'.[65] However, Crokey was not only granted a *habeas corpus* (26 January), but also gave 'good proofs' to the Committee for Petitions, and having described Smyth's 'powerfulness and practice' he secured the appointment of a new inquiry, more or less on his own terms, as has already been demonstrated. The result saw Smyth's trial being kicked very firmly into the long grass.[66]

What emerges vividly at this point is that Smyth remained watchful, ready, and active, and that costs regarding 'law with Crokey' continued to accumulate even though the trial was on hold. Smyth made further brief visits to London, paid retainers to attorneys each term, and incurred Hudson's fees regarding skirmishes over 'old costs'. He also paid substantial sums to William Jones and Mr Nevill to get the case back on track.[67] London expenses in Hilary term 1631 ran to £11, as Smyth instructed counsel to 'be prepared for the hearing of this cause' (£6). He complained to Lord Keeper Coventry that Crokey had delayed matters using an 'untrue' petition, and pleaded for a hearing on 'the first or second day' of Easter term, not least because Crokey had worked to delay completion of the latest inquiry.[68] Smyth's request was evidently granted, according to an annotated copy of his petition, and although additional delays cost him a further £12 in travelling to London, instructing counsel, and issuing subpoenas, the hearing finally took place on 15 June 1631, almost *five years* after the bill of complaint was submitted. As a result, Smyth expenses for Trinity term—over £23—were substantial but worthwhile. He was able to instruct lawyers (£6), and paid them for attending 'at the bar', for 'pleading and arguing of the cause' (£10), and for obtaining copies of the decree, alongside a bill of costs.[69]

VI

The final stage of this protracted process—the Star Chamber hearing at which Crokey was censured—was decisive, but it was also revealing and controversial. It repays attention, in terms of decisions by the defendants and the possibility that Smyth's aggressive and intimidatory tactics paid off.[70]

Predictably enough, Crokey complained about Smyth's 'many unjust suits', but also insisted that he 'caused a brief relation . . . to be printed' to 'inform the Parliament', that he refrained from 'publishing' it 'till the parliament was sitting',

[65] GA, D9125/1/13612/14.
[66] PA, HL/PO/JO/10/1/37; *LJ*, iv. 12, 13, 17–18; GA, S379/2/3/1/1; Crokey, *Complaint*, sig. B4. See: GA, S379/2/3/1/2.
[67] GA, D8887/6/102–4; D9125/1/13608/65–7; D9125/1/13612/15.
[68] GA, D9125/1/12023; D8887/6/104.
[69] GA, D8887/6/104; D9125/1/12023, 12008, pp. 91–2.
[70] Gardiner, *Reports*, pp. 38–9.

and that copies were not 'put to sale'. He protested that his intention was to 'lay the fault upon the plaintiff only', and not to 'lay scandal' upon the courts. He also maintained that the motivation for producing a catalogue of Smyth's 'practices' involved his sense of having been 'wronged', thereby confirming that his approach was rooted in a sense of natural justice, irrespective of legal judgments. Crokey's problem was that this made it difficult for him to accept, or defend himself against, the notion of 'libel' with which he was charged, particularly in a situation where Wright suddenly claimed he was instructed 'to sell' pamphlets on Crokey's behalf, and that he did so 'not thinking they were scandalous'.[71] This startling revelation—which Smyth had worked hard to substantiate—made Crokey suspicious that something was amiss, since it contradicted Wright's earlier testimony. Noting that the bookseller travelled to London 'to make defence at the hearing', Crokey alleged that Smyth 'came to Wright at his inn, and after some threatening speeches . . . they both agreed' what answer to give in court. The result, he protested, was that Wright was sent home with a promise 'to free him from the business in Star Chamber'.[72]

Such claims notwithstanding, the court's verdict was clear and emphatic. This was particularly true regarding the tactics and strategies of both men, not least once Smyth's counsel reiterated the 'scandals' of Crokey's book, demonstrated that it was written by 'a servant of the now master of the Court of Wards', and showed that printing cost £9. Judges accepted that the books were available commercially, and although Ralph Wright was cleared, Thomas Wright was fined £100, because printing a libel was not 'warrant enough to any bookseller to put them to sale'. Like Crokey, who was fined £200, Wright was ordered to be imprisoned in the Fleet, and any promises made in return for explosive testimony seem not to have been honoured. Having dismissed Crokey's 'pretence'—that the aim was merely to inform Parliament—the court decided that the pamphlet was 'framed falsely and mischievously . . . to scandalise the plaintiff *and* the courts of justice'. Smyth, meanwhile, was described as 'a discrete and honest man', who 'carried himself fairly and well . . . in all his proceedings'.[73]

Smyth was doubtless satisfied with the verdict, paying 30*s*. to copy the decree, and 20*s*. to engross his bill of costs since 1626, which involved a shade over £206.[74] Even at this stage, the difficulties involved in achieving complete satisfaction left him with choices to make. Crokey had 'fled into Ireland', later explaining that he had already absconded by the time that Smyth—'being powerful with . . . Lord Keeper Coventry'—secured the 1631 hearing. This left Smyth with little prospect of recovering costs, although he issued a subpoena against Crokey in the hope of doing so, but he even faced difficulties getting money out of Wright. Smyth's

71 Gardiner, *Reports*, p. 39.
72 Crokey, *Complaint*, sigs B4v–C.
73 Gardiner, *Reports*, pp. 39–40; GA, D9125/1/12008, pp. 92–6; S379/2/3/1/3.
74 GA, D8887/6/104.

determination was plain to see: he prosecuted a commission of rebellion against Wright, who made an 'untrue affidavit' and 'endeavoured in vain to discharge himself' (April 1632). Reluctantly, Smyth accepted just £40 in August 1632, 'the importunity of friends overpressing me'. Wright was discharged, Smyth 'desiring he may more wisely hereafter carry himself than to wrong any other as he hath done me'.[75] By this time, the court had also discharged Crokey—nominally, and *in absentia*—from the Fleet prison.[76]

VII

The battle over Crokey's pamphlet revealed Smyth at his most powerful and effective. Irrespective of whether his 'practices' and 'power' lay behind Thomas Wright's decision to change his story, Smyth demonstrated a willingness and ability to devote considerable resources to pursuing a legal judgment and investigating Crokey's activities. He exploited a substantial network of friends and family, undertook forensic analysis, and behaved like a 'toothdrawer' towards witnesses and defendants. The affair also reveals the care with which he thought about litigation.

Nevertheless, Smyth's victory in 1631 belies a more complicated story, and not just because Crokey dragged proceedings out so effectively, to Smyth's cost and frustration. Crokey appeared much better connected than at other stages of the dispute, and he too put considerable thought into the confrontation with Smyth. He tried to calibrate arguments in ways that would do maximum damage without committing *lèse majesté*, and pushed the boundaries of what could be done with printed texts. Striking evidence has emerged about how texts were constructed, printed, and distributed; about the innovative use of printed breviates, petitions, and pamphlets; and about the promiscuity of print media. Crokey experimented with using print to fight legal and parliamentary battles, and encountered both problems and possibilities when blurring the line between texts that reached discrete audiences and those that were more public. It is noteworthy that Star Chamber condemned Crokey not just for printing and selling a libellous text, but also for contravening parliamentary protocols; ruling—as they had done previously—that the printing and dispersal of Crokey's book, 'upon pretence' of giving peers information about 'the state of the case', was 'utterly unlawful'. This was why the tract was condemned as 'libellous and scandalous', and the court

[75] GA, D9125/1/12008, pp. 92–7; S379/2/3/1/3; Crokey, *Complaint*, sigs B4v–C; D9125/1/13608/70v; D8887/6/104.
[76] GA, D8887/6/105.

made the general point that 'to . . . print briefs of a cause before the hearing, and to divulge and publish them, is to be accounted scandalous and libellous.'[77]

Crokey thus revealed why printed petitioning and lobbying was treated with such suspicion: he demonstrated that texts could not neatly be categorised as unproblematically 'private' or worryingly 'public'. Here too, surviving evidence offers novel ways of grappling with crucial topics like readership, reading practices, and the reception of printed texts. Crokey's texts blurred such distinctions, and were difficult to control in terms of their reach and impact, and at a time when printed petitioning and lobbying was in its infancy it was only to be expected that such practices caused Crokey trouble.

The 1631 decree symbolises new ways in which the Warrens Court dispute fosters understanding about how litigants thought and behaved. It helps to evaluate strategising, perceptions of legal processes, and reflections upon types of disputation. It also addresses larger issues about print and political culture. Not the least significant benefit of the surviving documentation is unprecedented detail about the circulation and readership of texts, and about reading practices, including the lending and borrowing of tracts, and their being passed from hand to hand, read communally, and discussed enthusiastically. Such evidence is normally only available in relation to highly seditious polemical texts, and the Warrens Court dispute provides dramatic evidence about contemporary fascination with, nervousness about, and acculturation to print media. Ultimately, contestation between Smyth and Crokey provides a different way of thinking about what was at stake in this long-running affair, and about its broader structural underpinnings and ramifications, something that will also inspire the remaining chapters of this book.

[77] Gardiner, *Reports*, pp. 39–40; GA, D9125/1/12008, pp. 92–6; S379/2/3/1/3. The key precedents here, from 1624 and 1629, involved printed petitions—also regarding complex legal cases—that were circulated beyond MPs and peers, and that were drafted by imprisoned lawyers. They had resulted in severe punishments. See: *LJ*, iii. 269–70, 2727, 273, 275–7, 281; *LJ*, iv. 20–1, 23; PA, HL/PO/JO/10/1/38 (Felix Kingston).

PART THREE
STRUCTURES

Lawsuits are types of enmities.

Leon Battista Alberti, *De Ichiarchia* (*c*.1468)

Introduction

When John Smyth reflected upon litigation in his famous *Lives*, he did so in one way that has attracted little attention. Well known are his complaints about 'troops of lawyers, attorneys and solicitors', and about the debilitating cost of litigation, but he also made a telling comment about his own experience, referring to 'the country malice and envy that rageth in this age with *the inferior sort*'. This was who he targeted for criticism, in terms of their 'recourse to Westminster Hall, our cockpit of revenge, upon each poor action and occasion'. More striking still was Smyth's comment that such behaviour involved 'the *civil wars* of my days', which were responsible for 'wasting more treasure and time' than the Wars of the Roses.[1] This section takes up such leads, and builds upon the analysis in Part Two, which argued that litigation revealed different ideas about, and expectations of, the legal system; that ideas could be generated by participating in disputation, and that they motivated further contestation. Part Three takes such conclusions further, addressing the possibility that Smyth's comments about 'the inferior sort' and 'civil wars' involved attitudes, values, and ideas that he brought to—and that were revealed by—litigation. It argues that litigation, of the kind undertaken by Smyth, Crokey, and their children, could be underpinned and driven by ideological issues, which served to motivate them, and which help to explain contemporary interest in the Warrens Court dispute. It suggests that resolving the mysteries with which we began—why the dispute went on for so long, and why it fascinated contemporaries—requires examining the structural issues at stake.

[1] Smyth, *Lives*, i. 242 (emphasis added). Smyth also referred to 'paper wars': Smyth, *Lives*, ii. 305.

This section reflects upon the connection between 'practice'—the behaviour associated with litigation—and 'structures'. This is territory with which historians are familiar, in relation to the power of social and political norms, and the impact of changes to how things were done. The relevant theoretical context involves the tension between 'structure' and 'agency', and ideas about 'habitus' and 'structuration', whereby structures—norms, rules, and routinized behaviour, as well as tacit, implicit, and shared know-how—might be more or less constraining, and both contestable and malleable. That is to say that 'structures' are influenced by conscious and unconscious action, as accepted practices are utilised and modified in the course of daily life, by people who have a sense of what constitutes the 'rules of the game', and of how these might be altered. Such ideas recognise that social 'structures' are produced and modified by activities that do not necessarily seek to effect radical change. They make it possible to focus upon competitive and conflictual activities: how disputations prompted innovation and creativity; and how individuals (not 'agents') found room for manoeuvre amid the inconsistencies and contradictions of normative frameworks.[2]

Here the aim is more modest, and involves using the Warrens Court dispute to identify the nature, severity, and visibility of societal divisions. Here too, there is value in returning to the insights of anthropologists who argue that 'social dramas'—as reflected in litigation and dispute resolution—help to identify 'hidden contradictions and conflicts', and divisions that might be persistent even if they are not always evident, and provide ways of revealing changes that occur 'unobtrusively'. They highlight 'structural vulnerability', if not always structural breakdown.[3] Such insights have proved useful for exploring the relationship between 'local detail' and 'global structure', and for demonstrating how 'trivial' localised disputes can 'get articulated with greater political and ideological differences', and 'promoted into conflicts of world-historical significance'. This involves a process of escalation: the amplification or worsening of differences over time, in ways that reveal their structural origins, perhaps only hazily.[4] For scholars of dispute resolution this has involved the possibility that such interactions had ideological dimensions. Litigation might thus involve—or raise—issues relating to honour and status; particular disputes might become more general over time; and it might be possible to distinguish between the ostensible issues involved and what was really going on. One reason for thinking that the genuine issues in a dispute might

[2] Anthony Giddens, 'The constitution of society: outline of the theory of structuration', in Gabrielle M. Spiegel, ed., *Practicing History* (London, 2005), pp. 124–4; William H. Sewell, 'A theory of structure: duality, agency, and transformation', *AJS*, 98.1 (1992), 1–29.

[3] Victor Turner, *Schism and Continuity in an African Society* (Manchester, 1957), pp. xvii, 124, 163, 232.

[4] Clifford Geertz, 'On the nature of anthropological understanding', *American Scientist*, 63.1 (1975), 52; Marshall Sahlins, 'Individual experience and cultural order', in Spiegel, ed., *Practicing History*, 111–20; Marshall Sahlins, 'Structural work: how microhistories become macrohistories and vice versa', *Anthropological Theory*, 5.1 (2005), 6, 24, 25.

not be evident from legal paperwork is that disputants need to formulate claims 'in such a way that the courts will be prepared to listen, probably transforming the original quarrel in doing so'.[5] Others insist not just upon the pressure for harmony—an 'ideology' that promotes conformist behaviour—but also that disputation involves more than merely solving problems, in terms of 'a political process, whereby divisions are created or overcome', and whereby 'ideologies are formed'.[6] All of this opens up possibilities for detecting the presence—and motivating force—of religious and political ideas.

Such insights are valuable for historical assessments about whether litigation was a normal method of solving problems. Litigation has been used to explore tensions—including social tensions—within local communities, and to make connections between discrete events, 'smouldering' conflicts, and 'deeper grievances', and to highlight animosities that 'escalate and expand' over time. Historians have noted how often claims about corruption were linked to religion, and have argued that legal cases occasionally provide clues about the values, emotions, and motivations of litigants. They recognise that legal claims in court could be a façade, and superfluous to the 'real' issues at stake, and that cases sometimes involved ideological differences that exacerbated disputes and made mediation and settlement difficult.[7] Hitherto, however, even the most successful attempts to untangle and contextualise protracted legal disputes have focused upon things other than their ideological depths and dimensions.[8]

This section explores such issues through the lens of the Warrens Court dispute, which is shown to have involved a kind of 'deep play'. It builds upon the idea that disputation was rooted in, revealed, and generated different ideas, and recognises that the ways in which rivals pursued the matter—beyond the point where victory would recoup their vast expenses—indicates the presence of other motivating factors, namely religious and political ideas. This is how Smyth understood the old Berkeley–Lisle dispute, and this section argues that the process by which a long-running dispute became a battle over Wotton school was neither accidental nor tactical, and that the school became a signifier of religious and political issues.[9] The dispute went on for so long because it was underpinned by ideological tensions, and even though the ideas of Smyth and Crokey were not expressed overtly, they are nevertheless recoverable. Teasing out these ideological

[5] John L. Comaroff and Simon Roberts, *Rules and Processes* (London, 1981), pp. 32, 117; Simon Roberts, 'The study of dispute: anthropological perspectives', in Bossy, *Disputes*, p. 22.

[6] Laura Nader, *Harmony Ideology* (Stanford, 1990), pp. 7, 291.

[7] Giovanni Levi, *Inheriting Power* (Chicago, 1988), p. 157; Barry Reay, *Microhistories: Demography, Society and Culture in Rural England, 1800–1930* (Cambridge, 1996), p. 58; Richard L. Kagan, *Lawsuits and Litigants in Castile, 1500–1700* (Chapel Hill, 1982), pp. 90–1; Thomas Kuehn, 'Nemo mortalis cognitus vivit in evo: moral and legal conflicts in a Florentine inheritance case of 1442', in Peter Coss, ed., *The Moral World of the Law* (Cambridge, 2000), pp. 113–33; Thomas Kuehn, *Law, Family and Women* (London, 1991), p. 150.

[8] Churches, 'Business at law'; Churches, 'False friends'.

[9] Smyth, *Lives*, ii. 332.

perspectives is tricky, and in the absence of overt statements about each man's beliefs their ideas might only be evident from sources that did not ostensibly record intellectual engagement. It will be necessary to recognise that the ideological perspectives of ordinary people—their 'social imaginaries'—might have been real but also 'latent', 'loosely structured', and 'unreflective', and perhaps inchoate and under-theorised.[10]

This will not be straightforward, and for all the richness of the surviving documentation we mostly lack the kind of correspondence that might be invaluable for recovering the attitudes and beliefs of protagonists, and for identifying their ideological perspectives.[11] Instead, it will be necessary to use extra-legal sources (including financial accounts, parish records, and estate papers), documentation relating to litigation, and evidence about litigants' responses to official policies and contemporary events. At the heart of this section is a study of mentalities. This is a well-known but not universally accepted approach, not least in terms of its suitability for analysing individuals, and societies in flux, but the following chapters highlight the value of accumulating clues about social attitudes, cultural taste, religious beliefs, and political ideas, from passing comments and from behaviour.[12] The chapters contend that such evidence—scrappy and allusive though it might be—is suggestive, permitting access to the political and religious attitudes of key protagonists.

Central to this process are the respective networks—and networking—of Smyth and Crokey. Networks are crucial for anthropologists interested in 'transactional' approaches, and for 'extended case studies' that place disputes within their wider social contexts; network analysis has provided a way of rethinking—without necessarily rejecting—traditional conceptualisations of associational behaviour involving 'class' and 'community'.[13] Networks—involving friends, family, and other associates—are central to all kinds of social interaction, although network analysis can be undertaken in many different ways, and historical engagement with its methods has not always been sophisticated. Many well-studied networks are excessively 'ego-centric', building outwards from key individuals, rather than 'socio-centric', in terms of recognising that networks could have many 'hubs', and that they might overlap in interesting ways, as those of Smyth and Crokey certainly did. Historians' networks also tend to be fairly homogenous, such that the relational ties connecting individual actors are more or less 'formal', 'affective',

[10] Magali Sarfatti Larson and Silvia Sigal, 'Does "the public" think politically? A search for "deep structures" in everyday political thought', *Qualitative Sociology*, 24.3 (2001), 291; Charles Taylor, *Modern Social Imaginaries* (Durham, NC, 2004).

[11] For an emphasis on correspondence: Churches, 'Business at law', pp. 937, 954; Churches, 'False friends', p. 52.

[12] Peter Burke, 'Strengths and weaknesses of the history of mentalities', *History of European Ideas*, 7.5 (1986), 439–51.

[13] Charles Phythian-Adams, ed., *Societies, Cultures and Kinship, 1580–1850* (London, 1993).

or 'intense', involving kinship, friendship, and shared lifestyles.[14] They often pay insufficient attention to the variety of roles that individuals fulfil within their networks, and the possibility that networks could be hierarchical, involving 'patronage' as well as people who served as 'bridges', 'agents', and 'brokers'. Finally, network analysis often concentrates upon their existence and shape, rather than on their 'uses', and on what can be learned from scrutinising the practices of those involved.

In other words, network analysis sometimes involves plotting, measuring, and quantifying connectivity, and establishing simplistic types of relationship that can be plotted diagrammatically.[15] However, there is considerable scope to explore how relationships were formed and used in everyday life, and how networks provided resources that could be mobilised to pursue specific goals, and in encounters with rivals. This has been done with commercial networks, by moving beyond the strong ties of patronage and trust associated with extended families and shared ventures, and by exploring tools and practices associated with the 'financial revolution', as well as the work of brokers and agents. It has also been done for the 'open' networks—rather than closed circles—that were central to the 'scientific revolution'.[16] In many ways this is precisely what has been undertaken above, in analysing how litigants like Smyth and Crokey pursued their suits strategically and tactically. It has already been shown that both men utilised heterogeneous, socio-centric networks, which involved many kinds of actor and many kinds of relationship, and which can best be observed and understood by observing practices. With both men, and particularly Crokey, it has been possible to observe how litigants drew upon diverse kinds of contacts, and managed to conjure—or muster—networks that might prove valuable. This was particularly clear in terms of those upon whom Crokey relied to distribute his pamphlets; a network that came about as he reached out to, and re-acquainted himself with, people to whom he had some prior connection, no matter how tenuous these ties may have been.

As such, the Warrens Court dispute highlights the importance of what network analysts call 'weak ties'. The premise here is that attention often falls too heavily upon certain kinds of ties, the strength of which is a factor of formal institutions, endurance over time, and emotional intimacy or intensity. What also needs to be

[14] Alec Ryrie, 'John Knox's international network', *Studies in Church History Subsidia*, 14 (2012), 96–115; Esther Mijers, *News from the Republick of Letters* (Leiden, 2012).

[15] Henning Hillmann, 'Mediation in multiple networks: elite mobilisation before the English Civil War', *American Sociological Review*, 73.3 (2008), 426–54.

[16] Jon Stobart, 'Personal and commercial networks in an English port:', *Journal of Historical Geography*, 30.2 (2004), 277–93; Larry Neal and Stephen Quinn, 'Networks of information, markets and institutions in the rise of London as a financial centre, 1660–1720', *Financial History Review*, 8.1 (2001), 7–26; David S. Lux and Harold J. Cook, 'Closed circles or open networks? Communicating at distance during the scientific revolution', *History of Science*, 36.2 (1998), 179–211.

appreciated is that some networks involve, depend upon, and gain strength from, less formal associations, and from connections within extended, open, and amorphous networks, not least in terms of individuals who serve as 'bridges' between much more familiar kinds of network that operated within confined social, institutional, or organisational settings.[17] 'Weak ties' may have been particularly important to Crokey, who lacked Smyth's 'power', the latter of which rested upon status groups, institutions, and locality, and upon connections of kinship and employment.

This section argues that placing individuals within networks and communities permits the use of fragmentary evidence to gain biographical insights. The connections evident in the networks of Smyth and Crokey—not the strongest ties, but not the weakest links either—involved and *reveal* ideological affinity, even if these affinities did not necessarily result in overt political and religious activity. The following chapters demonstrate that even fairly loose networks—whether long-standing or newly conjured—could involve shared political and religious outlooks, and help to position individuals ideologically.[18] This is obviously perilous territory, because individuals do not automatically share the views of friends, associates, and family, let alone acquaintances. It is vital not simply to infer the views protagonists from the ideological positions of people with whom they interacted, and instead to undertake a calibrated exercise that distinguishes between contingent relationships—including those with lawyers—and more meaningful associations. The latter were purposeful and chosen, forged and found, even if they were informal and involved 'weak ties'. Not all such associations involved—or can be shown to have involved—ideological affinities, and the views of any one 'contact' might not be revealing. However, the cumulative effect of such evidence proves telling, particularly alongside cross-generational identities within particular families. Such networks help to reconstruct the mental worlds of Smyth and Crokey, to recover their religious and political beliefs, and to reassess their motivations, as well as to appreciate why the dispute generated so much interest, even if only in a localised fashion. This section argues that religious and political identities can be discerned, and that these were evident in how both men dealt with their dispute, and with Wotton school. It builds upon evidence that has emerged thus far—about how more people came to be informed about, and touched by, the Warrens Court affair—to suggest that such interest reflected understanding about its deeper significance, on the part of people intimately connected to and involved with the key protagonists, as well as with the locality. The fascination that contemporaries demonstrated reflected awareness of, and sympathy with,

[17] Mark S. Granovetter, 'The strength of weak ties', *AJS*, 78.6 (1973), 1360–80.

[18] Carlo Ginzburg and Carlo Poni, 'The name and the game: unequal exchange and the historiographic marketplace', in Edward Muir and Guido Ruggiero, eds, *Microhistory and the Lost Peoples of Europe* (London, 1991), pp. 6–7; Kate Davison, 'Early modern social networks: antecedents, opportunities, and challenges', *AHR*, 124.2 (2019), 456–82.

ideological positions that are sometimes difficult to detect. Such positions may also have been difficult to *express*, and this section will grapple once again with how to treat claims made during litigation. This section argues that, whether or not it makes sense to trust litigants' claims about plots, conspiracies, and violence, legal processes incentivised the modulation of ideological claims; that certain elements of a dispute might have been played down even as others were accentuated.

In short, this final section argues that the development of a richly-documented case study provides an opportunity to delve beneath the surface of litigation, and to tease out the deeper issues in play, in terms of ideas, attitudes, and beliefs that were brought to, revealed by, and generated during disputation, even if they were not necessarily made explicit in formal legal proceedings. It involves a methodology for using evidence about litigants and litigation to tease out structural issues that were—or became—relevant; an approach based upon the relevance of certain kinds of network analysis for understanding aspects of early modern life to which they have rarely been applied.

7

'Country malice', the 'inferior sort', and the Church of England

The Mental World of John Smyth

In 1615, John Smyth arranged for the repair of Nibley's church bells, and in 1639 he drew up contracts to replace them with five 'sufficient musical bells', by 'chipping and tuning' three devices, and casting two new ones. This was costly—over £100—and sheds light upon Smyth's beliefs and ideas. The task was complicated by the need to get episcopal approval, involving repeated journeys to the diocesan chancellor, and the ensuing delays suggest that the move was controversial. It is revealing that Smyth emulated decisions made elsewhere, stipulating that Nibley's bells should be 'as deep in note as [at] Slimbridge or Dursley, or half a note deeper', and consulting with Hugh Robinson, the notorious vicar of Dursley (and archdeacon), who was later hounded out of the parish by local Puritans.[1] That the period witnessed division amongst Nibley's parishioners seems clear: complaints led to churchwardens being called before the episcopal authorities more than once; and litigation regarding the church—involving Smyth's servant William Archard—took place in the late 1630s.[2] Such evidence implicates Smyth in activities that exposed religious divisions within Nibley, even if the precise nature of his behaviour, and of the ideas that drove him, remains elusive. This chapter grapples with the evidential issues involved in recovering Smyth's ideological 'identity', and assesses how political and religious beliefs structured his dispute with Benjamin Crokey.

That this requires attention reflects dissatisfaction with previous attempts to pin down Smyth's ideas, which involved using his colonial adventures, parliamentary career, and reading habits to associate him with the 'opposition' to crown and court, and with godly reformers. Such views can be challenged by reconsidering the evidence, grappling with Smyth's *mentalité*, and reflecting upon his social attitudes, cultural preferences, and responses to political and religious change. This means paying attention to passing comments and recorded behaviour, and situating Smyth within a network of 'confederates'. The effect will be to highlight traces of ideological controversy that had surrounded Wotton school since the late

[1] GA, P230/CW/2/1; *HMC 5th Report* (London, 1876), p. 358; GA, D8887/4/7; D9125/1/9778–9.
[2] GA, P230/CW/2/1; D9125/1/12025.

The Madman and the Churchrobber: Law and Conflict in Early Modern England. Jason Peacey, Oxford University Press.
 DOI: 10.1093/oso/9780192897138.003.0008

sixteenth century, and while Smyth's ideas, attitudes, and beliefs cannot be calibrated precisely, a rich body of evidence suggests that he was economically adventurous but socially and culturally conservative, loyal to the Stuart regime on issues of church and state, and anything but a Puritan. These traits were manifest in, and intimately related to, the dispute over Warrens Court.[3]

I

The idea that Smyth inclined towards 'opposition' rests upon a problematic reading of his personal and political activities, not least regarding overseas adventuring and membership of Parliament, both of which are better explained by his being an *arriviste* who sought to establish himself within Gloucestershire's gentry.[4] Correcting this misreading involves scrutinising Smyth's involvement with the Virginia Company, and contextualising his record as an MP, both of which can be documented in considerable detail.

Smyth's interest in Virginia needs to be understood in the context of his participation in other 'projects'. The most obvious involved the development of Warrens Court: a concerted push to enhance its productivity by rethinking the use to which it was put.[5] However, Smyth also sought other ways to improve his financial position. He became involved with the Fisheries Society and with Guiana, giving 11*s*. to a man who travelled to South America in 1614, upon the encouragement of a neighbour, Sir Thomas Roe.[6] Smyth's papers also reveal an interest in other enterprises, from Mr Russell's 'artificial wine' to various tobacco ventures.[7] His commitment to Virginia was much more substantial, and having 'adventured' 50*s*. in the company's 1612 lottery he invested £37 in 1614. Perhaps encouraged by John Smith's *Description of New England*—purchased for 8*d*. in 1616—Smyth helped to develop Berkeley hundred on the James River (1619).[8] Smyth joined forces with other local men—George Thorpe of Wanswell, Richard Berkeley of Rendcomb, and Sir William Throckmorton—to develop a settlement, and his papers reveal the agreements made, the cost of securing ships and supplies, and lists of settlers, as well as servants' indentures. Smyth was willing to transport 'a good number of young men and maids', who could do the company 'good service' (May 1621), and duly despatched 'my four Virginia men', each with a

[3] Horn, *New World*, pp. 78–9. [4] Broadway, 'Political appropriation', pp. 3–4.

[5] See above, p. C1.P22, C1.P27.

[6] For Fisheries: GA, D8887/2/76. For Guiana: Bodl. MS Eng.Misc.e.6, fo. 87. For Roe: Joyce Lorimer, 'The failure of the English Guiana ventures 1595–1667 and James I's foreign policy', *Journal of Imperial and Commonwealth History*, 21.1 (1993), 1–30.

[7] Kingsbury, *Virginia*, ii. 233, iii. 365–7, iv. 79.

[8] GA, D9125/1/13608/29, 41; Bodl. MS Eng.Misc.e.6, fos 68v, 88, 91v; GA, D9125/113612/5; D8887/2/27. Smyth also read *Purchas his Pilgrimage*, which he then paid to 'exchange' (1615), as well as 'my old Lady Sandys travels' (1622): GA, D9125/1/13608/27, 53.

copy of Patrick Copeland's thanksgiving sermon (April 1622). Smyth also built houses and boats, and corresponded with governors like John Woodleafe and George Yeardley, and although he received depressing reports about slow progress, disease, and the 1622 massacre, he continued to promote the company's affairs—buying *Generall Histories of Virginia* and sending more supplies—until terminating his investment in 1624.[9]

What is difficult to demonstrate is that Smyth's financial interests were underpinned by oppositional politics. Some of his collaborators—like Thorpe and Arnold Oldisworth—probably hoped to resolve financial problems, and William Tracy of Hales had recently been imprisoned for debt, explaining that, since he would 'live in shame and disgrace in England', he had 'nothing but Virginia'.[10] Smyth's motivations were less clearly expressed, but his activities seem clear. He replaced the first governor, Woodleafe, because he was ineffective, and 'none of the wisest, providentist nor observantest of our directions', and in choosing Robert Pawlett as chaplain he sought to ensure scrupulous loyalty to the Church of England.[11] Berkeley Plantation was not meant as a 'city upon a hill'. Neither is there evidence that Smyth was involved in the factionalism that beset the company in London, or that he was close to its most controversial grandees, Sir Edwin Sandys and the earl of Southampton. His involvement in its internal workings was limited to membership of a small number of committees.[12]

Historiographically, the link between the Virginia Company and opposition politics involves connecting colonial activity with the political and parliamentary careers of those involved, and here the evidence does little to support the suggestion that Smyth had the profile of an 'opposition' MP. His election at Midhurst was more likely to have been facilitated by the Lewkenor family than by the earl of Southampton.[13] It is also difficult to place significant weight upon the fact that Smyth prepared—but did not deliver—a motion supporting 'free speech', spoke out against patents and monopolies (2 and 3 March), and supported parliamentary authority to punish the Catholic lawyer, Edward Floyd, for insulting the Elector Palatine.[14] Recent scholarship has questioned older claims about the

[9] GA, D8887/2/53; D9125/1/13608/41, 46, 49, 50; D9125/1/13612/7, 9; Kingsbury, *Virginia*, i. 477; iii. 109–14, 130–4, 136, 137, 138, 148, 151, 178–89, 190, 193–5, 197–214, 230, 248, 260–1, 266, 376, 381–94, 396–7, 402–5, 408, 412–15, 426, 435, 509, 589, 618, 674; Patrick Copland, *Virginia's God be Thanked* (1622); GA, D8887/5/11. Throckmorton eventually withdrew: Kingsbury, *Virginia*, iii. 271–4.

[10] Kinsgbury, *Virginia*, i. 535, iii. 289, 291, 367–70, 373–4, 395, 401, 409–12, 417. See: Horn, *New World*, p. 53. Oldisworth died in Virginia in 1621; Thorpe was killed in the massacre of 1622: *Commons 1604–1629*, vi. 514–15; TNA, PROB 6/14A, fo. 171. For Smyth's connections with Arnold Oldisworth: Berkeley, GPL 752, 896, 950, 1051, 1057.

[11] Kingsbury, *Virginia*, iii. 292–3, 374–405; Horn, *New World*, pp. 384, 390.

[12] Kingsbury, *Virginia*, i. 469, 472–3, 490, 496, 556.

[13] Broadway, 'Political appropriation', p. 4; Broadway, 'John Smyth', p. 80; *Commons 1604–1629*, ii. 415–16; Smyth, *Lives*, ii. 432.

[14] *CD 1621*, i. 81–2; v. 268, 282, 324, 358, 366, vi. 277; *CJ*, i. 536a; Edward Nicholas, *The Proceedings of the House of Commons in 1620 and 1621*, ed. Thomas Tyrwhitt (2 vols, Oxford, 1766), ii. 22.

nature and degree of conflict within early Stuart Parliaments, especially before the mid-1620s; challenging the existence of a coherent—let alone 'Puritan'—opposition, and emphasising instead court factionalism.[15] Writing about 1621, Conrad Russell insisted that the concerns raised by Smyth also animated the crown, and involved issues that were much less controversial than they would later become.[16]

Smyth's parliamentary career requires close scrutiny in the light of such 'revisionism'. His desire to become an MP might have reflected his Virginia interests, but he might also have sought parliamentary privilege because of his dispute with Crokey. More importantly, his record as an MP indicates that he was a marginal figure, who 'listened much and said little', and whose diary even Wallace Notestein thought 'whimsical'.[17] Both Smyth's diary and the detailed report he sent to Lady Berkeley—'a part of the journal of these last six days'—*related* proceedings more obviously than commented upon them, and little or no reference was made to the issues—parliamentary privilege and foreign policy—that soured relations, even though they directly affected men—Sandys and Southampton—with whom he has sometimes been linked, and who were arrested for adopting a more confrontational approach.[18] Smyth also ignored the controversy surrounding the duke of Buckingham, and emphasised good relations between Parliament and the king.[19] He considered it to be 'ignorance and indiscretion for a subject to force his prince', let alone 'by violent means'.[20]

What *can* be said is that Smyth attended regularly, even though he had business with the Berkeleys at Cranford, and that he worked hard, to the detriment of his health. This probably reflects Smyth's enthusiasm for his new role; he made a point of recording a payment of 2*s*. to the Serjeant of Arms, as well as purchases of 'paper books and ink for the parliament', and expenses in 'going to the parliament by water', not to mention money spent on 'parliamentary diet'.[21] He also acquired a bundle of 'separates', including the king's speech at the state opening, a catalogue of royal monopolies, and Francis Bacon's submission before the Lords.[22] Smyth also confessed that, having spent from 6am to 9am on a Sunday morning 'foolishly' writing to Lady Berkeley—'unbuttoned and undressed, whilst the messenger stayeth'—he grew ill 'with an ague . . . not able to hold my pen any longer'.[23]

Smyth's parliamentary career also goes some way towards supporting Russell's claims that MPs generally put local matters before 'the national interest', and were more interested in passing effective legislation than in promoting parliamentary power.[24] Smyth's concerns related to his locality and his own interests. He sat on a

[15] *CD 1621*, i. 83; Conrad Russell, *Parliaments and English Politics 1621–1629* (Oxford, 1979), pp. 4, 6–8, 14, 26.

[16] Russell, *Parliaments*, pp. 87–8, 92–3, 98–108. See: Robert Zaller, *The Parliament of 1621* (Berkeley, 1971).

[17] *CD 1621*, i. 79, 81. For Smyth's diary: BL, Add. MS 34121.

[18] Russell, *Parliaments*, pp. 123–44. [19] FSL, Z.e.1(22). [20] Smyth, *Lives*, i. 274.

[21] GA, D9125/1/13608/41, 45. [22] FSL, Z.e.1(12–16).

[23] *CD 1621*, i. 79, v. 321; FSL, Z.e.1(22). [24] Russell, *Parliaments*, pp. 8, 35, 37.

committee regarding Tewkesbury bridge (5 May), and even his speech on Durham's ambition to gain parliamentary representation reflected a determination not to diminish Gloucestershire's influence.[25] Smyth also contributed to debates about the cloth trade, which was vital to the county's economy, and his desire to 'abridge' the days on which wool trading took place at Blackwell Hall reflected a desire to reduce the travelling expenses of local clothiers, and to ensure that they could get home to 'observe…the sabbath day'. It also reflected a 'conservative' provincialism, and he spoke about preventing 'merchants' meetings' while also reflecting upon the 'beauty' of his county 'in Tuckmills and Tenters, far superior to the sixty goldsmiths in Cheapside'.[26] This outlook is also evident in Smyth's letter to Lady Berkeley, in which he described this last speech—by 'a member…dwelling within the hundred of Berkeley'—as being delivered 'in confutation of a burgess of London', and 'for the ease of his neighbour clothiers against the merchants there'.[27] Smyth's interventions regarding the tobacco and fishing trades defended the economic interests of the Virginia Company, and reflected a dispute between 'rival vested interests' more obviously than it did a desire to attack Spain.[28] His parochial attitudes even extended to the introduction of a private bill to protect the interests of the Berkeley family in Bosham (Sussex).[29]

The issues that occupied Smyth the most related to the dispute with Crokey. Smyth noted speeches regarding 'the swelling of the Chancery' and the need to 'ease the subject of exhorbitancy', and showed an interest in a bill about 'vexations and delays' within the legal system, and about excessive fees.[30] He was appointed to committees regarding bribery and Chancery reform, and took a keen interest in the fate of Lord Chancellor Bacon.[31] Smyth's own experiences may also have informed his interest in prisoners' grievances, and he described the warden of the Fleet as 'a most hateful abuser' of inmates.[32] Even more specific to Smyth's own battles were issues noted in his diary. These related to the statute of chantries, the protection of landowners from 'titles of concealment', and the need to limit the time devoted to private bills, as well as to motions to prevent petitions from being entered 'privately', and to ensure they were signed, received, and read in the petitioner's presence. Smyth also took an interest in 'protections', like the one Crokey received from Lord Stafford, and in banning 'private briefs', of the kind that Crokey deployed.[33] Thus, whatever the wider plausibility of Russell's argument, which will certainly be questioned in due course, revisionist accounts of the

[25] *CJ*, i. 553, 609. [26] *CJ*, i. 552; *CD 1621*, ii. 217, iv. 152, v. 294–5, 367, 379, 382.
[27] FSL, Z.e.1(22); Russell, *Parliaments*, pp. 94–5.
[28] *CJ*, i. 581; *CD 1621*, i. 81, v. 78, 261, 333–4, 344, 377–9, 419–20; Russell, *Parliaments*, p. 97. See: Zaller, *Parliament*, pp. 101–2.
[29] *CD 1621*, ii. 63, v. 253. [30] *CD 1621*, v. 321, 339, 345, 399.
[31] *CD 1621*, v. 349, 352; FSL, Z.e.1(22); *CJ*, i. 626b. See: Zaller, *Parliament*, pp. 20–1, 75–84, 92–7.
[32] *CD 1621*, v. 258, 329, 394. [33] *CD 1621*, v. 253, 337, 346, 355, 379, 399, 400; FSL, Z.e.1(21).

1621 Parliament make it necessary to rethink Smyth's politics, while his activity in the House reveals a conservative provincialism, and a preoccupation with issues relating directly to the Warrens Court dispute.

II

Rethinking the nature of 'opposition' also involves reassessing the light that Smyth's reading practices sheds upon his political and religious outlook. Here too it is possible to challenge claims that he was well disposed towards Puritans 'whose works he read', that his annotated books reveal someone who 'associated with provincial opposition to Stuart policies', and that he 'appropriated' texts 'against the royal prerogative'.[34] In fact, while Smyth's papers contain valuable evidence about the consumption and reception of contemporary literature, they do not support such an interpretation.

Smyth's accounts reveal extensive book-buying, and spending of around £6 per year with London's stationers, although what such purchases reveal is less clear.[35] Smyth frequently bought—and reminded himself to buy—almanacs, and was a keen follower of current affairs, via scribal separates and newsbooks ('currantoes'), the latter of which he acquired regularly from 1632 onwards, alongside instalments of the *Swedish Intelligencer*.[36] Doing so represented a conscious reaction to 'Simondsall newes'—'feigned inventions' devised by local 'clothiers, horsecarriers and wainmen... who weekly frequent London'.[37] Such habits were entirely conventional, and many other purchases were made on behalf of, or as gifts for, his employer, lawyers, and children.[38] Books that Smyth acquired for himself and his family are more important, but not necessarily more enlightening. These certainly included titles by Puritans, although many of these—the works of William Perkins, Lewis Bayly's *Practice of Piety*, and William Whately's *Bride Bush*—represented conventional reading, as did histories and chronicles, Augustine's *City of God*, Selden's *Mare Clausum*, and Sarpi's *Council of Trent* (twice), not to mention the *Anatomy of Melancholy* by his friend Robert Burton.[39]

While Smyth undoubtedly followed political and religious controversies—the 'Alured letter' against the Spanish match; Daniel Featley's 1624 account of the disputation between Francis White and John Fisher ('for my lady')—his shelves

[34] *CD 1621*, i. 76; Broadway, 'Political appropriation', p. 3.

[35] Bodl. MS Eng.Misc.e.6, fos 61v, 82v, 91v, 105v, 111, 114v, 121v; GA, D9125/1/13612/1, 8.

[36] Bodl. MS Eng.Misc.e.6, fos 41v, 92; GA, D9125/1/13612/1, 15; D9125/1/13608/29, 67, 70–v, 72, 76v; D8887/5/6, 16; D9125/1/13611/19, 21; D8887/9/122, 134; FSL, Z.e.1(19–21).

[37] Smyth, *Lives*, iii. 30.

[38] Bodl. MS Eng.Misc.e.6, fos 78, 83v; GA, D8887/2/31, 48; D8887/3/8; D9125/1/13612/3, 6, 8–10, 13–15; Berkeley, BB 109, fos 107v, 112.

[39] Bodl. MS Eng.Misc.e.6, fo. 51; GA, D9125/1/13608/41, 46, 50, 86; D8887/5/6, 18; D9125/1/13612/3, 7, 9, 14.

also housed conformist works, from Mocket's *God and the King* to the works of King James.[40] A volume that Smyth either owned or composed in the 1590s—'Apt and fit similes taken out of learned men's sermons'—included notes from William Tyndale's *Practice of Prelates*, but also from the Catholic Thomas Dorman's *Request to Mr Jewel*, and from orthodox divines, one of whom—Leonard Wright—attacked Puritan texts by 'Martin Marprelate'.[41] It might even be possible to detect a slight bias towards Arminian and anti-Puritan works, and while Smyth acquired the *Apologie* by George Hakewill, a Calvinist who suffered under William Laud, he also acquired Laud's re-working of Richard Field's *Of the Church*, and a work on the Sabbath by John Prideaux that was published to embarrass him by the Laudian, Peter Heylyn.[42] In the wake of William Prynne's notorious *Histriomastix*, Smyth showed an interest in James Shirley's *Triumph of Peace*, the performance with which other lawyers demonstrated loyalty to Charles I.[43]

The aspect of Smyth's reading most obviously used to link him with 'opposition circles' involves Sir Walter Raleigh.[44] Smyth certainly admired Raleigh, 'that prodigy of wit' who 'was not likely to stand in awe of mere majesty', and the two men may have been friends. Smyth acquired copies of Raleigh's letters and speeches, and annotated a scribal copy of the 'Dialogue between a counsellor of state and a justice of peace' (1615), although how to interpret these annotations is unclear.[45] Occasionally, Smyth saw personal concerns reflected in Raleigh's text: a passage about how 'a weak title that wears a strong sword hath commonly prevailed against the strong title that wears but a weak one' probably seemed relevant to Crokey. However, he read it before a modified version—printed as *The Prerogative of Parliaments*—became controversial, and probably saw it as a text that critiqued 'evil counsellors' and promoted cooperation between Crown and Parliament.[46] Smyth highlighted passages about counsellors who 'bare the great sway', about the dangers of 'tumultuous assemblies', and about popular support for the king, who had recently been 'betrayed' by 'those whom he trusted'. He noted passages about the need for monarchs to trust their own judgment; about grandees who had become 'hateful to the people' and 'insolent' towards 'princes that... advanced them'; and about it being better for subjects to open their purses 'willingly' than through 'violence'. He also noted Raleigh's endorsement of 'freedom of speech' (in Parliament), and of the advantages that accrued to monarchs who honoured Magna Carta. As such, Smyth was more interested in the issue of impeachment than in royal power, although he was intrigued by notions that the

[40] FSL, Z.e.1(18); GA, D9125/1/13612/9; D9125/1/13608/46; Bodl.MS Eng.Misc.e.6, fo. 129v.
[41] Bodl. MS Eng.e.3400; *HMC 5th Report*, p. 360.
[42] GA, D9125/1/13612/14; D8887/5/12; D9125/1/13608/72.
[43] FSL, Z.e.1(25).
[44] GA, D225/Z1; Broadway, 'Political appropriation', pp. 5–6.
[45] *CD 1621*, i. 83; FSL, Z.e.1(8–11).
[46] GA, D225/Z1; Noah Millstone, *Manuscript Circulation and the Invention of Politics in Early Modern England* (Cambridge, 2016), pp. 212–15.

prerogative was best employed to confront people who exploited their power to 'assist their own passions', 'punish and imprison . . . the king's poor subjects', and promote 'fortunes and factions'. Smyth's only *comment* contradicted Raleigh's claim that 'there was never any assembly so barbarous as not to answer the love and trust of their sovereign', saying 'yes, there has'. It signalled *disapproval* of recent agitation.[47] Thus, while it is difficult to gauge Smyth's response from his annotations, he probably sought consensus, feared the effect of conciliar government upon constitutional harmony, and worried about aggressive Parliaments.

III

In suggesting that Smyth was sympathetic towards Puritan 'opposition', conventional approaches are unconvincing, and it makes sense to focus instead upon what can be gleaned using other methods, beginning with his social world and mental outlook.

Smyth was preoccupied with social hierarchy, venerating the lineage of the Berkeleys—'this noble family', whose ancestry he traced back to Adam—and insisting upon the respect owing to him as a gentleman.[48] His will made explicit reference to 'the pews . . . by me heretofore builded [*sic*], where myself, wife and family do sit', and to his visibility as a patrician, who provided a 'dole of bread each Sunday . . . to seven poor folks in the church porch of Nibley'.[49] He was a proud patron of Nibley's almshouse, erected in 1601 and rebuilt after being 'maliciously' burned down in 1629.[50] In defending the requirement that pupils at Wotton school should honour him in their prayers, Smyth told Crokey not to 'reprehend their . . . flattery too censoriously, nor me of ambition or vain glory for avowing the same as *due unto me*'.[51] Such comments reflect a determination to defend his reputation. Smyth prosecuted people 'for words', brought one local man before the Court of Chivalry for calling him 'a knave, villain and beggar', and forced two others to disown a petition criticising his work as steward to the Berkeleys.[52] During the Warrens Court dispute, Smyth repeatedly denounced attempts to 'wound and slander' him, and protested about 'clearing my reputation, which is more dear unto me than my life'. He even claimed that, in defending himself as someone possessing the 'rank of a gentleman', he prevented others of 'great

[47] GA, D225/Z1. Cf. Broadway, 'Political appropriation', pp. 5–6.

[48] GA, D9125/1/12008, pp. 5–10; D8887/5/48; TNA, PROB 11/187, fo. 239. See: E. P. Tompson, *Customs in Common* (London, 1991), pp. 43, 46, 64, 86.

[49] TNA, PROB 11/187, fo. 239. See: GA, D9125/1/13611/4; D9125/2/5821; Bodl. MS Eng.Misc.e.6, fos 29, 55, 74, 75v, 76.

[50] GA, D8887/3/95–7, 112–14; D2957/354/33.

[51] GA, D9125/1/12008, p. 36 (emphasis added).

[52] Bodl. MS Eng.Misc.e.6, fos 125, 131; G. D. Squibb, *High Court of Chivalry* (Oxford, 1959), p. 38; GA, D8887/5/27.

eminency' from being 'assaulted' and 'wounded' through his 'sides'. For Smyth, personal reputation was bound up with the social order, and with the peace of a 'well-governed commonwealth'.[53]

Smyth was also adamant that the social order should not be threatened by the 'lower orders', and in bemoaning how Westminster Hall had become 'our cockpit of revenge', he railed against the 'country malice' and 'envy' of 'the *inferior sort*'.[54] This explains his determination to know whether legal witnesses 'were subsidy men or not', and to learn of their 'reputations or estates'.[55] In noting the 'miserable fate' of princes and grandees 'by flatterers'—'the cruellest of all beasts'—Smyth also opined that 'wise men' were 'never much affected with the applauses of the rude and unskilful vulgar', or with 'the vain and popular multitude'.[56] Smyth plainly believed that Crokey was misbehaving towards his superiors, referring to his humble background and limited means, and criticising him for giving up the 'honest' trade in which he had been 'bred'. This involved more than just a prejudice against urban life by a convinced man of the vale, although Smyth certainly described husbandry as 'the only vocation wherein innocency remaineth', and expressed disdain for cities where people 'busy themselves how to deceive and beguile one another'. It also involved a comment upon Crokey's poor 'stock', and he noted that 'this man... having no credit nor estate, careth not what he speaketh nor of whom.'[57] The implication was clear: men who lacked a meaningful stake in society had no place criticising their superiors.[58] This was why Smyth contrasted the 'gravity', 'integrity', and 'learning' of a schoolmaster like Edward Cowper with Crokey's ignorance. Crokey was accused of 'prattle', and of having done insufficient research, doubtless because he lacked formal learning. At the Wickwar hearing, Crokey allegedly produced two documents from Richard II's reign, and affirmed them to be true copies of records in the Tower, despite being unable to 'read one line of those old Latin records'. On another occasion, Crokey was 'urged to read' a Latin document, but 'neither could do it, nor yet could pronounce one Latin word of two or three syllables, other than in a ridiculous manner.'[59]

Smyth's social attitudes also emerged in relation to controversial rural policies. While many locals—not least in Nibley—strove to suppress the 'evil' caused by alehouses, Smyth was more tolerant. He rejected the reforming impulses that

[53] TNA, STAC 8/107/7; PA, HL/PO/JO/10/1/37; GA, D9125/1/12008, pp. 4, 88–9.

[54] Smyth, *Lives*, i. 242 (emphasis added), iii. 313.

[55] GA, D8887/8/6; D9125/1/13611/23v; D9125/1/11989/12. See: Hillary Taylor, 'The price of the poor's words: social relations and the economics of deposing for one's 'betters' in early modern England', *EcHR*, 72.3 (2019), 828–47.

[56] Smyth, *Lives*, ii. 151.

[57] Smyth, *Lives*, iii. 42; GA, D9125/1/12008, pp. 16, 43–4, 77.

[58] GA, D9125/1/12008, p. 10. See: GA, D8887/6/15. Smyth thus seems to betray an attitude that linked credibility to social status, for which see Steven Shapin, *A Social History of Truth* (Chicago, 1994), p. 238.

[59] GA, D9125/1/12008, pp. 9, 10, 35, 37, 57, 67.

closed one such establishment in Berkeley, bemoaning that it was now 'out of use for men of honest conversation', and for travellers seeking 'entertainment'.[60] Smyth also courted controversy by supporting policies to enclose common land. Such activities provoked considerable tension, but Smyth mocked local disorder as 'a rural reluctation'. He joined his employer—as well as friends like Oldisworth and Thorpe—in prosecuting men who obstructed the enclosure of the 'new warth' in Slimbridge (1611–18), and inflicted harsh punishments upon rioters and those who trespassed upon private land. He also insisted that common ground merely attracted the poor, who 'burden the township with beggarly cottages... where the greater part spend... their days in a lazy idleness and petty thieveries'. Smyth applauded royal policies to encourage enclosure, for 'the private benefit' of landlords and 'the general good of the commonwealth'.[61]

More striking still is Smyth's support for games and pastimes that were anathema to the godly. Some of these were specific to Gloucestershire, and Smyth praised traditions associated with 'Bluemead Sunday'—the second Sunday after Pentecost—when 'the younger sort of both sexes' gathered at Stinchcombe, 'to dance, leap, wrestle and disport themselves'. He was fond of activities on Cowley Pike Hill, 'where to behold young men and maids ascending and descending and... tumbling down, especially *on communion days*... bringeth no small delight'. He also celebrated the 'inbred delight' that 'gentry, yeomanry, rascality, boys and children' took in a game called 'Stoball', which 'not a son of mine, but at seven was furnished with his double stoball staves, and a gamester thereafter'. Smyth confessed to spending Sunday afternoons on Hodley's Green—'between our two houses'—watching local children 'run at Barley-breakes, dance in a ring, and such like sports', and in 1610 he recorded expenses associated with 'pulling the rope with Cam's men' upon Shrove Tuesday. As a defender of the 'Book of Sports' he bemoaned how such 'recreations' had been 'discontinued' by 'severe and rigid Catoes', deeming them to be 'laudable', like 'church-ales, wakes, [and] saints' feast days'. Citing Richard Carew and Robert Burton, Smyth, suggested that such traditions had 'no oppugners save wayward dispositions, and men of too stern a judgment'.[62]

Smyth's approval of precisely the things that troubled Puritans extended to other forms of entertainment, including 'stage plays'. From the 1590s onwards he witnessed—and arranged—dozens of performances at Berkeley Castle, by various companies of players and assorted musicians. Smyth oversaw payments to the Lord Admiral's 'fool', and provided money to indulge his master's passion for

[60] GA, D8887/4/21; D8887/1/35.

[61] Smyth, *Lives*, iii. 328; GA, D9125/1/13611/23-v; Bodl. MS Eng.Misc.e.6, fos 93, 102v; Chicago UL, MS 1465, folder 3. See: GA, D8887/4/4, 19; Smyth, *Lives*, iii. 303; GA, D9125/1/13612/5; D8887/3/5; Warmington, *Gloucestershire*, pp. 140–2; Horn, *New World*, p. 97. For controversy over the warth: GA, D8887/4/78, 81–5, 87–8, 93–5; Berkeley, GPL 715–1081, 1154–74.

[62] Smyth, *Lives*, iii. 10, 67, 151–2, 349–50. See: Richard Carew, *The Survey of Cornwall* (1602), sigs S4-T; Robert Burton, *The Anatomy of Melancholy* (1628), p. 257.

cards, defending such pastimes against those who believed that 'the hours may seem too many which this lord spent . . . at bowls, tennis, cockput, shufgrote, cards and dice'.[63] Moreover, these were not simply Lord Berkeley's tastes. Smyth himself spent money on gambling, on 'singers at my door', and on musicians at Stinchcombe, and occasionally visited London's playhouses, once paying 12*d.* to see *The World Goes Round* (1627).[64]

IV

Another means of illuminating Smyth's mental world involves the religious and political views of his 'confederates'. These have rarely been explored, and attempts to associate him with the Puritan leanings of neighbouring families like the Trotmans highlight the risks involved.[65] Nevertheless, the views of Smyth's closest associates are valuable, given the patterns that emerge.

Of course, not every connection is relevant for this kind of network analysis. It would be unwise to expect Smyth's lawyers to reveal a consistent political and religious 'identity', and he probably prioritised skill and eminence over ideological purity. It might be tempting to label some counsellors—Leonard Bawtry, Sir Thomas Chamberlain, and Richard Waltham—as Puritans, given the company they kept and the ministers they promoted, and Heneage Finch certainly spoke out against Arminianism.[66] Others, like William Jones, had serious reservations about policies like Ship Money.[67] Nevertheless, Bawtry was a controversial MP who was hissed in the Commons for defending the king's right to levy impositions, while a reputed Catholic like Sir Richard Weston ruled against Hampden over Ship Money, was impeached by the Long Parliament, and became a royalist, grumbling about 'these troublesome times'.[68] Others with Catholic ties likewise inclined towards royalism, like Francis Moore and Edward Norgate, the latter of whom protested against 'heresies, sects and schisms'.[69] Even Smyth's lawyers amongst the Trotman family are ideologically elusive, even if Samuel Trotman became connected through marriage to the Speaker of the Long Parliament, William Lenthall.[70]

[63] Berkeley, BB107, fos 13, 16, 19, 21, 29, 93, 94; BB10, fos 2, 9v, 13; BB110, fos 12–v, 16, 101v, 109; Smyth, *Lives*, ii. 363.

[64] Bodl. MS Eng.Misc.e.6, fos 9v, 82, 99v; GA, D9125/1/13612/9, 12.

[65] Rollison, *Local Origins*, ch. 5.

[66] Prest, *Barristers*, pp. 343, 361, 400; *Commons 1604–1629*, iii. 160–2, iv. 257–69; *ODNB*.

[67] Prest, *Barristers*, p. 374; *ODNB*.

[68] Prest, *Barristers*, pp. 343, 401; *Commons 1604–1629*, vi. 731–2; TNA, PROB 11/208, fo. 163.

[69] Prest, *Barristers*, p. 380; TNA, PROB 11/138, fo. 279; *CSPD 1639*, pp. 12, 47, 59, 82, 116, 144, 162, 180–1, 189, 213, 242, 248, 269, 271, 281, 330, 349, 355; TNA, PROB 11/215, fo. 64v.

[70] See: GA, D8887/7/100–1, 112; D8887/10/96; GA, D9125/1/13618; Prest, *Barristers*, p. 398; F. A. Inderwick, ed., *A Calendar of the Inner Temple Records* (5 vols, London, 1896–1901), ii. 27, 144, 359; GA, GDR/1630/133; Bodl. MS Eng.Misc.e.6, fo. 95; TNA, PROB 11/379, fo. 89; PROB 6/11, fo. 150v; Rollison, *Local Origins*, pp. 103, 107–8, 113.

Many of the Gloucestershire men with whom Smyth associated are also hard to fathom religiously and politically, and at least some became (lukewarm) parliamentarians. Smyth's will referred to 'worthy alliesmen and friends', a term used for local men to whom he made regular gifts, for employees like William Archard, and for relatives like John Browning, as well as for those who received mourning rings with the text 'be faithful'.[71] Of these, Stephen Fowler and Charles Jay both served Parliament, although their allegiance was questioned.[72] Many others were obscure, or died before the late 1630s, the point when the views of 'middling sort' characters often come into focus. These included Robert Smyth (*d.*1637), sometime mayor of Wotton, who allegedly joined the mob that intimidated Robert Pritchard, and John Togood, a servant of the Berkeleys whose funeral sermon was preached by their chaplain, Edward Vaughan.[73] Even the views of some gentry friends—with whom Smyth reportedly 'confederated'—are poorly documented. These include Sir George Huntley of Frocester (*d.*1623), an aggressive land encloser, Jasper Selwyn of Matson (*d.*1635), and Christopher Stokes of Stanshaw, and even Sir John Poyntz of Iron Acton (*d.*1633), sometime sheriff and MP.[74] George Raymond, who was nominated by Smyth to an inquiry (in 1616), and who provided information about Crokey (in 1626), became a controversial parliamentarian, but another, Nicholas Webb, is more elusive.[75]

Patterns emerge, however, from Smyth's broader network: men with whom he chose to work, and to whom he was connected by 'weak' ties. Few, if any of these inclined towards puritanism or parliamentarianism. Sir Edward Bromfield, to whose daughter John Smyth junior was married, was a forceful supporter of Ship Money, an opponent of puritanism, and a monopolist, who was removed

[71] TNA, PROB 11/187, fo. 239; *Vis. Gloucester 1623*, pp. 32, 149; *Vis. Gloucester 1682–3*, pp. 30, 171–3; GA, D8887/5/38, 80; D8887/10/79; GDR/1671/141; TNA, PROB 11/303, fo. 42v.

[72] For Stephen Fowler of Stonehouse (*d.*1671): *A&O*, i. 169, 230, 546, 966, 1083, 1136, 1237, ii. 35, 299, 467, 664, 1069; Warmington, *Gloucestershire*, pp. 79, 83, 92; *HMC 5th Report*, pp. 356–7; For Charles Jay: Warmington, *Gloucestershire*, p. 79; GA, D8887/1/70; D8887/11/44; *HMC 5th Report*, pp. 356–7; BL, Add. MS 34012, fo. 28. For gifts to such men: GA, D9125/1/13618.

[73] For Smith: Lindley, *Wotton*, p. 95; *Men and Armour*, p. 164; TNA, PROB 6/16, fo. 125. For Togood: GA, D9125/1/12014; TNA, PROB 11/175, fo. 179v; GA, D8887/9/133.

[74] For Huntley: Smyth, *Lives*, iii. 303; *Vis. Gloucester 1623*, pp. 93–4; TNA, PROB 6/11, fo. 27. For Selwyn: *Al. Oxon.*, iv. 1133; Prest, *Barristers*, p. 390; W. Paley Baildon, ed., *The Records of the Honorable Society of Lincoln's Inn. The Black Books* (6 vols, London, 1897–1968), ii. 20, 121, 214; *Men and Armour*, p. 30; GA, GDR/1635/91. For Stokes: *Men and Armour*, p. 215; TNA, PROB 11/316, fo. 203v; *Vis. Gloucester 1623*, p. 154; *Vis. Gloucester 1682–3*, p. 178. For Poyntz: *Commons 1604–1629*, v. 747–8; Berkeley, BB10, fos 8v, 9v.

[75] For Raymond: Warmington, *Gloucestershire*, pp. 79, 90–1, 102, 103, 117–18, 124, 126, 134–5; TNA, PROB 11/281/54; *CCC*, p. 1585. One Nicholas Webb was sheriff of Gloucestershire in the 1620s and 1630s, but it is unclear whether he is the same man who was mayor of Gloucester in 1643 and a parliamentarian: *Al. Oxon.*, iv. 1590; *A&O*, i. 966, ii. 1325; Samuel Rudder, *The History and Antiquities of Gloucester* (Cirencester, 1781), p. 147; Warmington, *Gloucestershire*, p. 63; PROB 11/212, fo. 238v. Another Nicholas Webb of Wotton (*d.*1635) was a clothier and cousin of Matthew Hale, who associated with Crokey's allies like Tobias Higgins and Albane Saunders, and with the Puritan vicar of Wotton, Thomas Ackson: TNA, PROB 11/169, fo. 192v; *Men and Armour*, p. 165.

from the aldermanic bench as a delinquent during the civil wars.[76] Smyth's attorney—and landlord—Michael Moseley was on the fringe of Laudian circles, through his 'loving friend' Roger Bates, rector of St Clement Danes.[77] Similar traits are evident with key allies in Gloucestershire, including Richard Berkeley of Rendcomb and his brother-in-law, Sir Thomas Roe. Berkeley supported Ship Money and the Bishops' Wars, participated in Gloucestershire's pro-episcopacy petition in 1641, and was named to the king's Commission of Array, for which he was declared a delinquent.[78] Roe likewise supported Ship Money, as well as the Forced Loan, criticised the 'passion' of the 1628 Parliament in demanding 'a shadow of liberty', and supported the king.[79] Many others—including Smyth's 'confederates'—similarly became royalists, including Arthur Kemis (*d.*1644) and Sir William Guise of Elmore (*d.*1643), who both travelled to Oxford and died within royalist quarters.[80] Another ally at least suspected of royalism was Anthony Hungerford of Black Bourton, whose family once lived in Down Ampney and held land in Nibley, and who provided Smyth with vital information about Crokey in 1626. Having sat in the Long Parliament, Hungerford faced punishment for travelling to Oxford, even if he claimed to have done so under duress.[81] Other local associates also suffered for their loyalism, including the attorney, Richard Dowsdwell, while Edward and Richard Wakeman of East Beckford were suspected recusants, who compounded for their estates and were kept under surveillance during the 1650s.[82]

Hungerford and Richard Wakeman are fascinating because they reveal another dimension of Smyth's royalist network, centred around Bristol's civic elite. In 1626, Hungerford encountered Crokey's pamphlet in the company of Thomas Colston, while Wakeman visited Crokey in prison alongside Giles Elbridge. Elbridge and Colston were both Merchant Venturers who held high civic office; both were part of Crokey's network that was co-opted by Smyth; and both were at the heart of Bristol's royalist community.[83] Elbridge, to whom Crokey was once close, became heir to Robert Aldworth's vast fortune, while Colston—who witnessed Elbridge's will (1644)—was removed from the city corporation for being

[76] Valerie Pearl, *London and the Outbreak of the Puritan Revolution* (Oxford, 1961), pp. 293–4.

[77] TNA, PROB 11/160, fo. 270; PROB 11/165, fo. 201.

[78] *HMC 5th Report*, p. 345; *CCC*, p. 1653; *Commons 1604–1629*, iii. 214; Badminton House, FmS/C1/1, 8, 9; FmS/C2/1.

[79] *Commons 1604–1629*, vi. 72–7.

[80] For Kemis: *Vis. Gloucester 1623*, p. 99; TNA, PROB 10/642, fo. 178. For Guise: *Al. Oxon.*, ii. 618; Warmington, *Gloucestershire*, pp. 36, 43, 181; TNA, PROB 10/639, fos 35–7v.

[81] GA, D9125/1/12014; D9125/1/13612/12; D2957/216/28; Smyth, *Lives*, iii. 270; *Men and Armour*, pp. 173–5; TNA, SP 23/175, pp. 451, 465, 475, 477; *CJ*, iii. 526.

[82] For Dowdswell: TNA, SP 19/116, fos 105–46; SP 23/156, fos 360–1; Warmington, *Gloucestershire*, p. 149; For the Wakemans: GA, D9125/1/12014; *Vis. Gloucester 1623*, pp. 174–5; *CCAM*, p. 746; *CCC*, pp. 88, 224, 739, 1929, 2746, 2982; TNA, SP 23/211, fo. 39; SP 23/247, p. 45; SP 23/128, pp. 206, 215; PROB 6/35, fo. 306; BL, Add. MS 34012, fo. 58v.

[83] GA, D9125/1/12014.

'forward and active' in the king's service. Also purged at the same time was another member of this group, Nathaniel Cole, who served as Elbridge's executor and remained a zealous opponent of political and religious radicalism into the Restoration.[84] This group can be widened further, to include Merchant Venturers like John Barker (*d*.1636) and Humphrey Hooke (*d*.1659), the Bristol MP expelled from Parliament in 1642, who became a leading royalist, albeit of a temporizing kind.[85] What makes this group intriguing is that it was associated with Laudian policies for the beautification of churches, and supported controversial local clerics, particularly Richard Towgood and Richard Standfast. Both were ejected from their livings in the 1640s, having proven themselves 'disaffected' by their 'printing, preaching and praying'.[86]

The value of such evidence lies in the cumulative effect of mapping Smyth's network. Not all of Smyth's relationships—even in his fight with Crokey—were ideologically driven, and some attachments reveal the power of kinship, gentry solidarity, and long-standing friendships. Nevertheless, his associates and allies tended to support controversial Caroline policies, Laudian reforms, and the royalist cause, and the ideological positions around which they coalesced became increasingly visible from the 1620s onwards, and may even have been rooted in cultural prejudices and socio-economic divisions.

V

Pursuing this idea involves using Smyth's behaviour to recover his religious opinions and beliefs. This includes tantalising clues from his accounts: donations to St Paul's school and the 'arch-Laudian' project for repairing St Paul's Cathedral; purchasing a wedding ring of 'fine gold' for his son's marriage (motto: 'in Christ alone two hearts made one'); and spending £3 on wine and music at the wedding celebrations.[87] It also involves Smyth's comments on religious issues, his

[84] TNA, PROB 11/167, fo. 21; Beaven, *Bristol*, pp. 185, 197–8, 223, 281, 283, 288; *CSPD 1625–6*, p. 301; *CSPD 1637*, p. 436; *CSPD 1637–8*, p. 231; McGrath, *Merchants*, pp. 127, 144, 148–50; Sacks, *Widening Gate*, pp. 50, 69–70; TNA, PROB 10/641, fo. 115; *CSPD 1645*, p. 208; *LJ*, vii. 644–5; TNA, SP 23/76, pp. 312–19; TNA, PROB 11/252, fo. 37v. For Cole (or Cale): *A&O*, i. 797–8; *CSPD 1661–2*, p. 319; *CSPD 1663–4*, pp. 37, 381, 433, 437, 477, 482; TNA, SP 29/68, fo. 9; *CSPD 1664–5*, p. 150; TNA, SP 29/109, fo. 185.

[85] Beaven, *Bristol*, pp. 185, 197, 222, 277; Sacks, *Widening Gate*, p. 51; BA, FCW/1636/1; TNA, PROB 11/171, fo. 238; PROB 11/290, fo. 9. See also: TNA, PROB 11/197, fo. 362; C 7/390/41; C 6/106/27; C 7/47/150.

[86] BA, M/BCC/CCP/1/2, fo. 116v; F/Au/1/20, p. 99; F/Au/1/22, pp. 26, 33, 101, 107, 164, 171, 229, 240, 298, 307; M/BCC/CCP/1/3, fos 47–8; *Walker Revised*, p. 178; Harlow, *Religious Ministry*, pp. 3, 165; TNA, PROB 11/373, fo. 206v; *Englands Memorable Accidents*, 89 (21–28 Nov. 1642), p. 91; Sacks, *Widening Gate*, pp. 226–8, 231–4, 238–9, 240–3. For Aldworth: Sacks, *Widening Gate*, p. 234; Reynolds, *Godly Reformers*, pp. 261–2; TNA, PROB 11/167, fo. 21.

[87] GA, D7115/1; D9125/1/13612/8, 15; *HMC 5th Report*, p. 345. See: Fincham and Tyacke, *Altars*, p. 270.

ambitions as a clerical patron, and his actions at Nibley chapel. Here too, Smyth's views and practices placed him at odds with local Puritans, and perhaps in agreement with Arminian and Laudian tendencies within church and state.

In Parliament and in his *Lives* Smyth was outspoken on church affairs. Referring to 'these devastating times' in 1621 reflected his concern about 'armies of divines', presumably those clerics who used 'sharp pens' to decry as 'sacrilegious' anyone who received tithes.[88] Smyth blamed the litigation that blighted his age upon those who demonstrated 'forwardness' in religion, and wrote dismissively of a 'lewd and factious knave' who accused Henry, Lord Berkeley of Catholicism.[89] While Smyth showed no evidence of being a Catholic, he was not troubled by the possibility of arranging marriages between members of the Berkeley family and recusants, and endorsed a conservative religious outlook. This may have involved tradition more obviously than deep theological convictions, but he was nostalgic for old practices like masses and sung prayers, which he believed could be practiced in a 'decent' and 'holy' manner, so that anyone other than 'a scholar to John Wycliff' would deem them compatible with 'the doctrine of... the church of England'. He praised chantry priests who lived 'chastely and honestly', by not frequenting alehouses and theatres, or indulging in 'unlawful games', mocking the idea that godly living was restricted to 'Puritans in these our times'. He also reflected fondly on times when 'monks, friars and nuns' were held in 'veneration', bemoaning that '*tempora mutantur et nos mutamur in illis*' [times are changing and we are changing with them].[90]

Such comments can usefully be supplemented by evidence about Smyth's behaviour in his locality.[91] His influence was theoretically constrained because, as a chapel of Wotton parish, Nibley chapel had been controlled by Christ Church, Oxford since the Reformation, but this did not stop him—or the Berkeleys—from intervening in its affairs. Smyth complained that the college made 'so poor an allowance' for local ministers 'that it scarcely sufficeth for the bread of those that serve at the altars', and when the college refused to enhance the income of Nibley's curates he paid them from his own pocket, not least in response to the 'clamour' of parishioners.[92] He may also have supported a formal deputation from Nibley to 'attend the Parliament' in 1640 or 1641, 'for the maintenance of their petition... for increase of maintenance'.[93]

More intriguing is Smyth's role in selecting Nibley's ministers, and although John Smyth junior complained about enduring clerics 'put upon us by the college', some were chosen publicly 'after evening prayers', and betrayed Smyth's influence.

[88] *CD 1621*, i. 83; Smyth, *Lives*, ii.361. [89] Smyth, *Lives*, ii. 370, iii. 313.

[90] Smyth, *Lives*, iii. 39, 260. See: BL, Add. MS 33588, fo. 60.

[91] GA, D8887/3/95; D8887/4/1–8; D9125/2/5818, 5820, 5822–3.

[92] Smyth, *Lives*, ii.169, iii. 260–1; Bodl. MS Eng.Misc.e.6, fo. 127v; Christ Church, Oxford, MS I.c.3, pp. 512–13, 518–19.

[93] GA, D9125/1/9780; D8887/4/12.

These included occasional preachers like Mr Hallows (1604), Mr Burte (1625), and Mr Norway (1633), and although such men preached 'by consent of the parish' it is noteworthy that they included a chaplain to the bishop of Gloucester (1631) and Lord Berkeley's own chaplain, Edward Vaughan (1631).[94] It is tempting to suggest that Smyth was involved in the appointment of Lewis Codrington as curate (1623), given that he too had ministered in Berkeley, although he subsequently helped to remove Codrington in 1634, perhaps for showing the Puritan sympathies—ignoring the parish perambulation—that caused him to be called before the episcopal authorities.[95] Codrington's removal made it possible for Smyth to secure the services of John Ham, to whom he was evidently close. Ham offered advice about 'erecting a schoolmaster', and about the 'pious policy' of educating 'those whom God and nature have made dear unto us' (1638).[96]

Ham's proximity to Smyth makes his views worthy of scrutiny. That this can be done reflects his attempt—after taking up the living at Harnhill (1641)—to dissuade Smyth's son from appointing Thomas Jackson as his successor. Jackson had evidently preached at Nibley in Smyth's absence, to the satisfaction of 'the multitude', who 'neglected' and 'despised' other preachers like Mr Brown and Mr Mitchman. Ham's concern—'in these distracted and schismatical times'—was that Jackson's former patron, the parliamentarian MP Sir John Potts, was known to favour Puritans, and that he was recommended by another parliamentarian, John Ashe of Freshford. Ham was 'doubtful' about Jackson's 'conformity', saying it was not 'so great as you and I wish', and he feared that parishioners—who were anxious to secure Jackson's services, and gave 20*s*. 'towards his pains'—'lacked sufficient judgment and penetration in a matter of this nature'.[97] While Ham survived the civil wars and Interregnum unmolested, more relevant is the fact that he resurfaced in 1662 to support a young cleric, Thomas Twittie, who sought a living that became free due to the nonconformity of the 'late usurper'. Ham attested that Twittie was 'orthodox in judgment', and a 'faithful subject to his Majesty', and joined forces with a notorious royalist divine, Paul Knell, as well as with local clerics who benefitted from the ejection of Puritan ministers.[98]

Smyth was out of step with local Puritans, and it seems likely that many inhabitants were unhappy with changes to the church for which he—as the most powerful local magnate—was almost certainly responsible. The churchwarden's book contains evidence not just about collections for poor soldiers, Irish

[94] GA, P230/CW/2/1; Bodl. MS Eng.Misc.e.6, fos 16v, 23, 24, 63v.

[95] GA, GDR/137, unfol.; GA, P230/CW/2/1.

[96] GA, P230/CW/2/1; TNA, PROB 11/187, fo. 239; GA, D9125/1/12025.

[97] GA, D8887/4/10–11; P230/CW/2/1. For Potts and Ashe: Mary Freer Keeler, *The Long Parliament, 1640–1641* (Philadelphia, 1954), pp. 312–13; *ODNB*.

[98] TNA, SP 29/58, fos 198, 201; *ODNB*; *Walker Revised*, p. 221.

vagrants, and exiled ministers from the Palatinate; about the response to church briefs; and about vigorous attempts to cull 'varmints' like hedgehogs, jays, and bullfinches. It also reveals contributions to the solidly conformist Chelsea College (20*s*. in 1617), and payments to the man—none other than John Bell—who rang to commemorate St James's day, the Gunpowder Plot and the failure of the Gowrie conspiracy.[99] It also records alterations to the church, and although re-edification and beautification were not always indicative of Laudianism, Smyth took steps that many Puritans would have opposed, and may even have been part of the 'parochial avant-garde', which did more than merely respond to official orders.[100]

The scheme of repairs at Nibley began in 1610, and while it was encouraged by the non-Laudian bishop of Gloucester, Miles Smith, it seems to have been given renewed impetus by Laud's activities as Dean (1616-21), and by the 1629 proclamation regarding church fabric, the 'first shot' in the Laudian campaign of beautification.[101] Changes were made to the parochial library, and while the King James Bible, the *Paraphrases* of Erasmus, and the works of John Jewel were all retained, an old prayer book was traded for a better version in 1622, and then replaced by a new one in 1637 (9*s*.), and by another edition in 1640. A new book of canons was acquired in 1635, and the following year Smyth donated a book of homilies, perhaps to the dismay of Puritans who craved sermons. In 1623, Smyth provided a silver communion cup (costing 25*s*., of which he paid half), and while such things were not intrinsically revealing about his views, they take on added significance alongside the payment of £2 to a carpenter to install a sommer donated by Lord Berkeley (1625), which seems to indicate the reintroduction of organ music. In the same year, the parish acquired a new communion table, before paying—in 1634—for 'drawing' it into what was presumably an altar-wise position. Thereafter, it was covered with a 'carpet', while the pulpit was adorned with a green cloth, 'with strings', although no mention is made of rails.[102] The following year Ham read out the controversial 'Book of Sports', and certified to the episcopal authorities that he had done so, while in 1637 wainscot was provided for the belfry, and in 1639 pews were re-arranged to permit the reintroduction of a rood screen, 'to part the church from the chancel'.[103] 1639 also saw steps to ensure that the parish clerk kept the church clean and tidy, maintained the clock, and rang the 'Coversell' bell twice a day between the feasts of St Michael and the Annunciation. Finally, in 1638–9 the

[99] GA, D9125/2/5815; P230/CW/2/1.
[100] Fincham and Tyacke, *Altars*, pp. 104, 237–49, 253, 273.
[101] GA, D9125/1/13611/4; P230/CW/2/1; Warmington, *Gloucestershire*, p. 139; Fincham and Tyacke, *Altars*, pp. 136, 237. See: Fincham, *Prelate*, pp. 90, 170, 273; B. Taylor, 'William Laud, dean of Gloucester, 1616–21', *TBGAS*, 77 (1959), 86–92.
[102] GA, P230/CW/2/1; D9125/1/13608/50v; Fincham and Tyacke, *Altars*, p. 140.
[103] GA, P230/CW/2/1; D8887/4/7.

churchwarden's paid 4*d.* for a copy of official prayers issued for Charles I as he set off to confront Scottish Covenanters, a move that led Puritans to question the king's authority to issue nationwide prayers. The parish also paid 4*d.* to the man who delivered the text, and 4*d.* to certify that a proclamation—presumably about Covenanters' 'seditious practices'—was read in church.[104]

Not all of these changes were straightforwardly Laudian, in terms of their timing and significance, and the churchwardens' accounts are frustratingly perfunctory. It is hard to be clear what kind of glazing was undertaken in 1639, and how divisive it might have been.[105] Nevertheless, such evidence is telling, and whatever drove Smyth's inclinations towards re-edification and beautification, it seems plausible to suggest that he was emboldened by the arrival at Gloucester of an anti-Calvinist bishop, Godfrey Goodman (1624), in the allegations against whom he took a close interest.[106] Many of the steps Smyth took were in line with Laudian policies, followed Laudian orders, and proved controversial, and it is striking how quickly the parish changed direction after 1640. This meant taking steps against recusants, and following instructions regarding the communion table, thereby confirming that it had been repositioned by Smyth.[107] In June 1642, Ham noted that Jackson delivered 'a short prayer for the king and a long one for the Parliament'; that he refused to say the Lord's Prayer; and that he honoured the wishes of parents who objected to the sign of the cross being used in baptism, something Ham could not 'in any way commend'.[108] The minister during the 1640s, Thomas Trotman, took the Solemn League and Covenant, styled himself 'presbyter', and adopted the *Directory*, purchased at a cost of 1*s.*6*d.* Long before then, the Smyth family admitted having lost control of the church. In 1642, they took back the silver communion cup that Smyth had presented, and thereafter John Smyth junior and William Archard refused to pay church rates.[109]

VI

Such evidence provides the context for exploring clear—although not voluminous—evidence that Smyth engaged with the Caroline regime as an unusually loyal member of the Gloucestershire gentry.

[104] GA, P230/CW/2/1; *A Forme of Prayer with Thanksgiving* (London, 1638); *A Prayer for the Kings Majestie* (1639); *National Prayers: Special Worship since the Reformation*, ed. Natalie Mears, Alasdair Raffe, Stephen Taylor and Philip Williamson (2 vols, Woodbridge, 2013–17), i. 363–5; *A Proclamation and Declaration to Inform our Loving Subjects* (1638).

[105] GA, P230/CW/2/1.

[106] GA, D2510/9. See: *ODNB*; Soden, *Goodman*, pp. 198, 202, 240; Fincham and Tyacke, *Altars*, p. 211.

[107] GA, P230/CW/2/1.

[108] GA, D8887/4/11.

[109] GA, P230/CW/2/1.

Here too, analysing Smyth's ideological identity requires distinguishing vital from circumstantial evidence. His willingness to secure a pardon at the king's coronation (26*s*.8*d*.), to accept the Forced Loan, and to compound for knighthood are not necessarily revealing, and some local men who opposed the Forced Loan later supported the king.[110] Within a divided county, however, Smyth *invariably* sided with the crown and the Berkeley interest. In 1614, he contributed to the benevolence (9*s*.4*d*.), and in 1624 petitioned Parliament against (Sir) Robert Poyntz of Iron Action, who contested the county seat with Sir Thomas Estcourt (an executor of Henry, Lord Berkeley), and who allegedly used menacing behaviour to defeat Sir Maurice Berkeley in a subsequent by-election. Indeed, Poyntz—who later opposed the Forced Loan—aligned himself against anti-Calvinist clergymen from Gloucester Cathedral, including Dr John Baber.[111] As has been shown, Poyntz also read and circulated Crokey's pamphlet. Somewhat more indicative is Smyth's support for Ship Money. This policy divided the county in interesting ways, with some future parliamentarians working conscientiously to raise the levy, and some future royalists proving obstructive, but here too Smyth was loyal. He paid his assessment, processed instructions, and planned to prosecute the sheriff—Poyntz—as one of those who 'pretend to be true servants to the king' while failing to punish 'refusers' (1638).[112] Finally, Smyth monitored local gentlemen who refused to support the first Bishops' War (1639), while personally supplying arms and men, and noting the need to 'procure further servants for Scotland'.[113]

The clearest evidence of Smyth's position as civil war approached involves parliamentary elections in early 1640. This episode is well known, demonstrating how consensual methods to 'select' MPs broke down, how social (and regional) divisions mapped onto political fractures, and how some notables neglected the possibility of mobilising voters along ideological lines, rather than as 'ballot fodder'.[114] The aim was certainly to strike a 'general accord', to give the county seats to Sir Robert Cooke, an opponent of Ship Money and a future parliamentarian from lowland Gloucestershire, and Sir Robert Tracy, a future royalist from the upland Cotswolds. However, while candidates and grandees attended alongside 'troops' of 'tenants and retinue', hopes that the result would be 'a matter of ceremony and formality' were undone, following the emergence of another candidate, Nathaniel Stephens of Eastington. Stephens had opposed Ship Money, and was 'much endeared to the vulgar', and he was 'cried up with no

[110] GA, D9125/1/13612/11; D8887/5/26; *HMC 5th Report*, p. 345; Warmington, *Gloucestershire*, p. 22.

[111] Bodl. MS Eng.Misc.e.6, fo. 94; GA, D8887/3/40; *Commons 1604–1629*, ii. 135–6, v. 748–9; *APC 1627*, pp. 125, 374, 449.

[112] GA, D9125/2/5813; D8887/4/69–76; D9125/1/13611/20; TNA, SP 16/386, fo. 160; Warmington, *Gloucestershire*, p. 22.

[113] GA, D2510/1/6–7; D9125/1/13614; *HMC 5th Report*, p. 345.

[114] Rollison, *Local Origins*, pp. 136–48; Warmington, *Gloucestershire*, pp. 16, 24–6.

less ardour and fervency' than if he had 'dropped out of the clouds for the purpose'. The result was 'eager competition' and a 'strong canvass'. Cooke was charged with 'infidelity' when some of his tenants were seen 'stickling for Stephens'; Stephens was accused of 'ungentleman-like' behaviour for reneging upon the 'compact'. It was at this point that social tensions emerged. Tracy expressed 'scorn' at being 'webbed and loomed', mocking the origins of Stephens's family as weavers, while others retorted that 'weavers might well enough rank with shepherds', like those found in the Cotswolds. The county seemed to be dividing 'into Cotswold shepherds and... Vale weavers', 'like the factions of the Guelphs and Ghibellines', which was thought to augur 'bad blood'. Tracy then used dubious tactics and 'misdemeanours' to undermine Stephens, whose subsequent petition complained about a man who shaved off his beard 'to be polled again', and intimated that things became violent and disorderly. The matter was investigated by the Committee for Elections, and Tracy was summoned as a delinquent, although nothing was resolved before the Short Parliament was dissolved.[115]

Less well recognised is that consensus was also threatened by the Berkeleys and by Smyth. In December 1639, Smyth requested electoral direction from his employer, and was eventually encouraged to back Sir Maurice Berkeley. The latter asked Smyth to remain 'unengaged' until it was known 'who will stand to be knights for our shire', and hoped to secure 'both voices'. Lord Berkeley then encouraged Smyth to support *both* Sir Maurice and Sir Baynham Throckmorton, the son of Smyth's colleague in the Virginia plantation. Sir Maurice was clearly a 'court' supporter; having been chided for opposing the Forced Loan he promoted war against the Covenanters, and both he and Throckmorton joined the royalist cause. Lord Berkeley resisted pressure from the Lord Chamberlain (the earl of Pembroke) to support Sir Ralph Dutton, a courtier and future royalist, and as late as February 1640 Smyth was urged to use all his 'means and power' for the Berkeley-Throckmorton ticket, with anyone 'in whom you have any interest'.[116] What he did next is unclear, but suspicions arose that he opposed any deal involving Cooke, who pleaded that a consensual outcome was being threatened by 'jealousies and unexpected canvassings', and who asked Smyth to send 'what voices you can'.[117]

If Smyth favoured Berkeley and Throckmorton over Cooke and Stephens, this probably reflected loyalty to his employers as well as anxiety over religious divisions. Cooke betrayed signs of religious radicalism, and had recently been called before High Commission, while Stephens showed Puritan 'zeal towards the

[115] TNA, SP 16/448, fos 165–v; Judith D. Maltby, ed., *The Long Parliament Diary of Sir Thomas Aston* (London, 1988), pp. 147, 153, 155–6; *CJ*, ii. 4, 6, 7.

[116] GA, D8887/2/89, 90; D8887/10/99–100; D7115/1, unfol. For Throckmorton: *Commons 1660–1690*, ii. 386.

[117] TNA, SP 16/448, fo. 165; GA, D7115/1; D8887/16/13.

zealous', and provoked John Dutton to exclaim that he 'would never... trust any man that wore his hair shorter than his ears'. He was also 'egged on' by 'a pack of... deprived, silenced or puritanically affected' clerics. These included notorious preachers like Humphrey Fox and John Geree (from Tewkesbury), as well as William Jones of Tytherington, a minister 'in whose very face a man may read schism and malice', and someone to whom attention will return. For some, an 'underhand canvass' of this kind heralded a House of Commons that would 'hold the king's nose to the grindstone and ruin the church'.[118]

Unfortunately, Smyth's involvement in the Long Parliament election is harder to trace. Sir Robert Cooke opted to sit for Tewkesbury, explaining to Smyth that the county needed to be 'sensible' and make a 'careful choice', which meant recognising the difficulty of unseating Stephens. He also suggested that the other county seat might be given to Sir Maurice Berkeley, while fearing that a consensual scheme might not survive 'strong solicitations'.[119] Smyth apparently recognised the wisdom of Cooke's plan. His refusal to help Sir Humphrey Tracy—a Ship Money sheriff and zealous royalist—reflected an appreciation that Stephens was unbeatable, rather than a difference of opinion. Smyth told Tracy that he had 'engaged his promise... unto others', presumably Berkeley, although the latter declined to stand, and it is unclear whether John Dutton, who eventually joined Stephens at Westminster, secured his endorsement. Dutton, after all, opposed Ship Money and entered Parliament as a reformer, even if he later became a royalist.[120]

VII

It is this accumulation of evidence—about Smyth's associates, attitudes, and behaviour—that makes it possible to turn, finally, to Wotton school, and to tease out evidence that the Warrens Court dispute involved well-established ideological divisions.

Central to Crokey's case was the claim that Wotton school was led away from its original mission to promote 'good literature and learning'. Accusations that Smyth effected its 'suppression' generated the dispute's bitterest moments, not least when Robert Pritchard seemed willing to 'discharge his conscience' by testifying on Crokey's behalf. It was at this point that Smyth allegedly tried to bribe the schoolmaster—with 'money and other rewards'—to 'forbear his testimony', before blocking an inquiry once it became clear that 'he could not corrupt the said Pritchard.' Smyth supposedly responded by raising a mob of 'riotous

[118] TNA, SP 16/448, fos 165v–6. [119] GA, D2510/10.

[120] GA, D8887/16/24; Warmington, *Gloucestershire*, pp. 26–8. For Tracy: ibid., pp. 22, 26–7, 29, 33, 51, 56, 88, 90, 105, 110, 113.

persons', who entered Pritchard's lands intending 'bodily hurt', threatened to 'set fire upon his house', and caused 'great terror' to his family.[121]

Smyth rejected the suggestions that Pritchard had been 'misused', and that he had undermined the school, and claimed to have taken control of its affairs to prevent others from doing so, rather than because he 'had not other house then to dwell in', as he once claimed.[122] Smyth's correspondence with James Duport—from the 1590s onwards—indicates that the fate of the school was entangled with the ancient Berkeley–Lisle dispute, and that as their quarrel came to a head in 1608 Duport was negotiating with both sides, since both peers sought the advowson and the patronage. Although Duport promised Berkeley that his 'best endeavours' would be used 'to bring it to your honour's hands', he also recommended keeping their correspondence 'from all men's eyes', lest Lisle (Robert Sidney, later 1st earl of Leicester) should recognise his ambitions and work even harder to secure control. Ultimately, Duport felt that Lisle offered 'a light price', and complained about 'gross speeches' by his 'agents', who suspected a 'plot' against their master. Duport characterised the latter as 'merciless men' and sensed that they would behave ruthlessly if thwarted. Smyth, he suspected, would not 'escape scot free', because Lisle planned 'to dive fair into his estate', and was hunting out ancient records to prove that the school lands were 'concealed'.[123]

This correspondence helps to explain why Duport struck a deal with Smyth, rather than with Lisle or Berkeley, and suggests that competition between the two noblemen was ideologically driven. Duport feared that John Staunton, vicar of Wotton and deputy schoolmaster, was helping Lisle, whose reputation as a fighter for international Protestantism would have been well known. Duport referred to Staunton's 'policy... in this business', and to suspicions that Lisle's 'pretence' was neither lawful nor '*godly*'. He noted that Staunton 'cast out... parables in the pulpit' about the school's affairs, worried about who might succeed him as master, and advised Smyth not to 'yield' to pressure from 'our Wotton magistrates... for a schoolmaster... of their placing'.[124] Given the religious debates that underpinned the Berkeley–Lisle dispute, and the puritanism of both the schoolmaster (John Duport) and his deputy (Staunton), it seems clear that the school's fate was intimately linked to religious divisions.[125]

Such evidence sheds light upon Smyth's awareness that the school would become controversial, and upon his management of its affairs. It explains why he remained in contact with James Duport, who sought support for his son (saying that 'the land is full of scholars' who were 'put to their shifts to live'), and who counselled Smyth to secure a new patent for 'Wotton schoolhouse' as

[121] TNA, STAC 8/107/7.

[122] Crokey, *Sacred Maiestie*, sig. A3v; TNA, STAC 8/107/7; GA, D9125/1/11996, 12008, p. 18.

[123] GA, D9125/1/11990. [124] GA, D9125/1/11990.

[125] Caroline J. Litzenberger, *The English Reformation and the Laity* (Cambridge, 1997), pp. 126–8; For Staunton: *VCH Gloucester*, ii. 404. For John Duport (*d.*1617): *ODNB*.

early as 1612.[126] It explains why John Berkeley advised Smyth that maintaining the school would bring 'trouble and scandal' (1618).[127] It might also explain why Smyth opposed the inquiry appointed in 1621, perhaps suspecting that it was (ideologically) loaded against him, and that this reflected Crokey's role in selecting the commissioners.[128] Beyond this, it explains Crokey's suspicion about the direction the school would take under new management, and raises questions about whether Smyth, like Berkeley and Lisle, had an ideological agenda. As already noted, Smyth denied doing anything to 'overthrow, impeach or hurt the . . . school', swearing that he improved its finances, funded a new schoolmaster, and increased his income from 40*s*. to £12.[129] He certainly spent money 'prettying' the schoolhouse, repairing its walls and 'glassing' its windows (1609–18).[130] However, when Smyth appointed a new master in 1632, an agreement was imposed whereby the 'overplus' of funds generated by higher rents—in line with the 1623 decree—was earmarked to reimburse his expenditure upon the 'needful and better repair of the . . . schoolhouse'. At the very least, Smyth displayed a hard-nosed attitude towards the school's finances.[131]

Crokey's concern involved more than money, although he certainly questioned Smyth's claims on this point. It also involved Smyth's 'false shows . . . of a *pious* intent', and his 'dissembled *piety*'.[132] This probably involved concerns about the school's admissions policy, and Smyth dealt with those who nominated candidates, exerted control over scholarships, and admitted the children of friends, like Charles Guise (1628).[133] Meanwhile, a Puritan like Edward Stephens encouraged Smyth to admit 'poor children' wisely, favouring boys who were 'ingenious and tractable for learning', and who would be 'profitable' to 'church and commonwealth'.[134] Such comments suggest a concern that Smyth—like Bacon and Ellesmere—believed that the country was 'overproportioned' with 'poor scholars', that education diverted country folk from the plough, and that grammar schools

[126] GA, D9125/1/11990; D9125/1/13608/24. [127] GA, D8887/2/52.

[128] Commissioners included an anti-Calvinist civil lawyer, Dr John Baber, and the Laudian minister of St Nicholas in Bristol, Thomas Tucker, who became vicar of Berkeley before being ejected in the civil wars: Soden, *Godfrey*, pp. 164–5; Harlow, *Religious Ministry*, p. 168; Reynolds, *Godly Reformers*, p. 261; *Walker Revised*, p. 321; *LJ*, viii. 550, 685. However, the majority were tolerant of puritanism, including John Thornborough (Bishop of Worcester), George Salterne (steward of Bristol), Rowland Searchfield (bishop of Bristol), Dr John Seaman (Chancellor of Gloucester), and Miles Smith (Bishop of Gloucester), who famously clashed with Laud: William Prynne, *The Antipathie of the English Lordly Prelacie* (1641), ii. 313; Reynolds, *Godly Reformers*, p. 262; *ODNB*; GA, D9125/1/12008, p. 66; TNA, PROB 11/142, fo. 39; Brian P. Levack, *The Civil Lawyers in England, 1603–1641* (Oxford, 1973), p. 268. For Crokey's naming of the commissioners: BL, Harl. MS 6803, fos 56v–7.

[129] Crokey, *Sacred Maiestie*, sig. B3v; GA, D9125/1/12008, p. 18.

[130] Bodl. MS Eng.Misc.e.6, fos 45v, 47v, 66v, 107v, 111, 115, 121v, 128v, 130v. For payments to scholars: GA, D8887/2/28.

[131] GA, D9125/1/12024. [132] Crokey, *Sacred Maiestie*, sigs A3v, C4v (emphasis added).

[133] GA, D8887/5/90; D8887/9/63. See: GA, D9125/1/12008, pp. 36, 85; D733/7/1; S379/2/8/1.

[134] GA, D8887/15/100.

would 'breed traitors'.[135] Smyth was perhaps suspected of promoting a social agenda at odds with the founder's charitable intentions.

Crokey clearly worried about the school's constitution, not least given the zeal with which Smyth oversaw new arrangements. Smyth spent £5 to get the Attorney General's advice, and paid clerks and lawyers to prepare regulations, before laying out £10 'towards my Wotton school letters patent' after paperwork was 'new drawn' by Coventry's clerks.[136] Having gone to such lengths, Smyth was pleased with the outcome, referring to 'apt and exquisite ordinances . . . for the reglement of the school and scholars', prepared with the 'grave advice' of the Lord Keeper, the bishop of Bristol, Thomas Chamberlain, William Jones, and Robert Heath. He also acknowledged that the old regulations were 'not well agreeing with *these times*'.[137]

The new ordinances seem straightforward, although they placed the school firmly in Smyth's grip. Their goal was to support people who had 'small means and ability' for 'breeding up' their children in 'good literature and learning', as well as to make loans to poor weavers, and to bind apprentices in 'honest trades', 'for the avoidance of idleness'. However, they also sought to ensure that the school would never be 'suppressed or otherwise violated', emphasising the need to appoint 'sober, discreet, learned and religious schoolmasters', who would receive a 'competent and reasonable' stipend as well as a 'convenient' house and schoolroom (at a rent of 4*d. per annum*). Masters were to be single, and were prohibited from holding another 'incumbency, dignity or promotion spiritual', and the maximum charge for teaching was 6*d.* per quarter. The ordinances also detailed the twenty-four parcels of land that would generate the school's income. However, Smyth's authority was considerable. Technically, the school was entrusted to local men from Wotton and Nibley, to minimise the chance of malfeasance, but significant responsibilities were vested in people to whom he was close—his half-brother, Anthony Gulson, and Arnold Oldisworth of Bradley—and who may have been beholden to him. Indeed, while Oldisworth and Gulson were empowered to choose new schoolmasters, Smyth regained control almost immediately, when Lord Berkeley granted him the patronage (December 1624). It was thus Smyth's responsibility to maintain a 'learned and godly schoolmaster', charged with 'instructing and teaching . . . in true religion, literature and good manners', to 'the praise of God' and 'good of the church and commonwealth'.[138] It was also in his power to interpret what this meant, and to appoint men who could put his vision into practice.

[135] David Cressy, 'Francis Bacon and the advancement of schooling', *History of European Ideas*, 2.1 (1981), 65–74; Christopher Wase, *Considerations Concerning Free Schools* (1678), pp. 1, 45, 50.

[136] GA, D9125/1/12008, p. 32; D9125/1/13608/49; D9125/1/13612/8.

[137] GA, D9125/1/12008, pp. 36, 85, 11996 (emphasis added).

[138] GA, D2957/354/7, 9; D9125/1/11987; S379/2/2/1/3. Oldisworth and Gulson were required to be involved in all decisions. For a subsequent agreement about 'overplus' money: GA, D2957/354/14.

What worried Crokey was how these ordinances would be implemented. Noticeably, in the late 1630s Smyth boasted that the school 'flourisheth' according to statutes 'fitting the *present time* and the doctrine of the Church of England', and Crokey was concerned by new prayers, to be used 'each day in the school'. These were printed in 'little pamphlets', with hundreds of copies being 'dispersed . . . over the whole country', as Smyth admitted and as his accounts confirm. Crokey's concern may have been puritanical; these were set prayers, one of which honoured the founder, Lady Berkeley. However, he also recognised that they portrayed Smyth as 'the only preserver of the school', and that the master and scholars 'twice a day pray for Smyth their patron'.[139] They were also modelled on prayers introduced at St Paul's School in 1602, apparently on the advice of Lancelot Andrewes, a leading anti-Calvinist.[140]

Crokey was also concerned about the calibre of men Smyth nominated as schoolmasters. He was unimpressed by Smyth's first nominee, Edward Cowper, whose appointment—following the resignation of John Duport—cost Smyth £5 15*s*., and who was described as a 'fellow servant to Lord Berkeley'.[141] Smyth admitted that the new master was 'sometimes my schoolmaster and tutor', saw him as someone that Crokey was 'pleased basely and falsely to scandal and traduce', and insisted that he was 'admired and commended of all good men', for 'gravity, integrity of life, profound learning and exquisite knowledge'.[142] However, Crokey pointed out that Cowper 'never exercised the place'; although he remained as schoolmaster until his death (1632), he served instead as rector of Seagrave (Leicestershire), where Lord Berkeley was patron. This contravened the ordinances, and left the school to deputies.[143] Initially, this meant Robert Pritchard, licensed as a tutor in 1609 and paid for teaching until 1617, as well as for his 'pains in preaching' as curate of Nibley. Pritchard, however, was not Smyth's nominee, having begun as deputy to John Duport, and it is significant that someone so closely connected to the school eventually endorsed Crokey's reservations about its management, and that Smyth removed him.[144] Thereafter, Smyth nominated William Wilmot (1618) and Henry Rugge (by 1623), and

139 Smyth, *Lives*, iii. 402 (emphasis added); Crokey, *Complaint*, sig. A4v; GA, D9125/1/12006, 12028, p. 7. Smyth paid 16s. to Mr Fletcher (Miles Flesher) for 250 copies in 1626: GA, D9125/1/13612/11; Henry R. Plomer, *A Dictionary of the Booksellers and Printers . . . 1641 to 1667* (London, 1907), p. 76.

140 GA, D9125/1/12008, p. 36. See: Michael McDonnell, *The Annals of St Paul's School* (London, 1959), pp. 169–70, 291–2. The 1602 ordinances were criticised by the Calvinist—but anti-Puritan—Bishop of London, Richard Bancroft.

141 GA, D733/4/1; D9125/1/12008, p. 18; Bodl. MS Eng.Misc.e.6, fo. 43v; GA, GDR/S1/17; HL/PO/JO/10/1/296; Crokey, *Sacred Maiestie*, sig. A3.

142 GA, D9125/1/12008, p. 9. See: Berkeley, BB 107, fos 18v, 33, 41v, 54, 90; BB 10, fos 1v, 36, 75; GA, D9125/1/11996.

143 Crokey, *Sacred Maiestie*, sig. B3v; Bodl. MS Eng.Misc.e.6, fo. 80; GA, D2967/354/54; D9125/1/13608, fo. 70v; TNA, PROB 11/162, fo. 41.

144 *VCH Gloucester*, ii. 404; Bodl. MS Eng.Misc.e.6, fos 43v, 45, 47v, 48, 49v, 51, 55, 56, 58v, 63v, 66v, 76v, 78v, 90v, 94, 98, 107, 110, 111v, 120v–1. See: TNA, E 134/14Jas1/Mich28.

although both are fairly obscure, Rugge offered Smyth loyal support during the dispute with Crokey, before eventually moving to Youghall in Ireland, where he was living in 1642.[145] Wilmot, not yet a deacon let alone an ordained minister, subsequently became rector of Monksilver (Somerset), but left in 1642 and died in Oxford two years later, presumably as a royalist.[146]

Smyth's appointments of men who were—or became—controversial is perfectly clear. Cowper's successor was John Turner (1632), endorsed by Smyth for having 'behaved . . . to the general liking of all good people', and for having 'enlarged the fame and reputation of the said school'.[147] However, Turner—Smyth's nephew—caused controversy upon moving to a living at Rede (Suffolk) in 1640, and during the civil wars he was sequestered and imprisoned, after refusing to relinquish control over the vicarage and glebe lands. He then sued parishioners who paid tithes to the new incumbent.[148] Equally intriguing is the appointment of Joseph Woodward as Turner's successor (June 1640). Woodward was the son of a local tanner, and was 'bred a scholar' in Wotton school, and the deeds for his appointment highlight the need to 'teach, instruct, rule and govern', according to the 'tenor' of the ordinances, as well as for 'beautifying' the school, for 'better furnishing it', and for buying 'such books as the said patron and schoolmaster shall think fittest'.[149] Woodward's appointment *seems* intriguing because, following his appointment to the living at Dursley (1647), he became one of Gloucestershire's most prominent Puritans, who helped to organise the *Testimony* that local Presbyterians produced in 1648.[150] In 1640, however, Woodward showed 'very little seriousness', and 'much frequented the company of . . . gentlemen whose character for virtue or ability was not very eminent'. It was only through the persuasion of godly clerics like Samuel Spring—and the experience of being attacked by dogs on his way home from the alehouse—that Woodward converted to puritanical ways. He was only appointed to Dursley after the 'malignant' incumbent, Hugh Robinson, was run out of town by godly zealots, and ridden backwards on a horse to Gloucester, in the style of a skimmington.[151]

The picture that emerges about the school remains sketchy, in terms of its history, culture, and personnel, but the evidence suggests that it was a focal point for religious divisions for some time, and that Smyth was suspected—perhaps with

[145] GA, D2957/354/7; D9125/1/12008, p. 36; TNA, C 66/2332/21; *HMC 5th Report*, p. 346.

[146] GA, S379/2/2/1/3. See: GA, GDR/27A; GDR/142A; *Al. Oxon.*, iv. 1654.

[147] GA, D73/17; D2957/354/10; *VCH Gloucester*, ii. 405.

[148] Crokey, *Complaint*, sig. A4v; *Al. Oxon.*, iv. 1520; *CSPD 1640*, pp. 409, 414; *Walker Revised*, p. 346.

[149] GA, D733/4/1; *VCH Gloucester*, ii. 407; GA, D2957/354/11–12. See: GA, D8887/15/101.

[150] *Al. Oxon.*, iv. 1677; Elrington, 'Survey', p. 95; Rollison, *Local Origins*, pp. 38–9; Warmington, *Gloucestershire*, p. 171. Woodward died *c.*1662: GA, GDR/1661/83.

[151] Edmund Calamy, *The Nonconformist Memorial* (3 vols, London, 1802), ii. 234–9; *Calamy Revised*, pp. 456, 545; Rollison, *Local Origins*, pp. 38–9. Robinson later took the Covenant, supported Parliament and found a living in Hampshire: *Walker Revised*, p. 176; *The Peoples Plea* (1646, BL, E328/3). George Thomason said he was '*formerly* a great malignant'.

good reason—of taking it in a religious direction that was less appealing to, or open to, Puritans.

VIII

Evidence relating to Smyth's political and religious beliefs is tantalising rather than definitive, and his behaviour sometimes reveals the strength of social connections and kinship ties, and an attachment to the Berkeley family, rather than 'ideology'. Nevertheless, the cumulative effect of these evidential shards seems clear, and while conventional approaches—about Smyth's colonial interests, parliamentary career, and reading—do not support the idea that he was a puritanically inclined member of the 'opposition' to early Stuart regimes, sources regarding his networks, attitudes, and religious and political behaviour indicate that he was socially, culturally, and intellectually 'conservative', with a nostalgic attachment to a world widely challenged by the godly. Smyth was loyal to the crown, and was more comfortable with—and willing to promote—people and practices that were anti-Calvinist and perhaps Laudian, and that led towards royalism. Perhaps there was more than meets the eye in courts describing Smyth as 'conformable'.

This chapter has argued that Smyth's 'mental framework' can be discerned, socially, culturally, and ideologically, and that the concept of *mentalité* has validity for individuals as well as collectivities, and for dynamic situations as well as static societies. It has highlighted possibilities for studying people who left little explicit evidence about their ideas and beliefs, by observing behavioural responses to contemporary events, and using evidence about the people with whom they chose to associate and work, even without developing strong ties and lasting relationships. Handled carefully, such methods provide telling clues about ideological identities, which in Smyth's case was more or less coherent, consistent with developments in political and religious culture, and connected to issues at the heart of the Warrens Court dispute. What comes into focus is how Smyth viewed this affair in ideological terms.

The sense that Smyth was out of step with contemporary Puritans and parliamentarians can be demonstrated with one final example of his clerical patronage, involving the advowson of Hoby (Leicestershire). This was a living over which Smyth sought control from the mid-1630s, and having agreed a price of £80 his 'remembrance' for Michaelmas 1635 noted the need to perfect a 'breviate', with a view to appointing Thomas Rawson after the death of the incumbent, Matthew Scampton. The position finally became vacant in late 1640 or early 1641, and Smyth recognised that the 'next presentation' would 'prove litigious'. He advised Rawson to be 'ready to go to the Bishop of Lincoln'—Smyth's old friend, John Williams—which meant knowing 'where my lord bishop is' at all times, 'whether at Lincoln, Bugden or at Westminster'. Plans were made to object to any rival candidate, and to get 'a friendly letter' from Lambert Obsbaldeston, sometime headmaster of Westminster school, canon of Westminster, and friend of Williams, even though he was deemed untrustworthy. Smyth himself petitioned Archbishop Laud when moves were made to appoint a rival, John Rhodes.[152] Such planning paid off. Smyth gained control of the advowson, and chose Rawson for the living (July 1642), after providing money to grease administrative wheels at Lambeth. Here too, however, Smyth backed a controversial candidate, whose arrival in Hoby immediately revealed religious divisions, as Rawson backed the king, clung to the Prayer Book, and resisted Puritan reforms. When Rawson was ejected from the living in 1646, his wife refused to leave the rectory until she was dragged out 'in a barbarous and inhumane manner', whereupon she took refuge in a nearby church.[153]

This episode might be thought to involve family loyalty; Rawson was Smyth's nephew, and Smyth hoped that one of his own sons would eventually secure the living. However, when placed alongside other surviving evidence it seems likely that Smyth backed Rawson aware of, or because of, his political and religious inclinations. The two men were *not* well acquainted, and Smyth only knew how to locate him through other relatives. Indeed, Rawson was actually 'commended' to Smyth by his son, John Smyth junior, suggesting that the latter should likewise be subjected to scrutiny.[154]

[152] GA, D9125/1/13611/12; D8887/2/35; D9125/1/13608/90; D8887/5/38; D8887/10/36; LB, MS 3549/213. Osbaldeston had recently been censured in Star Chamber for siding with Williams against Laud; Smyth said 'have care and caution, that Mr Osbaston look not himself or friend of his in face, whilst he pretendeth most friendship to you; the heart of man is unsearchable.' See: *ODNB*.

[153] LB, MS 3549/224; GA, D8887/10/101; *Walker Revised*, p. 243; Fiona McCall, 'Scandalous and malignant? Settling scores against the Leicestershire clergy after the first civil war', *Midland History*, 40.2 (2015), 238, 240; Bod. MS Walker.c.1/64, 218; MS Walker, c.11, fos 34–v. See: LB, MS 3549/224–5.

[154] GA, D88876/10/36.

8

'The many-headed multitude'

The Royalism of John Smyth Junior

In 1647, John Smyth junior, heir to the Warrens Court estate, managed a sizeable charitable bequest left by Hugh Perry of Wotton-under-Edge. The aim was to secure apprenticeships for local boys, and to provide a weekly lecture, a daily service at Perry's almshouses (which still exist), and an 'usher' for Wotton school. That Smyth acted alongside royalists (Sir Robert Poyntz), 'pragmatic conservatives' (the lawyer Matthew Hale), and parliamentarians (Edward and Nathaniel Stephens), might suggest he was a moderate figure, who sought to heal rather than foment the divisions ravaging the county.[1] Indeed, while Smyth is less well known than his father, he has been depicted as someone who took sides reluctantly, and who pursued a settlement with Benjamin Crokey.[2] This chapter offers an alternative reading of Smyth's career, arguing that although he differed from his father—he grudgingly followed his wishes by becoming a lawyer, and was much less litigious—he could be combative, and his responses to religious and political divisions require careful consideration. He also proved *willing* to take over the Warrens Court dispute.[3]

Smyth's career was not entirely straightforward, and recovering his ideas and attitudes involves scrutinising experiences and behaviour, and confronting methodological challenges about civil war 'allegiance'. These are often thought to involve the accessibility of 'popular' attitudes, in terms of deference, 'agency', and ideological awareness; the relevance of 'national' issues in 'local settings'; and the legibility of 'neutralist' tendencies. Considerable scholarship exists on the importance and implications of various motivating factors, in terms of 'legal constitutionalism' and 'religion', as well as on the relationship between neutralism, moderation, and 'localism', and historians have weighed the advantages of biographies, prosopographies, and community studies.[4] This chapter reiterates the value of well-documented individuals for exploring responses to shifting

[1] GA, D2957/354/59. See: GA, P379/CH/1; D1193/1/1.

[2] Howes, 'John Smyth', p. 215.

[3] *CCC*, p. 948; TNA, SP 23/196, p. 533.

[4] Buchanan Sharp, *In Contempt of all Authority* (Berkeley, 1980); David Underdown, 'Community and class: theories of local politics in the English Revolution', in B. C. Malament, ed., *After the Reformation* (Manchester, 1980), pp. 161–2; Ann Hughes, 'Militancy and localism: Warwickshire politics and Westminster politics, 1643–1647', *TRHS*, 31 (1981), 51–68; Clive Holmes, 'Colonel King and Lincolnshire politics, 1642–1646', *HJ*, 16.3 (1973), 451–84; John Morrill, *The Nature of the English Revolution* (London, 1993); G. E. Aylmer, 'Collective mentalities in mid-seventeenth-century England:

The Madman and the Churchrobber: Law and Conflict in Early Modern England. Jason Peacey, Oxford University Press.
 DOI: 10.1093/oso/9780192897138.003.0009

circumstances, in terms of John Smyth junior's relationship with local elites during the 1640s. This involves emphasising that his public image—neutral and 'delinquent'—belies the complex way in which he grappled with personal, local, and national issues, and a story with wider significance for understanding gentry behaviour. Smyth suggests that 'neutralism' could be skin deep, masking fairly clear positions; that 'localism' could be strategic; and that contemporaries were capable of reflecting upon how people 'presented' in public through deception and disguise.[5]

Smyth's overt responses to tests of allegiance need to be understood in relation to local and personal interests, but not *localism*, and as reflections of strategic behaviour. Smyth's public persona was not straightforwardly emblematic of his personal convictions. He was fundamentally a royalist, whose responses to church reform and activities as a patron echoed those of his father. At the same time, he made tactical decisions based upon pragmatic thinking. Smyth sought to protect his family's interests, and the political and religious causes to which they were attached, even if his methods were subtle. Crucial here is evidence about Smyth's network, which helps to clarify his views and how they related to 'national' issues, and also makes sense of his behaviour. The network is significant for understanding how ideological perspectives can be recovered, how contemporaries navigated difficult circumstances, and how the Warrens Court dispute developed. It demonstrates that ideological issues motivated ongoing resistance to Crokey's demands, and connected Wotton grammar school with the civil wars, and reveals the methods by which Smyth operated. Understanding the final phase of this protracted affair requires a more sophisticated understanding of Smyth's experience and activity, which indicates that he possessed both the motives and skills to undermine Crokey.[6]

I

John Smyth junior's response to political and religious division within Gloucestershire undermines the idea that he strove 'not to take sides', or did so 'reluctantly and tentatively'. He was committed to the royalist cause, while recognising the need to behave pragmatically and avoid an open confrontation

iv. Cross-currents: neutrals, trimmers and others', *TRHS*, 39 (1989), 1–22; Peter Lake, 'Puritans, popularity and petitions: local politics in national context, Cheshire, 1641', in Thomas Cogswell, Richard Cust and Peter Lake, eds, *Politics, Religion and Popularity in Early Stuart Britain* (Cambridge, 2002), pp. 259–89; Roger Howell, 'Neutralism, conservatism and political alignment in the English Revolution: the case of the towns, 1642–9', in John Morrill, ed., *Reactions to the English Civil War, 1642–1649* (London, 1982), pp. 67–87.

[5] Ann Hughes, 'The king, the parliament, and the localities during the English Civil War', *JBS*, 24.2 (1985), 237; Hughes, 'Militancy', p. 68.

[6] GA, D7115/2, unfol.

with local parliamentarians. He also recognised that such a position was 'almost impossible' to sustain.[7]

Smyth's impossible mission became evident in the months leading to war, and as he followed news from Westminster—especially Strafford's trial—his response to demands from local reformers involved foot-dragging.[8] He apparently ignored a summons to attend a meeting—at Mr Portlock's in Cirencester (February 1642)—to take the Protestation, and as the county's parliamentarian leadership coalesced his loyalty came into question.[9] His reaction to demands for money and troops navigated a path between resistance and compliance, and the questions he addressed to local officials suggested he was stalling, raising suspicions about his zeal. The parliamentarian, John Gorges, exclaimed that the 'mutinous language' of local people was explicable given the dilatoriness of men like Smyth, who needed to mobilise resources.[10] Smyth also showed an interest in royalist sentiment across the country, and his obfuscation made him a target for parliamentarians. He acquired the petition from Lancashire's 'true Protestants' (May 1642), and a statement on accommodation by the Yorkshire gentry (September 1642), and although he read Parliament's militia ordinance he was disinclined to mobilise the trained bands (August 1642). He repeatedly ignored requests to attend parliamentarian meetings to discuss 'great and weighty affairs', and to plan the county's defence 'in these times of extremity and danger'. When Smyth was asked to supply dragoons for a muster at Chipping Sodbury, a pointed reference was made to support from other quarters.[11]

Nevertheless, Smyth's response was calibrated rather than obstructive, and both sides counted on his support, at least for a while. News about the battle of Edgehill prompted him to raise money and troops for Parliament, while resisting further demands in December 1642. He explained that, while he was 'unwilling to be found backward', his horses were 'unserviceable' or already 'in this service'.[12] It was later claimed that Smyth provided Parliament with £140 and two horses, but only for 'diverse weeks'.[13] At the same time, the king's supporters expected him to join the royalist cause. Alongside Thomas Veel, Smyth was called by the royalist grandee, George Lord Chandos, to attend a meeting at the Ram in Cirencester (August 1642), to consider the distracted state of the kingdom, and newsletters from the Berkeley household assumed that he was loyal to the king.[14] They did so despite him ignoring a summons to discuss reports about a royalist army being

[7] Howes, 'John Smyth', p. 215; GA, D7115/2, unfol.; *HMC 5th Report* (London, 1876), p. 347.

[8] GA, D7115/1, unfol.

[9] GA, D2510/15; *HMC 5th Report*, p. 345; Warmington, *Gloucestershire*, pp. 32, 34.

[10] GA, D8887/4/24; D7115/1, unfol.; D2510/11–12; *HMC 5th Report*, p. 347; Warmington, *Gloucestershire*, p. 32.

[11] GA, D7115/2, unfol.; D2510/21, 22, 25; D8887/11/10; *HMC 5th Report*, pp. 345–6.

[12] GA, D7115/2, unfol.; D2510/28; D8887/15/87.

[13] TNA, SP 23/196, pp. 546–7.

[14] GA, D7115/2, unfol.; *HMC 5th Report*, p. 346. See: Nick Poyntz, 'The attack on Lord Chandos: popular politics in 1642', *Midland History*, 35 (2010), 71–88.

mobilised in the Midlands (October 1642). Smyth was not named in the king's Commission of Array, and showed neither the conspicuous loyalty of Sir Richard Ducie and Sir Robert Poyntz, nor the willingness to fight displayed by his brothers (Thomas and William), but he was a quiet rather than a lukewarm loyalist.[15] This is evident from his correspondence, which indicates how close he remained to royalists like Isaac Bargrave, and from his behaviour once civil war arrived in Gloucestershire.[16]

II

Smyth's actions early in the civil war reflected a desire to support the royalist cause while protecting Berkeley family interests, and since these were more or less incompatible he avoided an open confrontation with parliamentarians. Smyth's, behaviour—if not necessarily 'allegiance'—was situational.

Like his father, John Smyth junior had a lengthy and loyal relationship with the Berkeleys, which influenced his behaviour. As late as 1675 Lord Berkeley sent him a new year's gift comprising 'my arms well done with my titles, which I hope and believe will be very acceptable to you', recognising that Smyth served as steward all his adult life. During the 1640s this involved protecting the family's financial interests.[17] While he appeared to be keeping his head down as war broke out, Smyth organised a petition in which tenants and servants sought their master's permission to guard Berkeley Castle, in 'these times of danger'. When the castle was occupied by parliamentarians Smyth resisted attempts to furnish supplies, explaining that he lacked the 'authority' and 'power' to do so, even if he wanted to 'accommodate' their demands, and even if resources were available. Tellingly, Smyth recognised the folly of being obstructive, adding that it might be possible to provide coal if 'well-willers' would 'pay for it', and that he would 'bear a double share'. Smyth distanced himself from the parliamentarian cause while also promising to help.[18]

Thereafter, Smyth's attempts to serve the family involved protecting them from all sides. In January 1643, he secured the release of one of Berkeley's servants, William Thorpe, who was detained by parliamentarians as a malignant, and who felt unable to 'endure . . . this imprisonment, being publicly affronted, disgraced . . . [and] beaten'.[19] Smyth responded by supplying 'credible information' that Thorpe was seized 'upon small or no just cause'.[20] He also aided royalists like Sir Maurice

[15] GA, D7115/2, unfol.; D2510/23; *HMC 5th Report*, p. 345; Northamptonshire RO, FH133; Warmington, *Gloucestershire*, pp. 33, 35–6. For Thomas and William Smyth: *CCC*, p. 865; TNA, SP 23/179, pp. 542–62; GA, D8887/3/74; D8887/12/15.

[16] GA, D8887/11/7.

[17] GA, D8887/2/93, 96, 98, 102, 104.

[18] *HMC 5th Report*, p. 356; Berkeley, SB87, unfol.; GA, D8887/11/9, 11.

[19] GA, D8887/1/36.

[20] GA, D8887/1/37.

Berkeley and Richard Berkeley, who expressed thanks for his 'friendly care' in protecting their estates from sequestration. Amid the turmoil of the late 1640s, Smyth offered 'assistance and advice' to Lord Berkeley, at the moment when London's apprentices engaged in the 'uproar' that presaged the Second Civil War.[21] To royalist grandees, meanwhile, Smyth justified Lord Berkeley's inactivity in the king's cause, explaining to Sir Edward Hyde that Berkeley was ill at home in London, and that revenues from his estates had failed, even if this was somewhat misleading (January 1644).[22]

Smyth's actions reveal loyalty to the king rather than just to the Berkeleys, but also the need to remain on friendly terms with parliamentarians. In February 1643, he seized the opportunity afforded by Prince Rupert's victory at Cirencester by entering Berkeley Castle, and although he held it only briefly, he did so as a royalist rather than merely as steward, and it was as a royalist garrison that the castle surrendered to Parliament (11 February). Smyth was briefly imprisoned before making his way to Oxford, where he allegedly became a commissioner for fining parliamentarian prisoners and enlisting them for the king's service. When Berkeley castle was re-taken following the arrival of royalist forces in the summer of 1643, Smyth made it a base from which to support the garrison at Bristol.[23] The new governor, George Maxwell, naturally requested money and supplies, and Smyth provided a loan of £24 the following day, before furnishing additional provisions, unlike many of the 'country people' whose 'baseness' Maxwell bemoaned.[24] Although Smyth's familial loyalty probably led him to prepare Lord Berkeley's petition to the House of Lords regarding parliamentarian 'outrages' (May 1643), he also used contacts in Oxford to help friends in London whose estates had been seized for delinquency.[25]

It is also tempting to suggest that Smyth's reading habits—as far as they can be reconstructed—reflected the concerns of a committed royalist. We lack the detailed accounts that reveal his father's book-buying, but it is nevertheless possible to scrutinise—and detect patterns within—Smyth's collection of scribal separates, and amid the texts he copied from pamphlets. These include the letter from the Oxford Parliament to the earl of Essex (January 1644), a satirical attack upon the Solemn League and Covenant, and the oath tendered to royalist peers at York. They also include the commission by which Charles I empowered the earl of Glamorgan to treat with Irish confederates, and the controversial articles

[21] Badminton House, FmS/D1/5; GA, D2700/QT4/1–2; D8887/2/91–2, 94–5.

[22] GA, D7115/2, unfol.; *HMC 5th Report*, p. 347.

[23] GA, D7115/2, unfol.; Berkeley, SB87, unfol.; *HMC 5th Report*, pp. 346, 356; TNA, SP 23/196, p. 539.

[24] GA, D7115/2, unfol.; D8887/1/38; D2510/33; *HMC 5th Report*, p. 346; BL, Add. MS 18980, fo. 117.

[25] *HMC 5th Report*, p. 356; Isaac Jeayes, *Descriptive Catalogue of the Charters and Muniments . . . at Berkeley Castle* (Bristol, 1892), p. 340; *HMC 4th Report* (London, 1874), p. 367; *LJ*, vi. 69; GA, D8887/11/21–2.

subsequently concluded (September 1645), as well as the king's letter to the Marquess of Ormonde announcing his flight to the Scots (May 1646), the letter from the Scots announcing his arrival, and his response to the Newcastle Propositions (July 1646). Finally, they included one of Charles's messages to Parliament during the Newport Treaty (September 1648). While it is dangerous to read too much into the acquisition of particular texts, Smyth's papers indicate a determination to follow the actions, arguments, and fate of the king and his allies, more obviously than to trace the deliberations of his opponents.[26]

Whatever Smyth's intentions, he was treated as a royalist by Parliament. His estate was sequestered, and articles were submitted against him (September 1644), for refusing to surrender Berkeley Castle, encouraging men to take up arms, and impressing men into royalist service, and for joining the king in Oxford. Smyth compounded for his delinquency (November 1645), and was fined £600 (January 1647), and although more or less inactive thereafter, he faced ongoing suspicion. In 1655, amid threats of royalist risings, Smyth was subjected to the decimation tax and forced to pay £30 *per annum*, despite protesting that his income was below £200, that his personal belongings were worth less than £10, and that he supported a large family.[27] As a Gloucestershire royalist he was required to submit bonds for good behaviour, and his movements to and from London were monitored. Cavaliers clearly expected him to join a plot against the republican regime in 1659, although Smyth claimed that 'nothing was done' by himself or his family.[28]

III

Given this track record, Smyth loyal service to Charles II's government might seem predictable, and yet evidence relating to this period clarifies his attitudes and ideas, and illuminates his activity *before* 1660, during the dispute with Crokey.

Smyth became a leading figure within Restoration Gloucestershire, although he was not exactly of the first rank, and not above criticising government policies. He proved assiduous in collecting taxes, while resisting excessive zeal on the part of the state, likening excise officials to 'Egyptian taskmasters'.[29] Having failed to defend Hearth Tax collectors who encountered opposition, Smyth was warned not to prejudice the royal revenue 'wilfully' and 'inconsiderately', but was adamant about protecting the poor, especially clothiers.[30] He opposed moves to place

[26] GA, D7115/2, unfol.
[27] *CCC*, p. 948; TNA, SP 23/196, pp. 516, 539, 546; GA, D8887/3/71; D8887/5/52; D8887/11/36.
[28] GA, D8887/5/53–4; D8887/11/119; BL, Add. MS 34012, fo. 51; Add. MS 34014, fos 48, 67.
[29] GA, D8887/16/72; D8887/3/41–4.
[30] BL, Add. MS 33589, fos 18–21, 25, 39, 41, 43, 45, 47, 49–51, 52–3, 55, 57.

Gloucestershire under the jurisdiction of a revived Council of the Marches, and was called before the Privy Council for perceived negligence in providing timber from the Forest of Dean (1665).[31] However, while questions were occasionally asked about his performance during the civil wars—he was even prosecuted by the Attorney General (Sir Geoffrey Palmer) in 1663—Smyth protested about being 'faithful . . . unto the late king's interest and unto the interest of his now majesty', styling himself a 'sufferer in the time of distraction', and insisting that he 'never had any office, place or employment under . . . the usurped powers'. This perhaps involved admitting that he accommodated parliamentarian officials.[32]

Elsewhere, Smyth's loyalism was perfectly clear. As a JP he responded zealously to 'seditious reports that fly up and down', ensuring that culprits were 'brought to their trials'. He insisted that recusants should take the oaths of allegiance and supremacy, and pursued nonconformists, dispersing a Wotton conventicle in ways that provoked violent resistance. The local bishop, William Nicholson, welcomed his pursuit of 'refractory' dissenters, and although Smyth licensed Presbyterian meeting houses following the Declaration of Indulgence (1672), he quickly revived harsher measures.[33]

Smyth's loyalty—to the regime and the Berkeleys—was also evident during parliamentary elections. In 1640, he declined to support Sir Humphrey Tracy, who became a leading royalist, albeit on the basis that Tracy was unlikely to win, and having taken a lead from his father, 'from whom I may not depart'.[34] After 1640, the family's power was eclipsed, and electoral influence was wielded by the county committee, the army, and congregational ministers, but its fortunes were revived during the protectorate. This saw the return of George Berkeley, heir to George, 8th Lord Berkeley, alongside others who probably received their backing (Christopher Guise, Matthew Hale), despite opposition from religious radicals.[35] In the case of George Berkeley, success reflected a willingness to accommodate Presbyterians, on issues like offering the crown to Cromwell, albeit as a royalist, and following the Restoration the family—and Smyth—backed loyalists.[36] In 1660, Smyth supported Thomas Overbury, who plotted against Interregnum regimes, before bowing to pressure from George, 9th Lord Berkeley, who chided

[31] Howes, 'John Smyth', p. 224; BL, Add. MS 33589, fos 29, 81; GA, D8887/12/27, 33–5.

[32] GA, D9125/1/13625.

[33] GA, D8887/15/88; *HMC 5th Report*, p. 348; BL, Add. MS 33589, fos 60, 62v, 69, 75–6; 78–v; *CTB*, 7 (1681–5), p. 769; *HMC 5th Report*, pp. 347–8. See: Warmington, *Gloucestershire*, p. 186; David Rollison, 'Property, ideology and popular culture in a Gloucestershire village, 1660–1740', *P&P*, 93 (1981), 70–97, Smyth's decision to employ a Quaker—Walter Clement—as was probably taken *despite* his religious sympathies: GA, D8887/12/83, 100, 104.

[34] GA, D8887/6/24.

[35] John Nickolls, ed., *Original Letters and Papers of State* (London, 1743), pp. 125–6; GA, D2768/1/1; Warmington, *Gloucestershire*, p. 124.

[36] *CJ*, vii. 521, 538; John Towill Rutt, ed., *Diary of Thomas Burton* (4 vols, London, 1828), ii. 136; BL, Add. MS 33589, fo. 15; *CSPD 1657–8*, pp. 357, 372; *CSPD 1659–60*, pp. 36, 126, 170–1, 264.

him for failing to seek his approval, and who favoured Matthew Hale and another royalist plotter, Lord Herbert of Raglan. Berkeley asked Smyth to act 'in pursuance of my desires', and to get 'friends and tenants' to attend the election, in a fruitless attempt to block an old parliamentarian, Edward Stephens.[37]

Smyth's instinct was to support known royalists. In 1661, he almost certainly backed Sir Baynham Throckmorton, a sufferer in the royalist cause, because Berkeley encouraged him to 'engage' local 'friends and tenants', and because Throckmorton asked for help. Although Berkeley refrained from imposing upon voters too much, seeking to 'concur' with the 'sense and inclination of the county' and with 'honest clothiers', Smyth was less reticent. He made another unsuccessful attempt to back Lord Raglan, against a candidate—John Grobham Howe—whose loyalty was much less clear.[38] In a 1664 by-election, Smyth offered 'friendly advice' to Overbury, in the vain hope he would stand for a seat that became vacant following Throckmorton's death.[39]

Smyth's loyalism remained evident in subsequent elections, even as members of his family moved in other directions. During the Exclusion Crisis, Smyth's son, Edward, promoted Whig candidates, and even stood as an exclusionist himself, receiving support from the earl of Shaftesbury and being 'a mighty man with Dr [Titus] Oates'. Smyth himself remained faithful, particularly during the 'horrid and dangerous' Popish Plot.[40] In Gloucester's first election in 1679, he took 'care and trouble' to support Lord Berkeley's son (Sir Charles Berkeley), whose subsequent withdrawal left the field to an exclusionist, William Cooke, son of the old parliamentarian, Sir Robert Cooke.[41] In the next election, Charles Berkeley was more determined. He defeated Cooke with help from Smyth, whose employer was thankful that his steward had 'power and interest enough' to defeat 'hotheaded and unreasonable men' who would 'put us all in disorder'.[42] It was only after the election that Charles Berkeley backed exclusion, claiming during the 1681 county election that 'there never was more need of sober men' and 'true lovers of their country', and that if Parliament was dissolved 'God knows when we may have a new one.' Berkeley thus forfeited the help he sought from Smyth—so that 'I may not go unattended to the election'—who recommended 'declining the county and sticking to the city'. Charles was returned at Gloucester, but only by promising to 'behave... well to the king'. Less clear is Smyth's role in the county election, where is son was an unsuccessful Whig candidate.[43]

[37] GA, D8887/2/97. For Overbury: *ODNB*.

[38] *HMC 5th Report*, p. 345; GA, D8887/2/99–100; *Commons 1660–1690*, i. 236–7.

[39] GA, D8887/12/26.

[40] GA, D8887/2/106; *HMC 5th Report*, p. 347; *Commons 1660–1690*, i. 414–16.

[41] GA, D8887/2/108. [42] GA, D8887/2/107.

[43] GA, D8887/2/113; *Commons 1660–1690*, i. 236–7, 241.

IV

Smyth's record of loyalty was long and consistent, and involved more than just fidelity to the Berkeleys. It confirms that his apparent reticence about choosing sides in 1642 reflected the need to tread carefully, and to preserve as much influence as possible with parliamentarians, locally and nationally. He was pragmatic, but shared his father's attitudes and beliefs, something that also becomes apparent from his response to religious reform and his own clerical patronage.

This is important territory because Smyth's papers offer little direct evidence about the Warrens Court dispute. This is not because he neglected the school's affairs. He secured a new lease of its lands in 1647, and exerted influence over admissions, such that by 1655 his sons dominated the student body. Smyth also exploited the opportunity to appoint a schoolmaster, and the circumstances surrounding his one nominee—Thomas Burton (1647)—are intriguing. The lease that Smyth secured—'very carefully'—kept the master 'in awe', by insisting that further grants should be made 'upon request', without fine or increase in rent, and that Burton should enter a bond—in £300—to 'resign upon request'.[44] Religiously, Burton was perhaps uncontroversial. He hailed from Wotton, and remained in post until his death in 1697, and surviving the Restoration—despite what Smyth called an 'illegal' attempt to arrest him in 1663—suggests that he was untainted by puritanism or parliamentarianism.[45] The same cannot be said of other ministers with whom Smyth associated.

The most obvious of these was Thomas Jackson, already discussed as someone too puritanical for Smyth's tastes, and whose 'conformity' was 'not so great'.[46] Jackson's behaviour troubled Smyth, who planned to petition Parliament against him (June 1642), in line with his response to demands for church reform.[47] The text of Gloucestershire's 'root and branch' petition is lost—only 'heads' survive—but it secured 3,000 signatures, and was delivered to Parliament by Thomas Pury and Nathaniel Stephens (February 1641).[48] On this Smyth's position was clear, and he helped to organise a counter-petition in support of episcopacy, participating in an organisational meeting in Thornbury, and reflecting upon a gratifying level of support for the 'general petition'. Smyth wrote of 'abounding numbers', and rallied local people by responding to 'pulpit discourses' that dismissed supporters—'us'—as 'papists, common drunkards, base and lewd livers'. He also worried that episcopalians might be 'called to account' by local Puritans, but encouraged 'more than ordinary . . . endeavours' to gather signatures, ahead of a

[44] GA, D9125/1/12030/30; D8887/5/52.

[45] GA, D2957/354/13; *VCH Gloucester*, ii. 407; *Al. Oxon.*, i. 227; GA, GDR/S1/17. See: Howes, 'John Smyth', p. 224; GA, D8887/5/87–9; D8887/12/27.

[46] GA, D8887/4/10–11.

[47] GA, D7115/2, unfol.

[48] GA, D9125/1/725; Warmington, *Gloucestershire*, pp. 31–2; TNA, C 231/5, fo. 528.

further meeting at Cirencester.[49] Smyth signed the petition himself, alongside men who became the county's leading royalists (December 1641).[50]

Smyth's religious views also come into focus either side of the Restoration, when opportunities arose to make clerical appointments outside Gloucestershire. In January 1659, he was approached by Thomas Reading, a relative of Wotton's former schoolmaster, Edward Cowper, on behalf of a son who was 'fitted for the ministerial function'. Reading sought to secure the living at Seagrave (Leicestershire), but having secured a nomination from Oliver Cromwell he also recognised the likelihood of a dispute. He was advised that the nomination would 'stand firm', but also wanted to secure 'a presentation' from Lord Berkeley, whose 'noble family' his ancestors 'honoured and served'. Reading approached Smyth 'knowing' that 'it resteth in your power to procure his peace and favour with my lord'.[51] Smyth's response is not recorded, but he probably supported another candidate, Thomas Audley, who was nominated by Berkeley sometime before July 1658, and who eventually secured the rectory in 1660. Audley is an intriguing figure, who helps to clarify Smyth's views. He was ejected from Cromhall during the civil wars, but petitioned Cromwell in the hope of securing the position at Seagrave, acknowledging the lawfulness of the protectoral regime, and protesting that he was targeted for 'differing in judgment and opinion', not for scandalous behaviour. Audley insisted that he never acted against the Cromwellian regime, and pointed out that he was approved by Gloucestershire's 'triers'—the panel appointed to vet clerical appointments—as a preacher in Nibley, and presented to Woodchester rectory (1656).[52] This suggests that Audley was conformable to the Restoration church, sufficiently out-of-step with Puritans to be deemed 'ill-affected' in the 1640s, but uncontroversial enough to find favour thereafter, with an odd alliance of grandees.

First, Audley secured support from Sir Richard Ducie of Frocester, who nominated him to Woodchester. Ducie was hugely controversial, having been imprisoned for delinquency in 1643, before escaping to Bristol and then causing trouble upon returning to Gloucestershire. This involved confrontational 'carriage' towards sequestrators and the county committee: he launched vocal assaults upon officials—'knaves' and 'plundering rogues'—and forcibly resisted attempts to seize his cattle *in lieu* of taxes that he refused to pay. Ducie repeatedly mustered mobs, 'armed with pike, guns, bills and clubs', who 'made a stand' and reclaimed his cattle 'violently', amid shouts of 'come let's charge them to the devil.' Eventually, the governor of Gloucester raised a troop of 200 musketeers, who

[49] GA, D8887/11/1; Warmington, *Gloucestershire*, p. 31.

[50] BL, Add. MS 11055, fos 130v–1; GA, D7115/1, unfol.; D2510/13–14; *HMC 5th Report*, p. 345; Warmington, *Gloucestershire*, p. 31.

[51] GA, D8887/11/111.

[52] *CSPD 1658–9*, p. 188; TNA, SP 18/183, fos 198–206; *Walker Revised*, p. 171; Elrington, 'Survey', p. 95.

'beset his house' in the small hours—'before he was aware'—and took him prisoner, as Ducie threatened to wreak revenge 'if ever the king come to his crown again'. He was forced to pay £3,300 to compound for his estates.[53] Ducie was a paradigmatic 'cavalier', who hated Puritan ministers. He behaved in 'a very uncivil way' towards the minister sent to Cromhall by the Westminster Assembly of Divines, turning him out of the parish 'so that the man, his wife and children are like to perish'. He was also accused of taking from 'Mr Pritchard, a poor godly minister' the tithes awarded by the Committee for Plundered Ministers, as 'an augmentation of maintenance'.[54]

It is telling that Audley proved acceptable to Ducie, but he also received support from men with different beliefs and backgrounds. This included clerics—mostly from Gloucestershire—who were unmolested by the parliamentarian authorities, and who survived the Restoration, including Jonathan Pritchard of Cromhall, the man from whom Ducie withheld money. These were moderate Puritans, and Audley was also backed by Matthew Haviland of Holy Trinity, Queenhithe, who was ejected in 1662.[55] Finally, Audley was endorsed by local JPs—Richard Corbet, William Sheppard, William Oldisworth, James Clutterbuck, and John Dorney—who were stalwarts of county administration during the Interregnum.[56] At least two of them—Sheppard and Dorney—had actually been involved in punishing Ducie, damning him for behaving with 'a high hand', for 'forcible resistance', and for 'great riots upon our officers', as well as for 'scornful and contemptuous words'. In 1647, they called Ducie someone 'by whose example' many delinquents 'took the boldness to withhold and deny payment of their rents'.[57] In 1658, they backed his nominee as vicar of Woodchester, even though Ducie was deemed suspicious by the regime.[58]

Audley's attempt to secure the living at Seagrave highlights the possibilities that existed for non-Puritans in the Cromwellian church, and the cooperation that occurred between royalists and Presbyterians, not least in opposition to Independents and congregationalists. The latter proved more disruptive and confrontational, and were invariably removed from their livings in 1662, and they sometimes engaged in dissident behaviour thereafter, and faced further harassment.[59] That there was a fundamental breach within Gloucestershire puritanism is clear: one of Audley's supporters, the JP William Oldisworth, was targeted by local radicals, who claimed that he was subjected to divine fury—the famous plague of Fairford frogs—for refusing to protect a separatist congregation

[53] TNA, SP 23/213, pp. 391–7; *CCC*, p. 1017. See: GA, D340a/C1/7–11; Warmington, *Gloucestershire*, pp. 85–6.

[54] TNA, SP 23/213, pp. 396, 401–2, 410.

[55] TNA, SP 18/183, fos 198–206. For Haviland: *Calamy Revised*, p. 252.

[56] *CSPD 1658–9*, p. 188; TNA, SP 18/183, fos 198–206.

[57] TNA, SP 23/213, pp. 401–3.

[58] BL, Add. MS 34012, fo. 16v.

[59] Warmington, *Gloucestershire*, pp. 114, 125; *Calamy Revised*, pp. 41, 204, 249, 256, 380, 490, 519.

from a mob.[60] It is thus telling that Smyth supported Audley during the early 1650s. He preserved the petition that, as minister of Nibley, Audley submitted to the Committee for Plundered Ministers, seeking an enhanced salary, a move supported across the parish (1651). Audley's promise—that he took the 'late Engagement', and was 'desirous to live peaceably under the present government'—was an admission that his loyalty was in doubt.[61] In church affairs as in politics, Smyth capitalised upon possibilities for cooperating with local parliamentarians, even if his own inclinations remained doggedly anti-puritanical.

V

Such evidence—regarding royalism, electoral influence, and clerical patronage—suggests that Smyth sometimes pursued pragmatic strategies, to help the Berkeleys, protect his own interests, and undermine radical Puritans, while remaining loyal to the crown and the established church. As such, and to the extent that Smyth pursued the Warrens Court dispute during the 1640s, his determination to defend his family's interests ought to be regarded as being driven by ideological factors, as his father's had been. Indeed, there are two direct ways in which Smyth's religious and political views—and his behaviour—impinged upon the contest over Wotton school.

First, a key aspect of Smyth's royalism involved his flight to the royalist garrison of Bristol following the surrender of Berkeley Castle to parliamentarians, and the people with whom he associated. Smyth not only re-located to Bristol, but also became steward of the city's Tolzey Court (15 December 1643).[62] This appointment was made during the mayoralty of Humphrey Hooke, who had been removed as the city's MP for serving as a Commissioner of Array (May 1642), and came in the wake of the capitulation to royalist forces (July 1643), and the controversial decision to send the king £10,000. Smyth's appointment formed part of a process by which royalists consolidated their grip on local administration, and just days after taking up the role he joined a delegation that travelled to Oxford to find ways of raising even more money. Subsequently, Smyth was involved in securing a general pardon, which cost the city £40.[63]

Smyth's appointment made his allegiance perfectly clear, but it also revealed 'weak ties' to a network that was directly relevant for the Warrens Court dispute, and that loomed large in Crokey's complaints about 'power' and 'practices'.[64]

[60] Warmington, *Gloucestershire*, pp. 113, 171–2; Andrew Warmington, 'Frogs, toads and the Restoration in a Gloucestershire village', *Midland History*, 14 (1989), 30–42.

[61] GA, D8887/4/12. See: GA, P230/CW/2/1.

[62] BA, M/BCC/CCP/1/4, p. 47; GA, D8887/15/92.

[63] BA, M/BCC/CCP/1/4, p. 64; F/Au/1/22, pp. 299, 303; TNA, SP 23/196, pp. 546–7.

[64] See above, pp. C3.P50, C4.P34–C4.35, C4.P48–C4.P49, C6.P24, C6.P28–C6.P29, C7.P25.

Smyth served the king alongside Thomas Colston—one of his father's informers in 1626—and two ministers, Richard Towgood and Richard Standfast, both of whom received bequests in Hooke's will.[65] Such men were at the heart of Bristol's royalist community, as were two others who were accused of conspiring against Crokey, Nathaniel Cole (or Cale), and Giles Elbridge, another beneficiary of Hooke's will. It was Colston and Elbridge who liaised with the royalist governor, Lord Hopton, presenting him with a butt of sack and two hogsheads of claret, and it was their faction that appointed Cole to the common council on the same day. It was also Colston who—like Smyth—travelled to Oxford repeatedly, not least to replenish the king's coffers.[66] It was the surviving members of this group who were removed from their church livings (Towgood, Standfast), and from the corporation (Hooke, Colston, Cole), following the recapture of Bristol by parliamentarian forces (August 1645). At that point, Smyth resigned his post and returned to Gloucestershire, upon passes issued by Edward Massey.[67]

Smyth's royalist ties extended beyond the city's corporation to its cathedral close. In 1648, Cole helped Smyth to convey £5 to Thomas Howell, who was made bishop of Bristol by the king in 1644, only to be removed by Parliament the following year.[68] Smyth also associated with George Williamson, yet another beneficiary of Hooke's will, who served as vicar of All Saints and cathedral prebend before falling victim to the parliamentarian purge in 1645. Williamson demonstrates the coherence of this royalist grouping and its survival after the Restoration, and sheds further light upon Smyth's forceful defence of the established church. In January 1661, Williamson and Standfast offered Smyth 'a small stipend' to 'assist our poor church' with 'advice in point of law'. They sought to know how to recover church lands sold by Interregnum regimes, from purchasers who were 'loath to vomit up their sweet bits' and who went about 'to make us their prey'. Williamson wondered whether it would be possible to 'make a seizure and demand possession' of what such people 'detain from us', acknowledging that, although 'the thing is just', there might be 'danger and difficulty in it'. He sought guidance about 'how... to proceed with safety in recovering our means' from 'the hands of these harpies'.[69] Smyth's response is unknown, but he certainly retained links with Standfast, who as canon sought his help in 1667, regarding a dispute between the cathedral and Sir Christopher Guise of Elmore. This argument,

[65] BA, M/BCC/CCP/1/3, fos 118v, 120, 122; M/BCC/CCP/1/4, pp. 5–6, 8; F/Au/1/22, pp. 170, 227. For Hooke's will: TNA, PROB 11/290, fo. 9.

[66] BA, M/BCC/CCP/1/4, pp. 33, 35–6, 44–5, 48, 101.

[67] *A&O*, i. 797–8; BA, M/BCC/CCP/1/4, pp. 129, 136; Harlow, *Religious Ministry*, p. 3; *CCC*, p. 1191; TNA, SP 23/76, pp. 311–19; GA, D8887/15/93; D7115/2, unfol.; TNA, SP 23/196, p. 529. See: Sacks, *Widening Gate*, pp. 238–46.

[68] GA, D7115/2, unfol.; *ODNB*; *Walker Revised*, p. 1; BL, Add. 34012, fo. 12.

[69] GA, D8887/12/8. For Williamson: *Walker Revised*, p. 179; Harlow, *Religious Ministry*, pp. 169–70. For lasting ties between Smyth and Hooke: Chicago UL, MS 1465, folder 3; GA, D8887/11/72, 75.

regarding repairs at a local church, evidently resulted in Guise 'letting fall some language as if they intended us some trouble in the Chancery'.[70]

Smyth was committed to the king and his church, and associated with men who shared such beliefs, and such confederates were also instrumental in undermining Crokey. However, there is another dimension to Smyth's behaviour during the 1640s that strengthened his hand in this regard, involving his ability to mobilise friends in high places, both in Gloucestershire and at Westminster. This might seem counterintuitive—that a royalist could mobilise parliamentarians against one of his enemies—but these were the rewards for a non-confrontational approach during the civil wars. Whether or not this loomed large in Smyth's thinking, the upshot was that he secured the means to protect himself against Crokey's campaign, and it is possible that the attempt to maintain harmonious relations with parliamentarians involved more than just the avoidance of unnecessary conflict over demands for military mobilisation. Smyth certainly hoped to muster support on behalf of the Berkeleys, and members of the family who expressed thanks for his 'friendly care' regarding sequestrations and compositions explicitly referred to his mobilisation of 'friends'.[71]

Smyth's endeavours to capitalise upon good working relationships with parliamentarians are evident after Berkeley Castle surrendered to Parliament in 1645. This involved securing an order to protect the castle, and getting permission for Lord Berkeley to approve its new governor, after which Smyth protected both its fabric and contents. To achieve this, Smyth worked with two men, Charles Jay and Stephen Fowler, who were family friends—his father's 'alliesmen'—but also local committeemen. It was Jay who warned Smyth about threats to sell the estate, and to destroy the castle, and it was with him that Smyth liaised once attempts were made to dismantle its fabric, resulting in forceful lobbying of the county committee (September 1646). Smyth courted controversy by criticising Parliament's decision, and then launched an investigation into the plundering that took place, but he also mobilised support at Westminster, helped by the fact that Lord Berkeley continued to sit in the House of Lords. Thus, whatever reassurances Smyth gave Sir Edward Hyde about Berkeley's royalist sympathies, he insisted to others that his employer remained loyal to Parliament. In protesting against plans to slight the castle, Smyth emphasised that the homes of no other *parliamentarian* peers had been threatened in this way, and even appeared before the Lords to support one of Berkeley's petitions in person (November 1646).[72] Subsequently, Smyth liaised with parliamentarians and republicans to deal with anti-enclosure 'disorders' which threatened the Berkeley estates. Thus, amid threats that the

[70] GA, D8887/12/54. See: Sacks, *Widening Gate*, p. 299.

[71] Badminton House, FmS/D1/5; GA, D2700/QT4/1–2; D8887/2/91–2, 94.

[72] *LJ*, vii. 591, 623, 630, 646, 656; *LJ*, viii. 11–12, 507–8, 571; *CSPD 1645–7*, pp. 156–7; *HMC 5th Report*, pp. 356–7; *CJ*, iv. 629; Berkeley, SB87, unfol.; GA, D8887/11/44; Warmington, *Gloucestershire*, p. 79.

'mounds' of the 'new grounds' at Slimbridge would be 'riotously cast down' by a 'rude multitude', Smyth secured help from the House of Lords and Council of State, both of which supported his attempts to mobilise soldiers, 'until the rioters shall be found out and conveyed to the common gaol'. Thereafter, Smyth was able to broker a settlement with local residents.[73]

Similar themes emerge regarding Smyth's own estate, which inevitably faced sequestration for 'crimes against the Parliament'.[74] Striking here is the protection offered to Smyth's property, which the county committee permitted him to lease to William Archard, for a rent of £40 (May 1645). Only once this was done did Smyth begin the process of compounding, admitting that he had served the royalist cause in Bristol (November 1645). Smyth also maintained good relations with local officials by endeavouring to supply gunpowder to Berkeley Castle, and by offering barrels of beer to local soldiers.[75] Such behaviour did not give Smyth complete immunity, and he certainly suffered difficulties: Archard claimed to have been harassed for Smyth's rents in 1646, and Smyth protested that his estate was 'very much wasted' by plundering. He was also required to provide free quarter, and complained about attacks by 'the many-headed multitude'.[76] Nevertheless, he mobilised support within the county, and did so in intriguing ways. In November 1645, Smyth persuaded the Committee for Sequestrations to let him nominate witnesses for examination by the county committee. This resulted in testimonials that he was present at Berkeley Castle 'accidentally' in February 1643—having been out hunting—and that he held it 'not... for the king against the parliament', but only to preserve Berkeley's 'goods and evidence'. Deponents attested that he surrendered it 'without... one shot made'; that he fled to Oxford to avoid 'extreme plundering'; and that he did not serve the king as a commissioner for fines. These were predictable claims, made by servants and tenants of the Berkeley family, and by men to whom he was close, including William Archard and Robert Maundey. Maundey claimed to know that one piece of evidence against Smyth bore a forged signature, having served as his clerk for 'twelve years now last past'. Nevertheless, Smyth also received support from at least one member of the county committee, who justified his flight to Oxford, and from parliamentarian soldiers who were captured at Cirencester and conveyed to Oxford. They explained that Smyth paid their 'ransom' money and effected their 'discharge'. This suggests a willingness and ability to mobilise support from across the political spectrum, although such

[73] GA, D8887/11/71, 73; *LJ*, viii. 200, 611; *CSPD 1650*, p. 218; Howes, 'John Smyth', p. 222.
[74] TNA, SP 23/196, pp. 513–14, 537; GA, D8887/11/36.
[75] Howes, 'John Smyth', p. 217; *CCC*, p. 948; GA, D7115/2, unfol.; D8887/6/28.
[76] Howes, 'John Smyth', p. 217; Warmington, *Gloucestershire*, p. 83; GA, D8887/11/42; D7115/2, unfol.; D8887/15/89.

men may also have been dependents, and there are hints that they were coached by Smyth, who apparently drafted their statements.[77]

Eventually, Smyth's fine was set at £600, half of which he paid immediately (January 1647). However, as he grumbled about his treatment in the months that followed, Smyth was able to call upon the 'continued favours' of Nathaniel Stephens, knight of the shire, as he negotiated with another MP, John Ashe, chairman of the Committee for Compounding. Ashe sent Smyth a 'thundering letter' which 'threatened a storm', and Smyth hoped that Stephens might find a way of delaying further payments. To help matters, Smyth appealed to Ashe directly, in a letter containing 'Gloucestershire truth', and eventually mollified him with 'a brace of fat bucks', which Ashe was anxious to receive (August 1648).[78] Smyth also relied upon local contacts to mitigate other financial demands, not least the £30 for which he was assessed by the Committee for the Advance of Money. This was achieved by insisting that he had supplied money and horses for Parliament's service (however minimally), and by protesting how much he suffered through free quarter.[79] Although Smyth was subsequently assessed at £100 (April 1649), and threatened with sequestration, he once again used local commissioners—like Stephen Fowler—to get this reduced to a mere £16, which he paid in July 1651.[80]

The possibility opened up by such contacts is that Smyth mobilised support on other personal matters, in ways that undermined Crokey's campaign at Westminster. Smyth certainly sought help from one prominent parliamentarian, Bulstrode Whitelocke, about a petition he planned to submit in early August 1642. Although the petition does not survive, and Whitelocke's response was terse, it probably involved an attempt to block Thomas Jackson's appointment as minister at Nibley. Crucially, while Whitelocke thought it 'preposterous' for an MP to offer advice upon a petition 'before it comes . . . before us', he suggested that it was unlikely to find favour, and that objections were likely to 'frustrate your hopes'.[81] Whether or not Whitelocke proved willing to help on this particular matter, the episode's significance lies in Smyth's hope, or expectation, that he could secure support from a leading member of the Commons.

[77] GA, D8887/16/28–30, 32–4, 39, 42–4; Berkeley, SB87, unfol.; TNA, SP 20/2, fo. 9; SP 23/196, pp. 513–14, 523–5, 527, 532, 535, 537, 541–7, 549; *HMC 5th Report*, p. 356.

[78] TNA, SP 23/3, p. 388; GA, D8887/14/11; D8887/5/50. See: GA, D8887/11/59–60, 63–4.

[79] *CCAM*, ii. 826; TNA, SP 19/114, pp. 26–8; Warmington, *Gloucestershire*, pp. 86–7. See: BL, Add. MS 33588, fo. 61; GA, D8887/1/39.

[80] *CCAM*, ii. 826; TNA, SP 19/114, pp. 29–30; GA, D8887/5/51.

[81] D7115/2, unfol.

VI

Smyth's appeal to Whitelocke, like his attempts to protect Berkeley Castle and exploit connections with Stephens, is important. It provides the final evidence for assessing his allegiance and ideological identity, as well as his motivations and actions regarding Warrens Court.

A case like Smyth's is significant, historiographically and methodologically, for highlighting the complexities surrounding 'allegiance'. Surviving evidence demonstrates how Smyth navigated the challenges he faced, the things he wanted to achieve, and the objections made against him, as well as the possibilities that existed for mitigating harsh treatment by parliamentarians. It reveals more than just the willingness of royalists to keep their heads down in the face of local parliamentarian strength. Smyth had good reasons not to be seen to be acting too clearly against Parliament, not least because he needed to remain on friendly terms with people who could undermine his ability to serve his employer and protect Berkeley Castle. At the same time, he was determined to oppose church reform, and willing to imperil his own interests by serving the king. His calculations about how to achieve such goals were calibrated in such a way that he remained hopeful about exerting influence over parliamentarian decision-making, at Westminster as well as locally. Smyth's case is also valuable because reaching such conclusions depends fairly heavily upon network analysis.

Being able to position John Smyth junior is also beneficial for understanding the Warrens Court dispute, in terms of why and how he confronted ongoing pressure from Benjamin Crokey. Smyth was forced to deal with Sarah Crokey's petition to Parliament in October 1648, an episode that is intriguing because, having initially been required to respond within a month, Smyth used delaying tactics, which resulted in him being given him until mid-February 1649 to produce a formal answer. This decision may obviously have reflected official preoccupation with more pressing business, as political and constitutional crisis loomed, and it was presumably taken without any inkling that the House of Lords was about to fall victim to a political revolution. Nevertheless, Smyth's contacts, and his determination to maintain a working relationship with parliamentarian grandees, make it plausible to suggest that he benefitted from having political capital at Westminster, beyond Lord Berkeley, one of a small group of peers who sat in the House on the very day that Sarah Crokey's case was kicked firmly down the road.[82]

However inscrutable this episode remains, reconstructing Smyth's response to the civil wars indicates how hard he worked to sustain and exploit parliamentarian contacts, and that this was done despite—indeed because of—his royalist

[82] GA, D8887/6/107–8; *LJ*, x. 529, 580; *HMC 7th Report* (London, 1879), p. 61; PA, HL/PO/JO/10/1/274.

inclinations. Smyth's civil war career also highlights a profound reluctance to assist local parliamentarians, unless it was absolutely necessary to do so, and much more obviously a willingness to serve the king. This reflected his determination to protect the Church of England as established by the end of the 1630s, and to support the victims of religious reforms during the 1640s and 1650s. Smyth proved himself loyal to the Stuarts, and opposed to Puritans and nonconformists, even if some of the clerics he patronised subsequently accommodated, and were accepted by, those who advocated 'healing and settling' during the Protectorate. Finally, Smyth's behaviour indicates that the men with whom he associated were very often the same as those with whom his father collaborated against Crokey. Such evidence indicates that John Smyth junior almost certainly viewed the Warrens Court dispute in ideological terms, and pursued it as part of wider attempts to resist religious reform and the 'many-headed multitude'. That this is how the contest—over both estate and school—was viewed at the time becomes even clearer by turning from the attitudes and behaviour of Smyth to the mental world of his opponents.

9

'For God's cause and the public good'

The Mental World of Benjamin Crokey

Within the records of St Katherine by the Tower—a London parish comprising wharves and warehouses—is evidence of a testamentary investigation that ran from July 1583 into early 1584, centred upon an ironmonger, Robert Crokey. The episode is murky—we have witness statements but not the interrogatories to which they responded—and the notes are scrappy, but Crokey was suspected of conning a Barber Surgeon, Robert Pike, who was aged, infirm, and 'speechless' on his deathbed. Crokey allegedly stole cash and jewellery to the value of £100, and prepared a will from which he would benefit, and it was the legality of this document that came under scrutiny. Some called Crokey an 'honest' man, and confirmed *his* story: that Pike asked him to 'make my will... as I will say unto you'; that he was 'well contented' with the results; and that Crokey declined a bequest precisely to avoid 'suspicion of corruption'. It was even suggested that Crokey took Pike's valuables to protect them, and handed them to officials under a 'bill of dotage'. Others claimed that Crokey was seen 'whispering' in the old man's ears, 'made himself an executor', and insisted on other people leaving the room while he dealt with Pike, and also that he sought to 'rifle', 'ransack', and 'shuffle away' possessions. Some contended that Pike refused to make a will, exclaiming 'I have had greater sickness than this and have escaped it.'[1]

The relevance of this story might not be immediately clear, and its meaning is uncertain. The matter was brought before Julius Caesar, commissary under the bishop of London (John Aylmer), but the upshot is unrecorded, although it is intriguing that the official version of Pike's will—recorded a few days before his death by Richard Chamberlain, one of Crokey's accusers—was not proved until 1586.[2] However, the incident merits attention precisely because its significance is unclear. This chapter argues that recovering the structural underpinnings of Benjamin Crokey's litigation involves difficult evidence, but that such material is revealing, about Crokey, about his ancestors, and about his awareness of their history and beliefs.

[1] LMA, CLC/199/TD/008/MS09740A, fos 2–50, esp. fos 2–3, 5, 8–9, 11, 16–v, 19, 21, 27–8, 29v, 31–3.

[2] TNA, PROB 11/69, fo. 226. See: L. M. Hill, *Bench and Bureaucracy. The Public Career of Sir Julius Caesar, 1580–1636* (Cambridge, 1988), pp. 9–10. For Chamberlain: LMA, CLC/199/TD/008/MS09740A, fo. 6.

The Madman and the Churchrobber: Law and Conflict in Early Modern England. Jason Peacey, Oxford University Press.
 DOI: 10.1093/oso/9780192897138.003.0010

What follows complements the treatments of John Smyth senior and junior, by establishing Crokey's religious and political 'identity'. This is not straightforward, and Crokey's many statements about the dispute make little explicit mention of ideological issues. Even his lengthy pamphlet concentrated upon legal matters, the procedural journey, and Smyth's 'practices', rather than upon religion or politics. It was ostensibly for libellous allegations, not political and religious dissidence, that Crokey was sentenced by Star Chamber. Nevertheless, there are hints that something else was involved. In turning a long-running inheritance dispute into a case about Wotton school, Crokey implicitly raised broader issues, and there is scope to suggest that he, like his opponents, was motivated by religious beliefs. Scrutinising these beliefs involves tantalising and frustrating evidence, including allusive phrases, spoken outbursts, and minor incidents, like the unknown sermon that Crokey planned to attend at St Paul's Cross when he was arrested at Smyth's behest (1621).[3] Individually, such snippets represent cryptic clues, but the hazy picture they produce comes into sharper focus with evidence about the ideas and behaviour of Crokey's friends, accomplices, and associates, to some of whom he was bound by fairly weak ties.

What follows represents another exercise in recovering the mental and ideological world of someone who left few explicit statements about their ideas and beliefs. However, while it shares something of the methodological approach used in earlier chapter—studying a loose but vital network of associates, and analysing allusive comments about socio-economic status, reform, and religion—it turns much more obviously to the issue of 'memory', which has emerged as a vital factor throughout the Warrens Court dispute. 'Memory' has become an increasingly important topic within early modern history, even if the term is used in many different ways. Here it refers not to formal reflections upon, and uses of, the past, as in memorialisation and historical writing, but to everyday recollections and reminiscences, and the historical 'baggage' lurking in people's minds.[4] This is partly about how contemporaries reflected upon the history of Wotton school, but also about Crokey's own 'identity'.

Ultimately, it is possible to reflect upon Crokey's cultural inheritance, and upon the dynamic of the Protestant reformation. Historians sometimes emphasise 'cultural memory', the 'continuity' of Puritanism, and the survival of localised

[3] TNA, C 3/338/8.

[4] Matthew Neufeld, *The Civil Wars after 1660* (Woodbridge, 2013); Edward Legon, *Revolution Remembered: Seditious Memories after the British Civil Wars* (Manchester, 2019); Judith Pollmann, *Memory in Early Modern Europe, 1500–1800* (Oxford, 2017); Andy Wood, *The Memory of the People* (Cambridge, 2013); Adam Fox, 'Remembering the past in early modern England: oral and written tradition', *TRHS*, 9 (1999), 233–56.

dissent,[5] but it has also been suggested that the Reformation 'aged' over time, progressing beyond its 'initial unruly phases' and becoming 'institutionalised'. It is argued that those born into—rather than converted to—Protestantism were less zealous, and that successive generations turned away from rebelliousness towards deference. Protestantism, on this account, witnessed an 'advance into middle age', and eventually towards a gerontocracy, with a loss of 'spontaneity' and 'enthusiasm' as younger generations abandoned 'youthful rebellion' for conformity with a status quo, and with 'elder statesmen'.[6] This chapter argues that the moderation of religious 'enthusiasm' is harder to trace than the persistence of Protestant—even Puritan—beliefs across successive generations of particular families. Robert and his son, Benjamin Crokey, highlight the potential for discerning religious meaning from allusive evidence, and suggest that cross-generational 'enthusiasm' was real even when it was not obviously signposted.

This chapter argues that one solution to the mysteries that prompted this book—why protagonists persisted with a dispute beyond the point where it made financial sense, and why the affair enthralled contemporaries—relates to the Puritanism of Benjamin Crokey, his associates, and his family.

I

Reconstructing Benjamin Crokey's ideological world involves teasing out religious beliefs and political attitudes, but it can usefully begin by demonstrating his ability to think about wider issues highlighted by the battle with John Smyth; something he associated with the 'general good'.[7]

The most obvious indication that Crokey saw deeper significance in the Warrens Court dispute involved reflections upon his socio-economic status, the credibility of his network, and his credentials as an independent agent. On one occasion, Crokey referred to his 'good repute and worth', and in 1625 he offered a certificate from the authorities in Bristol to prove he had once been a citizen of good credit and respect, 'before his declining in estate'.[8] Crokey contrasted the juries that he mustered, involving 'substantial men of good estate', with those organised by Smyth, involving 'simple men' from his family network.[9] He also

[5] Jacqueline Eales, 'A road to revolution: the continuity of Puritanism, 1559–1642', in Christopher Durston and Jacqueline Eales, eds, *The Culture of English Puritanism, 1560–1700* (London, 1996), pp. 184–209; David R. Como, *Blown by the Spirit: Puritanism and the Emergence of an Antinomian Underground in Pre-Civil War England* (Stanford, 2004).

[6] Alexandra Walsham, 'The Reformation of the generations: youth, age and religious change in England, c.1500–1700', *TRHS*, 21 (2011), 93–121.

[7] PA, HL/PO/JO/10/1/37.

[8] GA, D9125/1/12028, pp. 11–12; Crokey, *Sacred Maiestie*, sig. A2.

[9] Crokey, *Sacred Maiestie*, sigs E2v, C3v. See: Hillary Taylor, 'The price of the poor's words: social relations and the economics of deposing for one's "betters" in early modern England', *EcHR*, 72.3 (2019), 828–47; Robert Zaller, *The Parliament of 1621* (Berkeley, 1971), p. 93.

stressed that the battle with Smyth was conducted without financial backing from other people, and that he was no mere agent for unseen actors. It is true that Crokey admitted how friends once raised £100 to secure his release from prison (1620), even if only to complain about being 'so entangled' that 'no penny would be accepted', and about festering in gaol as a result.[10] More often, Crokey insisted that he worked 'at his own charge', 'without contribution of any', referring to 'great labour' and 'toil' and swearing that this was done with 'no benefit to himself'. He even incurred 'the *blame* of...his dearest friends for so great earnestness in a common cause generally neglected and violently opposed'.[11] Finally, he protested about fighting for the school for thirty-three years to his own 'ruin', 'none assisting him but his said daughter', who 'left all her fortunes, being an approved virtuous maid'.[12]

Asserting his independence was important to Crokey's image as a zealous campaigner for a higher cause, and his experience of disputation convinced him that the dispute highlighted the need for law reform. He was surely aware that bringing the matter before Parliament in 1621 was appropriate, given that concealed lands—and the patents opponents used to identify such property—were controversial, and had become the subject of proposed legislation.[13] Crokey helped to prepare the 'humble petition' of subjects who were 'grieved with Chancery proceedings', who '*of late* made divers complaints', and who demanded 'reformation', 'to prevent grievances in time to come'. This invoked legislation from the reign of Henry VI, which required litigants to 'pay good costs and damages' if cases 'proved not true', and bemoaned how an act intended 'for the good of the commonwealth' had fallen into disuse. It reflected upon 'crying complaints', 'tedious and chargeable proceedings', and 'needless suits', as well as upon 'chargeable motions', 'excessive fees', and 'intolerable dilatory expense'. Properly executed, the act would ensure that Chancery cases were 'fewer, shorter and truer', and that matters would be 'determined with more speed and less charges...to the content of subjects and prevention of many wrongs'.[14]

Crokey's petition showed an ability to generalise from his own experience, and to align himself with a reforming campaign. It was almost certainly submitted in 1621, and copies survive within the papers of the MP, Edward Alford, and within the Parliamentary Archive. The latter was signed by Crokey, and was 'retained to be further considered, nothing as yet done'. It was probably one of 'many petitions' referred to on 26 March, when a committee was appointed to consider Chancery reform. This timing is important because it places Crokey alongside reformers like George Norbury, who wrote about the 'abuses and remedies' of

[10] Crokey, *Sacred Maiestie*, sig. E2v.

[11] GA, D9125/1/11996; Crokey, *Sacred Maiestie*, sigs H3v–4.

[12] GA, D9125/1/12028, p. 2.

[13] *CD 1621*, ii. 210, iv. 147, vii. 343–4; *CSPD 1611–18*, p. 499. See: Stephen D. White, *Sir Edward Coke and the Grievances of the Commonwealth* (Manchester, 1979), pp. 56, 72–6.

[14] PA, HL/PO/JO/10/13/9.

Chancery, and the MP, Robert Phelips, who bemoaned the problems caused by protracted litigation, and described the court's 'unlimited power and abuse' as something under which 'we all groan'. Phelps made explicit reference to the statute Crokey hoped to revive.[15] Others too claimed that Chancery processes were a 'grievance to the subject', and that the 'six clerks'—including men employed by Smyth—inflated charges, delayed cases, and made themselves 'absolute officers', treating clients 'as they list'.[16]

Crokey demonstrated a reforming zeal in the public interest, a theme that re-emerged when discussing his Irish experience in the 1630s. As shown already, Crokey boasted about his 'famous design called the Flax business', insisting that it was pursued 'upon his own charge of livelihood', and that 'perfecting the said design' involved training local people and erecting bridewells. He also claimed to have been fêted as someone who might become 'the best commonwealthsman that ever came for Ireland', and his scheme represented an early example of attempts to employ—rather than merely punish or pay—the poor.[17] However, the episode is also relevant because Crokey gave evidence about it during Strafford's trial (1 April 1641), and because he linked Smyth with the lord deputy's corrupt and self-serving behaviour. Smyth allegedly encouraged Wentworth to monopolise the flax trade, precisely to undermine his opponent.[18]

II

Crokey's attempts to relate his litigation and Irish career to reforming ambitions, the public interest, and political corruption, provide the ideal backdrop to a discussion of his ideological beliefs. Pursuing the possibility that his defence of Wotton school reflected religious concerns involves paying close attention to rhetoric and tactics, not least in terms of those to whom Crokey appealed for support and assistance.

First, it is worth dwelling upon Crokey's allusions to God and religious issues, which were fleeting but frequent. Crokey mocked Smyth's 'dissembled piety', claiming that his opponent 'made false shows . . . of a pious intent for settling the school', and that when his scheme 'would not take' he 'began to make a show of a pious intent, to make and erect a new foundation of that school', even though this was done 'in his own name, and for his own glory'. Smyth sought 'to outface and

[15] *CD 1621*, vii. 204–7; BL, Harl. MS 6803, fos 27–8; PA, HL/PO/JO/10/13/9; *CJ*, i. 573–4; G. W. Thomas, 'James I, equity and Lord Keeper Williams', *EHR*, 91 (1976), 521–7. See: Zaller, *Parliament*, pp. 20–1, 92–7; White, *Coke*, pp. 49–50, 57–65.

[16] TNA, E 215/599.

[17] Crokey, *Complaint*, sigs B2–v; GA, D9125/1/12028, p. 9.

[18] *The Tryal of Thomas Earl of Strafford* (1680), pp. 67, 417–18; Crokey, *Complaint*, sigs B2v–3; Crokey, *Petition*, p. 9. Smyth's alleged co-conspirator—Carpenter—was expelled from the Irish Parliament for 'cruel and illegal proceedings': Jansson, *Proceedings*, iii. 286n13, 287n18.

blindfold the world, [so] that his former practices for supplanting thereof might not be seen', which explained his financial endowment of the school. Indeed, 'for divulging of that dissembled piety and bounty' Smyth also 'ordained' twenty-five feoffees to oversee 'his new false foundation'. Reflecting on his own travails, Crokey admitted that he might have succumbed to Smyth, if 'the special mercy ... of God' had not 'strengthened his weakness', in 'so sore a conflict' and 'so just a cause'. This cause was 'more precious than life itself', and Crokey cited the wisdom of Sirach: 'strive for the truth unto death, and defend justice for thy life ... God shall fight for thee against thine enemies' (Ecclesiasticus 4.28).[19]

Faith was central to how Crokey explained his purpose and experiences. Claiming to be unmoved by 'private ends', he demanded schoolmasters who would 'teach and instruct in good literature and learning', professing 'a charitable disposition for God's cause'.[20] Onlookers, he said, 'may marvel what God, by the petitioner with his daughter ... hath done and suffered, in defending and preserving the said school and lands ... being moved thereunto for God's cause'. Elsewhere, he referred to being motivated by 'God's cause and the public good'.[21] Justifying law reform, Crokey protested that the legal system generated grievances 'displeasing to God the author of truth', and his language sometimes reflected the rhetoric of supplicatory prayer. He wrote about 'oppressions' being 'laid in a just balance and ... rightly weighed', and of 'afflictions' that 'loudly cry for execution of justice', adding that a successful campaign for the school would be credited 'not unto me, Oh lord ... unto thy name be the praise'.[22] Finally, during his outburst at the Three Cups inn, Crokey allegedly called Smyth 'a churchrobber', 'a Jesuit', and a 'jesuitical fellow', and someone with 'a black conscience'.[23]

Such comments offer vague hints about Crokey's religious zeal; they were buried in texts that betrayed little evidence of ideological motivations, and were made in private conversations, and perhaps even in drink. Nevertheless, they should be taken seriously, particularly alongside Crokey's comment about the 'breaking'—rather than merely 'dissolution'—of the 1628 Parliament, as clues about the dispute's meaning, and about why it fascinated contemporaries.[24] Such comments might be thought to reveal Puritanism, or anti-popery, of a kind associated with claims about the value and fate of Parliament. It is intriguing that Denzil Holles, who was imprisoned for participating in the chaotic scenes at the end of the 1629 Parliament, and who became a leading parliamentarian, later drew attention to Crokey's case when defending the judicature of the House of

[19] Crokey, *Sacred Maiestie*, sigs A3v, C4v–D, H3v–4.

[20] GA, D9125/1/12027, sigs Av, A2; TNA, STAC 8/107/7; PA, HL/PO/JO/10/1/24. See: Sheffield Archives, WWM/StrP/24–5/340.

[21] GA, D9125/1/12028, p. 2; PA, HL/PO/JO/10/1/274. Crokey perhaps used a phrase like 'God's cause' more pointedly than other embattled litigants: PA, HL/PO/JO/10/1/25 (Weare, Martin); HL/PO/JO/10/1/26 (Fowler).

[22] GA, D9125/1/12027, sig. Av.

[23] GA, D8887/6/71.

[24] GA, D9125/1/12028, p. 9.

Lords.[25] It is also likely that Crokey's 'libel' was regarded as a form of political sedition, involving comments that undermined authority and threatened the public peace.[26]

It obviously might be objected that Crokey frequently sought support from the king and the episcopal authorities, submitting himself 'most humbly' to 'the consideration of His Majesty'.[27] Nevertheless, such tactics were hardly incompatible with Puritanism, which frequently revealed exalted expectations about royal power, particularly during the 1620s, notably in terms of the king being the fountain of justice.[28] Crokey's dealings with episcopal grandees also merit scrutiny, and while Smyth mocked Crokey's attempt to claim—'audaciously'—that one lawsuit was 'exhibited by the encouragement of a most reverend and worthy prelate', his petitions were certainly referred to a small group of prominent bishops, who were willing to authorise new commissions of inquiry, summon Smyth to hearings, and criticise his 'practices'.[29] An intriguing pattern also emerges in terms of the prelates to whom Crokey appealed, and from whom he secured assistance: John Thornborough (bishop of Worcester), Rowland Searchfield (bishop of Bristol), Miles Smith (bishop of Gloucester), John King (bishop of London), and George Abbot (archbishop of Canterbury).[30] He nominated Thornborough, Searchfield, and Smith to a charitable uses inquiry (1621), and claimed that Abbot 'well-informed himself' about Wotton school. Crokey also insisted that he visited Abbot, to whom he 'spoke... truth and soberness', boasting to Henry Townshend that Abbot put pressure on senior legal figures to expedite the case, and that he had 'good friends... chiefly the bishop of Canterbury with other bishops' (October 1618).[31]

Abbot's help also took other forms. According to Crokey, the archbishop responded to being 'fully acquainted' with Smyth's 'practices against the school' by sending a servant, John Harte, to visit the Chief Baron of the Exchequer (Sir Lawrence Tanfield), 'for traversing... undue proceedings' and 'reversing' a recent 'inquisition'.[32] Harte is an intriguing character, whose role in Crokey's litigation can be substantiated. He was 'a gentleman towards my lord's grace of Canterbury',

[25] Denzil Holles, *The Grand Question Concerning the Judicature of the House of Peers* (1669), p. 161.

[26] Alastair Bellany, '"Rayling rymes and vaunting verse": libellous politics in early Stuart England, 1603–1628', in Kevin Sharpe and Peter Lake, eds, *Culture and Politics in Early Stuart England* (London, 1994), p. 294.

[27] Crokey, *Sacred Maiestie*, sigs Dv, Fv.

[28] Richard Cust and Peter Lake, 'Sir Richard Grosvenor and the rhetoric of magistracy', *BIHR*, 54.129 (1981), 40–53; Hart, *Justice*, p. 33. See: Sheffield Archives, WWM/StrP/24-5/340. See also: R. W. Hoyle, 'Fountains of Justice: James I, Charles I and equity' Michael Lobban, Joanne Begiato and Adrian Green, eds, *Law, Lawyers and Litigants in Early Modern England* (Cambridge, 2019), pp. 79–113.

[29] GA, D9125/1/11996, 12008, p. 63; D8887/6/77.

[30] Crokey, *Sacred Maiestie*, sigs Ev, Fv–2.

[31] BL, Harl. MS 6803, fos 56v–7; Crokey, *Sacred Maiestie*, sig. F2; GA, D9125/1/12014; D8887/6/72.

[32] Crokey, *Sacred Maiestie*, sig. C4v. For Harte as a member of Abbot's household, see: LPL, MS 1730, fo. 7. I am grateful to Ken Fincham for this reference.

and Abbot described him as 'solicitor of my causes', and it is noteworthy that Crokey used him as a legal adviser, and called him as a witness in Common Pleas (February 1619–20). At precisely this time, another witness, John Strachey, encouraged Harte to fulfil a 'promise' made to 'your client Mr Crokey', confident that he could 'end that business'.[33] Abbot may thus have been the 'most reverend and worthy prelate' to whom Crokey referred when explaining that he was encouraged to pursue a new Star Chamber case against Smyth (early 1621).[34]

Abbot's significance lies in more than just his elevated position within the Church. Like the other bishops mentioned by Crokey, he was a staunch Calvinist, vigorously anti-Catholic, and lenient towards moderate Puritans, if not towards separatists.[35] Also noteworthy is Crokey's claim—made to Townshend—that he was advised to approach Abbot by Mr Proctor, chaplain to another prominent Calvinist and anti-Catholic, Toby Matthew (archbishop of York).[36] Crokey's reliance upon such clerics scarcely proves that that he was puritanically inclined, but it is significant that he turned to prominent Calvinists at a time when 'avant garde' Arminian ideas were becoming more prevalent, and as the authority of Abbot was on the wane. It certainly does not preclude the possibility that Crokey inclined towards some form of Puritanism, and other evidence suggests this was not just likely but also fairly certain.

III

Teasing out Crokey's religious ideas involves reconstituting his personal network, and identifying the figures upon whom he most relied for support. As with Smyth, this involves suggesting that Crokey's religious ideas were reflected in—and indicated by—friends and associates, and by the activities and practices with which they can be linked.

A key element of Crokey's network involved Bristol, in terms of the intriguing cast of citizens to whom copies of his pamphlet were sent, and with whom he associated. Of course, not everyone to whom Crokey can be linked was a friend or sympathiser, whose views illuminate his position. Some were probably approached due to their prominence and influence, and if the 'Cary' who received a copy of the tract was William Cary (*d.*1632), then he was probably chosen as a

[33] LPL, MS 1730, fo. 7; TNA, PROB 11/164, fo. 211; GA, D9125/1/12008, pp. 56, 61; D8887/6/79–80. See: LB, MS 3549/175.

[34] GA, D9125/1/12008, p. 63.

[35] *ODNB*; Susan Holland, 'Archbishop Abbot and the problem of "Puritanism"', *HJ*, 37.1 (1994), 23–43; Fincham, *Prelate*, pp. 46–7, 62, 197, 236, 238, 257, 264, 269, 283.

[36] GA, D8887/6/71. See: Rosamund Oates, *Moderate Radical: Tobie Matthew and the English Reformation* (Oxford, 2018), p. 154.

former sheriff and member of the aldermanic bench.[37] That ideological alignment was *not* what led Crokey towards many such men seems clear from the cases of Thomas Colston and Giles Elbridge, with whom he had strong personal connections, but who later emerged as opponents, and who demonstrated very different religious and political views.[38] The same may also have been true of George Knight (*d.*1659), if he was the person to whom a copy of Crokey's tract was sent. Knight, a local mercer, was the incumbent sheriff in 1626, and someone with whom Crokey had interacted in his trading days. He too associated with men who later displayed royalist sympathies, including the minister, Jacob Brent, who plotted to surrender Bristol to Prince Rupert in 1643, and who received a bequest in Knight's will.[39] Another who received Crokey's book, John Barker, had a similar profile. He was the city's mayor at the moment when Crokey's tract was distributed, and had recent experience as an MP, not to mention property interests in Wotton. However, while his will reveals enthusiasm for, and donations to, preaching and catechising, he also made bequests to his local bishop (George Coke) and Dr Edward Chetwynd, the cathedral's dean, and while these were not exactly enthusiastic Laudians, Barker was also close to three ministers—Richard Towgood, John Tilladam, and Richard Standfast—who became lynchpins of local royalism.[40]

Such evidence suggests that Crokey sent copies of his pamphlet to people who might not be sympathetic to his cause, highlighting the risks involved in using Crokey's associates to illuminate his ideological agenda. Nevertheless, it makes sense to distinguish between men to whom he turned as power-brokers and officeholders when the tract appeared, and those to whom he can be connected in other contexts, and alongside whom he *worked*.

This means drawing attention to how Crokey targeted, and had contacts within, Bristol's clerical community, and how at least some associates were puritanically inclined. He sent one copy of his tract to Abel Lovering (*d.*1643), sometime lecturer in the parishes of St Thomas and St Nicholas, and then vicar of Temple, the living to which he was presented by the city in 1639.[41] Another copy may have been sent to Richard Knight (*d.*1639), Lovering's predecessor at Temple.[42] It is unclear how obviously such men can be identified as Puritans, but there is no evidence that Lovering supported the royalist cause. More importantly, some of

[37] BA, M/BCC/CCP/1/2, fos 127, 137; Beaven, *Bristol*, pp. 185, 196, 222, 281; McGrath, *Merchants*, p. 109; BA, FCOB/3/8. It is possible that Crokey's book was sent to Mr Cary, minister of St Stephens: BA, F/Au/1/19, p. 283.

[38] See above, pp. C6.P24, C6.P28–C6.P29, C7.P25.

[39] Beaven, *Bristol*, pp. 197, 223, 299; TNA, PROB 11/296, fo. 245v. For Knight: BA, JStap/1/3, fo. 90. For Brent: BA, M/BCC/CCP/1/4, p. 28; *Walker Revised*, pp. 171–2.

[40] Beaven, *Bristol*, pp. 185, 197, 222, 277; *Commons 1604–1629*, iii. 130–1; BA, FCW/1636/1; TNA, PROB 11/171, fo. 238. Chetwynd was sometime vicar of Berkeley: Harlow, *Religious Ministry*, p. 149.

[41] *Al. Cant.*, iii. 108; BA, F/Au/1/18, p. 173; M/BCC/CCP/1/2, fo. 116v; M/BCC/CCP/1/3, fo. 91; M/BCC/CCP/1/4, pp. 28, 30–1; Harlow, *Religious Ministry*, pp. 62, 68, 159.

[42] BA, M/BCC/CCP/1/2, fo. 48; M/BCC/CCP 1/3, fo. 91; Edwin George and Stella George, eds, *Bristol Probate Inventories Part 1, 1542–1650* (BRS, 54, 2002), p. 110.

Crokey's Bristol associates were obviously Puritans. One of these was his legal adviser, John Price (*d.*1640), who left bequests to 'that exceeding reverend divine' Richard Watson, rector of St Mary Aldermanbury in London, and to another cleric, Thomas Westfield.[43] Watson and Westfield were committed Calvinists, who inclined towards moderate Puritanism of a kind that accommodated a version of episcopacy (Westfield became bishop of Bristol in 1642), and both were prominent in the early history of Sion College. Westfield was even appointed to the Westminster Assembly of Divines in the 1640s, even if he participated only minimally.[44]

Price suggests that, within a divided city, Crokey not only appealed to civic leaders, but also tapped into a godly network. Central here was the preacher William Yeomans (*d.*1633), who received a copy of Crokey's pamphlet and who was a key figure within Bristol's clerical community, as minister of St Phillips and lecturer at St Werburghs, where he received money from the city authorities. Yeomans' service as prebend of the Cathedral belied his godly activism, and he was inspirational within an underground network—including the grocer, Anthony Kelly, his wife Dorothy, and her second husband, Matthew Hazzard, minister of St Ewen from 1639—all of whom were instrumental in establishing the Broadmead Baptist church.[45] One member of that congregation described Yeomans as a 'zealous preacher', 'raised up' by God, who 'would not suffer... hearers to use any blind devotion as bowing at the name of Jesus' or 'profaning the sabbath'. Such zeal attracted Yeomans to 'awakened souls and honest minded people', who flocked to hear him 'and sat under his light near twenty years, keeping many fast days together in private houses'. Such followers also appealed 'to the lord to pluck the lordly prelates of the time', along with their 'superstitions'.[46]

Yeomans' circle is revealing. It included Alderman Mathew Haviland, who left money for Yeomans to preach a funeral sermon, secured funding for able lecturers, and established a city library with help from Archbishop Toby Matthew, 'for the furtherance of learning'. Haviland also took action against disorderly inns,

[43] BA, FCW/1639/4. Lovering was friendly with Robert Aldworth: TNA, PROB 11/167, fo. 21.

[44] *ODNB*; William Henry Milman, 'Some account of Sion College, in the city of London and its library', *Transactions of the London and Middlesex Archaeological Society*, 6 (1890), 79. See: Peter Lake, *The Boxmaker's Revenge: 'Orthodoxy, 'Heterodoxy' and the Politics of the Parish in Early Stuart London* (Manchester, 2009), pp. 315, 339. Watson and Price may have been related: TNA, PROB 11/176, fo. 400.

[45] *Al. Oxon.*, iv. 1701; BA, FCW/1633/5; George and George, eds, *Bristol Probate Inventories*, p. 81; D. M. Livock, ed, *City Chamberlains Accounts* (BRS, 24, 1966), p. 131; Harlow, *Religious Ministry*, pp. 2, 74n530, 170; Sacks, *Widening Gate*, pp. 231–4, 244–5; BA, M/BCC/CCP/1/1, p. 140; F/Au/1/16, p. 158; MC/BCC/CCP/1/2, fo. 34v. See: F/Au/1/18, p. 35; Roger Hayden, ed., *The Records of a Church of Christ in Bristol 1640–1687* (BRS, 27, 1974), pp. 13, 88–9, 310. For Matthew Hazzard: BA, M/BCC/CCP/1/3, fo. 98v; F/Au/1/22, p. 101.

[46] Hayden, ed., *Records*, p. 84.

taverns, and alehouses, and banned drinking on the sabbath.[47] Yeomans' network also included Richard Aldworth, the city's leading parliamentarian during the civil wars, and Aldworth's father-in-law, Alderman John Doughty, who left money that 'God may be praised and his word preached by Mr William Yeomans, my very loving friend and faithful pastor.'[48] Doughty was a divisive figure, and in 1623 Thomas Cicell was expelled from the Common Council for 'opprobrious and unreverent speeches' against him and the incumbent mayor. Cicell, who 'cared not a fart' for them, was clearly no Puritan, and was deemed guilty of 'loose carriage and behaviour', and of 'being often seen drunk'.[49] Doughty was also someone who, as the city's MP in 1628, collected six copies of parliamentary debates regarding 'the liberty of the subject', which were ordered to 'remain of record forever'.[50] Finally, it even seems clear that Yeomans' circle incorporated associates of Crokey, such as Thomas Baddam, the cooper with whom he launched a legal case about Warrens Court. Baddam's will was witnessed by Yeomans, as well as the bookseller, Thomas Wright, with whose family Yeomans was close.[51]

Evidence about Crokey's Bristol network might be fragmentary, but it is plausible to associate him with factionalism grounded in religious and socio-economic divisions. This conjuncture has been elucidated by David Harris Sacks, who highlighted tensions between 'mere merchants' within the Society of Merchant Venturers, including Robert Aldworth and Giles Elbridge, and their anti-monopolist opponents, and who tentatively mapped these divisions onto religious groupings, involving Laudians and Puritans respectively. According to Sacks, such divisions 'penetrated deeply' into the structure of Bristol politics, and the evidence presented here supports his argument. Crokey emerges as someone who, like Richard Aldworth, was associated with the Merchant Venturers, but who did not share their monopolistic and hierarchical vision of commerce, and who had interests in domestic trades as well as international commerce. Both men reacted against Laudianism and can be connected to the Puritan circle around William Yeomans, which involved small shopkeepers and craftsmen, and which provided the bedrock of local parliamentarianism, in opposition to the royalism of senior Merchant Venturers and their Laudian friends.[52] Dorothy Hazzard, of course, played a famous role on the barricades during the royalist siege in 1643.

[47] BA, M/BCC/CCP/1/2, fos 43v, 55v; M/BCC/CCP/1/1, pp. 118, 127; Hayden, ed., *Records*, p. 310; BA, FCOB/3/5. For the library: Oates, *Moderate Radical*, pp. 171–3.

[48] TNA, PROB 11/157, fo. 115v. See: Sacks, *Widening Gate*, p. 245.

[49] BA, M/BCC/CCP/1/2, fo. 110v.

[50] BA, M/BCC/CCP/1/3, fo. 6v.

[51] For Baddam: TNA, PROB 11/167, fo. 333; BA, FCW/1635/1. For Wright: McGrath, *Merchants*, p. 30; TNA, PROB 11/184, fo. 296; BA, FCI/1633–41/42, 46; TNA, PROB 11/162, fo. 111v.

[52] Sacks, *Widening Gate*, pp. 50–1, 69–70, 221–46, 299.

IV

Further evidence about Crokey's political and religious identity emerges from a parallel and overlapping network within Gloucestershire, particularly around Wotton-under-Edge. This can likewise be interrogated with evidence about those who distributed, and received copies of, his pamphlet. Here too, there are both problems and opportunities with assessing his ties to godly circles, and similar challenges arise regarding the ideological identities of particular individuals. Nevertheless, what emerges is the striking degree to which Crokey associated with, and relied upon, local Puritans, many of whom became parliamentarians after 1642.

As with the pamphlet's distribution in Bristol, analysis of copies that reached Gloucestershire involves methodological challenges, and his readership does not necessarily reveal his views. The beliefs of those who encountered his tract are not always apparent, and it is risky to deduce attitudes during the 1620s from evidence about the civil wars. In Gloucestershire, as in Bristol, Crokey probably reached out beyond known sympathisers, and could not always control access to his pamphlet. It is uncertain whether Crokey intended a copy to reach Philip Langley of Mangotsfield, who obtained it from his maid, to whom it was sent by the scrivener, George Hartwell. Langley became an inactive parliamentarian, albeit one who came under suspicion during the 1650s, and if he was targeted by Crokey then it may simply have been as a prominent gentleman and former sheriff.[53] Other people may have been identified despite their views. William Player of Mangotsfield (*d.*1637) was offered a copy by Thomas Wright, perhaps on Crokey's instructions, but may not have been sympathetic, given his fairly close friendship with the Laudian (and royalist) minister, Richard Towgood.[54] Other readers included Sir William Guise of Brockworth (*d.*1643) and Arthur Kemis of Frampton Cotterell (*d.*1645), both of whom 'confederated' with Smyth and ended their days as royalists in Oxford. It is unclear whether Crokey intended them to get sight of the tract, and the same may have been true of another future royalist, Edward Slaughter of Winchcombe, who was offered a copy by William Burford.[55] With other readers, religious and political views may have been less relevant to Crokey than their links to Smyth. These included Smyth's cousins, like William Hill, who as town clerk of Tewkesbury found himself imprisoned by both parliamentarians and royalists during the 1640s, as well as Edward and Richard

[53] *Vis. Gloucester 1623*, pp. 39, 103; *Vis. Gloucester 1682–3*, pp. 107–8; *A&O*, ii. 966, 1083; Warmington, *Gloucestershire*, p. 75; BL, Add. MS 34012, fo. 33.

[54] *Vis. Gloucester 1623*, p. 99; BA, FCW/1637/4; TNA, PROB 11/171, fo. 114.

[55] For Guise: *Vis. Gloucester 1623*, p. 73; *Al. Oxon.*, ii. 618; G. Davies, ed., *Autobiography of Thomas Raymond and Memoirs of the Guise Family of Elmore* (London, 1917), pp. 109–15, 119–20, 123, 170; Warmington, *Gloucestershire*, pp. 36, 43, 181; GA, D9125/1/12008, p. 25; TNA, C 21/C25/4; PROB 10/639, fos 35–7v. For Kemis: *Vis. Gloucester 1623*, p. 99; *Men and Armour*, p. 200; TNA, PROB 10/642, fo. 178. For Slaughter: *CCC*, p. 86; BL, Add. MS 34012, fo. 50.

Wakeman, to the latter of whom Crokey apparently showed a copy at the Three Cups inn in London. Both men were sequestered as royalists and suspected recusants.[56] Perhaps the most intriguing case involves Sir Robert Poyntz (*d.*1665) of Iron Acton, another man who received Crokey's pamphlet from Burford. Like many other readers in Gloucestershire, Poyntz later sided with the king, served as a Commissioner of Array, and was branded a delinquent for joining the royalist garrison at Bristol. In 1626, however, he may have been considered a worthy recipient, not just as a prominent JP and MP, but also as someone religiously and politically out of step with the Caroline regime. He was imprisoned for refusing to pay the Forced Loan, and may also have been an anti-Arminian; he later expressed a preference for 'the orthodoxical faith and religion *formerly* established in the Church of England'.[57]

Ultimately, it is easier to understand why Crokey may have targeted such men than to use them as guides to his religious and political views. It is more profitable to focus upon his associates and collaborators, including those who helped to circulate the pamphlet, although even here the picture is hazy. A case in point is John Dowle of Over (*d.*1638), nominated by Crokey to the charitable uses commission in 1618 and 1621. Dowle is hard to pin down ideologically, and it is possible that Crokey was attracted by his local eminence—he was sheriff in 1624—and his kinship with Peter Bird, one of Smyth's closest associates. Nevertheless, it has already been noted that there was a pattern to the men that Crokey nominated to such inquiries, in terms of their Calvinism and tolerance of Puritans, and it might be unwise to rule out ideological affiliation between the two men. Somewhat clearer is evidence about Dowle's son, John Dowle junior, who distributed as many as seventeen copies of Crokey's tract, and who was pursued by Smyth accordingly. Dowle was once described as the 'chief stirrer' of a 'mutiny' at the Middle Temple, which involved behaving 'insolently' and refusing to remove hats in the hall, which might indicate religious nonconformity.[58]

The same logic may also have drawn Crokey to others who distributed the pamphlet in Gloucestershire, including Jeffrey Webb, about whom little is known, as well as the soldier, John Leigh (*d.*1645). Leigh apparently received a copy from John Barker in Bristol, and might also have been given a copy by Lacy, a prisoner in King's Bench, whose father, John Lacy, was vicar at Tytherington and

[56] For Hill: Warmington, *Gloucestershire*, pp. 28, 77, 145; GA, D2688/1; *CCAM*, p. 859; TNA, SP 21/94, 316; GA, D9125/1/12009, 12014. For the Wakemans: *CCAM*, p. 746; *CCC*, pp. 88, 224, 739, 1929, 2982; SP 23/128, pp. 206, 215; *Al. Oxon.*, iv. 1554; TNA, PROB 6/35, fo. 306; BL, Add. MS 34012, fo. 58v.

[57] *Commons 1604–1629*, v. 748–9; *ODNB*; *CCC*, pp. 65, 76, 85, 102, 279, 1942, 2247, 2782, 2850; TNA, SP 23/210, p. 201; SP 19/155/95–6; *CCAM*, p. 1384; BL, Add. MS 34012, fo. 42; Warmington, *Gloucestershire*, pp. 22, 33, 159; TNA, PROB 11/321, fo. 238 (emphasis added).

[58] GA, D8887/6/66; BL, Harl. MS 6803, fos 56v–7; *Men and Armour*, p. 201; *Vis. Gloucester 1623*, p. 53; *Al. Oxon.*, i. 418; *Admissions MT*, i. 104; Hopwood, *MT Recs*, ii. 600, 607, 614–15, 616, 641–3, 645; BA, FCW/1638/3; TNA, PROB 11/178, fo. 108.

schoolmaster at Cam. Leigh subsequently participated in the tract's distribution, but also provided contacts within the local community. He hailed from Wotton, held property in Nibley, and undertook business with the schoolmaster, Edward Cowper, and even with Smyth, to whom he was perhaps related.[59] Indeed, the number of Crokey's associates who came from the Wotton area is striking. These included Albane Saunders, a mercer whose son attended Wotton school, Edward Tanner (*d.*1642), a clothing factor from Tetbury who was well connected within Wotton's textile community, and Hugh Deinton (*d.*1630), a weaver from Nibley.[60] They also included Edmund Grayle, the son of a Wotton yeoman, who became a physician at St Bartholemew's hospital (Gloucester), and one Dimery, a clothier from Cromhall, who helped distribute Crokey's pamphlets in the 1640s.[61]

Such men provided access to the networks through which Crokey's pamphlets circulated, as well as local knowledge, and they were well acquainted with Smyth. This emerges clearly with Albane Saunders, a trustee of the school lands, and Robert Pritchard (*d.*1663), labelled as a 'meddler' for distributing Crokey's pamphlet around the Wotton area.[62] Pritchard represents another of Crokey's contacts within Bristol's clerical community, having been presented to the parish of St Peter in 1622, before securing further patronage from the civic authorities. Unlike Yeomans, however, his religious views are hard to fathom: he played no part in royalist agitation during the 1640s, survived the civil wars and Interregnum, and avoided ejection in 1662. The only other hints regarding his views involve him treasuring a three-volume edition of the works of William Perkins (the only book identified in his will), and the nomination of a former royalist, Richard Towgood, as his executor.[63]

Pritchard was valuable because of his connection with Wotton and his palpable commitment to Crokey's cause, in which he too suffered. Pritchard was a former curate in Nibley (1612–16), and had taught at Wotton school before Smyth's time; he appears frequently in Smyth's financial accounts, for preaching, teaching, and undertaking repairs (1609–17).[64] Thereafter, the two men fell out spectacularly, apparently because Smyth feared that Pritchard 'did incline to the assistance of Crokey for righting the school'. Smyth allegedly 'set upon Pritchard with . . . high and threatening speeches', to get him to 'depart from the school', and when Pritchard refused to be intimidated Smyth reportedly mobilised a mob of twenty

[59] GA, S379/2/2/1/1; D8887/8/81; TNA, PROB 11/200, fo. 182v.

[60] *Men and Armour*, pp. 164, 175, 284. For Tanner: TNA, PROB 11/189, fo. 242. For Deinton: GA, GDR/1630/43.

[61] For Grayle: *ODNB*; *Al. Oxon.*, ii. 595; GA, D8887/9/50–1, 58–61. For Dimery: *Men and Armour*, p. 153.

[62] GA, S379/2/2/1/3.

[63] BA, M/BCC/CCP/1/2, fo. 144; F/Au/1/22, pp. 56, 127, 193, 261, 325; F/Au/1/23, pp. 46, 112, 174, 238, 306; F/Au/1/24, pp. 46, 110, 178, 262; F/Au/1/25, p. 60; F/Au/1/26, p. 64; F/Au/1/27, p. 60; Harlow, *Religious Ministry*, pp. 50, 163; BA, FCW/1663/2.

[64] See above, pp. C4.P50–C4.P51, C7.P50; Bodl. MS Eng.Misc.e.6, fos 45–v, 47v–8, 49v, 51, 55–6, 58v, 63v, 66v, 76v, 78v, 90v, 94, 98, 107–v, 115, 121; TNA, E 134/14Jas1/Mich28.

men, 'in outrageous and violent manner', who harassed Pritchard's pregnant wife and forced him to 'leave the school to Smyth'.[65] As noted already, Smyth did little to deny such stories, although he criticised Pritchard for showing 'no thanks for nine years' breeding and feeding', adding that '[i]gnorance made him err, for which I suppose him sorrowful.'[66] Thus, while Pritchard sent copies of Crokey's tract to men like Thomas Hewett (a brother-in-law), his real value probably involved his zeal, and his animus against Smyth.

Crokey pursued a logical strategy of fostering contacts in the Wotton area, identifying people who understood the Warrens Court dispute and moulding local opinion. This enabled him to capitalise upon local knowledge, and to exploit opposition to Smyth's manoeuvres and tactics, and he perhaps expected to find sympathy and support. In encouraging a Wotton chandler like Edward Olyver to disperse pamphlets, Crokey was relying upon kinship ties, but probably knew that Olyver had clashed with Smyth in the 1590s, in relation to local property claims. That particular dispute is murky, but Olyver was eventually forced to relinquish his financial claims, 'by all manner of actions, suits and demands', presumably under pressure from Smyth.[67] It is possible that he, like Pritchard, bore a grudge against Smyth that translated into support for Crokey. Morgan Ady may also have been approached on the assumption that he was disgruntled. Crokey took Ady into his confidence during meetings in King's Bench prison, and wanted him to distribute the pamphlet, unaware that he was helping Smyth to gather intelligence. Crokey was perhaps inspired by the fact that one of Ady's relatives—Gyles Ady of Frampton, 'a fellow of mean quality'—had recently been prosecuted for slander in the Court of Chivalry, having described Smyth as a 'knave, villain and beggar', apparently in a 'boasting manner'. Ady was imprisoned and forced to beg forgiveness, and Crokey perhaps recognised that this all stemmed from his being prosecuted by Smyth for violently opposing enclosures at Slimbridge.[68] Crokey may also have been aware of Ady's familial links with Puritan ministers, like Richard Hall of Beverston, who signed the Presbyterian testimony (1648) and suffered ejection from his living in 1662.[69]

Any assumptions that Crokey made about Morgan Ady's religious views may have been understandable, given the persistent association between local people (including clothworkers) and advanced forms of Protestantism.[70] In 1540, the local minister, John Andrews, faced official sanction for describing the 'laudable ceremonies of the church' as 'foolish, lewd and beggarly', and as being 'full of

[65] Crokey, *Sacred Maiestie*, sig. D. [66] GA, D9125/1/12008, p. 65.

[67] *Men and Armour*, p. 164; GA, D8887/7/19.

[68] *Men and Armour*, p. 165; TNA, C 2/Jas1/R6/3; GA, D9125/1/13608/70. See: Bodl. MS Eng.Misc. e.6, fos 125, 131; G. D. Squibb, *High Court of Chivalry* (Oxford, 1959), p. 38; Berkeley, GPL 715–1081, 1154–74; College of Arms, MS I.25, fos 42v–3; MS R.19, fo. 103; Berkeley, BB110, fo. 192v.

[69] TNA, PROB 11/295, fo. 5v. For Richard Hall: *Calamy Revised*, pp. 242–3; GA, GDR/1684/202.

[70] Rollison, *Local Origins*, chs 1, 5.

idolatry and superstition'. He also withheld confession, and appointed lecturers like Richard Turner, 'a man of ill fame' who preached 'erroneous, scandalous and seditious things' and held Bible-reading sessions at Kingswood, with locals 'congregating and flocking to him for that purpose'.[71] During this period Wotton witnessed 'great troubles... by reason of divers opinions' over church reform, and was home to one of the Marian martyrs.[72] It was probably such advanced Protestantism that prompted Lord Berkeley to assert his influence over the local church. Having appointed Robert Knight as minister during Mary's reign, he tried unsuccessfully to regain control of the advowson, which was granted to Christ Church, Oxford upon the dissolution of the monasteries. This decision was a source of frustration to Berkeley and Smyth, not least because the college made 'so poor an allowance to the ministers both of Wotton and Nibley'.[73]

Subsequently, the local area became a bastion of Puritanism. During the 1630s, controversy swirled around Wotton's minister, Thomas Ackson (*d.*1641), who was censured for refusing to read set prayers (1631), and who was described by Brian Duppa, Laudian dean of Christ Church, as being 'as cunning and as dangerous a Puritan as any in the pack'. Ackson courted trouble by prosecuting men, like John Cox of Combe, who sought to enforce Caroline policies, resulting in a dispute with Christ Church and an appearance before High Commission. He was reported to Laud after punishing parishioners for 'performing service commanded by the bishop'.[74] At his death Ackson was succeeded by a Presbyterian, Richard Kent, whose own successor Joseph Bowden (*d.*1672) was removed as a nonconformist in 1662. Such appointments reflected the mood amongst townspeople. Bowden continued to preach in Wotton after his ejection, with financial support from parishioners, and the town remained a hotbed of dissent and conventicling, as John Smyth junior discovered. Even Christ Church recognised the need to secure local approval for subsequent appointments.[75] In Nibley, meanwhile, Puritanism was latent during the 1630s, with church court records showing a marked increase in cases of local parishioners refusing to attend church, receive (or kneel at) communion, or respect the litany and set prayers as the Long Parliament approached.[76]

In moving beyond the idea that Crokey enlisted local people for practical reasons, such analysis is necessarily speculative. Nevertheless, it is justifiable

[71] GA, D3439/1/420; R. Perry, *Wotton-under-Edge* (Wotton-under-Edge, 1986), p. 59.

[72] GA, D3439/1/420; Lindley, *Wotton*, p. 43; Ben Lowe, *Commonwealth and the English Reformation* (Farnham, 2010), p. 144.

[73] Smyth, *Lives*, ii. 169; iii. 265–6.

[74] GA, GDR/137; *CSPD 1635–6*, pp. 81–2, 468, 476, 483, 493, 497, 518; *CSPD 1637*, pp. 37, 61; TNA, C 78/387/3; SP 16/354, fo. 249; Smyth, *Lives*, iii. 264. See: GA, D3439/1/419; GDR/1641/121.

[75] Perry, *Wotton*, pp. 61–2; BL, Add. MS 33589, fos 78–v. For Bowden: Thomas Edwards, *Gangraena* (1646), iii. 242; *Calamy Revised*, p. 62; Bodl. MS Walker c.7/26. For Christ Church: GA, D8887/5/91; Christ Church, Oxford, MS I.c.3, pp. 517–18.

[76] GA, GDR/137. For earlier: GA, D3439/1/299.

given how closely Crokey worked with local men whose Puritan credentials were unimpeachable. The most significant was John Staunton, who was perhaps the son of a Marian exile, and who became Wotton's most eminent Puritan in the late sixteenth century. He was involved in disputes with parishioners, who 'disgraced' him with 'scornful, scandalous and contemptuous speeches', not least by calling him 'woodcock' (i.e. simpleton or dupe).[77] He also served as deputy schoolmaster at Wotton in the 1590s, and like Pritchard tried to block Smyth's manoeuvring regarding the school and its land. Staunton was suspected of siding with Lord Lisle's interest against Lord Berkeley, not least by assisting them to get hold of crucial documents, and James Duport notified Smyth about his 'policy', and about the 'parables' he 'cast out' about the dispute 'in the pulpit'.[78] Whatever the risk of exaggerating the Puritanism of Crokey's Wotton network, the evidence about some of its members is unambiguous. In Staunton, he found someone who had useful knowledge and connections, and a track record of opposing Smyth over Warrens Court, and who was demonstrably a Puritan.

This link between the Wotton school dispute and Puritanism is evident most dramatically from Crokey's campaign against Smyth. This centred around Staunton and Edward Olyver, and occurred while Olyver was Wotton's mayor, and it can be reconstituted in detail. It involved gathering support for a certificate (or petition) in Crokey's favour, in ways that contextualise links he has already been shown to have had with local clerics. In petitions and pamphlets, Crokey boasted about mustering fourteen 'preachers of God's word of those parts', who would 'testify' to Smyth's 'powerfulness, cunning and contentiousness', and to his own 'prosecution of a charitable disposition at his own charge'. He also insisted that this certificate was signed by 'the mayor and burgesses of Wotton'.[79] Such claims are supported by a letter sent to John Smyth by Robert Smyth (5 August 1620), sometime mayor of Wotton, which noted that Crokey visited the town and 'caused a certificate to be made'. This represented Crokey's response to allegations that he would settle the school 'on his own head', out of 'malice' rather than a 'just cause', and that he lacked local support. Apparently, Staunton and Olyver sought to 'obtain as many hands as they can', with support from local ministers.[80]

On Robert Smyth's account, Crokey's clerical support came from leading Puritans. Of those named as having 'subscribed to the certificate', only one, Robert Woodroffe of Boxwell (*d.*1639), is hard to pin down, although it is noteworthy that his curate in the early 1630s, Francis Doughty, was repeatedly cited in church courts for refusing to read set prayers or wear the surplice. Doughty's

[77] Perry, *Wotton*, pp. 60–1; Lindley, *Wotton*, p. 228; GA, D3439/1/420; GDR/B4/1/2890; GDR/D1/320. For John Staunton senior: GA, D2940/1, part 1, p. 26; GA, GDR/1580/93.

[78] GA, D9125/1/11990.

[79] PA, HL/PO/JO/10/1/24; Crokey, *Sacred Maiestie*, sig. A2; BL, Harl. MS 6803, fos 56v–7; Crokey, *Complaint*, sigs A–v.

[80] GA, D8887/6/83.

successor (Richard Cox) was a signatory of Gloucestershire's Presbyterian testimony.[81] About the others the picture is strikingly clear. William Pilsworth (*d.*1655), minister of Ozleworth, was also questioned for refusing to read set prayers (1631), and for refusing to participate in the parish perambulation, something many Puritans regarded as superstitious. He was later described as a 'painful' preacher in the official survey of Gloucestershire livings (1650).[82] The vicar of Tytherington, William Jones (*d.*1661), who apparently received Crokey's pamphlet from Thomas Wright, subsequently supported the electoral campaign of the Puritan, Nathaniel Stephens, and was later approved as minister by the republican regime.[83] Samuel Heron or Hieron (*d.*1663), minister at Alderley, was friendly with Puritans in Bristol, and his son was apprenticed to Anthony and Dorothy Kelly, from William Yeomans' godly network. Hieron too was lauded in the 1650 survey, as a 'constant preacher', and later served as assistant to Cromwellian 'triers' and 'ejectors'.[84] Finally, Robert Smyth drew attention to Tobias Higgins (*d.*1647), the minister at Wickwar. He was probably the 'Hugyins' to whom Thomas Wright sent a pamphlet in 1626, and he later published a godly tract, *The Deafe Man Cured* (1641). In addition to being the father of two Puritan ministers—Obadiah, who succeeded him as an 'able preacher' at Wickwar, and Tobias, the 'able minister' at Cam—Higgins was well connected around Wotton, not least with one of Crokey's friends, Albane Saunders, and with the Puritan minister, Thomas Ackson.[85] This group is striking because three of the four who survived into the 1640s—Pilsworth, Hieron and Jones—signed the Presbyterian 'testimony' submitted by Gloucestershire ministers in 1648, while Jones became an army chaplain, and Hieron was ejected in 1662.[86]

Surviving evidence is partial, but demonstrates that Crokey's campaign was fuelled by Puritan enthusiasm, just as Stephens' electoral campaign would be in 1640, even if it only involved Puritanism of a moderate kind. However widely Crokey cast his pamphlets amongst power-brokers and opinion-formers, who may not have been sympathisers, his known associates and collaborators in Bristol and Gloucestershire were members of discrete and ideologically driven networks.

[81] GA, GDR/D1/41; *Al. Oxon.*, iv. 1676; Bigland, *Gloucester*, p. 236; TNA, PROB 11/114, fo. 174v; PROB 11/103, fo. 213v. For Doughty: GA, GDR/137. For Cox: *The Gloucestershire Ministers Testimony* (1648), p. 4.

[82] GA, GDR/137; Elrington, 'Survey', p. 95; TNA, PROB 11/247, fo. 306.

[83] GA, GDR/D1/292; *Al. Oxon.*, ii. 832; Elrington, 'Survey', p. 96; Bigland, *Gloucester*, p. 1329.

[84] Harlow, *Religious Ministry*, pp. 83–95; Elrington, 'Survey', p. 92; *Calamy Revised*, p. 255.

[85] GA, GDR/D1/308; GDR/1648/112; *The Deafe Man Cured* (1641). For Tobias junior (*d.*1655): TNA, PROB 11/247, fo. 9v; *Al. Oxon.*, ii.707; Elrington, 'Survey', p. 95. For Obadiah (*d.*1670): GA, GDR/D1/308; TNA, PROB 11/334, fo. 386; PROB 6/45, fo. 177; Elrington, 'Survey', p. 97; *Al. Oxon.*, ii. 706. For Higgins' Wotton connections: TNA, PROB 11/169, fo. 192v.

[86] *Gloucestershire Ministers*; *Calamy Revised*, pp. 301, 555. Other parishes visited—'to get hands of the ministers'—were Avening, Beverstone and Kingscott, whose ministers, including William Hall and Richard Hall were dead by 1642: GA, D8887/6/83; TNA, PROB 11/153, fo. 372v; GA, GDR/1631/252; GDR/1638/157; GDR/1639/127.

They provided contacts and local knowledge, and made a stand against Smyth, and did so through religious zeal.

V

Crokey's religious views can be discerned using personal networks, and were also evident within his wider family, highlighting the importance of familial memories and cross-generational identities.

It is possible to look forwards, to Crokey's daughter Sarah, who joined and then led the dispute over Warrens Court during the 1640s. Her ideological inclinations are probably revealed by her marriage, in 1648, to a London parliamentarian, Roger Calcott (*c.*1588–1652), treasurer for sequestrations in London and Middlesex, and receiver-general of the Elector Palatine's revenues.[87] By his death in September 1652, Calcott was in dispute with the republican authorities, over an apparent failure to declare his accounts, thereby ensuring that Sarah struggled to recover property seized by the government. This included £500 owed by the East India Company, and debts from Brian Walton, compiler of the polyglot Bible. This generated numerous petitions and meetings with the Commissioners for Compounding, and a demand that Sarah should pay £1,100 (May 1653), although Calcott's allegiance was never questioned.[88] More striking is the fact that, by the time of her death in 1663, Sarah was living as a widow—with 'little estate'—in one of London's most notorious Puritan parishes, St Stephen Coleman Street. That she too was puritanically inclined is evident from the bequests—worth £5—made to ten 'distressed' ministers, presumably nonconformists who were ejected from their livings the previous year.[89]

It is also possible to look back to earlier generations of Crokey's family, as Crokey did himself. Crokey's aunt, Anne Tempest, left money not just to Crokey, but also to the poor of her Bristol parish, tellingly described in the Puritan style (as 'Redcliffe' rather than 'St Mary Redcliffe'), and to Matthew Hazzard, a leading godly preacher.[90] It is tempting to look even further back, to Richard Moore, from whom Crokey inherited the dispute. In one of his final letters to John Smyth, as he prepared for death, Moore requested twenty shillings to pay a tailor for 'new apparell', so that he could make himself presentable for a visit by the bishop of Durham, Toby Matthew, the Calvinist friend of moderate Puritans, and someone with whom Crokey also had connections.[91]

[87] LMA, DL/A/D/002/MS10091/024; P69/TRI2/A/005/MS09241/001, fo. 107; TNA, STAC 8/34/3; TNA, SP 16/402, fos 11–12; Joseph Foster, ed., *The Register of Admissions to Gray's Inn* (2 vols, London, 1889), p. 207; TNA, SP 28/210/144; *CSPD 1650*, p. 385; *CCC*, pp. 171, 197, 245, 1251, 2058.

[88] Arthur Meredyth Burke, ed., *Memorials of St Margaret's* (London, 1914), p. 631; *CCC*, pp. 253, 258, 311, 315, 318, 622, 639, 2194, 2196, 2183, 3039–40; TNA, SP 23/72, pp. 611–12.

[89] TNA, PROB 11/310, fo. 21v. [90] BA, FCW/1641/4. [91] GA, D8887/6/41.

Given that Crokey's associates displayed godly leanings during battles with Smyth dating back to the sixteenth century, he was surely aware of his own family history. Crokey certainly asserted his family's respectable heritage, in the face of Smyth's tendency to belittle his status and intelligence, insisting upon their gentility and citing a grant of arms from Henry VII.[92] As such, he presumably knew the amazing stories that circulated about his father's first wife, Gertrude Crokey, not least via Foxe's 'book of martyrs', as an example of the 'strange dealing of the papists with the faithful'. According to Foxe's account—amply supported by documentary evidence—Gertrude Crokey was a 'godly matron' and 'fast Protestant' during the reign of Mary I, who was even accused of Anabaptism. The latter charge might have been concocted, by a 'naughty' Dutchman who was owed money by Robert Crokey, although it resulted in her being imprisoned in Antwerp on her way back from Gelderland, where she went to settle the affairs of her first husband, 'a stranger born'. Gertrude cleared herself, but more persistent were threats from the Marian authorities, which targeted her for having 'abstained herself from the Popish church', and for having 'shut her doors' against officials. She also mocked her minister, Doctor Francis Mallet of St Katherine by the Tower, and participated in surreptitious baptisms in private houses. Bishop Bonner referred Gertrude to his chancellor, and Mallet ensured that she was 'troubled on her deathbed', as he and one of Mary's chaplains encouraged her to return to the fold. Gertrude emerges as a defiant character, telling Mallet that Catholic sacraments were 'abominable', and that he would 'draw me from my Christ'. She even protested that her Protestant faith was fostered by Mallet's own sermons in days gone by, prompting a confession that he was 'deceived' in his youth 'by little new-fangled twopenny books'. Upon her death in 1558, Mallet insisted that Gertrude should be 'buried next to some highway', with 'a mark set up, in token that a heretic was buried there', although Robert Crokey was eventually allowed to bury her in unconsecrated ground. Gertrude's true loyalty may have been to the Edwardian prayer book. This can be inferred from the man from whom she sought advice when her conscience was troubled about attending Catholic services—to the point of believing that God had 'cast her off, and that she should be damned and never saved'. This was John Rough, a Marian martyr, who encouraged her to join his underground congregation, which was frequented by Dutch and French immigrants, and met in private houses in Wapping, Ratcliffe, and Limehouse, and in her own parish. Most members of this congregation accommodated the Elizabethan church, albeit as supporters of a hotter sort of Protestantism.[93]

[92] Crokey, *Complaint*, sig. C2.

[93] John Foxe, *Acts and Monuments* (1563), book 5, pp. 1825–6; John Strype, *Survey of London* (2 vols, 1720), Book 2, chapter 2, p. 8; Susan Brigden, *London and the Reformation* (Oxford, 1989), pp. 563–9, 580, 601–2, 617. See: LMA, DL/C/B/001/MS09168/11, fos 12–14, 165. For Rough: *ODNB*; Champlin Burrage, *The Early English Dissenters* (2 vols, Cambridge, 1912), i. 70–3.

Gertrude's experiences make it possible to return to the story with which this chapter began, and to her husband, Robert Crokey. The case against him in 1583 was far from transparent, and did not obviously involve religious controversy.[94] From what is known about early modern probate litigation, such cases mostly involved disputes over nuncupative wills, the mental capacity of testators, and the undue influence to which they were subjected. All of these were relevant on this occasion, although Crokey's defenders also claimed that Pike had agreed to raise the child of his bigamous wife, who had 'two husbands alive at once'.[95] However, there may have been more obvious religious dimensions, and claims were made about a history of 'controversy' between Crokey and one of his accusers, the Scotsman Richard Chamberlain (*d.*1595), who recorded the version of Pike's will that was eventually processed. This dispute resulted in 'scandalous speeches'.[96] It thus makes sense to reflect on the area where Crokey lived, since St Katherine's was a haven not just for merchants who wanted to evade the City's jurisdiction, but also for dissidents.[97] It was a parish beset by tension; Gertrude Crokey was betrayed to Bonner by the local bailiff, Robert Hemmings, and Robert Crokey remained friends with members of underground congregations. One witness who defended him in 1583 was an Aldgate shoemaker, Henry Frogg, from the Duchy of Cleves, who was a member of John Rough's congregation and hosted their meetings.[98] It also seems likely that Robert Crokey shared Gertrude's determined brand of Protestantism. He supported her during disputes with the Church authorities, and faced the threat of imprisonment, and only 'escaped their hands' through friendship with Mallet's commissary, Mr Hussey.[99] Crokey too was defiant, burying Gertrude on his own land, and if his nomination as warden of the Ironmongers Company in 1584 suggests that he escaped punishment over Robert Pike's will, then it is tempting to suggest that his absence from the company's records—and even its lists of liverymen—for the preceding eleven years reflected an obscure episode in the history of the Elizabethan Protestant underground.[100]

[94] See: A. P. House, 'The City of London and the problem of the liberties, c.1540–1640' (Oxford University DPhil, 2006), p. 165.

[95] LMA, CLC/199/TD/008/MS09740A, fos 35v, 39, 44, 45–v, 47v. See: Lloyd Bonfield, *Devising, Dying and Dispute. Probate Litigation in Early Modern England* (Farnham, 2012).

[96] LMA, CLC/199/TD/008/MS09740A, fo. 24. For Chamberlain: R. Kirk, ed., *Returns of Aliens Dwelling in the City and Suburbs of London* (4 vols, Aberdeen, 1900–1908), iii. 425; A. W. Hughes Clarke, ed., *The Registers of St Katherine by the Tower* (7 vols, London, 1945–51), i. 123.

[97] Hill, *Bench and Bureaucracy*, pp. 9–10; Irene Scouloudi, 'The strangers in the precinct of St Katherine by the Tower, c.1500–1687', *Proceedings of the Huguenot Society*, 25.1 (1989), 75–82; H. Gareth Owen, 'The liberty of the minories: a study in Elizabethan religious radicalism', *East London Papers*, 8.2 (1965), 81–97; Patrick Collinson, *The Elizabethan Puritan Movement* (Oxford, 1967), pp. 86–90.

[98] LMA, CLC/199/TD/008/MS09740A, fo. 47v; Andrew Pettegree, *Foreign Protestant Communities in Sixteenth-Century London* (Oxford, 1986), pp. 128–9; Brigden, *London*, p. 602; Scouloudi, 'Strangers', p. 78; Kirk, ed., *Returns of Aliens*, iii. 430; Burrage, *Dissenters*, i. 70–3.

[99] Foxe, *Acts and Monuments*, Book 5, pp. 1825–6.

[100] GL, MS 16967/1, fos 86, 102, 107v, 157, 172, 200, 201v; GL, MS 16988/2, fos 231v–336.

VI

Ending this chapter as it began, with tentative suggestions and cryptic evidence, is appropriate given its subject matter and methodology, and much remains unknown about Benjamin Crokey's network, and about his religious and political views. Nevertheless, it would be wrong to dismiss the clues peppered through Crokey's texts, and words that occasionally fell from his lips. He came from a fascinating family, whose advanced Protestant—or moderate Puritan—beliefs he probably recognised and shared. He certainly seems to have handed them down to his daughter. He does not fit the bill of someone from later generations of Protestant families whose zeal was less pronounced; instead he might be thought of as someone who shared the spirit of his forebears, even if he did not behave—or express himself—in the same way. His story was freighted with memories of previous generations, and a sense of familial identity seems to have been key to his thinking as he took up the fight that his ancestors began.

Crokey's Puritanism was veiled, and more or less excised from his petitions and pamphlets, doubtless for tactical reasons. However, the suggestion at the heart of this chapter is that what makes the Warrens Court dispute intriguing is the possibility that Crokey's zeal can be discerned through his practices and networks, and with a cross-generational case study. This involves piecing together clues, many of which are unspectacular, curious, or difficult to comprehend, and discerning the attitudes and beliefs of people with whom he chose to associate and work. It also involves suggesting that, while many members of Crokey's network do not come into focus unequivocally, and may not have been close personal friends, such men and women are valuable for betraying Puritan traits, of a kind that was perfectly apparent with his closest collaborators and most determined accomplices. In other words, since a significant section of Crokey's network was sympathetic towards Puritans, or demonstrably godly, this can plausibly be used to contextualise a wider group of associates, and to clarify Crokey's views. As with Smyth, comments by lawyers—about Crokey being 'unconformable' and deserving to have his ears 'cropped'—might have been telling, and were perhaps deliberate.

Such conclusions contribute the final answers to the puzzles with which this book began. They indicate that for Crokey the dispute dragged on because the stakes were high and ideological, and that, even if these were not made explicit, his perspective was comprehended and shared by people with whom he associated. Approaching the dispute from the perspective of Crokey's mental world indicates that it became bitter and protracted because it involved a long-standing bone of contention—Wotton school. It fascinated contemporaries precisely because the ideological fault lines symbolised by the school were profound and widely appreciated, not least by the 1640s. It is noteworthy that the Long Parliament encouraged Crokey to pursue his legislative goals at the very moment when investigations began into 'abuses' in the government 'free-schools', and the 'mis-employment' of their revenues. It is even tempting to speculate that, by his death in 1647, Crokey found himself in sympathy with political radicals like Richard Overton, who insisted that 'all ancient donations for the maintenance and continuance of free schools which are . . . converted to any private use, and all such free schools which are destroyed or purloined of any freedom . . . may be restored and erected again.'[101]

[101] *CJ* ii. 121–2; R. Overton, *An Appeale from the Degenerate Representative Body* (1647), p. 37.

Conclusion

The disputation analysed in this book—like the 'civil wars' and 'combat' to which litigation was likened by John Smyth and Thomas Middleton—apparently ended in the early 1660s, although it is unknown whether the protagonists, like Middleton's Tangle, repented of their litigious ways.[1] However, the meaning of the Warrens Court dispute, and of methods used to solve its mysteries, cannot be assessed fully without an important epilogue. This involves recognising that a contest stretching from the Reformation to the Restoration fizzled out—with Sarah Calcott's death—rather than being resolved, and that it resurfaced with renewed litigation, in new circumstances and with new personalities, between 1710 and 1725. This rehearsed familiar claims, and confirmed that a problematic school retained the capacity to animate local people and provoke heated debate. It also clarifies issues raising during earlier contestation, driving home central themes from the preceding analysis. Only once this has been addressed will it be possible to distil the book's findings and arguments, and outline the significance of its conclusions.

I

Having re-founded Wotton school in 1623, the Smyth family controlled its affairs untroubled for eighty years, not least by securing a new lease of its lands in 1647.[2] Things only began to unravel following the death of John Smyth junior (1692), and with the troubled fortunes of his descendants.[3] Smyth's heir, Edward, became a Middle Temple bencher, but died young (1700), shortly after a marital breakdown, while one of Edward's two surviving sons, James, fled to Hanover after murdering a neighbour. Apparently, he was 'never rightly *compos mentis*'; he was sent to a 'mad house', and died 'perfectly distracted' in 1709. Having been 'outlawed and attainted', a protracted battle ensued over the estate.[4] James's brother, George (d.1712), also had other problems. As a JP he courted controversy—and accusations of corruption—by pursuing coin-clippers, and

[1] Thomas Middleton, 'The Phoenix', in *The Collected Works*, ed. Gary Taylor and John Lavagnino (Oxford, 2007), 9.202–3, 15.340.

[2] Lindley, *Wotton*, p. 230.

[3] GA, GDR/1692/240.

[4] GA, D9125/1/12030/20–1; *CTB*, 3 (1702–7), pp. 146–7; *CSPD 1703–4*, p. 354; TNA, SP 34/37, fo. 26; *CTB*, 26 (1712), 28, p. 245; *CTB* 28 (1714), p. 249.

The Madman and the Churchrobber: Law and Conflict in Early Modern England. Jason Peacey, Oxford University Press.
 DOI: 10.1093/oso/9780192897138.003.0011

even feared assassination.[5] His estate was indebted by £4,000, making it necessary to get parliamentary approval to sell the rectory and impropriation of Chesterfield in Derbyshire (1714), amid desperate attempts to protect the legacies of George's children.[6]

It was in this conjuncture—a reversal of financial fortunes—that debates about the school re-surfaced, amid ongoing concerns that it—like other grammar schools—was being starved of funds and exploited financially. This was implied by the research behind Christopher Wase's *Considerations Concerning Free Schools* (1678), which only received a perfunctory reply to a request for information about Wotton school. One correspondent, John Giles of Arlingham, described the 1623 settlement as 'far different' from the original foundation, hinting that the Smyths had something to hide.[7] It became known that schoolmasters appointed since 1647 were obliged to renew the family's lease without increased rents; this happened in 1697 and 1706, and provoked demands for enhanced contributions from George Smyth, which he rejected following legal advice (1705). Legal action was eventually instigated by the Attorney General, at the request of the master, Samuel Bennet, and Richard Osborn of Wortley (1710).[8]

Renewed litigation generated another paper mountain and was controversial. It was alleged that the school's buildings were 'decayed' (and turned over to malting); that parents were forced to hire a teacher from London; and that the school was 'abused' by the family securing favourable leases 'at their pleasure'. Disagreements emerged about the estate's value, about bonds obliging masters to resign upon demand, and about the family having the 'whole government and management' of the charity. They were accused of admitting pupils from outside Wotton ('strangers and foreigners'), and of granting leases to 'favourites and creatures'.[9] Smyth rejected some of these claims, and the dispute became protracted, dragging on beyond his death (1712) and the death of his widow Margaret (1720), eventually being overseen by the guardian of their infant son. George Smyth assumed that the 1623 decree would be upheld, but a controversial survey eventually prompted a decree that the family had privileged its own interests over the school's. They were ordered to pay compensation and higher rents (£60 *per*

[5] GA, D8887/5/81–3; D8887/13/120; D8887/14/9, 41, 49; D8887/16, p. 34; *CJ*, xi. 776–7.

[6] *LJ*, xix. 629; PA, HL/PO/JO/10/6/238/3060; GA, S379/2/3/2/2; TNA, C 78/1337/3–4.

[7] Corpus Christi College, Oxford, MS 390/1, fos 141, 159–62; Chicago UL, MS 1465, Folder 3. See. W. Vincent, *The Grammar Schools* (London, 1969), pp. 173–9. I am grateful to Simon Brown for alerting me to the Wase collection.

[8] GA, GDR/S1/17; D8887/14/51; D9125/1/12030/22; S379/2/3/2/4; *VCH Gloucester*, ii. 407; Lindley, *Wotton*, p. 231.

[9] GA, S379/2/3/2/1–7; D9125/1/12030/1–37; D654/VII/4; D2957/216/9; TNA, C 11/1925/3; C 11/1925/5–6; C 11/2349/4; C 11/2332/7; C 11/2373/3; C 11/2568/28; C 11/2568/37.

annum), as well as legal costs (1718), even if the inevitable appeals dragged on before finally being rejected (1725).[10]

This litigation involved extraordinary echoes of earlier disputation, far beyond references to the 'great dispute' of earlier centuries, and to verdicts 'one way and the other'.[11] First, contestation involved familiar legal behaviour, as formal bills and replies led to objections, demurrers, and delays, amid repeated claims (and orders) that George Smyth's answers were 'evasive', 'insufficient', and 'impertinent'. Sounding like Crokey, Smyth dismissed lawsuits as 'vexatious', protested about 'confederacy' and 'fraudulent, indirect and unjust designs', and moaned about being rendered 'remediless by the strict rules of the common law'. He predicted 'charge and trouble', and when attempts at mediation—at the Bell Inn, Dursley—proved fruitless, Smyth was forced to spend costly time in London. By 1713 he had racked up legal charges of £500; by 1726 the affair had cost his family £800.[12]

Secondly, the affair witnessed familiar accusations against Smyth's family, regarding their abuse of power. One commissioner who investigated the matter was said to be a 'near relation' of George Smyth, and in the 1720s the family was accused of having 'under-husbanded' the estate, to reduce its value and mitigate unfavourable rulings. Smyth allegedly employed locksmiths to 'break open' the school's archive and take away documents. His opponents insisted that the 'settlement' of the earlier dispute had been illusory, and that old problems had never gone away. They explained that the family, being 'gentlemen of estate... and always backed with the authority of a JP, nobody durst stir in it'. It was their power and status that 'occasioned this affair to lie so long neglected'.[13]

Thirdly, explicit references were made to John Smyth senior ('old Mr Smyth'). He was accused of pursuing the dispute for 'private advantage', and his claims about improving the school were styled 'specious pretences'. Insisting that his descendants secured a 'great advantage' by the 1623 decree, and received 'ample satisfaction' for whatever legal costs were incurred (particularly after the re-grant of lands in 1647), the plaintiffs blamed Smyth for ensuring that the school lands were 'intermingled', and that the family paid artificially low rents. Witnesses even swore that Attorney General Coventry's case, which led to the 1623 decree, was 'carried on and obtained' by Smyth himself. On this point George Smyth actually agreed with them.[14]

Fourthly, in resisting their demands, George Smyth explicitly compared his 'adversaries' to Benjamin Crokey, who was decried for 'obstinacy and

[10] GA, D9125/1/9796, 12032, 12030/26, 31; S379/2/3/2/1, 4–7; D654/III/218; D2957/216/9. See: *VCH Gloucester*, ii. 407; Lindley, *Wotton*, p. 231; F. Hornsby and P. Griffin, *Katherine Lady Berkeley's School* (Wotton, 1984), ch. 5. For Margaret Smyth's will: TNA, PROB 11/579, fo. 62.

[11] GA, S379/2/3/2/7.

[12] GA, D9125/1/12029, 13601; S379/2/3/2/4, 6–7.

[13] GA, S379/2/3/2/3–4; D9125/1/12030/11, 30.

[14] GA, S379/2/3/2/6/1; S379/2/3/2/7; S379/2/3/2/4; D9125/1/12030/10, 16.

perverseness'. Smyth's tone was patrician; he accused the plaintiffs of 'malice' and of being 'horribly insolent', insisting they were 'persons not capable in law to sue me'. Following the example set by his great-grandfather, he mocked his opponent, insisting that Richard Osborn was once a 'poor scholar' at Wotton, through the 'kindness' of the Smyth family, and taking credit for 'the little share of learning' he possessed.[15] Remarkably, in boasting about local support and an 'outcry' against his opponents, Smyth even accused the plaintiffs of relying upon 'an old libel', pointing out that copies of Crokey's 1625 pamphlet—'a most scandalous roguish paper'—were 'handed up and down' around the Wotton area. He briefed lawyers with arguments and evidence from the 'folio', John Smyth's response to Crokey's allegations, which contained 'the marrow and elixir of my title'. Having also unearthed the 1631 Star Chamber decree against Crokey's 'libel', Smyth had it reprinted in Bristol by William Bonny, proprietor of the *Bristol Post Boy* (October 1712) (Fig. 13). That he spent £2 on what were no more than flyers suggests the text was distributed liberally, as Crokey's pamphlet had once been.[16] This was a

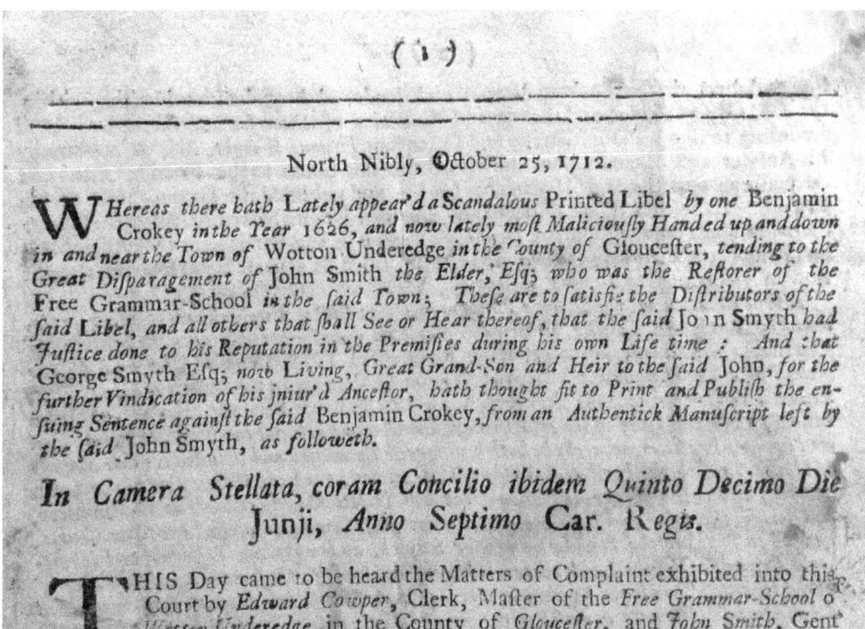
(1)

North Nibly, October 25, 1712.

WHereas there hath Lately appear'd a Scandalous Printed Libel by one Benjamin Crokey in the Year 1626, and now lately most Maliciously Handed up and down in and near the Town of Wotton Underedge in the County of Gloucester, tending to the Great Disparagement of John Smith the Elder, Esq; who was the Restorer of the Free Grammar-School in the said Town; These are to satisfie the Distributors of the said Libel, and all others that shall See or Hear thereof, that the said John Smyth had Justice done to his Reputation in the Premisies during his own Life time: And that George Smyth Esq; now Living, Great Grand-Son and Heir to the said John, for the further Vindication of his injur'd Ancestor, hath thought fit to Print and Publish the ensuing Sentence against the said Benjamin Crokey, from an Authentick Manuscript left by the said John Smyth, as followeth.

In Camera Stellata, coram Concilio ibidem Quinto Decimo Die Junji, Anno Septimo Car. Regis.

THIS Day came to be heard the Matters of Complaint exhibited into this Court by Edward Cowper, Clerk, Master of the Free Grammar-School of Wotton Underedge in the County of Gloucester, and John Smith, Gent

Fig. 13. North Nibly, October 25, 1712 ([Bristol,] 1712) [copy of Star Chamber sentence, 1631]. Gloucestershire Archives, D9125/1/12031. Reproduced by permission of Gloucestershire Archives.

[15] GA, S379/2/3/2/7; D9125/1/12030/11.
[16] GA, D9125/1/12029, 13601. For a copy: GA, D9125/1/12031.

blatant attempt to threaten a new generation of opponents, and it made Smyth's lawyers nervous. Nevertheless, Smyth was confident about using Crokey's libel as the 'foundation' of his defence, insisting that the broadside 'put a damp upon my adversaries, who have never held up their heads since in these parts but are blamed by all good men, for my great grandfather left too good a reputation behind him'. In claiming that opponents found themselves 'hated and discountenanced', Smyth noted that their ringleader, Osborn, was 'dubbed... Young Crokey', and felt confident that 'Old Smyth's' book would 'knock young Crokey on the head'.[17]

These events involved more than just a new battle along familiar lines; it was the *same* dispute, undertaken by people who consciously invoked earlier contestation. It involved simmering tensions that had never gone away, and an ongoing battle over memories and different versions of the school's history. George Smyth made much of witnesses who had 'heard' or been 'credibly informed' that his great-grandfather restored the school, and who claimed that John Smyth was 'always reputed and esteemed' as a benefactor who 'detected and rectified abuses'. However, this reputation was also *cultivated* after 1623. Thomas Burton believed this version of history because he saw 'a pamphlet printed... a great while ago', namely Smyth's 'ancient printed collection of prayers'. He and others had 'often seen' an 'inscription' set up in Smyth's honour in Wotton church, apparently by John Smyth junior (1669). Protecting John Smyth's reputation was the explicit aim of George Smyth's propaganda.[18]

This phase of the dispute generated attention and animosity, and involved using print to refresh people's memories about earlier contestation, and it too was underpinned by ideological divisions, rather than just the social tensions that George Smyth's comments blatantly revealed. The evidence here is hazy but tantalising. Disagreements occurred over Bennett's nomination as master in 1706: Smyth favoured another candidate, and Osborn and his allies only prevailed 'with much difficulty'.[19] Smyth, who knew his Sacheverell, was a Tory, uncomfortable with the Revolution settlement, albeit without supporting the non-jurors. In 1707 he clashed with a congregationalist minister, Joseph Twemlowe of Cam, who needed to remind him about the liberties that dissenters gained with the Toleration Act.[20] Osborn, while no dissenter, was almost certainly a Whig, if not necessarily a radical one. He was a proud episcopalian, but a devoted and godly supporter of the SPCK (Society for Promoting Christian Knowledge), and his bequests to Wotton's new co-educational Blue Coat school—as founder, treasurer, and trustee—noted that these would continue so long as it maintained 'the

[17] GA, D9125/1/12029. Osborne had been mayor in 1697: GA, P379/CH/1; D553/B2, fo. 42.
[18] GA, D9125/1/12030/35; S379/2/3/2/4.
[19] GA, D9125/1/12030/11, 35; S379/2/3/2/4; S379/2/3/2/2.
[20] GA, D8887/15/15; GA, D8887/16/34; D8887/14/49; GA, D9125/1/13601.

discipline of the episcopal church of England *as by law established*'. Like other SPCK colleagues, he was probably a latitudinarian, and a loyal supporter of the Williamite church.[21] In other words, renewed litigation over Wotton school reflected new kinds of religious division, and the ways in which old fault lines remained important, even if refracted through new lenses.

Even after 1725, key issues remained unresolved, and the legacy of seventeenth-century litigation was hard to forget, and occasionally recited.[22] The school's income was increased, but by less than some hoped; its trustees had greater security and independence, and laid plans for a new school building, but resentment lingered regarding the family's ongoing control over the nomination of masters and trustees (upon which Lord Berkeley sought to insist), and over the school's management. The lands remained 'intermingled'. Osborn was warned that his 'enemies' would prove 'busy' in obstructing the settlement, and disputes arose over particular schoolmasters, even as the family moved away from the area.[23] George Smyth's descendants settled in Shrewsbury, and then at Condover, and although a new mansion—which survives—was built on the site of Smalcombe Court, financial difficulties resulted in parliamentary approval being given for the sale of the Nibley estate, to raise £9,000.[24] This occurred in 1798, after Warrens Court was demolished, and after a final attempt—with difficulty, and amid fears that the 'rights and privileges' of the master remained in peril—to disentangle the school and family lands. The family finally admitted that the deliberate blending of different estates in the seventeenth century had caused serious problems.[25] Once an 'exchange' of lands was negotiated, the only real legacies of earlier troubles were the school's 'ordinances' (introduced in 1624 and endorsed as late as the 1830s), and its patronage, and one final echo of earlier problems was heard when the power to nominate masters was purchased by trustees in the 1840s. Their explicit motive was to stop the school from falling into 'improper'—'papist'—hands.[26]

[21] GA, D1193/15/10; P379/CH/1; TNA, PROB 11/587, fo. 218 (emphasis added). Another plaintiff, John Austin, helped to secure an augmentation for the vicar of Wotton: GA, D553/B2, fos 71, 109v. See: Eamon Duffy, 'Primitive Christianity revived', *Studies in Church History*, 14 (1977), 287–300; John Spurr, 'The Church, the societies and the moral revolution of 1688', in John Walsh, Colin Haydon, and Stephen Taylor, eds, *The Church of England, c.1689–1833* (Cambridge, 1993), pp. 127–42; Craig Rose, 'The origins and ideals of the SPCK 1699–1716', in ibid., 172–90.

[22] GA, S379/2/2/1/7; S379/2/3/3/1; S379/2/4/2.

[23] GA, S379/2/3/2/6/14, 17–18, 20, 24; Hornsby and Griffin, *Katherine Lady Berkeley's School*, pp. 65–6.

[24] TNA, PROB 11/975, fo. 221; PROB 11/978, fo. 46; Shropshire RO, 1536/7/1–2; Rudder, *Gloucestershire*, p. 575; GA, D8887/4/104; *LJ*, xxxiii. 45.

[25] GA, D9125/1/9797–9, 9801, 12030/26, 31; D3439/1/299; S379/2/2/3/6–7; Thomas Fosbroke, *Abstracts of Records and Manuscrips Respecting the County of Gloucester* (2 vols, Gloucester, 1807), i. 468–9; Hornsby and Griffin, *Katherine Lady Berkeley's School*, pp. 73–5; *VCH Gloucester*, ii. 408; Lindley, *Wotton*, pp. 231–8.

[26] Hornsby and Griffin, *Katherine Lady Berkeley's School*, pp. 80, 98.

II

Evidence about ongoing litigation, controversy, and religious disputation makes it possible to return to the puzzles with which this book began: why the Warrens Court dispute went on for so long, and why it fascinated contemporaries. Solving these mysteries has been difficult, involving twists and turns, difficult episodes, and a large cast of characters, and piecing together the story has involved evidential and methodological challenges. Surviving source material is voluminous, but partial and asymmetrical, and in the absence of extensive correspondence the dispute's meaning needs to be recovered using material—account books, writs, subpoenas, and legal papers, as well as Smyth's 'remembrances' and Crokey's petitions—that clearly does not reveal the whole story. The evidence makes it possible to say *what* occurred more obviously than *why* things happened. The historian is confronted with claims, counterclaims, and lurid allegations, and incompatible versions of events, and there is obviously a danger that things which have the 'fascination of a jigsaw puzzle' for the author might not be so appealing to the reader.[27]

Nevertheless, this book has contended that an interrogation of the Warrens Court dispute is worthwhile, methodologically and historiographically. The aim was not to arbitrate between rival accounts, but to fathom the logic and thinking on both sides, and as such this incompatibility between rival perspectives was a help rather than a hindrance. As an example of dispute resolution it offered a rare chance to subject early modern litigation to the 'extended case method', in which lawsuits are scrutinised within a 'social drama'. This meant studying *interactions*—regarding litigation and interpersonal relations—during protracted contestation. It meant scrutinising the dispute's many phases, involving attempts at reconciliation and arbitration, the willingness to behave more aggressively and engage in tactical escalation, and the risk of frustration and embitterment. And it meant analysing the attitudes and behaviour of protagonists who instigated, inherited, and bequeathed the dispute, as members of overlapping and interlocking networks. As a *longue durée* microhistory it was recognised that making sense of proceedings, people, and incompatible contemporary interpretations involves addressing phenomena that seem mysterious, characters who appear incomprehensible, and episodes that look extraordinary. This involved three stages of analysis.

The first stage traced a multi-stage dispute through the courts, demonstrating that both sides persisted with their claims despite, but also because of, repeated failures to secure a definitive judgment. Both sides grappled with legal uncertainties—arcane and intricate processes, jurisdictional complexity,

[27] Giovanni Levi, *Inheriting Power: The Story of an Exorcist* (Chicago, 1988), p. 43.

inconsistent and unpredictable verdicts—as well as legal possibilities; they had legal motives and methods for pressing on; and they were given reasons to think they might prevail. The basis of the dispute—things contested and arguments deployed—changed over time, as old litigants died and new ones appeared, and as litigants dwelt on both the matter and the manner of their contest; on legal issues, procedural grievances, and how the affair was conducted. What initially looked like an inheritance dispute—regarding leases which did not have many years left to run—became a contest over the fate—and alleged despoiling—of a free grammar school funded by the lands in question. Eventually, it turned into a libel case, and along the way litigants confronted issues like chantry lands, concealed lands, and defective titles, not to mention allegations of forgery, champerty, and maintenance. In tracing the legal rationale and legal proceedings, Part One also revealed how the dispute became much more acrimonious—and perhaps violent—over time.

The second stage—Part Two—approached matters from a different angle, capitalising upon amazing documentary evidence by exploring the practices and skills involved in the 'labyrinths and perplexities' of litigation, and exploiting a rare opportunity to observe and scrutinise tactical and strategic thinking. This meant observing the obsessive zeal with which litigation was pursued, the arduous work involved, and the stupendous amounts of time, money, and energy expended on 'toils, turmoils, troubles and disquiets'.[28] It revealed how litigants grasped opportunities to make themselves more effective, exploiting the role of a London inn like the Three Cups as a hub for West Country folk, and utilising the logistical opportunities offered by the capital's prisons. It also involved considering the 'sharp practice' that litigants apparently used to bend the rules, in terms of collateral suits, vexatious litigation, delaying tactics, and the weaponising of motions, bills, subpoenas, and affidavits, in various courts and contexts. Litigants sometimes used behaviour—deliberately and unapologetically—that is otherwise mostly observed in the allegations made by disgruntled appellants and concerned onlookers, and that have been treated with scepticism by historians. It emerged that litigation could be based upon a complex variety of short- and long-term aims, which did not necessarily involve the desire to win particular cases. This revealed that both sides employed subtle tactics, of a kind that had become integral to legal manoeuvring, but that were also controversial, not least as legal and procedural logic led litigants to behave tendentiously. The result was that both sides traded blows about ruthless behaviour, about conspiracies and combinations, and about power, corruption, and violence, as well as about ignorance and even madness. This involved something other than dishonest mischief-making;

[28] Smyth, *Lives*, ii. 302, 305.

it entailed differences of opinion about what constituted proper and improper conduct.

In this analysis 'practice' played a double role. It was argued that scrutiny of everyday practices, processes, and behaviour reveals litigants' thinking, rationale, and logic, and that litigants' claims about 'practices'—bad behaviour—provide a different perspective on their motivations. What emerged was that litigants approached the dispute in a determined and careful fashion, and had more or less different—and incompatible—perceptions and expectations of the legal system, in terms of how it did and should work. Crokey berated Smyth as 'a lawyer by practice', indicating that what he found objectionable about his opponent's behaviour was precisely what Smyth thought made him successful. Crokey wanted a system that would give him justice, by getting to the 'truth'; what he faced were processes where Smyth ultimately outmanoeuvred him legally. It was his attempts to understand and explain what was happening that led Crokey to demand reform, and call out what he considered bad practice, the abuse of power, and 'corruption'. It was this that led him to appeal beyond the courts—to Parliament, the king and the archbishop of Canterbury—and ultimately down the road that ended with a libel prosecution in Star Chamber. The dispute revealed competing ideas about the legal system; ideas that were revealed but also generated by litigation. Disputants sometimes worked 'with the law', by mobilising people and resources, developing skills and acting strategically, even to the point of manipulating processes and rules. However, there was a risk they would think and act 'against the law' when they concluded that it could be arbitrary, rewarding 'might' rather than 'right', and serving as a net into which they might become trapped, even to the point where they engaged in resistance.[29] The existence of competing or evolving ideas about the law helps to explain why the dispute persisted for so long, and why relations became more tense, as mounting suspicion and animosity decreased the chances of a harmonious settlement, and as escalatory tactics became more likely.

The final stage built upon this evidence about ideas and thinking, and Part Three focused upon the ideological 'structures' by which the dispute was underpinned. This involved a methodologically complex investigation of how to use surviving evidence—most of which does not involve overt expressions of religious and political thinking—to reconstruct protagonists' mental worlds. This meant piecing together fragmentary material—allusive comments, behaviour, and responses to events, as well as evidence about the people with whom disputants chose to collaborate—to discern ideological attitudes, even if only tentatively. Smyth emerged as a conservative-minded anti-Puritan, who accepted or accommodated Laudian innovations. His son, John Smyth junior, was a committed

[29] Patricia Ewick and Susan S. Silbey, *The Common Place of Law* (Chicago, 1998).

royalist, albeit one who needed to behave pragmatically. Crokey and his daughter, Sarah, were Puritans of some kind, in keeping with a family tradition of advanced Protestantism. What also emerged was that religious issues may always have been at the heart of the Warrens Court dispute, and of contestation over Wotton's grammar school; the school may always have been the root cause of disagreement, even if it did not always provide its ostensible rationale. On both counts, understanding the ideological dimensions of the dispute provides a different way of understanding why it became so protracted, and why it fascinated contemporaries. What litigants knew, and onlookers recognised, was that the Warrens Court dispute highlighted topical issues, from corruption to concealed lands, and that a range of legal, political, and religious controversies were playing out in local communities and everyday lives. In such circumstances, local institutions—like charitable schools—were prone to become lenses through which contemporaries reflected upon their times, providing focal points for experiences and memories, and helping people to understand their age.

III

The wider significance of these findings relates to the severity and *visibility* of political and religious division in early modern England, the role of the legal system in dealing with disputation, and the methods and approaches needed to analyse conflict and consensus. Smyth noted 'how deep the seat of malice is... in the bosom of any enemy implacably offended', and competing sides in the Warrens Court dispute were at odds over money and land, but also over politics and religion, and the issue at the heart of the dispute—the tiny grammar school in Wotton-under-Edge—was emblematic of ideological fault lines within local and national society, and perhaps a test case regarding the direction in which the country was moving.[30] The area was divided, religiously and politically, but also economically, socially, and culturally, making it tempting to invoke a modified version of David Underdown's model of geography, land-use, and cultural division in southern England. As Smyth recognised, and as the 1640 elections revealed, Gloucestershire was divided between the 'wolds' and the 'vales', with the upland Cotswolds being characterised by sheep-corn husbandry, nucleated settlements, and tight manorial control, and the lowland areas to the west of Wotton being dominated by wood-pasture and dairy production, weak manorial structures, and skilled artisans. The cultural differences between these areas mapped to some degree onto political and religious fault lines, which divided 'Cotswold shepherds' and 'Vale weavers', the latter of whom inclined towards

[30] Smyth, *Lives*, i. 275.

Puritanism and parliamentarianism. During the 1640s the Vale of Berkeley became a bastion of Presbyterianism, although not of more radical forms of Puritanism. It was also the area where traditional customs faced most opposition, unlike in Cotswold villages, where Whitsun revels, maypoles, and traditional games survived much longer.[31]

Wotton and Nibley, and other clothing towns like Dursley and Cam, represented the places where these two worlds met, as Smyth recognised. They were located under the Cotswold escarpment, and were 'evenly partaking of hill and vale'. As such, and given Smyth's strong connections to Berkeley Castle, it is tempting to depict him as someone out of place, and perhaps out of time, in this part of the county.[32] As a supporter of enclosure and the Berkeley interest, and as an opponent of Puritanism, Smyth was almost certainly a controversial figure around Nibley and among local Puritans, and certainly reflected that his activity and behaviour caused 'much talk'. It is noticeable that by the early seventeenth century the customs and games he lauded were features of Cotswold life—and of places like Tetbury, Rodmarton, Stinchcombe, Cowley, and Bisley—rather than of lowland areas.[33] Indeed, in an area where many people remembered the convoluted history of Wotton school—and its clerics—since the Reformation, as well as repeated contestation over the lands by which it was funded, it was logical that the school's fate attracted local attention, and became something local people observed through the lens of religious divisions. Crokey, Smyth, and the people with whom they worked came from different sides of a divided county, and the same is also true in nearby Bristol. There too, the fault line between litigants' networks was socio-economic as well as religious and political, involving tensions between monopolistic overseas traders, who inclined towards Laudianism and royalism, and less affluent domestic tradesmen, who provided the bedrock of local Puritanism and parliamentarianism.[34]

What makes the Warrens Court dispute intriguing is that these tensions did not come to the surface, a fact that raises important questions about the legal system in early modern England. Failing to recognise the affair's religious and political depth—that the ostensible issues at state, and claims made in court, were not necessarily what it was *about*—will merely render it anomalous and inexplicable, and make it harder to relate to the historiography on litigation and dispute resolution. This is because scholars have often stressed that litigation was not only commonplace but also effective; that although 'vexatious' behaviour was

[31] See: David Underdown, *Revel, Riot and Rebellion: Popular Politics and Culture in England, 1603–1660* (Oxford, 1985); John Morrill, 'The ecology of allegiance in the English Revolution', *JBS*, 26.4 (1987), 451–7; Neil Davie, 'Chalk and cheese? "Fielden" and "Forest" communities in early modern England', *Journal of Historical Sociology*, 4 (1991), 1–31.

[32] Smyth, *Lives*, iii. 10, 122.

[33] Smyth, *Lives*, ii. 319; Warmington, *Gloucestershire*, pp. 36, 40, 136–9, 145–8; Horn, *New World*, pp. 70–5, 81–90, 93, 244.

[34] Sacks, *Widening Gate*, pp. 50–1, 69–70, 221–46, 299.

possible, it was not normal; and that most cases were entered into tactically—to promote composition—and settled quickly and informally.[35] Studied as a kind of microhistory, however, the dispute sheds light upon early modern litigation as a 'normal exception' to recognised behaviour. As noted earlier, this term refers to the idea that mysterious characters and extraordinary episodes are worthy of study because what appears to be 'exceptional' may actually have been 'normal', especially for those on the periphery of society. Here, the 'exceptional norm'—'the anomalous isolated incident' and 'apparent exception'—refers to the possibility of challenging schematic distinctions between the 'extraordinary' and the 'everyday', not least by observing extreme versions of mundane, everyday phenomena.[36] Microhistorians have used 'ordinary' or 'everyday' life—and well-documented people and places—to recover beliefs and values, and 'things that take place when nothing seems to be happening'. They have shown how ordinary communities, everyday lives, and prosaic activities sometimes involved 'extraordinary' episodes, and how disputes 'exposed and intensified' divisions that already existed, that were otherwise hard to perceive, and that were more serious than the stakes seemed to warrant.[37] Beyond this, exaggerated episodes make it possible to calibrate what was and was not normal, and what represented the boundaries of normal behaviour.[38] As Thomas Kuehn argued, disputes that appear to be extraordinary—in terms of either length or bitterness—might actually have been integral to legal culture.[39]

It is in this context that the Warrens Court affair offers important insights into early modern litigation, and that the methods used here have wider relevance. This particular dispute may have been protracted and perplexing, and mysterious in terms of the interest it generated, but it may merely have involved an exaggerated form of dispute resolution, and one that contemporaries saw as regrettable but predictable, or at least comprehensible. Given the evidential and methodological challenges involved in studying litigation, what makes it extraordinary might be our ability to subject it to detailed scrutiny, rather than the fundamental issues and practices involved.[40] The analysis of litigation undertaken here has hopefully involved methods and arguments which can stimulate further work, on the complexity of cases and disputes, the complexity of rules and processes, and

[35] Steve Hindle, *The State and Social Change in Early Modern England, 1550–1640* (Basingstoke, 2002), pp. 83, 85; Christopher Brooks, 'A law-abiding and litigious society', in John Morrill, ed. *The Oxford Illustrated History of Tudor and Stuart Britain* (Oxford, 1996), pp. 139–55.

[36] Victor Turner, *Schism and Continuity in an African Society* (Manchester, 1957), p. 231; Paul Boyer and Stephen Nissenbaum, *Salem Possessed. The Social Origins of Witchcraft* (Cambridge, Mass., 1974), p. xii.

[37] Levi, *Inheriting Power*, pp. xv–xvi; Boyer and Nissenbaum, *Salem Possessed*, p. 47.

[38] Arlette Farge and Jacques Revel, *The Vanishing Children of Paris* (Cambridge, Mass., 1991), pp. 4–5.

[39] Thomas Kuehn, *Law, Family and Women* (London, 1991), p. 53.

[40] J. A. Sharpe, '"Such disagreement betwyx neighbours": litigation and human relations in early modern England', in Bossy, *Disputes*, pp. 167–9, 172.

the complex ways in which litigants thought and behaved. Tracing a long dispute across time and multiple jurisdictions makes it possible to observe phenomena that are not visible through formal legal records, not least how ostensibly unconnected cases became entangled. However quickly and easily individual suits were resolved, the larger disputes to which they related were a different matter. It also makes it possible to identify a range of different forces and tendencies that affected the dynamic of specific disputes, and to show how, in an iterative and multi-jurisdictional process, litigants needed to respond to circumstances, adapt to moves made by opponents, and deal with possibilities for making progress, as well as with the obstacles, setbacks, and frustrations they encountered, whether legal or procedural. This sometimes encouraged conciliation, but it also resulted in matters becoming more controversial and more public, making escalatory and extra-legal gambits more likely, and producing dramatic unintended consequences. What is suggested by this analysis is that the worst case scenario, involving a ratchet effect and attritional litigation, while not necessarily inevitable, was not intrinsically unlikely. Political scientists have used game theory to show that tit-for-tat behaviour can be logical for individuals as part of ongoing interactions, and beneficial for all concerned; it can provide the basis for co-operation. The dispute over Warrens Court confirms that it also involves behaviour—'once a feud gets started'—that can lead to indefinite animosity, especially if either party becomes intolerant of retaliation by others, as sometimes happens in situations of unequal status and power. In this situation, 'interactions can spiral downward into a long series of mutual punishments.' One solution to this problem is thought to involve the 'rule of law', but as this book has shown, this requires a legal system that is regarded as being fair and equitable.[41]

That the methods needed to interpret the Warrens Court dispute have wider relevance seems clear from the fact that other legal disputes revealed similar phenomena. Henry Elsynge's response to other petitioners who turned to Parliament in 1621 indicates a concern to resolve legal issues that had been unresolved for a long time, and to address 'oppressions' and problems caused by the 'greatness' of certain litigants.[42] Other petitioners complained about protracted litigation that resulted in 'infinite charge' and 'utter ruin', but no 'final end and determination', and some of these cases were regarded as 'notorious' and in need of attention, but also as disputes where it would be almost impossible to reach an amicable settlement that would satisfy anyone.[43] The contest between Leonard Loveis (or Lovyes) and Robert Doyly of Lincoln's Inn—which also reached Parliament in 1621—involved three decades of litigation ('so long and tedious a suit'), apparent settlement, and then new suits, and it generated serious allegations about sharp behaviour, 'corrupt and indirect practices', and rulings

[41] Robert Axelrod, *The Evolution of Cooperation* (London, 1990).

[42] HEH, EL6473, EL6920, EL7932.

[43] HEH, EL5975, EL5977.

that were 'contrary to all law and equity'.[44] Such cases remain tantalising and difficult to interrogate, but analysis of the Warrens Court dispute suggests that such claims may have been substantive rather than merely formulaic.

Occasionally, there are hints about the possibilities that exist for subjecting other disputes to similar scrutiny, with revealing results. Underdown's analysis of Dorchester in the early seventeenth century teased out ideological tensions from the behaviour of different networks, and found evidence of opposing and incompatible cultures and mentalities in local litigation, and indeed in struggles over a grammar school. Whether or not it makes sense to liken Benjamin Crokey to the Puritan minister John White, it is certainly tempting to draw parallels between John Smyth and Matthew Chubb, the powerful anti-Puritan who had a very particular 'vision of the ideal community' and the 'social order', who was opposed to 'reform', and whose charity was more showy than substantial. Chubb too faced accusations of financial impropriety regarding charitable funds and proved to be a 'formidable enemy'.[45] Similarly, it might be tempting to compare Crokey to John Lilburne, whose preoccupation with ensuring that the courts provided ordinary people with mechanisms for preserving liberties and securing justice reflected not just personal experiences of 'tyranny' but also his family's involvement in a protracted and acrimonious land dispute dating back to the 1540s.[46] Likewise, there is scope to probe contemporary claims about characters known to Smyth, like William Rowles, who was notably litigious, and 'a common mover, stirrer up and maintainer of suits in law amongst his neighbours in many courts in this kingdom', not least because he was 'turbulent and troublesome' in other respects, as a 'nightwalker', sabbath-breaker, and instigator of disputes with local people about 'their long and ancient common'.[47]

Other legal disputes are also tantalising. The correspondence of David Evans, steward to the earl of Bridgewater during the 1620s and 1630s, reveals litigants scuttling around London to navigate the legal system, zealous manoeuvring across a range of courts, and careful thinking about strategies, tactics, and procedural complexities, and the assiduous monitoring of moves made by opponents. It also reveals a willingness to comment upon the behaviour of other litigants, amid claims about 'frivolous' suits and long-lasting disputes, as well as the close working relationships that existed between litigants, lawyers, and other officials.[48] Precisely the same things emerge from a protracted familial dispute between Thomas Wood and Leonard Scurr, over property in Beeston, Yorkshire. This was another

[44] *LJ*, iii. 74; HEH, EL7934–7, EL7940–5. See: TNA, PROB 11/214, fo. 157; STAC 8/195/1; PROB 10/639/86; STAC 8/127/15; C 2/Jas1/D7/54.

[45] David Underdown, *Fire from Heaven* (New Haven, 1992), esp. pp. 30, 32–6, 46, 59, 151–2, 156, 224–6.

[46] Michael Braddick, *The Common Freedom of the People: John Lilburne and the English Revolution* (Oxford, 2018), p. 29.

[47] GA, D8887/10/95.

[48] HEH, EL6477.

contest—from the early 1650s to the late 1670s—comprising many separate suits, and involving 'difficulty', 'uncertainty', and 'doubtful' outcomes. It too generated grumbling about 'how chargeable the law is', and about being 'led in the dark... by lawyers', who were 'all for self-ends, let their client's cause go how it will'.[49] It too involved difficult characters, 'high words', and a willingness to behave ruthlessly. Wood's pursuit of legal costs repeatedly led to Scurr being imprisoned in the Fleet, where he was pursued with new subpoenas in the hope that he might eventually agree to 'a right understanding', and that there might be 'no more money spent in law'. Scurr was accused of subtlety and cunning, of vexatious and delaying moves, and of 'insolency', as well as of 'clamorous' and confrontational behaviour. He was characterised as a 'rogue', a 'knave', and a 'subtle politician'. Complaints were also made about his 'unjust dealing', 'scurvy tricks', and 'devilish policy', about his willingness to escalate matters with petitions to the higher powers, and about his ignorance of the law. It was even suggested that he was 'not right within'. More importantly, this was another dispute marked by religious and political divisions. The land in question had been sequestered for royalism, leading to a long fight with the Commissioners for Compounding, and Scurr was a godly preacher who was eventually deprived in 1662. The dispute was also tinged with violence, and only came to an end with the murder of Scurr and his family, who were 'burned in their beds' in 1680.[50]

Such evidence suggests that the Warrens Court dispute was far from unique, and that there might be other cases where protracted and bitter litigation can be brought into focus when official records are supplemented by private papers. It is this possibility—that the dispute with which Smyth and Crokey became embroiled was at the extreme end of a spectrum of early modern disputation—that makes it useful for testing historiographical claims about how the legal system had an 'enabling' effect, and served as a 'functional means of dispute settlement'. Litigation has sometimes been depicted as one of the 'weapons of the weak'—a means of solving problems and exercising 'agency'—and has become central to arguments about the emergence of a participatory state, in which local communities were integrated into national life, and in which office-holding fostered stability and orderly government. However, there exists a tension between the argument that litigation was a normal and useful everyday business, and historians' sense that legal processes were slow, costly, and open to abuse by vexatious (and powerful) litigants. What emerges from the Warrens Court dispute—which generated some of the most well-known contemporary complaints about lawyers and litigation—is a less optimistic picture about the early modern legal system, in

[49] HEH, HM82070, 82077, 82097, 82113, 82118.

[50] HEH, HM82072, 82075–6, 82079–82, 82085–7, 82097–9, 82102–6, 82184. See: TNA, C 10/100/167; C 10/49/143; C 10/108/132; C 10/92/120; E 134/1659/East6; C 10/57/128; *The Royalist Composition Papers* (6 vols, Manchester, 1891–1942), ii. 15–17; *CCC*, pp. 1090–1; Edmund Calamy, *The Nonconformists Memorial*, ed. Samuel Palmer (2 vols, London, 1775), ii. 555.

terms of its effectiveness and what litigants made of it.[51] Key here is the need to recognise that legal behaviour could be more or less acceptable, more or less savvy, and more or less sharp, and not to reify—and minimise the existence of—'vexatious' disputation. It is also important to recognise that rhetoric about 'conspiracy', 'corruption', 'powerfulness', and even violence was not necessarily exaggerated; it could sometimes be substantiated and can occasionally be verified. What emerges from the Warrens Court dispute is that the 'vexatious' and 'sinister' aspects of litigation need to be taken seriously, and that they involved contested modes of behaviour, about which contemporaries reached very different judgments.

The Warrens Court dispute also indicates that legal cases could be tense, and that litigation could reflect and enhance animosity, and perhaps generate disharmony, to the point where it involved 'a form of proxy violence'. It suggests that, while litigation involved people from all walks of life, and was not merely a tool of the elite, it could be a profoundly difficult and frustrating business, and indeed a dispiriting and disillusioning one, which could make matters worse as well as facilitate the resolution of disputes.[52] It could highlight inequalities of power, and reveal social tension, snobbery, and patrician attitudes. It could foster critical ideas about law and politics, and create new incentives for contestation, and the shared language of the law needs to be explored from the perspective of ordinary citizens as well as from the perspectives of the state and the elite. Litigation may have integrated people into a political system *and* acted as a 'solvent' of deferential attitudes, and it certainly provided a means of developing and articulating ideas about justice, corruption, and arbitrary power, as well as about social and economic relationships. In other words, the 'commoning' of the law was a matter of experience as well as of print culture, and the 'lawmindedness' that emerged from the rise of litigation may have involved disappointed expectations about what the legal system could offer. The fact that litigation could be underpinned by ideological divisions without making these divisions clear indicates that a legal system which was 'imbricated in the fabric of social life' might actually serve as a 'barometer of a breakdown in social relations', and of the severity of religious and political conflict.[53]

[51] June Starr and Jane F. Collier, *History and Power in the Study of the Law* (Ithaca, 1989), p. 12; Alan Macfarlane, *The Justice and the Mare's Ale* (Oxford, 1981), pp. 196–8; Prest, *Barristers*, p. 3. See: Hindle, *State and Social Change*, pp. 89–93; Steve Hindle, 'The micro-spatial dynamics of litigation: the Chilvers-Coton tithe dispute, Barrows vs Archer (1657)', in Michael Lobban, Joanne Begiato, and Adrian Green, eds, *Law, Lawyers and Litigants in Early Modern England* (Cambridge, 2019), pp. 159–62.

[52] Martin Ingram, 'Law, litigants and the construction of 'honour': slander suits in early modern England', in Peter Coss, ed., *The Moral World of the Law* (Cambridge, 2000), p. 146. See: Sharpe, 'Litigation and human relations', pp. 167–9, 172; Lawrence Stone, 'Interpersonal violence in English society, 1300–1980', *P&P*, 101 (1983), pp. 28–32.

[53] Brooks, *Law*, p. 277; Craig Muldrew, 'The culture of reconcilation: community and the settlement of economic disputes in early modern England', *HJ*, 39.4 (1996), 915. See: John Walter, '"Law-mindedness": crowds, courts and popular knowledge of the law in early modern England', in Lobban, Begiato and Green, eds, *Law, Lawyers and Litigants*, 164–84.

Finally, the Warrens Court dispute provides a novel means of engaging with debates over the nature and severity of ideological division in early modern England; over the degree to which local communities witnessed religious and political contestation, and over how this related to affairs in Parliament and national developments. It provides a means of connecting the 'politics of the parish' with 'high' politics, and of tracing the ideological underpinnings of the English revolution. Key here is the observation that the Warrens Court dispute was underpinned by ideological issues, as well as by memories of conflict and family traditions of religious partisanship, even though these were not signposted, and did not obviously come to the surface. This indicates that legal cases sometimes had hidden depths, and raises questions about what was happening when litigants took their cases out of the courts and laid them before the higher authorities, or indeed the public. Having recognised the value of 'revisionist' analysis of 'opposition' in the Jacobean parliaments, there is also scope to use the Warrens Court dispute to challenge some of the larger claims made by historians like Conrad Russell. Central to Russell's account was the idea that Parliament, as a 'place of last resort for those disappointed by verdicts in lawsuits', was a forum in which to 'transact business', more obviously than it was a place where ideological conflict played out. It was regarded, he claimed, as an effective means of resolving 'little businesses'; issues that 'may have concerned members and their constituents more than some of the great matters which are more familiar to us'. More broadly, revisionist historians argued that political and religious conflict was more obviously evident in machinations and discourse at a national level than it was in provincial England, an argument that was central to the claim that previous generations of historians had overplayed the degree of conflict within the country in the decades before the civil wars.[54]

What the Warrens Court dispute suggests, by contrast, is that in Parliament, as in the law courts, there were reasons to downplay the ideological elements of local disputes that were—and were recognised by local onlookers as being—driven by religious and political issues. This perhaps reflected a pragmatic desire to ensure that matters were heard and resolved, but it raises questions about whether local communities witnessed political and religious divisions to a degree that has not been appreciated, and how historians can do justice to such tensions. With the Warrens Court dispute we are confronted by a case that fascinated contemporaries not just because it was libellous, but also because they understood what it was about; because they could see things that the dispute barely makes visible to historians, at least without extremely close scrutiny. This suggests the possibility of offering a different—but compatible—response to revisionism from the one

[54] Conrad Russell, *Parliaments and English Politics 1621–1629* (Oxford, 1979), pp. 36–7; Alan Everitt, 'The county community', in E. W. Ives, ed., *The English Revolution, 1600–60* (London, 1968), pp. 48–63; R. Howell, *Newcastle-upon-Tyne and the Puritan Revolution* (Oxford, 1967), pp. 334–49.

offered by some 'post-revisionist' historians of local communities, in terms of how to detect religious and political divisions within provincial society, and in terms of whether 'little businesses' really reflected localism.[55] The Warrens Court dispute opens up the possibility not just that religious and political divisions existed—and are evident—within local communities, but also what was happening when 'little businesses' reached the law courts, Parliament, and even the monarch and the Privy Council. It suggests that many other legal disputes and cases that came before Parliament may have been more ideologically freighted than can easily be demonstrated. Such a case ought to leave us pondering—if not quite in Straussian ways—the layers of meaning that might lurk beneath the surface of legal bills and parliamentary petitions, and the possibility that the degree of ideological conflict that can be observed by focusing on what happened at the centre fails to do justice to what was happening in the localities.

It is this possibility that justifies describing this analysis of the Warrens Court dispute as a microhistory. The 'archive grubbing' involved has emphatically not involved the kind of 'archival fetishism' that is sometimes said to involve unfounded assumptions about the possibility of securing unmediated access to what happened in the past.[56] This book has employed a cache of archival papers that is peculiar and dizzyingly rich, in order to offer a detailed examination of a particular if protracted episode, but it has done so precisely in order to expose the problematic claims about 'truth' with which historians must grapple, as litigants and onlookers at the time grappled. It is the archive that makes it possible to analyse practices and strategies, to recover the mental worlds of contemporary litigants, and to reflect on how power, ideology, and conflict suffused the early modern world. Using a microscopic lens—and the kind of papers that often lie neglected within the 'legal' sections of family archives—has made it possible to observe an otherwise hidden world of early modern litigation, and previously hidden phenomena that have much wider significance. This was a world in which disputants were capable of engaging in vexatious and indirect practices, of pushing the boundaries of acceptable behaviour, and of revealing, exacerbating, and generating disputes of an extremely serious nature. It was also a world in which litigation could be underpinned by ideological divisions, even when these were not made explicit. Such findings suggest that historians might need to rethink the nature, severity, and *visibility* of ideological conflict—as well as the ideological interplay between centre and locality—within early modern England. It might be necessary to revise their sense of the meaning and significance of local litigation, a phenomenon that was extremely common but that is rarely subjected to thorough

[55] Ann Hughes, 'Local history and the origins of the Civil War', in Margo Todd, ed., *Reformation to Revolution* (London, 1995), pp. 252–71; Clive Holmes, 'The county community in Stuart historiography', *JBS*, 19.2 (1980), 54–73; David Harris Sacks, 'The corporate town and the English state: Bristol's "Little businesses", 1625–41', *P&P*, 110 (1986), 69–105.

[56] See Dominic LaCapra, *History and Criticism* (Ithaca, 1985), p. 92.

scrutiny. Of course, microhistories do not necessarily answer all of the questions they pose. In some ways, they magnify 'both knowledge and bafflement', and offer 'not proofs but historical possibilities'.[57] Nevertheless, the possibilities offered by this study are not just that 'every county had more or less the civil war within itself'—as Lucy Hutchinson claimed—but also that historians have more work to do to discern the connections between litigation and conflict—whether socio-economic, cultural, or ideological—in early modern England.[58]

[57] Thomas Cohen, *Love and Death in Renaissance Italy* (Chicago, 2004), p. 224; Natalie Zemon Davis, *The Return of Martin Guerre* (Cambridge, Mass., 1983) p. viii; Clifford Geertz, *The Interpretation of Cultures* (New York, 2000), p. 29.

[58] Lucy Hutchinson, *Memoirs of the Life of Colonel Hutchinson*, ed. James Sutherland (Oxford, 1973), p. 60.

Bibliography of Manuscript Sources

All Souls College, Oxford

MS 117 Humphrey Dyson catalogue of books

Badminton House, Gloucestershire

FmS Berkeley of Rendcomb papers

Beinecke Library, Yale University

Osborn a22 John Smyth, 'Commentary on John Seton's Dialectica'
Osborn fb151 John Smyth, 'Lives of the Berkeleys'

Berkeley Castle, Gloucestershire

BB Bound Books
SB Select Books
GPL General Papers Legal

Bodleian Library, Oxford

MS Eng.e.3400 'Apt and fit similes taken out of learned men's sermons'
MS Eng.Misc.e.6 John Smyth accounts
MS Walker John Walker collection

Bristol Archives

F/Au Bristol corporation: chamberlains' accounts
FC/AB Bristol corporation: apprentice books
FCI Bristol diocese: administrations
FCOB Bristol diocese: will book
FCW Bristol diocese: wills
JStap Bristol corporation: Staple Court
JTol Bristol corporation: Tolzey Court
M/BCC/CCP Bristol corporation: common council proceedings
SMV Society of Merchant Venturers

Bristol University Library

DM104 Kingswood Abbey papers

British Library

Add. MS 11055 Letters of Bishops
Add. MS 18980 Prince Rupert correspondence
Add. MSS 33588–9 John Smyth papers
Add. MS 34012 Returns made by Major Generals
Add. MS 34014 Returns made by Major Generals
Add. MS 34121 Parliamentary diary of John Smyth
Add. MS 49381 Letter of Robert Burton to John Smyth
Harl. MS 6803 Edward Alford papers

Chicago University Library

MS 1465 Smyth of Nibley papers

Christ Church, Oxford

MS I.c.3 Book of Evidences of Christ Church property

College of Arms, London

MS I.25 Earl Marshal's books
MS R.19 Court of Chivalry cases

Corpus Christi College, Oxford

MS 390/1 Christopher Wase papers

Folger Shakespeare Library, Washington DC

V.b.298 John Smyth legal and historical papers
Z.c.13 Muniments of title relating to Gloucestershire
Z.c.3 Muniments of title relating to Buckinghamshire
Z.c.30 John Smyth papers
Z.e.1 John Smyth papers

Gloucestershire Archives

D73 Lady Katherine Berkeley's grammar school, Wotton-under-Edge
D225 Denison-Jones family
D340a Ducie family of Tortworth
D553 Wotton-under-Edge town trust
D654 Goldingham and Jotcham of Wotton-under-Edge, solicitors
D733 Lady Katherine Berkeley's grammar school, Wotton-under-Edge
D1193 Wotton-under-Edge charities
D2404 North Nibley papers
D2510 John Smyth papers
D2688 Giles Geaste's charity, Tewkesbury
D2700 Beaufort family of Badminton
D2768 Tewkesbury papers
D2940 Notes on chapels in Vale of Berkeley
D2957 Gloucestershire deeds
D3439 Hockaday abstracts
D4431 Sir Thomas Phillipps Gloucestershire collections
D7115 Smyth family papers
D8887 Smyth family papers
D9125 The Gloucestershire Collection
GDR Gloucester diocesan records
P230 North Nibley parish records
P379 Wotton-under-Edge parish records
S379 Lady Katherine Berkeley's grammar school, Wotton-under-Edge

Guildhall Library, London

MS 16988 Ironmongers' Company: warden's accounts
MS 16967 Ironmongers' Company: court minutes

Henry E. Huntington Library, San Marino, California

EL Ellesmere Papers
HM82049-82280 Thomas Packes newsletters to Thomas Wood, 1642–95

Herefordshire Archives and Record Centre

BB2 Clive family of Whitfield and Perrystone

Lambeth Palace Library

MS 1730 Archbishop George Abbot accounts
MS 3512 Matthew Hale papers

Library of Birmingham

MS 3549 Fletcher collection

London Metropolitan Archives

CLC/199 Records of St Katherine's by the Tower
DL/A/D Diocese of London marriage allegations
DL/C/B Diocese of London commissary court
P69/BRI Parish records St Bride, Fleet Street
P69/TRI2 Parish records Holy Trinity, Minories
P82/GIS Parish records St Giles in the Fields

The National Archives

C 2 Chancery: pleadings
C 3 Chancery: pleadings
C 6 Chancery: pleadings
C 7 Chancery: pleadings
C 10 Chancery: pleadings
C 21 Chancery: country depositions
C 66 Chancery: patent rolls
C 78 Chancery: decree rolls
C 93 Chancery: commissioners for charitable uses
C 181 Chancery: entry books of commissioners
C 231 Chancery: crown office docket books
E 133 Exchequer: barons' depositions
E 134 Exchequer: depositions
E 190 Exchequer: port books
E 215 Exchequer: commission on fees
PC 2 Privy Council registers
PRO 30/38 Star Chamber writ books
PROB 6 Prerogative Court of Canterbury: adminstrations
PROB 10 Prerogative Court of Canterbury: Oxford wills
PROB 11 Prerogative Court of Canterbury: wills
REQ 1 Court of Requests: books
SP 12 State Papers Domestic: Elizabeth I
SP 14 State Papers Domestic: James I
SP 16 State Papers Domestic: Charles I
SP 18 State Papers Domestic: Council of State
SP 19 Committee for the Advance of Money
SP 23 Committee for Compounding with Delinquents
SP 28 Commonwealth Exchequer Papers
SP 29 State Papers Domestic: Charles II
SP 34 State Papers Domestic: Anne
STAC 5 Star Chamber proceedings: Elizabeth I
STAC 8 Star Chamber proceedings: James I

New York Public Library

*ZL-214 Smyth papers

Northamptonshire Record Office

FH Finch-Hatton MSS

Parliamentary Archive, London

HL/PO/JO Main Papers

Sheffield Archives

WWM Wentworth Woodhouse Muniments (Strafford papers)

Shropshire Record Office

1536 Condover Hall papers

Westminster City Archives

SMWSt Margaret's Westminster parish records

Index

For the benefit of digital users, indexed terms that span two pages (e.g., 52–53) may, on occasion, appear on only one of those pages.